From After Effects to Flash
Poetry in Motion Graphics

Tom Green and Tiago Dias

friendsof
DESIGNER TO DESIGNER™
an Apress® company

From After Effects to Flash: Poetry in Motion Graphics

Credits

Lead Editor
Chris Mills

Technical Reviewer
Charles E. Brown

Editorial Board
Steve Anglin, Ewan Buckingham,
Gary Cornell, Jason Gilmore,
Jonathan Gennick, Jonathan Hassell,
James Huddleston, Chris Mills,
Matthew Moodie, Dominic Shakeshaft,
Jim Sumser, Keir Thomas,
Matt Wade

Project Manager
Beth Christmas

Copy Edit Manager
Nicole Flores

Copy Editor
Ami Knox

Assistant Production Director
Kari Brooks-Copony

Production Editor
Kelly Winquist

Compositors
Dina Quan, Lynn L'Heureux

Artist
April Milne

Proofreaders
Liz Welch, Lori Bring

Indexer
Tim Tate

Interior and Cover Designer
Kurt Krames

Manufacturing Director
Tom Debolski

To William Hanna, Dean of the School of Media Studies at the Humber Institute of Technology & Advanced Learning in Toronto, who shares my passion for digital media and has supported me every step of the way. Thanks, William.
—Tom

To my girlfriend, Anjanee, who supported me throughout the writing of this book, and learned to accept my working moods.
—Tiago

CONTENTS AT A GLANCE

CONTENTS

CONTENTS

ABOUT THE AUTHORS

Tom Green is currently professor of Interactive Media in the School of Media Studies at Humber College Institute of Technology & Advanced Learning in Toronto, Canada. He has written seven books on Macromedia technologies, and many articles for numerous magazines and websites, including the *MX Developer's Journal*, *Community MX*, *Digital Web Magazine*, and *Computer Arts*. He has spoken at over 20 conferences internationally, including Adobe Max, NAB, FITC, MX North, Digital Design World, TODCON, and SparkEurope. You can contact Tom at tom@tomontheweb.ca.

Tiago Dias started to get into Flash around the time of Flash 3, after seeing his first Flash site. He started off by doing freelance work on the side from his day job as a network/systems engineer. On the motion graphics side of things, he got a lot of After Effects and Premiere experience at multimedia school in Zurich. From those humble beginnings, he now works as a video producer and Flash developer at a corporate television and news production company based in London with subsidiaries around the world—this is Tiago's ideal job, as it combines two of his favorite technologies!

In his free time, he writes tutorials on Flash and After Effects for various communities, tries to go snowboarding every time the sun is shining in the Swiss Alps, or hops on a plane to visit new countries. He currently lives and works in Zurich, Switzerland.

ABOUT THE TECHNICAL REVIEWER

 **Charles E. Brown** is one of the most noted authors and teachers in the computer industry today. His first two books, *Beginner Dreamweaver MX* and *Fireworks MX Zero to Hero*, have received critical acclaim. He has also been a Fireworks MX contributor for the *MX Developer's Journal*.

In addition to his busy writing schedule, he has conducted frequent seminars for the PC Learning Center (www.pclearningcenter.com) on such topics as Java programming, the Macromedia Studio MX environment, and the Microsoft Office environment.

Charles is also a noted classical organist, pianist, and guitarist, and studied with such notables as Vladimir Horowitz, Virgil Fox, and Igor Stravinsky. It was because of his association with Stravinsky that he got to meet, and develop a friendship with, famed artist Pablo Picasso. Charles can be contacted through his website at www.charlesebrown.net.

ACKNOWLEDGMENTS

The Internet is an odd place. People can meet and develop close working relationships with others they have never met in person. This is exactly how I wound up with my coauthor Tiago Dias. As is so typical of the Internet, Tiago and I live at opposite sides of the planet, and yet we have worked so well together on this book you would think we share an office. Not bad for two guys who have never met. There isn't one project in this book where I explained my idea to Tiago and he didn't bring it to life in a way that went far beyond what I considered possible. It looks like he and I are in this for the long haul, and I couldn't be happier.

I would also be remiss in not acknowledging a couple of people from the Adobe crew who helped make this book possible by answering questions and generally steering us in the right direction. First up is Steve Kilisky, the After Effects product manager who essentially told me I was crazy if I didn't do the book when I first blew the idea by him at Adobe Max in 2005. The other individual is Scott Fegette, community manager at Adobe, who never failed to answer a question or tell me if I was way off base when I breezed an idea by him. Thanks guys.

I would also like to thank Shawn Pucknell, who gave me several opportunities to stand up in front of my peers at the Toronto Flash User Group, FlashinTO, which he founded, in order to demonstrate much of what Tiago and I were discovering as we wrote this book. I would also like to thank him for taking a risk and inviting me to the "belly of the beast"—Los Angeles—to do a session on After Effects for Flash designers at FITC Hollywood. It proved that Tiago and I were on the right track.

Naturally, my editor at friends of ED, Chris Mills, has had a major positive influence on this book. It took him less than a week to approve the concept when I first approached him with my idea, and he has been riding herd on this merry band of explorers ever since. Along the way, Chris and I have developed a solid professional relationship, but most important of all, we have become good friends.

Finally, the task of writing these things means I hole myself up in my office, and become moody and generally difficult to live with as I mull over what to do next or how to explain a technique. It takes a very unique individual to put up with it, let alone understand why, and my wife, life partner, and best friend for over 30 years, Keltie, somehow puts up with it.

Tom Green

ACKNOWLEDGMENTS

When Tom contacted me a few months ago asking me to coauthor his newest book, I just had one thing to say to him, and that was a clear "Yes, Tom." So Tom, a big thank you for giving me the opportunity to be part of it—it was a lot of fun working with you . . . even though both of us live on opposite sides of the planet!

I would like to thank Claudio Cappellari from Toscano Records in Zurich, who created three awesome custom-made soundtracks for this book. It was quite an experience working together with a musician to create a custom track, which matched my imagination and fulfilled my wishes.

I would like to thank Chris Mills at friends of ED and David and Andy for being good buddies and always giving me great feedback on all of the projects I created for the book. Finally, a big thanks has to go to my family and my girlfriend who accepted my regular "no time" moods. Thanks guys!

Tiago Dias

INTRODUCTION

The concept for this book, like most book ideas I develop, was more accidental than deliberate. I was approaching the last chapter of my previous book for friends of ED—*Foundation Flash 8 Video*—and was getting nervous. The plan for the chapter was to explore preparing and deploying Flash video for mobile devices. What was making me nervous was the Flash Lite 2 Player was still in beta and Macromedia, now Adobe, wasn't giving us any sort of idea of when it would be ready for the market. In the midst of this "nervousness," my doorbell rang. It was the man from UPS, and he was delivering a copy of the Adobe Creative Suite Production Studio Premium.

What immediately caught my attention was that Flash Professional 8 was included with the bundle. It made sense because the ability to create and work with Flash video was a major feature of the application. Then the idea hit me: kill the mobile chapter, and instead do a few exercises that demonstrated how Adobe After Effects content can be used in Flash movies. I will admit I played it safe with that chapter, but the ability to include some of the After Effects in Flash content started rattling around my subconscious. I found the whole concept extremely intriguing and, without the pressure of a book deadline, took a few weeks to explore what I could do.

I also took some time to see what others in the Flash community were up to, and, as it turns out, After Effects was not on most of the Flash community's radar. Most of the people I talked to were intrigued with the stuff they could do with code or were simply trying to get a Flash video to properly stream. I then started talking to the guys at Adobe, and, as it turns out, they were also intrigued with the potential of how Flash and After Effects could play with each other and what they could do to bring the two applications closer to each other. I was told, "Let us know what you find out." The next step in the process was to start nosing around the After Effects community. They too found the concept intriguing, but either tended to view Flash as nothing more than another output format or simply didn't have the time to "learn another goddamn application."

What I learned from all of this is that both the "Flashies" and the After Effects guys were intrigued with the concept, but there was really nothing out there to get them started or interested. The entire field was wide open and unexplored. This explains why this book uses a "dragon hunt" as its theme. This also explains the opening paragraphs of Chapter 1:

"We are going to start our journey through After Effects and Flash by launching a search for dragons. There is a historical myth that assumes English mapmakers in the 1500s, not knowing what lay in the Arctic, would add the legend 'Here be dragons' to their maps. We say 'myth' because the only known reference to that phrase is on the Lenox Globe, which can be found in the New York Public Library. Still, the phrase has stuck and makes for a rather great jumping-off point for our exploration of the unknown.

"In many respects, the workflow and relationship of Flash and After Effects is uncharted and out there in 'Dragon Country.'"

The purpose of this book, therefore, is not to be the definitive work of its kind when it comes to the relationship between After Effects and Flash Professional 8. It is too early for that one. The purpose of this book is to show you some of the things Tiago and I have discovered as we journeyed through Dragon Country and to encourage you to undertake your own dragon hunt. If you do, you will discover what Tiago and I did: that this is fun stuff.

Book structure and flow

The book starts by introducing you to using After Effects to create a project destined for Flash in Chapter 1. Chapter 2 walks you through what you need to know to move an After Effects project through the Flash Video Encoder and to play the video in Flash using the FLVPlayback component, and shows you how to build a custom video player. By the end of these two chapters, you will have discovered the workflow between these two applications is more efficient and simple than you may have first thought.

Once you understand the workflow, we walk you through some examples to show you how text-based motion graphics effects (Chapter 3) in many cases can be more easily done in After Effects than in Flash. We show you how to import the animations into Flash and manipulate them in Flash movie clips, and we even show you how to create a banner ad for playback through Flash.

Chapter 4 shows you the ability of After Effects to create alpha channel video. Once you understand that, we then show you how to have the video interact with Flash content on the stage through the use of ActionScript. The chapter also answers a very common question: "How do they create those iPod ads?"

With alpha channel video out of the way, we then dig deeper into working with text and show you how to use Flash cue points and XML to provide closed-caption video; and then we really start to roll by blurring text in Flash and After Effects, adding lens flares in After Effects, having text on the Flash stage interact with a lens flare created in After Effects, and showing how you can work with Illustrator CS 2, Flash, and After Effects to create a rather fascinating text mask. Chapter 5 concludes with the production of an animated poem that uses audio and a variety of text effects to create an amazing motion graphics project.

The midpoint of the book, Chapter 6, is where we explore a variety of special effects you can create, from drop shadows to explosions, and how to mix and match them in After Effects and Flash. This is also the point where we challenge you to stop looking at video as video and instead regard it as "content." To do this we involve you in a Flash/After Effects challenge by asking a simple question: "What is Flash content and what is After Effects on the Flash stage?" This is an important question because the answer has rather interesting implications for the future of Flash video.

The balance of the book stays with that question and shows you how to create stunning visual effects that use content from a variety of sources, such as exploding text, letters shaped like fish swishing their tails, and text created in After Effects interacting with text created in Flash. We also look at the use of 3D in After Effects for your Flash projects, the use of parenting relationships in After Effects to create complex animations that can be used in Flash, audio visualization, Flash content interacting with blobs of goo, and bending video around geometric shapes in Piccadilly Circus.

All of these projects are designed not to show off but to get you to understand that After Effects and Flash together form a content creation powerhouse and, more importantly, how they can combine to expand your creative horizons and skill set.

As I am writing this, I am in a hotel room 15 floors above the Las Vegas Strip preparing to do a couple of sessions at Adobe Max designed to get the Flash and After Effects user communities to join me on the same dragon hunt to which you have been invited. It should be fun, but that isn't what has me "cranked." I can hardly wait until this time next year and the year after to see what Adobe, you, and your fellow explorers have discovered. That is the real payoff.

Tom Green

Layout conventions

To keep this book as clear and easy to follow as possible, the following text conventions are used throughout:

Important words or concepts are normally highlighted on the first appearance in **bold type**.

Code is presented in fixed-width font.

New or changed code is normally presented in **bold fixed-width font**.

Menu commands are written in the form Menu ➤ Submenu ➤ Submenu.

Where we want to draw your attention to something, we've highlighted it like this:

> *Ahem, don't say we didn't warn you.*

Sometimes code won't fit on a single line in a book. Where this happens, we use an arrow like this: ➡.

```
This is a very, very long section of code that should be written all ➡
on the same line without a break.
```

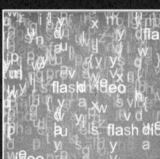

We are going to start our journey through After Effects and Flash by launching a search for dragons. There is a historical myth that assumes English mapmakers in the 1500s, not knowing what lay in the Arctic, would add the legend "Here be dragons" to their maps. We say "myth" because the only known reference to that phrase is on the Lenox Globe, which can be found in the New York Public Library. Still, the phrase has stuck and makes for a rather great jumping-off point for our exploration of the unknown.

In many respects, the workflow and relationship of Flash and After Effects is uncharted and out there in "Dragon Country."

Until the acquisition of Macromedia by Adobe in 2005, Flash and After Effects lived in separate worlds and solitudes. Adobe was quite succinct in their motivation behind the acquisition of Macromedia. When asked for the reasoning, those involved in the acquisition, both at Adobe and Macromedia, summed it up in one word: "Flash."

Though Flash 8 covers a lot of web ground, the most groundbreaking aspect of Flash 8 was the inclusion of a number of serious video tools designed for the creation and deployment of video on the Web. Within hours of the completion of the Adobe/Macromedia deal, Adobe released updated versions of its media creation and editing tools, and among them was a new version of Adobe After Effects 7, which pushed the application into new territory. With Flash Professional 8 and After Effects 7 under the same roof, we have been handed two tools that were absolutely made for each other and will inevitably also be drawn closer to each other over the next few years.

Just to give you an idea of how these two applications integrate, consider the following:

- You can export an After Effects Composition directly into the Flash 8 Video Encoder.
- Alpha channel use in video is now available in Flash and After Effects and contains a range of "industrial-strength" keying tools.
- Vector animations, created in After Effects, can be directly imported into Flash movie clips and manipulated in Flash.
- Motion graphics created in After Effects can be easily and seamlessly incorporated into Flash movies, thanks to the FLVPlayback component.
- After Effects offers the Flash designer access to a full complement of powerful filters and graphic effects, including 3D, that are simply unavailable in Flash Professional 8.

The neat thing about these points is they just scratch the surface of what you can do with these tools. In many respects, these five points are the land masses on those early English maps, and the time has arrived to see whether there really are dragons out there. Let's go dragon hunting.

The After Effects workspace

If you have used After Effects prior to this release, you are in for a rather pleasant surprise when you open After Effects. One of the more common complaints about the application, until this release, was the cluttered workspace. Palettes would sit on top of palettes, and many After Effects developers referred to this condition as **paletosis**. Now all of the palettes, which are now referred to as **panels**, as shown in Figure 1-1, dock with each other, and they can be moved around and collapsed to meet your unique needs.

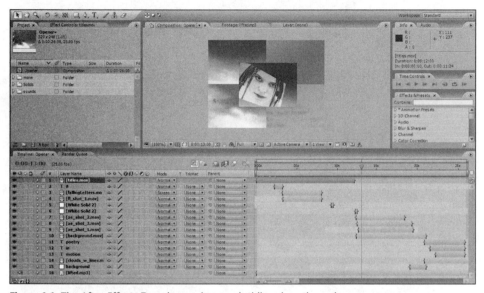

Figure 1-1. The After Effects 7 workspace is a much tidier place these days.

> *We aren't going to get into customizing the workspace, adding or subtracting panels, or a long discussion on what each panel does. We are assuming that you know the real basic stuff already, and are at the stage where you are itching to be creative!*
>
> *Many After Effects users will use a dual-monitor setup for their work. The main screen will be reserved for the* Project *and* Composition *panels while the timeline and other panels will be moved to the second monitor.*

As you can see, each of the panels is now **tabbed**. This means you can bring the panel you need into focus by simply clicking a panel tab. You can also change the order of the panels in the grouping by simply clicking the **gripper**—the dots beside the panel name—and dragging the selected panel to one side or the other. You can also create new panel groups— you want the Composition and Effects & Presets panels in the same place. Here's how:

1. Click the gripper beside the Effects & Presets panel and drag the panel onto the Composition window.

When the panel is over the Composition window, you will see the window essentially divide into five pieces. Each of these pieces is a potential location for the Effects & Presets panel.

> *Each of the pieces is called a **drop zone**.*

2. Drag the panel over the slice on the left side of the Composition window. When the slice darkens (see Figure 1-2), release the mouse, and the panel drops into position beside the Composition window (we will generally refer to this as the Comp window from now on).

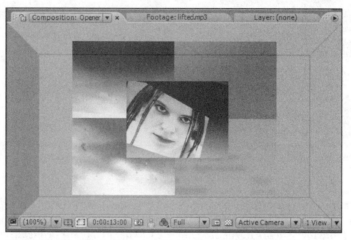

Figure 1-2. The Effects & Presets panel is about to be dropped into a location to the left of the Comp window.

3. Drag the Effects & Presets panel back to its original position.

> *If your workspace becomes a bit disorganized you can always return it to the After Effects 7 default condition by selecting* Window ➤ Workspace ➤ Reset "Standard". *You will see a dialog box asking you whether you really want to do this. Click* OK *and the panels will change to the grouping you saw when you first installed After Effects 7.*
>
> *How do you know whether a panel is selected? It will have a solid yellow line surrounding it when you click it.*

Creating an After Effects project

The plan for this chapter's project is to have you assemble a short video, about 30 seconds, that serves as an opener for a Flash movie devoted to this book. To get yourself going, you'll need the Exercise folder within the Chapter 1 code download from the friendsofED site. The download will consist of a series of very short QuickTime movies and an MP3 file.

Obviously you are going to be involved in the "end game" of this process. The actual project followed a typical workflow that started with a storyboard. Once the storyboard was approved—a rather short process considering there are only two of us—the various bits and pieces for the project were created, tweaked, and then output as a series of QuickTime movies to be used in the assembly of this project. If you are familiar with After Effects, you are probably wondering, "Why the heck don't you just create the whole thing using the features of After Effects in After Effects?" This is a valid question, but the purpose of this chapter is to get you used to working with the application and outputting a file for use in Flash Professional 8. Everything in this project is covered elsewhere, in one form or another, in this book.

Let's get busy and build a movie:

1. Launch After Effects 7.

When the application finishes launching, you are essentially looking at an empty workspace. That empty workspace actually is the project.

2. Select File ➤ Save As and you will be prompted to give the file a name. Navigate to the Exercise folder, name the file Opener, and click the Save button.

The file you will be saving has the extension of .aep. This format is used by After Effects to store the references to any footage you may be using as well as any effects and so on that you may be applying to a Composition. By saving the After Effects project (AEP) file to the same folder as the assets to be used, everything is in one location. This is especially handy in situations where one person uses the Mac version of After Effects and another uses the PC version and a project needs to be shared among the team. If everything is in the same folder, neither individual will be asked for missing files, volumes, or directories.

Creating a Composition

Having created the project, the next step in the process is to create a new Composition. Here's how:

1. Select Composition ➤ New Composition or press Ctrl+N (PC) or Cmd+N (Mac) to open the Composition Settings dialog box shown in Figure 1-3.

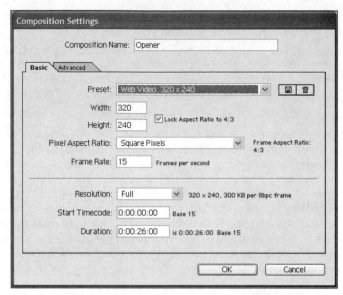

Figure 1-3. The Composition settings for this project determine the size of the stage, the media used for playback, and the length of the timeline.

2. In the Composition Settings dialog box, specify the following settings:

- Composition Name: Opener
- Preset: Web Video, 320✕240
- Frame Rate: 15
- Resolution: Full
- Duration: 0:00:26.00

Though there are a number of Composition presets that ship with After Effects, you only need to concern yourself with Web Video output. This will yield the stage size you need, which fits right into the traditional web video size ratio of 4:3. Pixel Aspect Ratio simply asks you what type of pixel to use and, again, because the medium used to view the video will be a computer screen, you will choose the square pixel of a computer screen.

> *You can also create a new Composition by clicking the* New Comp *button—it looks like a frame from a film—in the* Project *panel.*
>
> *The most common dimensions for video destined for Flash are 320✕240, 240✕180, and 120✕90.*

3. Click OK to accept the settings and to close the Composition Settings dialog box. If you subsequently want to change one of these settings, select Composition ➤ Composition Settings to reopen the Composition Settings dialog box.

When you close the dialog box, you will see your Comp in the Project panel. Its icon looks like a frame from a piece of film. Now that the Comp has been created, you can concern yourself with bringing in the various assets you will need to assemble the video.

> *Here's a neat little trick. Though you can change the Composition settings by selecting* Composition ➤ Composition Settings, *you can also do it without using a menu. If you right-click (PC) or Cmd-click (Mac) on the gray area in the* Composition *panel, a menu appears where you clicked. Select* Composition Settings, *and the* Composition Settings *dialog box will appear.*

Importing media into a project

Bringing videos, audio, images, and other files into an After Effects project is a rather uncomplicated process. Here's how:

1. Select File ➤ Import ➤ Multiple Files. When the Import Multiple Files dialog box, Figure 1-4, opens, navigate to your Exercise folder.

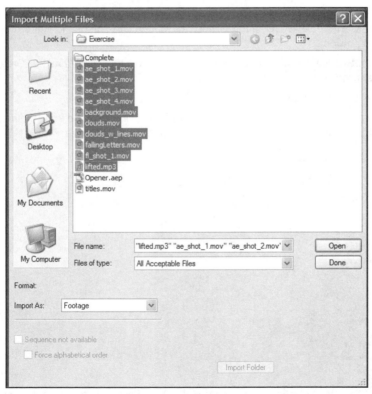

Figure 1-4. You can import files into a Comp either singly or in groups.

2. Press the Shift key, and with the Shift key held down select the ae_shot_1.mov file and, at the bottom of the list, the file named lifted.mp3. Click Open and all of the selected files will appear in the Project panel.

3. Select the final file in the list, titles.mov, and click the Done button.

The Import Multiple Files dialog box is a real productivity booster. You may have noticed the dialog box, unlike many other applications, remained open when you clicked the Open button. This avoids multiple trips to the Import Multiple Files dialog box and, best of all, by placing all of your assets—photos, line art, video, and audio, for example—in one place that can accessed in one central location.

> *You don't have to use the menu to import multiple items into After Effects. Open the window where the items to be added to the project are located and drag and drop them into the* Project *panel.*

If you are familiar with Flash, the Project panel is quite similar to the Flash Library. Like the Flash Library, the Project panel can also become a rather disorganized place. Let's add a bit of organization to the Project panel before we continue creating the Comp.

4. Click the Folder icon at the bottom of the Project panel. A new folder will appear. Name the folder Video and deselect the folder. Drag all of the video files into this new folder.

5. With the Video folder deselected, create a new folder named Audio. Drag the MP3 file into this folder and deselect the folder.

6. Create a new folder named Solids.

7. Click the Layer button (it looks like a small paint brush) in the Project panel, and the folders will move, in alphabetical order, under the Comp (see Figure 1-5).

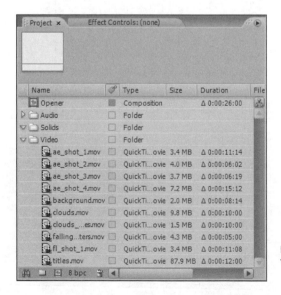

Figure 1-5. Bringing order to chaos in the Project panel

You may have noticed we kept asking you to deselect the folder before adding another to the Project *panel. If a folder is selected, the new folder will be placed in the selected folder.*

If you are a seasoned After Effects user, you may be questioning why we created a folder for solids. When a solid is created in After Effects, it will be placed in a Solids *folder. If one isn't in the* Project *panel when a solid is created, a* Solids *folder will be added.*

Layers and timelines

With the assets in place, we can now turn our attention to assembling the project. Remember, an After Effects movie, at its most elemental, is nothing more than a series of assets placed on top of each other and set to appear at different times in the video. This is the purpose of the timeline. Once an asset is moved from the Project panel to the timeline, it can be manipulated in what seems to be an infinite number of ways.

You can get an item from the Project panel onto the timeline in two ways, as you'll see by following these steps:

1. Select the titles.mov clip in the Video folder and drag it to the Comp window. When you release the mouse, the clip appears both in the Comp and on the timeline. What you may not have noticed is that the clip is not centered in the Comp window. It is placed wherever you drop it because the point of your mouse is regarded as being the location of the clip's center point.

2. Select the titles.mov clip in the timeline and press the Delete key to remove it from the timeline.

3. Select the titles.mov clip in the Project panel and drag it onto the timeline. This time, when you release the mouse, the clip is centered in the Comp window.

4. Drag the Current Time Indicator, which we refer to as the **playback head**, on the timeline across the video, and you will be able to see a preview of the clip's contents (as shown in Figure 1-6) as you drag it backward and forward across the clip.

There are other ways to preview a clip. The first is to simply double-click the clip in the Project panel. This will open the QuickTime player. Staying with the Project panel, another method is to double-click the item's Preview icon at the top of the Project panel. Another method, if the clip is in the Comp, is to click the Play button in the Time Controls panel.

You can also turn layer items on or off. To turn off the visibility of a layer, click the Video switch—the eyeball on the left side of the layer strip—and the item on the layer will turn off in the Comp window. Click the icon again and the layer becomes visible.

If you scrub across, or even preview, the clip, you will notice there is a rather large "hole" in the clip. It starts at about the 3-second mark and lasts about 5 seconds. Also, we are talking about Flash *8*, and the artist seems to have forgotten this rather important fact. Let's fix this error.

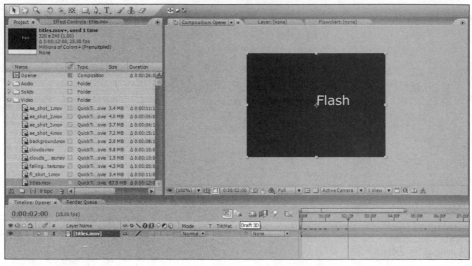

Figure 1-6. The clip on the timeline is also visible in the Composition panel.

Adding and manipulating timeline objects

Objects on the timeline are not static. They can be manipulated using the timeline. This is because all objects on the timeline have properties such as size, duration, and opacity. Here's how to change object properties:

1. Drag the playback head to the 0:00:02:00 mark on the timeline. This is the point where the word is fully formed with no movement. Clicking the time code in the upper-left corner of the timeline will open the Go To Time dialog box. Enter the time in the dialog box and click the OK button to go to that precise point in time.

2. Click the Text tool on the toolbar—if your tools aren't visible, select Window ➤ Tools—click the Comp window once and enter the number 8.

> As soon as you click the mouse, a new Text layer is created on the timeline and the name of the layer will be the text you enter.
>
> There are a couple of ways of looking at time in After Effects. Time as displayed in the timer located in the Comp window is **hours:minutes:seconds:frames**. If you expand the magnification of the timeline, you will notice that you are looking at time on a frame-by-frame basis. Neither is the best way of using time, and you will discover as you become more competent with After Effects that both methods work equally as well.

3. Change to the Selection tool, click the number, and drag it to a point to the right of the word *Flash*. Release the mouse.

4. Select Window ➤ Character to open the Character panel (see Figure 1-7). With the Text tool, highlight the number by double-clicking it and specify these text properties in the Character panel:

- Font: Verdana
- Style: Regular
- Size: 36 points
- Color: White

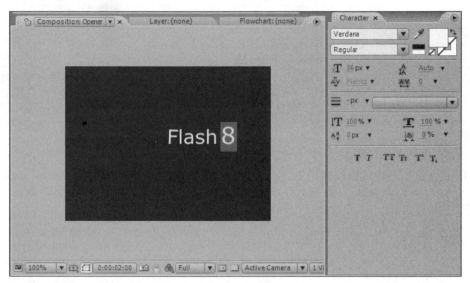

Figure 1-7. Use the Character panel to format text that is selected in the Comp window.

5. Close the Character panel by clicking the panel's close button.

If you look at the timeline, you will see a new layer has been added to it. The problem with this layer is its duration. It lasts for the duration of the entire movie. It needs to be trimmed so that the number appears at the 2-second mark on the timeline and disappears after being visible for only 1 second. Here's how to fix that:

You will notice that the layer strip, on the timeline, appears to be enclosed in curly brackets. The bracket on the left is the **In point** for the clip and the one on the right is its **Out point** (see Figure 1-8).

Figure 1-8. A layer's duration is set by creating its In and Out points on the timeline.

1. At the bottom of the timeline panel is the zoom slider. Drag it to about the mid-point of the zoom indicator line.

2. Drag the new layer's In marker to the location of the playback head on the time-line.

3. Drag the playback head to the right until the word *Flash* disappears. Drag it slightly to the left until it reappears.

4. Drag the layer's Out marker to the location marked by the playback head.

> Moving the In and Out points of a clip is called **trimming**.
>
> If you prefer to "do it by the numbers," you are in for a treat. Right-click (PC) or Cmd-click (Mac) on a column name, for example, Layer Name, in the timeline. This will open a context menu. Select Columns ➤ In and a column named In will be added to the timeline. The time shown in that column is the In point. Click and drag that number to the left or right, and the In point and the time shown in the column will also change.

5. Save the project.

There is still a bit of work to be done because the original storyboard called for this number to appear at about 500% of its size and then shrink it down to its final size of 36 points. Here's how:

1. Select the 8 layer and press the S key to open the layer's Scale property on the timeline.

2. Drag the playback head to the start of the 8 layer sequence.

3. Click the stopwatch to the left of the Scale property. This adds a keyframe, as indicated by the diamond, at the position of the playback head.

4. Double-click a scale percentage value and enter 500. Press Return (Mac) or Enter (PC). The number will grow larger.

5. Drag the playback head to the end of the sequence and set the Scale value to 100%. The number will shrink and another keyframe will appear. If you scrub the playback head across this animation, you will see the number shrink to its final size as shown in Figure 1-9.

6. Drag the 8 layer under the layer below it. Now you know how to move layers from one position in the order to another position.

7. Save the project.

> The chain icon beside the word Scale, if selected, will scale an object equally on the horizontal and vertical axes. Deselect the chain icon and you can distort the scaling by entering different scale percentages for the horizontal and vertical values.
>
> You don't have to manually enter the numbers used to scale a selected object; if you click and drag a value to the right, the Scale value increases, and if you drag to the left, the Scale value decreases.

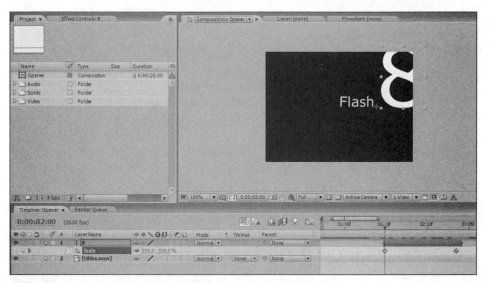

Figure 1-9. Like in Flash, objects in After Effects can be scaled through the use of keyframes.

Applying a transfer mode

If you are a Photoshop, Fireworks, or Flash user, you are quite familiar with the **transfer modes**, which are also referred to as the **blend modes** in Flash 8. Apply these effects to an object on a layer, and you wind up with some rather interesting color interactions with the content in the layer below it. The neat thing about these effects in After Effects is they aren't static. Instead they apply to objects that move. In this section, you will apply a screen transfer to remove the solid black background of a video.

1. Select the fallingLetters.mov file in the Video folder and drag it to the timeline under the 8 layer you just created.

2. Drag the clip so its In point is directly under the Text layer's Out point at 0:00:03:01.

3. Drag the fl_shot_1.mov clip under the fallingLetters layer onto the timeline.

4. Drag the playback head to 0:00:06:09 and drag the In point of the clip to the play-back head. Drag the layer strip—it is called the **duration bar**—and align its In point with the In point of the clip, at about 0:00:03:01, above it on the timeline.

If you scrub the playback head across these two clips, you really won't see anything because the falling letters are on a black background that covers the clip below it.

5. Select the Falling Letters clip and, in the Mode area of the layer, click the word *Normal*. When the Transfer Modes pop-up menu appears, select Screen.

If you scrub the timeline now, you will see the black has disappeared and the content in the video clip below it is now visible.

You will now notice that even though the In and Out points of the fl_shot_1.mov roughly match those of the Falling Letters clip, there is still a bit of the clip visible—a colored area—beyond those two points. This tells you that you need to shorten the clip.

6. Place the cursor at the end of the duration bar in Layer 4. The cursor will change to a double arrow. Click and drag the left edge of the colored area to the Out point of the clip, which is about the 8-second mark on the timeline.

7. Drag the playback head to the start of the movie and click the Play button in the Time Controls panel. Notice now how the white letters, shown in Figure 1-10, fall from the top of the Comp to the bottom of the Comp, and they appear to be falling over a pinkish textured background. The Screen mode removed the black background.

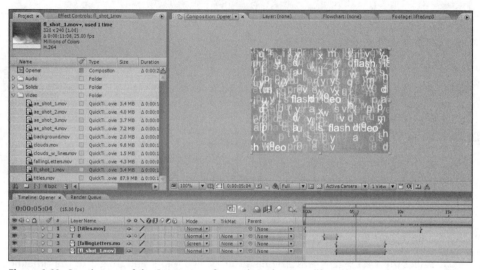

Figure 1-10. Creative use of the Screen transfer mode makes your life easier.

8. Save the project.

Creating and using solid layers

A solid layer, or **solid**, does exactly what the name says: it is a layer that contains a solid color shape. The really interesting thing about such layers is they can range in size from 1 pixel by 1 pixel up to 32,000 pixels square and can be any color you wish. You are now probably thinking, "That's interesting, but what are they used for?" In many cases, they are used as a background for a new graphic or animation, and, because they are layers, they can be manipulated in the timeline just like any other content on a layer.

In the case of this exercise, the solids will be used to act as a transition between scenes. The first part of the animation talks about Flash 8. This solid will give the viewer a visual clue that we are about to change the subject. The user will see a brief flash of white and new content will start to appear. Here's how:

1. Select Layer ➤ New ➤ Solid to open the Solid Settings dialog box shown in Figure 1-11.

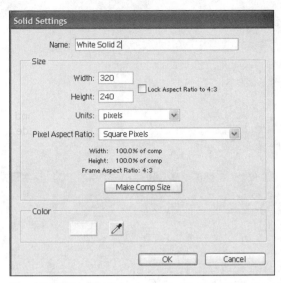

Figure 1-11. Use this dialog box to create solid color backgrounds for your projects.

2. Name the solid White Solid 2 and don't change the dimensions.

3. Click the Color chip in the Color section and, when the Color Picker opens, select white as the color.

4. Click OK to close the dialog box. The solid is now added to the Project panel and to the timeline. Delete the solid from the timeline. We'll put it back in a moment.

> *You may be looking at the* Project *panel and wondering where the solid went. Open the* Solids *folder. All solids are added to this folder if it exists, or After Effects will create one for you when you create your first solid.*

5. Move the playback head across the timeline until the timer in the Comp window displays 0:00:09:08.

6. Drag the solid from the Solids folder to the bottom of the timeline. Set the solid's In point to match that of the playback head.

7. Drag the playback head to the right until the timer in the Comp window displays 0:00:09:11. Set the solid's Out point to this mark on the timeline.

8. Drag another copy of White Solid 2 to the bottom of the timeline and set its In point to 0:00:12:03 and its Out point to 0:00:12:08. You will now have a white solid that will act as a transition between the video in Layer 1—Titles.mov—and the next section of the video as shown in Figure 1-12.

9. Save the movie.

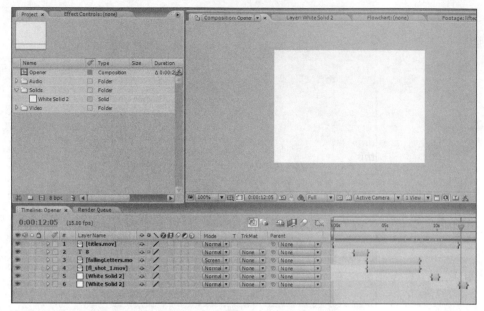

Figure 1-12. Solids perform a variety of use functions in After Effects.

Transforming and manipulating video clips

The next section of this small video will show the user some of things that can be done using Flash and After Effects. The plan is to use four clips for this process. One clip will serve as the background for the demo (background.mov), and the remaining three clips (ae_shot_1.mov to ae_shot_3.mov) will show what the applications can do.

The plan is to scale two of them (Clips 1 and 3) to 25% of their original size, and the third one will appear over the background clip at 50% of its original size. Finally, as each of the three clips finishes, it will fade out. In many respects this could be a rather complex and intimidating process. It isn't if you follow the first rule of digital media creation: *Let the software do the work*. Here's how:

1. Open the Video folder and drag ae_shot_2.mov to the bottom of the timeline.
2. Drag the playback head to the 0:00:12:08 mark and drag the video until its In point aligns with the playback head.

Obviously this video is too large for our purposes. It is to sit in the middle of the screen and appear above three other videos. It will need to be reduced to 50% of its current size.

Before we do that, this is a good time for a short break to talk about the timeline and what a cluttered place it can be. If you twirl down a layer to expose its properties, you may notice that the list takes up quite a bit of screen real estate. If you have a complex project with, say, 25 layers, trying to twirl down each layer and adjust its properties while showing all of the other layers and their properties would require a monitor the size of a drive-in movie theater screen. This is why it is so important that you start learning how to show only the property required for the layer. In this example, the video will need to be scaled and its opacity adjusted. Each of the properties that affect an object on the timeline has a keyboard equivalent that will open only that property. We will be using this technique in this section and throughout the book.

3. Select the layer containing the new video clip and press the S key to open the Scale properties.

4. Double-click one of the Scale values and change it to 50. The video will reduce to 50% of its original dimensions while still remaining centered on the screen in the Comp window.

5. Press the T key to open the Opacity settings.

6. Drag the playback head to the 18-second mark and click the stopwatch beside the word *Opacity* to add a keyframe.

7. Drag the playback head to the Out point of the clip and change the Opacity value to 0% as shown in Figure 1-13. When you press the Return/Enter key, a new keyframe will be added at that point.

Figure 1-13. The clip will fade out between the two keyframes.

8. Drag the ae_shot_3.mov file to the bottom of the timeline and align its In point with the previous video's In point.

9. Select the video and add the following properties:

- Position: 80,60 (press P on the keyboard)
- Scale: 50%
- Opacity: 100% at 0:00:18:11, 0% at the Out point

10. Drag the ae_shot_1.mov file to the bottom of the timeline and align its In point with the previous video's In point. Set the Out point to 0:00:19:04.

11. Select the video and add the following properties:

    - Position: 240,180 (press P on the keyboard)
    - Scale: 50%
    - Opacity: 100% at 0:00:18:11, 0% at the Out point

12. Save the file and click the Play button to preview your work so far. It should resemble Figure 1-14.

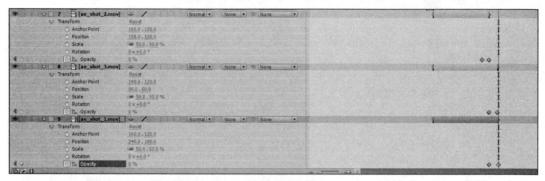

Figure 1-14. The videos are positioned, scaled, and their opacity set.

Animating text in After Effects

One of the hallmarks of motion graphics is animated text. Though the effects you will create here can be done just as easily in Flash, the purpose here is to get you comfortable using the timeline. Later on in the book, Chapter 3 to be exact, you are going to discover how to create text effects that make these ones look like a bike with training wheels.

Still, the ability to animate text and embed that animation into an After Effects project is a core skill when it comes to working with After Effects. The first thing you need to know is that all text goes on a Text layer and that you can edit the text directly in the Comp window and change the font, style, size, color, and other properties of the text.

In many ways, a Text layer is no different from any other layer in After Effects. Content on these layers can be manipulated, have effects applied to them, and so on, much as you have done with video to this point in the chapter. Another really neat feature of a Text layer is that text can be copied from Photoshop, Illustrator, and Flash and pasted directly into it. This is because After Effects supports Unicode characters. Just to prove to you that it can be done, one of the authors copied and pasted the first paragraph of this section into an After Effects Text layer. The results are in Figure 1-15.

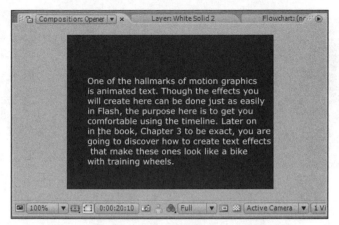

Figure 1-15. Text can be copied and pasted into After Effects from many other applications . . . including word processing programs.

Let's start animating the title of this book!

1. Select the Text tool, click the Comp window once, and enter the text poetry. Drag this new Text layer to the bottom of the timeline. Select the new Text layer in the timeline, press the P key, and set the position to 160,120.

2. Select Window ➤ Character to open the Character panel. Use these settings to format the text:

  - Font: Verdana
  - Size: 30 px
  - Style: Regular
  - Color: 5C6FE6 (light blue)

> *To change the color of any selected text, click the Color chip in the* Character *panel and click the color you wish to add. If you know the RGB or hexadecimal color values, you can enter them, as shown in Figure 1-16, directly into the* Color Picker.

Figure 1-16. Either click a color or enter the values directly into the Color Picker.

3. Set the In point for the text to match the Out point, 0:00:19:04, of the layer directly above the text. Also set the Out point for this layer to 0:00:25:14.

4. Move the playback head to the start of the Text layer and press the S key to open the layer's Scale properties. Change the Scale value to 315%.

5. Use the following values to scale the text four more times:

Time	Scale Value
0:00:21:14	100%
0:00:22:21	100%
0:00:23:12	350%
0:00:24:03	100%

You may be wondering why there are two keyframes with a Scale *value of 100%. If we didn't add that second keyframe, the text would scale from 100% to 350% between the keyframes. The intention is to have the text scale up to 350% in less than a second, meaning there has to be that second keyframe.*

6. If you scrub the playback head across the layer, you will see the text grow and shrink. It will also need to fade out as well. Press the T key to open the Opacity properties. Add the following keyframes and Opacity values:

Time	Opacity Value
0:00:21:13	100%
0:00:21:24	0%
0:00:22:21	0%
0:00:24:03	90%
0:00:24:14	0%
0:00:25:14	0%

The remaining three text layers will follow the lead of the Poetry *layer. The text will grow and shrink and fade in and fade out as the playback head moves across the timeline.*

7. Select the Text tool and enter the text in. Drag this in layer under the Poetry layer. Set the In point for this layer to 0:00:21:14 and the Out point to 0:00:25:14. Press the P key and set the position to 160,120.

8. Apply the following Scale values to this layer:

Time	Scale Value
0:00:21:14	350%
0:00:22:10	100%
0:00:23:14	100%
0:00:24:07	350%
0:00:24:14	115%

9. Press the T key to open the Opacity properties. Add the following keyframes and Opacity values:

Time	Opacity Value
0:00:21:14	100%
0:00:22:14	0%
0:00:23:14	3%
0:00:24:14	90%
0:00:25:08	0%
0:00:25:14	0%

10. Select the Text tool and enter the text motion. Set the In point for this layer to 0:00:22:08 and the Out point to 0:00:25:14. Press the P key and set the position to 160,120.

11. Apply the following Scale values to this layer:

Time	Scale Value
0:00:22:08	350%
0:00:22:14	100%
0:00:24:07	115%
0:00:24:14	315%
0:00:25:14	100%

12. Press the T key to open the Opacity properties. Add the following keyframes and Opacity values:

Time	Opacity Value
0:00:22:14	100%
0:00:23:10	0%
0:00:24:07	3%
0:00:25:00	100%
0:00:25:14	0%

13. Save the file. Your text should be scaled and faded as in Figure 1-17.

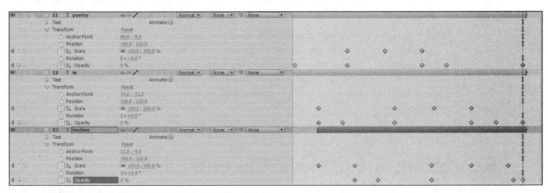

Figure 1-17. The text is scaled and faded using the timeline.

14. Drag the playback head to the 21-second mark of the timeline and drag the clouds_w_lines.mov file to the bottom of the timeline. Set its In point to the 21-second mark as well.

15. Save the file and click the Play button in the Time Controls panel to preview the movie.

There is one last bit of housekeeping to do before we lay in the soundtrack. There needs to be a bit of a transition out of the videos that play just before the text appears.

16. Drag the background.mov file from the Video folder to the bottom of the timeline. Set the In point of this clip to 0:00:19:04 and the Out point to 0:00:21:00. Open the Opacity properties for this clip and change the Opacity to 100% at 0:00:20:00 and to 0% at 0:00:21:00.

Adding audio to your project

As you have seen earlier in this chapter, you can import audio directly into your project. The audio file formats that can be imported are as follows:

- Advanced Audio Coding (AAC)
- AU
- Audio Interchange File Format (AIFF)
- MP3
- Video for Windows (AVI or WAV)
- WAVE (WAV)

If your projects are inevitably destined for playback in Flash, you may as well stick with the MP3 format, because all audio in Flash is converted to this format when your Flash movie plays.

1. Open the Audio folder in the Project panel and drag the Lifted.mp3 file to the bottom of the timeline.
2. The audio file will run the length of the movie. If you want to preview the file, select Composition ➤ Preview ➤ Audio Preview (Work Area) and the audio will play. If you want to preview the video, with the audio track, click the RAM Preview button in the Time Controls panel. The entire movie will be moved to RAM and will play back. Just be aware that a RAM preview plays a bit slower than a regular QuickTime video.

Rendering the project: the end game

With all of the assets in place, the time has arrived to create the video that will be used in Flash. The process is not terribly difficult to understand and, in many respects, is easier to do for Flash than were the video to be prepared for broadcast or other medium.

The reason is the video you will output does not really need to be compressed. To the average video developer, that last statement is rather heretical, but it is true. When you convert this video from a QuickTime movie to the FLV format used by Flash, you will be compressing the video using what is called a **lossy codec**. That means one of the reasons these video files are relatively small is because information is lost during the compression. When you convert the video to Flash's FLV file format, you will be applying yet another lossy compressor to the file. This means a lot more information is lost, and, to be gentle, there is the inevitable degradation of video quality.

In this final section of this chapter, you will be creating the QuickTime video that will be converted to an FLV file in the next chapter.

Let's get busy.

1. Select Composition ➤ Add to Render Queue. This will place the entire Comp you have created into the Render Queue and will launch the Render Queue panel shown in Figure 1-18.

Figure 1-18. The Render Queue panel is where projects are transformed into videos.

The panel is divided into two areas. The top of the panel is where the Composition is rendered. This sort of explains the Render button. The bottom of the panel is where you will actually decide which settings will be used before you click the Render button.

If you have rendered several movies, they will be listed in the bottom half of the panel. To remove a previous render job, select the name and press the Delete key.

2. The next step in the process is to click the Best Settings link. This will open the Render Settings dialog box shown in Figure 1-19.

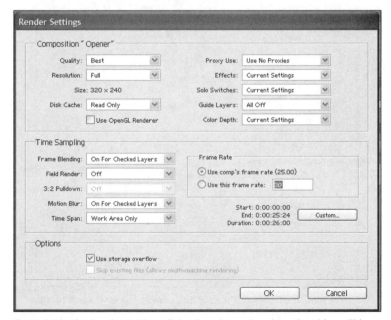

Figure 1-19. The Render Settings dialog box determines how the video will be created.

3. The dialog box shows the default values that will be applied when the video is created. For our needs we really don't need to change anything here. Click the OK button.

> *Though we are ignoring the settings in the* Render Settings *dialog box, one of the more important areas is the* Field Render *pull-down in the* Time Sampling *area. If you are creating footage for broadcast, the odds are really good the footage needs to be interlaced. This means alternate lines of the video are displayed. In the digital universe this can play havoc with a video. This setting should always be set to* Off *when preparing video for computer output.*

4. Click the Lossless link in the Output Module area. The Output Module Settings dialog box that opens is the key to the project (see Figure 1-20). It is in this dialog box that you determine the how the video will be formatted.

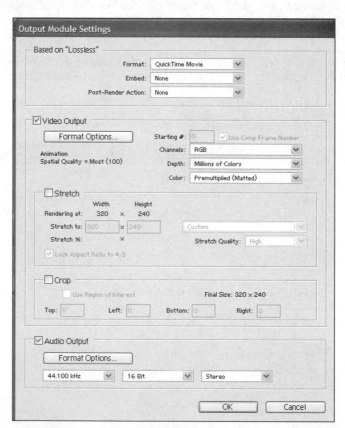

Figure 1-20. The Output Module Settings dialog box is where the video to be rendered receives its formatting instructions.

5. Click the Format pull-down menu in the Based on "Lossless" area at the top and select QuickTime Movie from the various choices available.

6. Select None in the Embed pull-down. This option allows you to embed the project into the final video file. All this serves to do is to add to the final file size and is not needed.

> *If you don't have QuickTime 7 installed on your PC, you can select* Video for Windows *or* Windows Media *from the Format pull-down. Both formats can be used by Flash.*

7. The next section is the Video Output area. This is where you will choose how the project will be compressed by selecting the appropriate codec. Click the Format Options button.

The goal of compression is to reduce the data rate—how much data flows into the video player—while maintaining image quality. Video destined for the Web might need to be compressed at a ratio of 50:1, 60:1, or higher. Lossless compression, where no essential data is lost, can compress by no more than 30:1. Thankfully we deal with humans, and human perception is not only based upon what we actually see and hear but also on what we think we see and hear. This means video can use lossy compression and still have acceptable quality. Though you can apply increasing amounts of lossy compression, the higher the value, the greater the sacrifice in quality.

The easiest way to reduce the file size of a video is to reduce its physical dimensions and/or its frame rate. For example, reduce the frame rate of a 30-frame-per-second video to 15 fps, and the data is reduced by 50%. Even so, there is still a huge issue to face. Reducing the physical size of the video, and its frame rate still does not reduce the bit-rate flow of the video. Digital video uses compression to control the flow, and there are two types of compression: **temporal** and **spatial**.

Temporal compression, sometimes known as **interframe compression**, sets aside just enough memory for one frame. When the video moves from the first frame to the second frame, all that happens is that the compressor looks at the first frame and simply paints over the things that changed.

By recording the changes between frames, rather than the frames themselves, you don't need a lot of extra data to be processed. Unfortunately, when there is a big change—a pan or a zoom—the process starts all over.

Spatial compression, or **intraframe compression**, is totally different. It looks at the frames in the video as being nothing more than a bunch of pixels with pretty colors. Sometimes referred to as **run-length encoding**, this method records consecutive runs of color and can achieve significant data stream reductions in areas where nothing changes. This system really falls apart when things change.

These two concepts are where your video headaches really start because they are at the core of the most common compression schemes used. The issues you will confront around working with video involve not only whether the compression is temporal or spatial, but whether the compression is **lossy** or **lossless**.

Lossless compression is good, and you should use it if you are going to be subsequently compressing the movie for web playback. The file will reduce—usually between 10% and 50%—but the files are still huge. If you are targeting a video for compression in the Flash Video Encoder, lossless compression is the way to go. When you compress an already compressed movie—a video that uses Cinepac or Sorenson compression is compressed in the Flash Video Encoder as well—there will be a definite loss of image quality.

As you may have guessed, lossy compression loses information . . . forever. Even so, the file-size reductions can be significant. In certain instances, these reductions can be in the order of 100:1, as is the case with Sorenson Squeeze.

The amount of the compression is under your control, but understand, *lossy compression introduces artifacts to your image.* As the file size starts decreasing, the severity of the artifacts increases. They usually first appear as blotches in areas of fine shading. At high compression, prepare to lose fine details and encounter a nasty sharpening effect called **ringing**.

8. When the Compression Settings dialog box opens, select Video from the multitude of codecs from the Compression Type pull-down (see Figure 1-21), drag the slider to the Best setting, and click OK to close the dialog box. The Video codec is a lossless codec and is ideal for our needs.

Figure 1-21. The Video codec is a lossless codec.

Compression and decompression are accomplished by a set of mathematical calculations called a **codec**, which is short for **COmpressor/DECompressor** or **enCODer/DECoder**. Codecs compress data as it is encoded and decompress it for playback. In order for a video to be played, it must be decompressed by the same codec used to compress the video. This explains why, in certain instances, you are asked by your computer to find the codec for a video you may want to watch.

9. Click the Audio Output check box and select Mono from the Stereo pull-down.

If you do not click the Audio Output check box shown in Figure 1-22, the audio track will be ignored when the video is created.

Figure 1-22. If you don't select the Audio Output check box, the audio track won't be added to the video.

Remember, video is always composed of two tracks—an audio track and a video track. In fact, when you create a video, the audio is compressed using a separate codec from that used by the video compressor. The choice of mono really is a serious one. The average person with a sound system connected to their computer really won't get the benefit of true stereo simply because the boxes enclosing the speakers are most likely more expensive than the speakers themselves. As well, simply reducing the sound from stereo to audio has the effect of cutting the size of the sound file by 50%.

10. Click OK to return to the Render Queue. Click the Output To link to open the Save As dialog box. Navigate to the folder where you will be saving the final video and click OK. You will be returned to the Render Queue.

11. Click the Render button.

Clicking the Render button starts the video creation process. You will see a progress bar, shown in Figure 1-23, move across the window, and you will also see each frame of the video being rendered appear in the Comp window. When the process finishes, a chime will play.

Figure 1-23. The video is being created.

> *If you want to remove a Comp from the Render Queue, select it in the* Render Queue *panel and press the Delete key.*

12. Save the file. This will create an AEP file that retains all of the project settings. This is an extremely valuable file in situations where changes need to be made to the video.

13. Quit After Effects 7.

14. Locate the QuickTime file you have just created and open it in QuickTime (see Figure 1-24).

Figure 1-24. The project playing in the QuickTime player.

Summary

This chapter has lived up to its title—"From Concept to Final Product in After Effects 7." It also started us on our dragon hunt.

You started off the chapter by learning how to create a project and a new Composition in After Effects. In many respects, once you learn how to create a new Composition in After Effects, you will repeat these steps innumerable times as you create motion graphics for use in Flash 8. The key aspect of the Composition is ensuring you maintain the 4:3 aspect ratio of the video's dimensions and that you use square pixels. They are important when the video is used in Flash.

You were also shown how to add content to the timeline, how to trim content to specific durations on the timeline, and how to move clips and layers around in the timeline. We also showed you how manipulate the content by adding keyframes to a layer and scaling or changing the opacity of a clip between those keyframes. In many respects, you have discovered there is very little difference between a keyframe in After Effects and its Flash counterpart.

We also showed you how to add and format text, how to create a new solid, and how to add audio to the project.

The chapter finished by using the Render Queue to output the final QuickTime movie.

In the next chapter, we continue our dragon hunt by converting the video you have created to an FLV file, and you will learn how to play the video through the new FLVPlayback component. We are also going to show you how to create your own custom player in Flash that does everything the FLVPlayback component does but in a space that is rather small. See you there.

1

2 FROM FINAL PRODUCT TO UPLOAD IN FLASH PROFESSIONAL 8

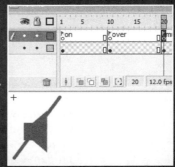

In the previous chapter, you created a video using After Effects. In this chapter, you prepare the video for playback in Flash Professional 8 and upload it to your website.

The phrase "prepare the video for playback in Flash Professional 8" is what has really gotten the attention of web developers and their clients. Ever since the late 2005 introduction of Flash Professional 8, it seems like video has exploded across the Web. One of the reasons, as you will soon discover, is that Adobe pulled off the impossible: they made web video more feature-rich but easier to create and deploy than ever before. Almost overnight, it seemed, web video moved from being seen as an interesting feature to a must-have element in websites.

In this chapter, we are going to do the following:

- Convert a QuickTime video to Flash Video (FLV) format.
- Use the Flash components to play the video.
- Create your own custom video player for Flash.

A brief word on streaming

Before you convert the video created in the previous chapter to the Flash Video format, you must understand the following:

- Flash Video streams into the Flash Player from your web server.
- The decisions you make before you create the video will directly impact whether the viewer has a positive or a negative experience with the video.

The key word is *stream*, which is a fancy word that describes the flow of information from the server to the SWF in the web page. The best way of envisioning a stream is to regard it as being like a river that connects a lake in a mountain to a lake in a valley. The water flows smoothly from the lake in the mountain, down the river, and into the lake in the valley. The water in the river moves at a constant speed, and the water rarely overruns the banks of the river, flooding the town that straddles the river. Let's assume that a rather large rainstorm occurred over the lake in the mountain and a foot of rain falls into the lake. That amount of water will rush out of the lake, down the river, flood the town, and eventually run into the lake in the valley, causing it to overrun its banks. It is no different with Flash Video.

When it comes to **streaming**, the river is the connection, or **pipe**, between the server and the Flash Player. The width of the connection, **bandwidth**, determines how much information can flow into the Flash Player, and how fast the river flows is the **data rate**. If too much information flows down the pipe, it will clog the Flash Player, and the user will experience inordinate wait times; video that plays, stops, replays; or even video that is jerky. It is the prudent Flash designer who has not only a design strategy in place but also a bandwidth strategy as well.

In very basic terms, streaming is the distribution of real-time or live audio or video through the Internet.

For the purposes of this discussion, there are three primary characteristics that define streaming media:

- It enables real-time or on-demand access to audio/video content through the Internet. That means the audio or the video plays immediately—there is no delay.

  The ability to provide on-demand content can't be understated. Any video you produce can be accessed at any time from anywhere.

- It is transmitted by a media server application (for example, a Flash Media Server or Real Media Server) and is played back and processed by a client player application (in this case Flash Player 8 or RealPlayer) as it is received.

  In basic terms, the video is transferred to a web page using a server application such as a web server or a Flash Media Server and is displayed in a browser using a client application such as Flash Player 8. The rate the data is fed into the client by the server is, in general terms, the stream. This stream of data into a Flash Player is the key issue surrounding the successful delivery and playback of a video. If too much information is moving into the client, it can't keep up. When this happens, the information is buffered. A **buffer** is nothing more than a place where enough data is stored to start playing the video and to play it successfully through to completion. Videos that take an inordinate amount of time to load and play or that start and stop are symptomatic of a developer who didn't pay attention to the stream of data from the server to the client.

Though a hallmark of web media technologies is that a file has to download before it starts to play, Flash moves in a different direction. It uses a **progressive download**, which starts the video playing before the download completes.

- Streamed files are received, processed, and played when they arrive, and no residual copy of the video is left behind.

  This is true of files that are streamed to Flash Player 8 through a Flash Media Server. FLV files arriving via your regular web server will wind up in the browser cache. Obviously, if security of the files is paramount, the Flash Media Server is a logical solution.

The importance of data rate

One of the fundamental maxims of working with digital video is this: *Data rate controls quality. Bandwidth controls the user experience.*

Regardless of which computer platform is used, the pipe is your prime consideration, and when it comes to creating and playing Flash video, *always keep an eye on the pipe.*

The pipe can make or break the user's experience. If he or she has a lot of bandwidth, such as a T1 line in a corporation or high-speed Internet at home, that user can view full-length movies with little or no disruption. If the user is in a remote or rural situation, the odds are very good he or she has a dial-up modem, meaning his or her bandwidth is limited.

To wrap your mind around the differences, think of a highway tunnel that goes under a lake. If the tunnel is part of a four-lane highway, thousands of cars simply approach the tunnel and zip through it at the posted speed. This is because the tunnel's entrance is the same width as the highway.

Now abruptly reduce the diameter of the tunnel from four lanes to one lane each way. Now thousands of cars have to squeeze into one lane of traffic and reduce their speed to a crawl as they approach the tunnel's entrance and proceed into the tunnel; we have all experienced how infuriating such a delay can be. The cars in this example represent data, and how fast they move represents the data rate. Think of a T1 line as being the tunnel for the four-lane expressway and the single-lane tunnel as dial-up service, the highway is the server, and the user is the poor guy behind the steering wheel in the car.

It goes without saying that when you plan to deliver video, you need to have a solid bandwidth strategy in place for the user, the server, and the video. The server bandwidth strategy must take into account the maximum number of users that can access the video at any one time. The last thing you need is for your user to get into the middle of a traffic jam waiting to download and view the video.

When it comes to the user, you need to be aware of the width of the tunnel up ahead. You need to leave enough room for the data stream but also other Internet activities. Not doing this is quite similar to having a transport truck sitting at the side of the road and jutting out into traffic. Things will stop or seriously slow down as the cars reduce their speed to avoid driving into the back of the truck. In a dial-up situation, a user with a 56.6K connection can drive along the highway at 56.6 kilobits per second (Kbps). When it comes to video, a target data rate of 40 Kbps, which leaves room for other activities, is normal.

So what is data rate? Data rate is simply the amount of data (cars on a highway in our analogy) transferred per second to the user's computer. This in turn determines the bandwidth required to play the video. The data rate calculation is

Data rate = (w $\times$ h $\times$ color depth $\times$ frames per second)/compression

Let's do the data rate calculation for the video created in the previous chapter. The video's values are

- Width: 320
- Height: 240
- Color depth: 24
- Frames per second: 15
- Compression: 60 (The benchmark compression ratio for both ON2 Flix and Sorenson Squeeze is 60:1.)

Data rate = (320 $\times$ 240 $\times$ 24 $\times$ 15)/60

Data rate = (27,648,000)/60

Data rate = 460,800

The data rate for the video at 15 frames per second (fps) is 460,800 bits per second (bps), or 461 Kbps. The second line of the calculation is there for a deliberate reason. If you were to apply no compression to the video, you would use a data rate of about 27.6 million bps. To deliver that video, you would need an Internet connection the size of the tunnel between Britain and France. Toss in the compression, and the video can safely be delivered to most users.

If you are creating video for Internet delivery, use these common data rates for delivery of the FLV file to the Flash Player:

Connection type	Data rate
Dial-up	60 Kbps
DSL	Between 150 and 300 Kbps
Cable	Between 200 and 300 Kbps
T1 or T3 line	150 to 430 Kbps

The Flash Player supports a maximum data rate of 4 megabits per second (Mbps).

One final consideration in regard to data rate is that the number shown in the compression applications is a bit disingenuous. If you use the FLV Encoder and use the Medium default setting, you set the data rate of a video to 400 Kbps. This is not the final data rate. Remember, video is composed of both an audio track and a video track. The number you set affects just the video track. If you look at the data rate for the audio track, it was set to 96 Kbps. This means the data rate for the video is 496 Kbps.

Keyframes and streaming

Other factors that could impact the user experience are frame rate and keyframe placement.

Frame rate is the speed at which a video plays. One of the more common frame rates for digital video is 29 or 30 fps, which matches the North American video standard of 29.97 fps. Another common frame rate is 24 fps. Regardless of which one you have been handed, there will be occasions when you may wish to reduce the rate such as in low-bandwidth situations. If you want to lower the frame rate, you should use equal divisions of the source frame rate. For 30 fps, use 15 fps, 10 fps, 7.5 fps, and so on. For 24 fps, use 12 fps, 8 fps, 6 fps, and so on.

Be careful when you consider playing with the frame rate. Your FLV frame rate should be as close to the Flash frame rate as possible. The reason is the audio track in the video—it always plays back at the original frame rate. Let's assume you create an FLV file that uses 24 fps. Place that in a Flash movie that plays back at 12 fps. The video portion will play at 12 fps, but the audio will zip along at 24 fps . . . a nasty scenario to say the least.

Keyframes in video, in many respects, are similar to keyframes in Flash. In video, a keyframe contains all of the data in that frame—where they part company is in what happens between the keyframes. In video, the frames between the keyframes are called **difference frames**, also referred to as **delta frames** by techie types. Difference frames remove the stuff that doesn't move or change from each frame between the keyframes. This means the file size is reduced. Now let's be very careful because a bad decision here can ruin your work.

If you were to stand at the side of a major city intersection and shoot cars and people walking by, there is going to be a lot of change and very few difference frames. Now say you were to take your camera into a farmer's field and shoot some footage of a tree. There wouldn't be a lot of change, meaning there could be a lot of difference frames. This explains why a 30-second video of a Formula One race is a lot larger in file size than that of a 30-second video of a tree in a field. Fewer difference frames means larger file size. The problem is, if you spread out the keyframes in the Formula One video, the figure quality degrades and looks blurry. We wish we could say to you there is a hard-and-fast rule about keyframe frequency, but there isn't.

Before you encode the video, watch the video and see whether there is a lot of movement both in the video and with the camera. This will determine the keyframe frequency.

By spreading out the keyframes, you can have quite a positive impact upon the final size of the FLV file. What you don't want to do is to think all video is created equally. If there is a lot of motion—a Formula One race—you will need more keyframes. If you have a "talking head" video—a tree in a field—you can get away with fewer keyframes. The bottom line is this decision is up to you, but it is the prudent developer who reviews the entire video prior to converting the file to FLV.

> *If you are going to be building a custom video controller that contains a scrubber, one keyframe per second is the benchmark.*

Frame size

Another major factor to consider is the physical size of the video. The larger the video is on screen, the greater the demand it places on bandwidth. Common video sizes are listed here:

- **NTSC**: 640×48
- **PAL**: 768×576 (This is the European standard.)
- **Wide screen**: 720×576
- **Flash Video**: Pick a number

Obviously, creating an FLV file at 720×576 is going to pose a huge issue to the poor viewer. This is why most FLV files use 320×240, 240×180, 160×120, and 80×60. Even so, the astute developer keeps the user, not the technology, foremost in mind, creating the video by targeting the bandwidth.

A larger video—320×240—requires more screen real estate. It will also have a higher resolution and better quality. The downside is a larger file size and a rather large appetite for bandwidth, making it difficult, at best, for the poor user with a dial-up connection.

On the other hand, a smaller video—240×180 or 160×120—has a smaller browser footprint, and the trade-off will be a decrease in resolution and detail. The upside, of course, is a smaller file size and a reduced bandwidth requirement.

When you use the Flash 8 Video Encoder or any other application that creates the FLV file, you will be asked the following questions regarding how the FLV file will be created:

- What bit rate will be used to stream the video?
- What frame size will be used to present the video?
- What frame interval should be used for the keyframes?

So much for theory, let's get to work.

Creating the FLV file using the Flash 8 Video Encoder

When you installed Flash Professional 8 onto your computer, you also installed a "side application" named the Flash 8 Video Encoder. The sole purpose of the Video Encoder is to convert a video file such as a MOV, AVI, or WMV file into the Flash Video format, which has the .flv extension. Keep in mind that FLV files can only be used with Flash. They can't be viewed by any other media player, and even then FLV files can only be viewed in Flash using either the FLVPlayback component or through an ActionScript-controlled player you construct.

Before you start converting your After Effects videos to the FLV format, you need to have a deployment strategy in place. This strategy asks a simple question:

What version of the Flash Player will be targeted?

The answer will determine which codec will be used in the Flash 8 Video Encoder to compress the video and the components you can use. If you are targeting Flash Player 6 or 7, you can't encode a video containing an alpha channel (which allows you to define transparency levels in your video), and you can't use the new FLVPlayback components in Flash 8. Though you can use both of the codecs—Sorenson Spark and ON2VP6—that come bundled with the Video Encoder, it is better you stay with the Sorenson Spark codec. In fact, if you choose one of the presets aimed at Flash Player 7, the default codec will be the Sorenson Spark codec.

1. Launch the Flash 8 Video Encoder. In both the Mac and the PC versions of Flash, the Video Encoder can be found in the Flash application folder on your hard drive. On the PC, the application can be found at C:\Program Files\Macromedia\ Flash 8 Video Encoder. On the Mac, it can be found at MacintoshHD\ Applications\Macromedia\Flash 8 Video Encoder.

2. When the Video Encoder opens, locate the video prepared in the previous chapter (a copy of the file, FinalOpener.mov, can be found in the Exercise folder within the Chapter 2 code download), and drag and drop it onto the interface. When you release the mouse, the video will drop into place, and you will be shown the compression to be applied to the file and whether the file has been encoded as shown in Figure 2-1.

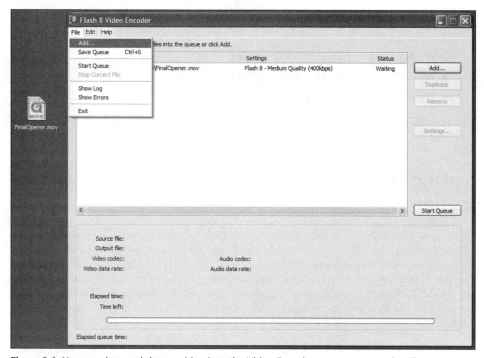

Figure 2-1. You can drag and drop a video into the Video Encoder or you can use the File menu.

Another method of adding a video to the Video Encoder is to select File ➤ Add *or click the* Add *button as shown in Figure 2-1, and, when the* Open *dialog box appears, navigate to the folder containing the video.*

The next step is not to click the Start Queue button, which will start encoding the video using a preset value. You are about to discover you really don't need to use the presets. Leave them to the rookies.

3. Select the file and click the Settings button to open the Flash Video Encoding Settings dialog box. When it is open, click the Show Advanced Settings button to bring up the Advanced Settings options as shown in Figure 2-2.

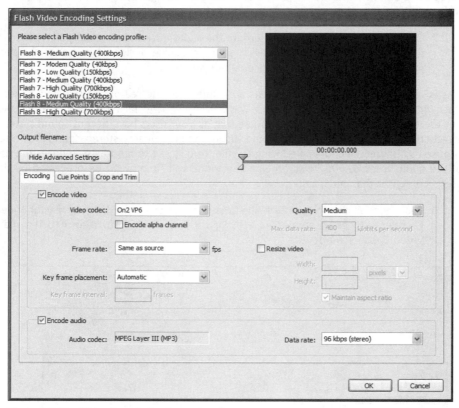

Figure 2-2. The Video Encoder's advanced options

When you click the Show Advanced Settings button, the entire interface opens. At the top, the pull-down menu presents you with a number of preset encoding values. These presets are aimed at either Flash Player 7 or Flash Player 8. If you choose a Flash 7 preset, the Sorenson Spark codec will be used, and, if you choose a Flash 8 preset, the ON2VP6 codec will be used for the compression. You can also scrub across the video using the scrub button and even set the In and Out points for the encoding by dragging the sliders under the scrubber.

The next areas ask how you wish to treat the video and the audio tracks in the video.

4. Make sure the Encode video box is checked and select ON2VP6 from the Video codec pull-down menu.

5. Click the Quality pull-down menu and select Custom from the choices.

6. You will now notice that the Max data rate area is no longer grayed out. Enter 300 as the Max data rate.

The number you just entered into the Max data rate area is an arbitrary number. The decision regarding data rate is one we consider as being subjective, not objective. The reason, as we pointed out earlier, is that data rate determines quality, and no two people can ever agree on a definition for quality. The best advice we can give you here is to experiment with various rates and determine which settings best suit your quality needs.

7. Check the Encode audio box to ensure the audio track will be encoded into the FLV file. Not selecting it will result in your producing a video for the deaf. Select 48 kbps (mono) from the Data rate pull-down menu.

This is another area where all decisions are subjective. The reason we selected a mono track with a relatively medium data rate was because we are "falling in love with the user, not the technology." You can't just assume that all your users have decent sound systems attached to their computers that would justify medium-quality stereo sound. You may choose to disagree, of course. Reducing the file from stereo to mono also reduces the size of the audio track by 50%, which means the sound will stream and be processed by the user's computer that much faster.

8. Click once in the Output file name area and name the file Opener. If your Video Encoder settings resemble those in Figure 2-3, click OK to return to the main Video Encoder window.

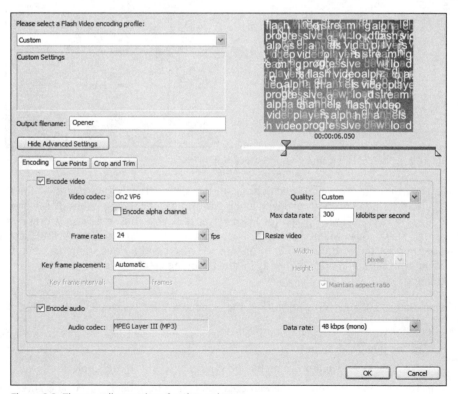

Figure 2-3. The encoding settings for the project

9. When you return to the Video Encoder window, click the Start Queue button. The process will start, as you see in Figure 2-4, and you will be shown the progress of the encoding process and the settings used. If you make a mistake, you can always click the Stop Queue button. To return to the encoding settings, select the video in the Video Encoder window and select Edit ➤ Reset Status.

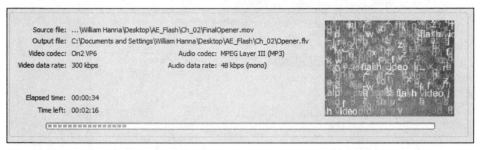

Figure 2-4. The video is being encoded.

When the encoding finishes, the FLV file will be placed in the same directory as the QuickTime MOV that was just encoded. At this stage, you can select the file in the window and click the Remove button to remove the video from the queue. If you do remove the video, you won't be deleting the original video. In fact, a dialog box will open that reassures you this isn't the case. If you realize you made a mistake with one of the settings, and you haven't removed the video from the queue, select the video and then select Edit ➤ Reset Status. This essentially tells the Video Encoder the video is going to be encoded, and, when you click the Settings button, the encoding settings applied to the video will be intact.

10. Quit the Video Encoder.

You are now in for a very pleasant surprise. If you open the folder containing the QuickTime movie and the FLV file you just created, you will notice that the video is 19MB in size, while the FLV file you just created is about 1.5MB. This is quite normal, and, when you create and test the video player in the next exercise, you will also discover a serious file-size reduction does not mean a major quality sacrifice on your part.

> *The FLV file you created can only be read by the Flash Player. You can't double-click the FLV file and preview the video. If you wish to do that, head over to* www. download.com *and do a search for FLV players. They offer the current version of FLV Player (at the time of this writing it is 1.3.3.) of one of the best, by Martijn de Visser.*

If you are a hardcore After Effects user, you have probably read this section and wondered why we were wasting our time. You can create the FLV file right out of After Effects 7 by selecting File ➤ Export ➤ Macromedia Flash Video (FLV), *as demonstrated in Figure 2-5. You are absolutely correct, but doing so opens the Flash 8 Video Encoder. By reviewing the application, you now know how to use the window that opens when you choose that menu item in After Effects.*

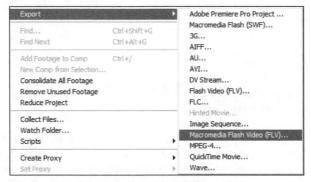

Figure 2-5. You can go directly to the Video Encoder from After Effects using the Export menu in After Effects.

Playing an FLV file in Flash Professional 8

Now that you have created the FLV file, you are half the way there to getting the video to play on a website. The balance of this chapter is designed to show you four ways of accomplishing this task:

- Use the new Flash 8 FLVPlayback component.
- Use the Flash 6-7 MediaPlayback component when Flash Player 6 or the Flash Player 7 is your target player.
- Use the FLVPlayback UI controls to create a custom player.
- Create your own player.

You should be aware the last two methods will require the use of ActionScript to make the player fully functional. If you have never been exposed to ActionScript, don't let that get in your way. The code presented will get you up and running in no time and does not get into the really advanced stuff you can do with ActionScript. In fact, the code to be presented is the absolute minimum you need to know to stream video.

The other thing to keep in mind is you are eventually going to have to use ActionScript in your video endeavors. You won't be able to avoid it. Let's look a couple of scenarios, shall we?

You are the master of your After Effects universe and have decided to permit the world to marvel at your After Effects prowess on your website. The design is quite radical, and the design of the FLVPlayback component simply doesn't mesh with your design. Though you can change the look and feel of the component, in the hands of someone who is new to Flash or has a basic understanding of ActionScript, changing a component is not recommended. You will need to create your own video player, and, to do that, you will need to create your own custom controller.

In the second scenario, your work is going to appear in an ad on one of the major sites out there. The problem is, you have been told that the SWF file you create for the video can be no more than 30K in size. Considering the fact the FLVPlayback component adds 37K to a SWF file, you are going to have to create your own player to fit.

You may be looking at those two scenarios and thinking, "As if that will ever happen!" We can assure you, it will. The standard file size for a SWF file in any rich media ad on a page is around 40K, and the car and movie companies are not using the components for that very reason. They are creating their own custom players to meet that constraint. Another example is CNET.com, who make extensive use of Flash Video on their site and use their own custom controller. Try navigating to www.cnet.com and looking around the site for a bit.

Using the Flash 8 FLVPlayback component

This is where everybody starts with Flash Video because it is both easy to do and "code free."

1. Open a new Flash document and save it to the Chapter 2 Exercise folder—we'll leave what to name the file up to you. The reason for this is "basic self-defense." By having the FLA and the FLV files in the same folder, you will never lose the path to your video.

2. Select Window ➤ Components to open the Components panel.

3. Click FLVPlayback—Player 8 once and when it opens drag a copy of the FLVPlayback component to the stage. You will most likely see a big black box (shown in Figure 2-6) with an FLV icon in the middle. If there are controls visible, they are the ones assigned when the component was last used.

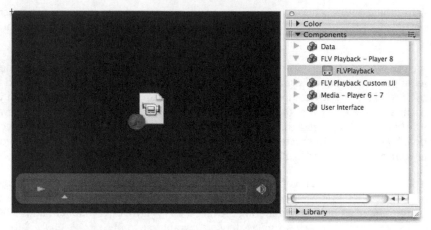

Figure 2-6. The component is on the stage.

4. Click the component on the stage once and then select the Parameters tab in the Property inspector. This is where the video is added to the component.

5. Double-click the contentPath area of the component to open the Content Path dialog box (see Figure 2-7). Click the Browse button (the folder icon) to open the Browse for FLV File dialog box. Navigate to the folder containing the FLV you just created. Select the FLV file and click the Open button. The dialog box will close and the name of the selected FLV file will appear in the Content Path dialog box.

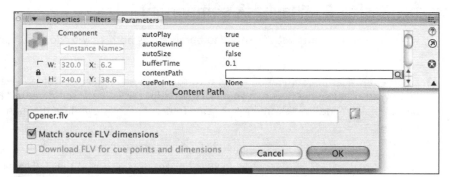

Figure 2-7. The FLV file to be added to the component is select through the Content Path dialog box.

6. Select the Match source FLV dimensions check box. The neat thing about this check box is it reads the height and width metadata that was added to the FLV file when you created it. This means, for example, if you have an FLV file that is 723 pixels wide and 124 pixels high, the component will automatically spring to those dimensions. Click OK to close the dialog box and return to the Parameters panel in the Property inspector.

If you see a path such as C:\Documents\My Documents\Videos\myVideo.flv *in the* contentPath *area, you are about to experience a world of hurt. That path will be hard-wired into the SWF file, and, when you try to play the video from your website, the SWF file will follow the path and inform whoever was unlucky enough to select the video that the path can't be found. This is why it makes sense to place the SWF file in the same folder as the FLV file.*

Yes, you can use a remote location for your FLV files. If you have a number of them in a folder on your site, you can set the path to http://www.mysite.com/FLVfolder/myVideo.flv.

7. Scroll down the parameter list and double-click the Skin area to open the Select Skin dialog box. Select SteelExternalAll.swf, as shown in Figure 2-8, from the list.

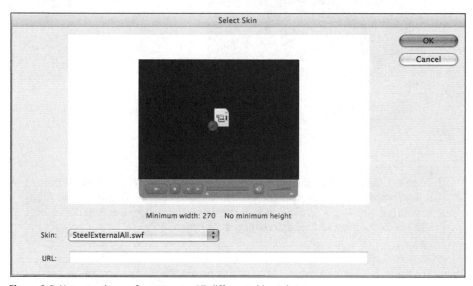

Figure 2-8. You can choose from among 27 different skin styles.

There are a couple of things to be aware of when choosing a skin. Pay attention to the minimum width number associated with the skin. If the FLV file is only 240 pixels wide and the minimum width is 270 pixels, the controller will not fit the video. The other thing to be aware of is if you choose one of the skins with "over" in its name, the controller will appear over the video. In this case, you have a decision to make. If you want the controls to be visible for the entire video, set the autoHide property in the Parameters tab—the one just under the Skin parameter—to false. The controls will appear over the video and will hide what is under them. If you set the autoHide parameter to true, the controls will appear anytime the user rolls over the video.

Yes, you can change the look and feel of a skin. No, we are not going to discuss how to accomplish this in this book. The reason is reskinning a component is not exactly an easy task to accomplish, and, if you don't know what you are doing, you can easily break the component.

8. Save the movie and test it by pressing Ctrl+Enter (PC) or Cmd+Return (Mac). The movie will be exported as a SWF file and, when it finishes exporting, the Export dialog box will close and the video will start playing as shown in Figure 2-9. When you finish the video, click the close button to return to Flash.

Figure 2-9.
The video playing in the skin

The SWF file you created should be regarded as being a test SWF file. Testing a Flash movie is not the same as publishing a Flash movie. Though a SWF file is created when you test the movie, it is common practice to select File ➤ Publish Options *in Flash when creating a SWF file.*

Obviously there is a lot of wasted space in this movie. The video sits on an overly large stage. Next, you'll fit the stage to the video and along the way discover a rather nasty gotcha associated with the FLVPlayback component.

1. When you return to Flash, select the component on the stage and then click the Properties tab of the Property inspector.

2. Set the X and Y coordinates for the component to 0. The video will now tuck up against the top-left edge of the stage.

3. Click the stage once and then click the Size button in the Property inspector. This will open the Document Properties dialog box.

4. Click the Contents button and click OK. When the dialog box closes, you will notice that the stage has shrunk to fit the video.

Not quite. In fact . . . "GOTCHA!!!"

5. Click the component on the stage, and, using the left or right arrow key, nudge the component until you can see the stage. As you can see from Figure 2-10, the controls are actually off of the bottom of the stage. This means if you were to publish the movie and post it to a website, the video would have no controls. Let's fix this nasty situation right now.

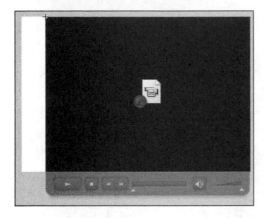

Figure 2-10.
The stage shrinks to fit only the video portion of the component.

6. Click the stage and click the Size button to return to the Document Properties dialog box. Change the height setting from 240 to 280 pixels. When you return to the stage, select the component and reset its X and Y coordinates to 0.

7. Save and test the movie.

That is all you need to know to get yourself going with video in Flash. Still, there are a couple of things to keep in mind when using the FLVPLayback component:

- The component only works in Flash Player 8. If your target player is Flash Player 7 or lower, you can't use this component.

- When you publish the video, you will have two SWF files appear in the folder. One will contain the name of the Flash movie, and the other will have the name of the skin applied to the component. Both of these files must be in the same folder for the component to work.

Targeting video for Flash 7 or lower

There will be instances when the target player for video will be Flash Player 7 or even Flash Player 6. This could be a situation, for example, where the video is being placed in a rich media advertisement and the specifications preclude the use of Flash Player 8. In this case, you can use the MediaPlayback component in the Media - Player 6 - 7 area of the Flash Components panel. Here's how:

1. Open the file created in the previous exercise. Select the FLVPlayback component and delete it.

2. Open the Components panel and open the Media - Player 6 - 7 component strip.

3. Drag a copy of the MediaPlayback component to the stage and set its dimensions to 320 by 240 and its X and Y positions to 0 in the Property inspector.

4. Select the component on the stage and select Window ➤ Component Inspector. When the Component inspector opens, click the Parameters tab and specify the following settings:

- FLV
- FPS: 24
- URL: Opener.flv
- Automatically Play
- Use Preferred Media Size
- Control Placement: Bottom
- Control Visibility: On

5. If your settings resemble those shown in Figure 2-11, save and test the movie.

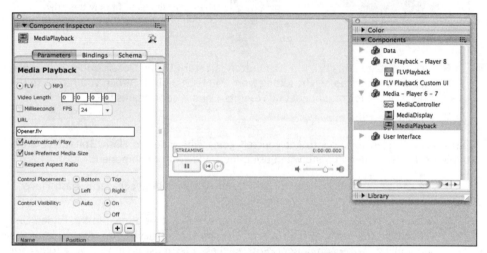

Figure 2-11. The style used for the MediaPlayback component is called Halo.

Using the FLVPlayback Custom UI components

This section answers a question that may be nagging at you: "That's all well and good, guys, but what if I only need a minimal set of controls?"

This is a valid question because there will be occasions when the full set of controls in the component is a bit overdone. It could be a situation where your clients are being given an opportunity to view their videos on a staging server, and all you really need is to give them the ability to play a video, fast forward through the video, pause/play the video, and even reduce the video's volume. Each of these features is available to you as a separate control. Follow these steps to create just such a video project:

1. Open the Controls.fla file located in the Chapter 2 Exercise folder. All we have done for you is to add an FLVPlayback component, with no skin, to the stage and create layers for the controls and the scripts you will write.

> *You may notice that we have locked the* Actions *layer. This is a common practice among Flash developers. By locking the* Actions *layer, you can't add content such as text or figures to the layer that will hold the ActionScript. Even though the* Actions *layer is locked, you can still add your script to it.*

2. Open the components window and open FLV Playback- Custom UI.

3. Select the Controls layer and drag a copy of the BackButton, ForwardButton, PlayPauseButton, and Volume components to the stage the video as shown in Figure 2-12.

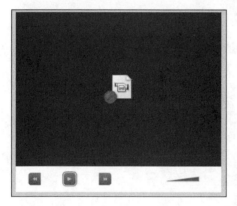

Figure 2-12.
The components are on the stage and ready to be wired up with ActionScript.

> *When components are dragged from the* Components *panel to the stage, a copy of the component is placed in the Library. When you drag a copy of the PausePlayButton component, copies of the PauseButton and PlayButton components, as well as the PausePlayButton component, are placed in the Library.*

With the components on the stage, you can now turn your attention to making them work. This will be accomplished through the use of ActionScript. Before you write the code, you must give each component a name—**called** and **instance name**—so that Flash knows what to do when a button is clicked.

1. Select each component on the stage, and in the Property inspector give them the following instance names:

   - FLVPlayBack: myVideo (see Figure 2-13)
   - BackButton: btnBack
   - PausePlayButton: btnPlay
   - ForwardButton: btnForward
   - VolumeBar: btnVolume

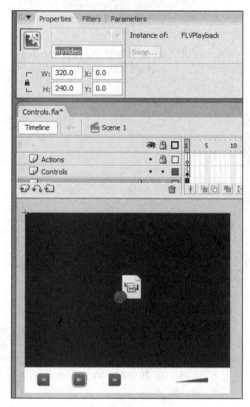

Figure 2-13.
Instance names are added in the Property inspector.

2. Click the first frame once in the Actions layer and press the F9 key to open the Actions panel. If you are using a Mac, F9 opens Expose. To open the Actions panel on a Mac, press the Option+F9 keys.

3. When the Actions panel opens, click once in the Script pane and add the following code:

```
myVideo.playPauseButton = btnPlay;
myVideo.backButton = btnBack;
myVideo.forwardButton = btnForward;
myVideo.volumeBar = btnVolume;
```

If you have never written ActionScript before, you may be looking at this and wondering, "Huh?" If you have never used the components, you may also be wondering the same thing.

These components are already smart enough to control a video. All you have to do is point one to the video component and tell Flash that the component being clicked has an instance name. Thus the first line of code, in English, reads "The btnPlay component is the instance name for playPauseButton, which turns the video, playing through the FLVPlayback component named myVideo, on and off."

> *If you are new to ActionScript, you may notice that some words such as* backButton *are blue and others are black. The words in blue are keywords used by ActionScript, and they must be spelled and capitalized exactly the way you entered them. If you enter* backbutton, *the word would be colored black, Flash wouldn't have a clue what you are talking about, and the* back *button simply wouldn't work.*

4. Save and test the movie. When you click the Play button, the video, as shown in Figure 2-14, starts playing.

Figure 2-14. The video is under the control of the buttons added to the stage and coded in the Script pane.

Creating a custom video player

To this point in the chapter you have been using the tools provided in Flash to create a video player. Though the tools are both easy to use and powerful, there will come a time when either due to space constraints or the need "for something different" you will start looking at creating your own custom player. A great example of this is the first exercise in this chapter. The final file size for the SWF file is 34K. On the surface this may seem like a relatively small size, but you can create a custom player that essentially performs all of the same tasks in a space that is 10K or less. In the Flash universe, "small is beautiful."

How is this possible? Pair a video object with ActionScript.

When you open the Flash Library and select the Library options pull-down menu, you will see a menu item named New Video. This is the video object, and when it is placed on the stage, you can use ActionScript to feed a video stream into it and to manage the stream.

We are going to start this chapter's final exercise in precisely that manner and then start building upon the exercise to the point where you will have created a fully functional video controller that fits in a very small space. Along the way, you will also learn how to deal with a rather complex project. How do you deal with complexity? From a position of simplicity.

When building this sort of thing, you just don't start constructing and coding until you reach the end of the task. That is a surefire recipe for failure. Instead, determine what needs to be constructed and coded, build and code it, and then test it. In short, build a bit and test it. Build a bit more and test it. In this way, if there is a mistake or an issue, it is dealt with immediately, you know exactly where the problem occurred, and, best of all, it won't ripple through the entire project.

In this project, we are going to

- Stream video into a video object.
- Create a pause/play button that will pause and play the video.
- Create a rewind button that will scoot the video's playback head back to the start of the video.
- Create a scrubber bar that will allow the user to jog forward and backward in the video.
- Create a button that turns the sound on and off.

Each one of these techniques will be contained in a file that can be found in the Completed folder within the Chapter 2 code download. If you have never really dug into ActionScript, each of the files will show you how a project is constructed and how one bit of code builds upon the others. As well, each of the following exercises is designed to move through ActionScript in a straight line from basic to somewhat advanced in a controlled manner. Along the way, you will obtain a firm grasp of the video techniques and code used for the remainder of this book.

Let's get busy.

Streaming video into a video object

First off this isn't going to be as difficult as it may first appear. There really are only three steps involved in the code, and, if you can remember six lines of code, you are in the game.

The steps are

- Connect.
- Stream.
- Play.

1. Open a new Flash document and set the stage size to 320 pixels wide by 240 pixels deep. Double-click the layer name and rename it Video.

2. Open the Library panel and click the Library panel options button to open the Library's pull-down menu. Select New Video (see Figure 2-15).

Figure 2-15. Video objects are added to a movie using the Library's pull-down menu.

3. When the Video Properties dialog box (shown in Figure 2-16) opens, be sure that Video (ActionScript controlled) is selected. The name for the symbol is irrelevant, but feel free to add one. Click OK to close the dialog box. When it closes, a little icon that looks like a video camera will be sitting in your library.

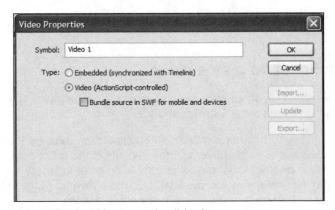

Figure 2-16. The Video Properties dialog box

4. Drag the video object from the Library to the stage, and, making sure the object is selected on the stage, give it these values in the Property inspector:

- Instance name: myVideo
- Width: 320
- Height: 240
- X: 0
- Y: 0

When you finish, you should see what looks like a box with a big X through it on the stage as shown in Figure 2-17. That's all you need to do for the Video layer. Lock the Video layer by clicking the lock button on the layer strip.

Figure 2-17. The video is ready to be "wired up" with ActionScript.

5. Save the file to the Chapter 2 Exercise folder.

Using ActionScript to play a video

Remember, there are only three steps here, so it isn't as complicated as you may think. Once more, the steps are connect, stream, and play.

The first step is managed by what is called the NetConnection class. All it does is to manage the connection between the server and the SWF file in the user's browser. Once that connection is made, another class named NetStream is used to manage the flow of data between the SWF file and the server. The final step uses a **method** of the NetStream class (method being a fancy term for action) to actually play the video.

1. Add a new layer to the timeline and name it Actions. Lock the layer and press the F9 (PC) or Option+F (Mac) keys to open the ActionScript Editor.

2. Click once in the Script pane and enter the following code:

```
var nc:NetConnection = new NetConnection ();
nc.connect (null);
var ns: NetStream = new NetStream(nc);
myVideo.attachVideo(ns);
ns.play("Opener.flv");
```

The first two lines give the connection a name—nc—and check to make sure the connection is made between the web server and the computer. The next line tells Flash to start the stream in the NetConnection, and the line after that says any video placed into the stream is fed into the video object on the stage. The last line tells Flash which video plays on the stream.

2

A couple of things that you may have noticed as you entered the code is the pull-down box that appeared when you entered a colon or a left bracket in the code and the use of var. *That box that appears is called a* **code hint** *and, if you are unsure of the correct spelling of a term, double-click the one you are looking for and it will be added to the code. The use of* var *indicates we are* **strict data typing** *our variables. This means the variable name can only have the properties of the class associated with it and nothing else. For example, if the variable* ns *were given the value of* tomato, *Flash will kick out an error message saying that* tomato *is not a part of the* NetStream *class.*

What's with the variable names such as ns *and* nc? *You can use any name you wish for a variable, but we prefer to use names that actually mean something. We could just as easily have used* GreatRiverofFlowingData *for the* NetStream, *but to us* ns *is a bit more succinct.*

3. Save and test the movie. The video should play in the video object on the stage as shown in Figure 2-18.

Figure 2-18. Six lines of code is all it takes to stream a video into a video object on the stage.

As we progress through the various steps in this exercise, you will find the files in the Chapter 2 Completed *folder. The file for this exercise is* CustomPlayer1.fla.

Creating buttons to control video playback

Now that you have the video playing, you can turn your attention to creating the controls that allow the user to rewind the video, fast forward to the end of the video, and to pause and play the video.

Before you start, it is important that you understand how controls work when it comes to working with Flash Video. The controls don't control the video. The controls manage the stream. This is an important concept to grasp because there is nothing in ActionScript that is aimed at, for example, pausing a video. To pause a video, you pause the NetStream.

You are also in for a rather pleasant surprise in this exercise. You are going to create the buttons, and we are going to show a rather neat way of adding the control symbols to the button without having to actually draw them. Let's get started:

1. Add a new layer to your timeline, below the Actions layer, and name it Control.
2. Select the Rectangle tool and click the Corner Radius button in the Options area of the toolbar and when the dialog box opens, enter a corner radius of 5 pixels and click OK.
3. In the toolbar, turn off the stroke and set the fill color to a dark gray or a black. Draw a rectangle on the stage and use these settings in the Property inspector:
   - Width: 310
   - Height: 25
   - X: 5
   - Y: 205
4. Click your rectangle once and select Window ➤ Color. In the Color Mixer panel, select Linear from the Type pull-down. This will add a gradient to the shape. Obviously it isn't quite correct, so let's fix it.
5. The pointers in the gradient color area are called **crayons**. Drag the black crayon on the left of the color bar to the middle. Click the left edge of the color bar once and another black crayon is added.
6. Double-click the crayon you just added. This will open the Color Picker. Change the color to the light gray on the left—#CCCCCC. Do the same thing for the crayon on the right side. When you change the colors, you will notice the bar on the stage (see Figure 2-19) changes to reflect your choices.

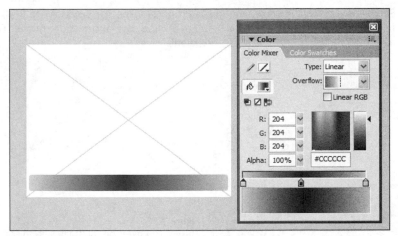

Figure 2-19. The gradient is added to the rectangle.

7. With the rectangle selected on the stage, click the Gradient tool in the toolbar. You will notice that the bar suddenly contains a rotate icon and a handle. Due to the fact we need this bar's gradient to run from top to bottom, the rotate handle is about to get a workout.

8. Click and drag the rotate handle to the left. When the handle is directly above the gradient, release the mouse. Now click and drag the square handle with the arrow downwards until it just touches the top edge of the rectangle as shown in Figure 2-20.

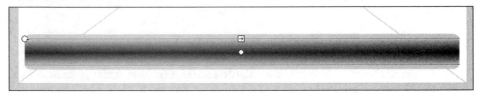

Figure 2-20. The rectangle now has a bit of a 3D look to it.

Obviously a shape with solid colors in the gradient that sits over a video is not exactly going to result in a pleasant experience for the viewer. Here's how to fix it:

9. Right-click (PC) or Option-click(Mac) the shape and select Convert to Symbol from the context menu. When the Convert to symbol dialog box opens, name the symbol Control Bar and select Movie Clip as its behavior. Click OK to close the dialog box. The symbol will appear in the Library, and the thin blue box surrounding the object on the stage indicates it is a symbol.

Now that the object is a movie clip, you can do some rather neat stuff with it. Let's push its opacity back so the viewer can see the video through the control bar.

10. Select the bar on the stage, and in the Property inspector, select Alpha in the Color pull-down list. Change the Alpha value to 60 and save and test the movie. The bar, as shown in Figure 2-21, is not so prevalent.

Figure 2-21.
The control bar is on the stage, and the time has arrived to add the control buttons.

11. Lock the Control layer and add a new layer above it named Buttons.

12. Select the Button layer and then select the Text tool.

> Switching between the tools in the toolbar can be a tedious process. If you really want to add zip to your production time, use the keyboard to select tools. For example, in the preceding step, pressing the T key will select the Text tool. To see the key associated with a particular tool, just place the cursor over that tool, and the resulting tooltip will tell you which key is associated with it.

13. Click the stage once and press the 9 key. Select the text, and in the Property inspector set the font to Webdings, the color to red (FF0000), the text type to Static, and the size to 18 pixels. Click the Text tool again and press the 4 key. You have just created the play and rewind buttons for the controller.

> The Webdings font, which is installed on both Macs and PCs, contains a number of symbols that are commonly used as the icons for video control buttons. You can see all of the symbols in the font by simply double-clicking the font in your PC's Fonts folder or by opening the Font Book utility on your Mac and choosing WebDings in the Font list. Being the nice guys we are, here are the controls and their associated keys:
>
> Play: 4
> Back: 3
> Rewind: 9
> Fast Forward: Colon
> Pause: Semicolon
> Volume: Capital X

14. Move the rewind button to the left side of the bar and place the play button just to the right of it. Select the rewind button and convert it to a movie clip named Rewind. Do the same thing with the play button but name it Play.

15. Select the Rewind movie clip and give it the instance name of mcRewind. Select the play button and give it the instance name of mcPlay as shown in Figure 2-22.

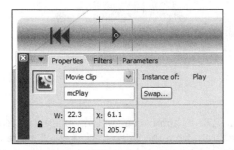

Figure 2-22.
The play button is converted to a movie clip and given the instance name of mcPlay.

You may be wondering why the instance name starts with mc. *When you have a lot of symbols on the stage, that prefix tells you exactly the type of symbol you are dealing with and avoids confusion. Other prefixes we use are* txt *for a text instance,* btn *for a button instance, and* cpt *for a component instance.*

With buttons in place, it is now a simple matter of writing the code that controls the video.

16. Click the frame in the Actions layer once and open the Actions panel. Click once in Line 7 of the Script pane and add the following code:

```
mcPlay.onPress = function() {
  ns.pause();
}

mcRewind.onPress = function () {
  ns.seek(0);
}
```

The first line of each function essentially says "When the button is clicked, do the stuff below." In the case of the play button, we are using the pause() method. The fascinating thing about this method is that by not putting anything between the brackets—True or False are the only values that can be put between the brackets—the button acts like a toggle switch, pausing and playing the video each time it is clicked.

The rewind button uses the seek method to simply scoot back to the start of the video—seek (0)—and the video will start playing from that point onward. If you do use the seek() method to navigate through a video, be aware that it can only use a whole number as the value. This means you can't use 1.5 to go to the 1.5-second mark of the video. The other thing to keep in mind about this method is the fact it will show you the keyframe that is closest to the time. For example, assume the FLV file has been encoded at a frame rate of 24 fps with keyframes that are spaced out by 48 frames. This means the first keyframe in the video is at the 2-second mark. If you were to use seek(1), you won't be shown the frame at second 1; the video's playback head will move to the 2-second mark of the video and show you that frame instead.

17. Save and test the movie.

> *The file for this part of the exercise is named* CustomPlayer2.fla *and can be found in the Chapter 2* Completed *folder.*

Turning the audio on and off

This next technique, on the ActionScript skill scale, is approaching intermediate. The reason is the audio in an FLV file is in a track separate from the video track. As well, there is no audio control method in either the NetStream or the Video classes. The audio track instead has to be controlled by the ActionScript Sound class.

This means you are going to have to put the audio track into a separate movie clip and control its volume through the use of an ActionScript Sound object. As well, you are about to learn how to move around inside a movie clip's timeline even though the movie clip is on the main timeline. Though it all sounds rather technical, it is rather simple to accomplish. Here's how:

1. Create a new layer in your movie and name it Volume.

2. Select the Text tool and enter an uppercase X. If you don't see a volume icon, change the font to 18-point Webdings and set the color of the text to red (FF0000). With the text selected, convert it to a movie clip named Volume. With your new movie clip selected, give it the instance name of mcMute.

3. Open the library and double-click the Volume movie clip to open it in the Symbol Editor.

4. Add a new layer named Actions and add keyframes in both the Actions layer *and* Layer 1 at Frames 10, 20, and 30. You can add a new keyframe by right-clicking (PC) or Ctrl-clicking (Mac) on the frame. Another way is to select the frame and press the F6 key.

What you are going to do is to change the volume icon depending on whether the sound is playing and whether the mouse is over the icon or not. This accounts for the four keyframes. The first one will indicate the audio is playing. The second will indicate whether the mouse is over the icon while the audio is playing. The third will indicate whether the volume is off, and the fourth will indicate whether the mouse is over the icon while the volume is off.

5. Click once in the keyframe in Frame 1 of the Actions layer. Name this frame on in the Frame input box in the Property inspector. These names are called **labels** and are indicated by a little flag in the keyframe.

6. Click the keyframe in Frame 10 of the Actions layer and name the frame over. Switch to the Text tool, select the icon, and change its color to yellow (#FF0000).

7. Click the keyframe at Frame 20 of the Actions layer and name it mute. Select the Line tool and draw a red line (see Figure 2-23) across the volume icon.

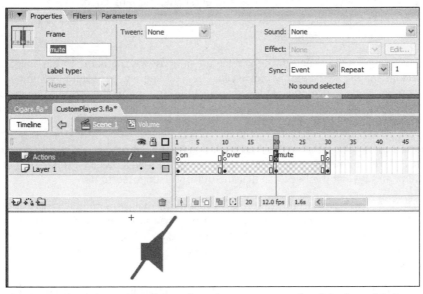

Figure 2-23. The various states of the volume button are created and the frame labels are added to the movie clip's timeline.

8. Add a keyframe in Frame 30 of both layers. Name the keyframe muteOver and change the color of the line and the volume icon to yellow (#FF000000).

9. The final step is to select the first keyframe in the Actions layer, open the ActionScript Editor, and enter the following code:

```
Stop();
```

If you didn't have the stop() action in that first frame, the movie clip would play, and each of the button states in the movie clip would flash on and off. Not a good situation.

With the various states of the button created, you can now turn your attention to writing the code that controls the audio track in the FLV file.

1. Return to the main timeline, select the keyframe in the Actions layer, and open the ActionScript Editor. Click once in the Script pane and enter the following code:

```
_root.createEmptyMovieClip("mcVol",_root.getNextHighestDepth());
mcVol.attachAudio(ns);
```

To pull the sound out of the FLV file and have it managed by the Sound class, you will first need to place the sound in a movie clip. Of course, you haven't created that movie clip in the library, but ActionScript allows you to create movie clips on the fly while the Flash movie is playing. The first line does just that. It uses the createEmptyMovieClip() method to create a new movie clip with the instance name of mcVol and puts it on the main time-line—_root. As you know, all movie clips occupy a unique position on the stage, and the getNextHighestDepth() method places the new movie clip at the next available depth above the content on the stage.

2. Press the Return/Enter key twice and enter the following code:

```
var FLVSound:Sound = new Sound(mcVol);
FLVSound.setVolume(100);
```

The first line gives the sound in the FLV file a name, assigns the name to the Sound class, and puts the sound in the empty movie clip. The next line sets the sound's volume to 100. That number is the full volume setting. If you wanted to turn off the sound, you would use 0 as the setVolume() parameter or, if you wanted the sound to be half volume, it would look like this: setVolume(50).

With the sound dealt with, the time has arrived to let the button do its job and manage the sound. Before you merrily start coding away, it might not be a bad idea to take a moment and think about what the heck it is that the button is supposed to do.

The first thing it will do is to turn the sound on and off. That is the simple answer. In actual fact, it will turn the sound on if the sound isn't playing and vice versa. If the sound is play-ing, the user sees an icon without a stroke through it, and, if the user rolls over the volume icon, it changes color. What on the surface appears to be rather simple suddenly becomes a tad complex when it comes to execution.

Actually, we put that in there to scare you. When you start planning interactivity, it is best to plan out what happens before you write the code and to write it down, in plain English, before you flame up the ActionScript Editor. For example, here's how we approached what happens when the user rolls the mouse over the volume button:

- When the user rolls over the mcMute button . . .
- . . . check to see whether the sound is playing.
- If it is playing, go to the frame label named over in the mcMute movie clip.
- If it isn't playing, go to the frame named muteOver in the mcMute movie clip.

What you just read is what programmers call **pseudocode**. Pseudocode is nothing more than a plain language description of the logic to be used when the code is written. Now, how does that translate into ActionScript?

3. In the Script pane, press the Return/Enter key twice and enter the following:

```
mcMute.onRollOver = function() {
  if(FLVSound.getVolume() ==100){
  this.gotoAndStop("over");
}
else{
  this.gotoAndStop("muteOver");
 }
}
```

Having dealt with what happens when the user rolls over the button, let's now turn our attention to what happens when the user rolls the mouse off of the button and what happens when the button is clicked.

> *Using the keyword* this *in the code is how you move around inside a movie clip on the main timeline. When the user rolls over the* mcMute *movie clip (*this*), Flash knows it is to go to the timeline of the movie clip just clicked or rolled over and to go to and stop on the frame name inside of the movie clip. The name is between quotes because Flash isn't smart enough to figure out the name is a string of letters. If you didn't have the quotation marks, Flash would think the name is a variable of some sort.*

4. Press the Return/Enter key twice and enter the following code:

```
mcMute.onRollOut =  function() {
   if(FLVSound.getVolume() ==100){
   this.gotoAndStop("on");
}
else{
This.gotoAndStop("mute");
}
}

mcMute.onRelease = function() {
   if(FLVSound.getVolume() ==100){
      FLVSound.setVolume(0);
   this.gotoAndStop("muteOver");
   }
   else{
      FLVSound.setVolume(100);
      this.gotoAndStop("on");
   }
}
```

5. Save and test the movie. Notice how the button reacts to the cursor as shown in Figure 2-24.

> *You may have noticed that, except for a couple of minor differences, the code for the* onRollOut *and the* onRelease *events is exactly the same as the* onRollOver *code. If you are lazy like us, just copy and paste the* onRollOver *code and make the minor changes.*

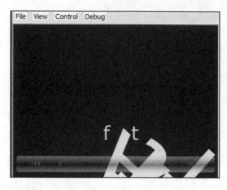

Figure 2-24.
The sound is off and the cursor is not over the volume icon.

The file for this part of the exercise is named CustomPlayer3.fla *and can be found in the Chapter 2* Completed *folder.*

Showing the user the loading progress of an FLV file

We finish the construction part of the chapter with a technique that is somewhere around the middle of intermediate-level techniques.

One of the keys to Flash design is the ability to provide the user with some sort of visual feedback regarding what is going on in the movie. If you have ever arrived at a Flash site where the first thing you saw was a preloader, you have experienced this feedback. In this exercise, you are going to construct a preloader of sorts, only it will show the user the loading progress of an FLV file. Where this widget differs from a regular preloader is that the video will start to play at some point during the loading process, and the widget will continue to show the progress while the video plays.

This is due to a streaming feature of Flash Video that is called a **progressive download**. Unlike most streaming video technologies, Flash doesn't need to have a large amount of the video in the player before the video starts to play. Instead, Flash keeps an eye on the information being downloaded, and, when enough of the FLV file has loaded to smoothly play, the video starts to play. While it is playing, the rest of the FLV files continue to download.

To understand how a loading progress indicator works, you only need to understand how to create a percentage value. At any point in time, the graphic being used to visually represent the amount downloaded will have a width or height that matches the percentage of the file that has downloaded at any point in time. If half of the FLV data has loaded into the Flash Player, the width or height of the graphic will also be half of its width or height.

Another little trick is not to look at the bar used as the loading indicator as being a graphic of a bar, Instead, regard its length or its height as being representative of the total amount of data to be loaded. So much for theory; let's get busy:

1. Open the file you have been working on and create a new layer named Loader.

2. Select the Rectangle tool and set the stroke color to black and the fill color to white. With the Loader layer selected, draw a rectangle on the control bar. As Figure 2-25 shows, ours is 160 pixels wide by 10 pixels high.

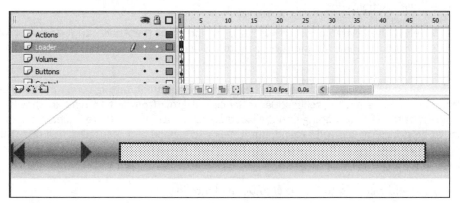

Figure 2-25. The progress indicator is drawn and placed on the stage.

3. Double-click the object on the stage to ensure you have both the stroke and the fill selected, and convert it to a movie clip named Loader.

4. Open your Library and double-click the Loader movie clip to open the Symbol Editor.

> The reason for the movie clip is the white fill will be used to visually show loading progress. This means the rate at which the fill grows from left to right will be determined by ActionScript. The best way of doing this is to convert the object under the control of ActionScript to a movie clip symbol.

5. Click the fill once to select it, and convert the selection to a movie clip named loadBar.

6. With the loadBar movie clip selected, select Modify ➤ Timeline ➤ Distribute to layers. When you click that menu item, you will notice that two layers are visible in the movie clip. One layer will be the load bar that will grow and the other will contain the stroke around the load bar. Name the new layer Stroke.

> You can also right-click (PC) or Ctrl-click (Mac) the loadBar movie clip and select Distribute to layers from the context menu.
>
> If you want to make the bar somewhat transparent, select the movie clip and reduce its Alpha value in the Color area of the Property inspector to 40%.

7. Select the loadBar movie clip and give it the instance name of mcLoadBar. Click the Scene 1 link to return to the main timeline. Click the loadBar movie clip on the main timeline, and give it the instance name of mcLoader in the Property inspector.

With the housekeeping out of the way, you can now turn your attention to wiring up the load bar with ActionScript.

8. Select the keyframe in the Actions layer and open the ActionScript Editor. Scroll down to the end of the rewind button function and press the Return/Enter key twice.

Before you start writing the code, let's take a minute and think through what needs to be done. In broad terms, the mcLoadBar instance will grow from left to right to show the progress of the FLV file loading into the video object. In actual fact, there is a bit more that has to be done. The bar will expand, but it needs to expand at a predetermined rate. This means Flash will have to constantly check how much of the FLV file has downloaded at any point in time and will change the width of the bar to reflect that amount.

To do this you will need to tell Flash to do the following:

- Every one-tenth of a second, check how much of the FLV file has loaded into the video object.
- When the check is done, calculate the percentage of the video that has loaded.
- Change the width of the mcLoadBar movie clip to match that percentage.

Looks suspiciously like pseudocode, doesn't it?

The check will be done using an ActionScript function called setInterval(). This function requires two parameters. The first will be the function to be performed, and the second is how often to perform the function, and that time is measured in milliseconds. The function called will be the one that does the calculations and resizes the mcLoadBar movie clip.

9. Click the mouse once on the new line in the Script pane and enter the following code:

```
var loadProgress =  setInterval(loadStatus,100);
var amountLoaded:Number;
```

The reason for the variables is at some point you may wish to change or even turn off the setInterval() function. The variable name is called the **interval ID**. The second variable is the result of a calculation that will be changing ten times each second.

10. Press the Return/Enter key twice, and you can now start writing the loadStatus function:

```
function loadStatus() {
  amountLoaded = ns.bytesLoaded/ns.bytesTotal ;
  mcLoader.mcLoadBar._width = amountLoaded * 160;
}
```

The first line uses two properties of the NetStream class—bytesLoaded and bytesTotal—to determine the percentage of the FLV file that has loaded. The number will be a number between 1 and 0. This means if half of the FLV file has downloaded, the amountLoaded value will be .5.

The next line uses the value from the previous line to set the width of the load bar. The first bit says to look at the mcLoader clip and to go inside the mcLoader clip to the mcLoadBar clip and change its width to the value of the previous calculation multiplied by the width of the load bar (160 pixels) and show that on the stage.

11. Save and test the movie (see Figure 2-26).

Figure 2-26.
The FLV file has loaded into the SWF file.

If you don't see the progress bar move across the interface, the odds are almost 100% you are testing the movie from your hard drive. If you really want to experience what the loader looks like, you will need to place the video in a folder on your website and load the FLV file into this movie from there. If you open the CustomPlayer4.fla *in the* Chapter 2 Completed *folder and check the code you will notice the play method uses a URL—*ns.play ("http://www.tomontheweb4.ca/FLV/Opener.flv")—*for its parameter, not the FLV file name. Feel free to use this URL, which belongs to one of the authors, to do a remote test, or use your own. It's your choice.*

Earlier in this chapter you created a video player using the FLVPlayback component. If you go back and check the file size of the SWF file for that project, you will see it weighs in at 34K. The final SWF file size for this exercise, which essentially has the same functionality as the component, is 2K. The exercise that used the three FLV UI components weighs in at 38K. Obviously, using a custom player makes sense in situations where file size is critical.

Publishing your video player

The end game of the process is actually publishing your SWF file. Again Flash offers you quite a high degree of flexibility when it comes to preparing this file. You can choose which version of ActionScript will be used, which Flash Player version will be used, and even whether the HTML page that holds the SWF file will be produced.

When it comes to video, there are a few things, in no particular order, you need to be aware of:

- If you are using a progressive download—the video streams from your web server—the SWF file and the FLV file should be in the same folder.

- If you use the FLVPlayback component, be sure the SWF file for the controller is in the same folder as the Flash SWF file.

- If you are using a Flash Media Server or a Flash Video Streaming Service, the NetConnection is to an RTMP address, and the reference to the FLV file in the NetStream.play() method should not contain the .flv extension.

- You can have the FLV files in a different location and play them by using an absolute path to the file, rather than placing an FLV file or files in the same folder as the Flash SWF file. This is a great way of managing multiple videos and players that use the same video.

Let's publish this project.

1. Select File ➤ Publish Settings. When the Publish Settings dialog box opens (see Figure 2-27) the Flash SWF file and the HTML options will most likely be selected.

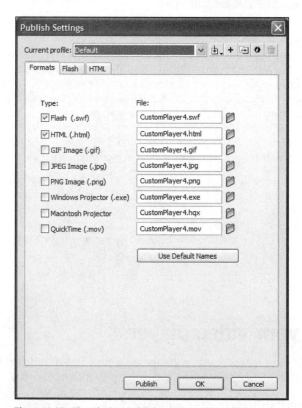

Figure 2-27. The Flash 8 Publish Settings dialog box

Another way to access the Publish Settings *dialog box is to click the Flash stage once and click the* Settings *button in the* Publish *area of the Property inspector.*

If the SWF file is destined for placement in a Dreamweaver 8 or GoLive CS2 document, feel free to deselect the HTML *option. All this option does is create a web page containing the object and embed tags necessary to hold the SWF file. If you do deselect the* HTML *option, the* HTML *tab in the dialog box will disappear.*

2. Click the Flash tab to open the Flash settings as shown in Figure 2-28.

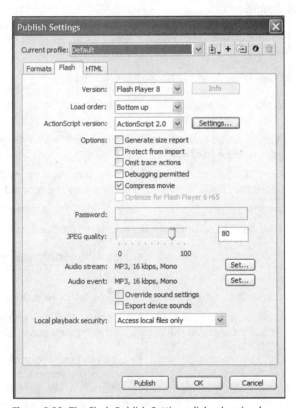

Figure 2-28. The Flash Publish Settings dialog box is where you can choose your target Flash Player.

This area is where you have to make some decisions. The first is the target player to create. The Version pull-down will present you with a full list of Player options ranging from Flash Player 9, the latest version of the Player on the street, to FlashLite 2.0, which is used for mobile devices such as cell phones.

If you choose Flash Player 7 or lower, you may be presented with an alert box telling you that certain features of your project can't be published. For example, using the FLVPlayback component and then selecting Flash Player 7 is a great way of kicking off this alert. If you see it when you are creating the Flash movie, open the Publish Settings *dialog box and change the Flash Player version.*

Your next decision is whether to use ActionScript 1 or ActionScript 2. Explaining the differences between the two is well out of the scope of this book. Still, all ActionScript presented in this book uses ActionScript 2 and, if you are publishing to Flash Player 8, it is advisable to select ActionScript 2.

The load order controls the way the layers are loaded into the Flash movie. The default, Bottom up, loads from the layer at the bottom up to the top layer.

There are also a number of options to choose from, as listed here:

- Generate size report: You will be shown, in the Output panel, the size of the data contained in the movie.
- Protect from import: Users won't be able to right-click a SWF file in the web page and download it to their hard drive.
- Omit trace actions: Coders love to use the trace command to see how things work. Select this before the movie is published and they will be ignored.
- Debugging permitted: Select this to remotely debug a Flash movie.
- Compress movie: Select this to create the smallest SWF file possible.

Changing the JPEG and Audio compression settings will override any settings you have made in the Library.

3. Click the Formats tab to return to the Formats panel. Deselect the HTML option.

4. Click the Browse button to navigate to the folder that will contain the SWF file. Click the Save button and you will return to the Formats panel.

The absolute last thing you want to do now is to click the Publish button. If you check the path in the SWF area, you will notice it is the path to the folder where you just saved the SWF file (see Figure 2-29). Clicking the Publish button, to be gentle, would be a fatal error because that path will get embedded into the published SWF file, and users will be asked where it is when they try to view it. Not a good situation for either of you.

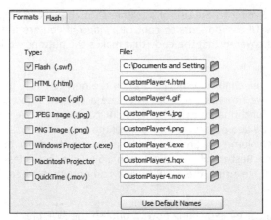

Figure 2-29. Click the Use Default Names button to clear the path out of the SWF file.

5. Click the Use Default Names button and the path will be stripped out of the SWF file.

6. Click the Publish button. You will see a dialog box showing you the progress of the publishing operation. When it disappears, click OK to close the Publish Settings dialog box.

Summary

This has been quite a long chapter, but if you have reached this point in the book you should now understand how Flash videos are created in After Effects and how they are encoded and deployed in Flash.

We started the chapter by explaining how streaming works and the importance of data rate. We then walked you through how to use the Flash 8 Video Encoder to convert the video created in Chapter 1 into the FLV file needed for this chapter. We then showed you how to get it to play in Flash.

As you may have discovered, a lot of possibilities are open to you. We showed you how to use the FLVPlayback component, how to add a skin, and how to deal with a rather sneaky gotcha associated with this component. We also showed you how to use the component designed for use in situations where Flash Player 7 or Flash Player 6 is the target player. Obviously, relying on components give you a "code-free" video deployment option, but there will be times when the component simply does fit the design or the space requirement for the project.

To do this, we eased you into the use of a "skinless" FLVPlayback component and how to use the FLVPlayback UI components to control a video. If you are just getting into using ActionScript, you discovered that the code that makes the buttons work is not terribly difficult to write.

The next section of the chapter, especially if you are new to Flash, moved you right into Dragon Country as we showed you how to create a custom video player that contains much of the same functionality as its component counterpart. We showed you how to stream a video into a video object, how to control the video with a play/pause button, how to turn the video's volume on and off, and finally how to show the user the loading progress of the video. Best of all, you did it with a SWF file that is less than one-third the file size of the SWF file using the FLVPlayback component created at the start of the chapter.

We finished the chapter by explaining how to publish the SWF file that will play the video from Chapter 1 and some of things to be aware of during the publish process. It was a lot of ground to cover, but the good news is everything you will do in Flash over the balance of this book will be a variation on the themes in this chapter.

Speaking of Flash ... did you know there is some really cool stuff you can do with text in After Effects that can also be used in Flash? To find out more, turn the page.

3 MOTION GRAPHICS AND THE PRESET TEXT EFFECTS IN AFTER EFFECTS

When it comes to the subject of **motion graphics**, the first place where designers tend to look is **text in motion**. This idea was first explored by Flash artists such as Hillman Curtis, Todd Purgason, Yugo Nakamura, and Brendan Dawes, and since then the term *motion graphics* as become intimately associated with text movement in the Flash page. This is not a negative, and there is a tremendous amount you can do with text in Flash.

One of our favorite examples of text-based motion graphics is about as elemental as one can get with text and Flash. Created by a talented Korean artist living in Seoul, Young-hae Chang, her site, www.yhchang.com, is a collection of web-based musings that are elemental, risqué, and heavy with irony. The words seen in Figure 3-1 hit the screen and dance in time with a 1950s jazz beat and drag you along for the waltz.

ØR WEB METAPHYSICS SUCH AS:

Figure 3-1. From Young-hae Chang's "Artist's Statement No: 45,730,944: The Perfect Artistic Web Site"

Yugo Nakamura takes type and motion graphics to a whole different level. He has created an example (available at his site, www.yugop.com/) called the "Typographic Book Search." Using the Amazon search engine, Yugo creates a list of the top-selling books in a variety of categories, and, when you make a selection, the name selected is drawn using copies of the book where the name appears (see Figure 3-2).

Figure 3-2. Yugo's name is constructed using copies of the friends of ED book *New Masters of Flash*.

Whether it is movie titles, product names, or even blocks of text, putting type in motion is an extremely effective technique. It is not surprising, therefore, to learn those who have mastered it are huge film buffs and have closely studied the film work of Saul Bass (*Psycho*) and Kyle Cooper (*Nixon* and *Donnie Brasco*). The key to understanding the use of text as a motion graphic is understanding that such factors as time and dimension contribute to creating text that isn't read on a static printed page, but from a computer screen where it is in motion. This raises such issues as the readability and legibility of the text that moves and is only visible for a finite amount of time. If text in motion can't be read or understood, you have failed in your job.

Though the intention of this chapter is not to turn you into a Kyle Cooper, Saul Bass, or Young-hae Chang, we are going to get you used to working with the medium of text and demonstrate how After Effects 7 offers the Flash artist an amazing suite of creative tools expressly designed for motion graphics. Rather than overwhelm you, we are going to start our hunt for motion graphic dragons with the **text animation presets** in After Effects.

Text animation presets

After Effects ships with well over 250 text animation presets, which you can apply, change, and even stack on top of each other. What is not as well known, on the Flash side of the pasture, is that many of these presets, after they are applied to some text, can actually be dropped, intact, into Flash and edited even more in Flash.

Obviously, reviewing each one of those presets would require a separate, companion volume to the book. Still, it is rather simple to review each one. When you open After Effects, select Help ➤ Animation Preset Gallery. The menu that appears (see Figure 3-3) will list all of the animation preset categories available to you.

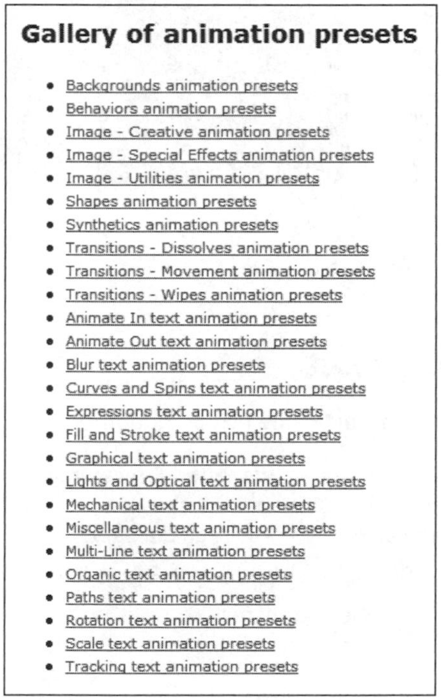

Gallery of animation presets

- Backgrounds animation presets
- Behaviors animation presets
- Image - Creative animation presets
- Image - Special Effects animation presets
- Image - Utilities animation presets
- Shapes animation presets
- Synthetics animation presets
- Transitions - Dissolves animation presets
- Transitions - Movement animation presets
- Transitions - Wipes animation presets
- Animate In text animation presets
- Animate Out text animation presets
- Blur text animation presets
- Curves and Spins text animation presets
- Expressions text animation presets
- Fill and Stroke text animation presets
- Graphical text animation presets
- Lights and Optical text animation presets
- Mechanical text animation presets
- Miscellaneous text animation presets
- Multi-Line text animation presets
- Organic text animation presets
- Paths text animation presets
- Rotation text animation presets
- Scale text animation presets
- Tracking text animation presets

Figure 3-3. The listing of the animation presets in the Help menu

When you click a category, another window (as shown in Figure 3-4) will open. Inside this window are examples of each preset animation. Each animation has the effect applied to the name of the effect. In this way, if you are at all curious about what an animation looks like—Helicopter, for example, really doesn't tell you much—you can select its category and see whether the motion or animation effect is what you were expecting.

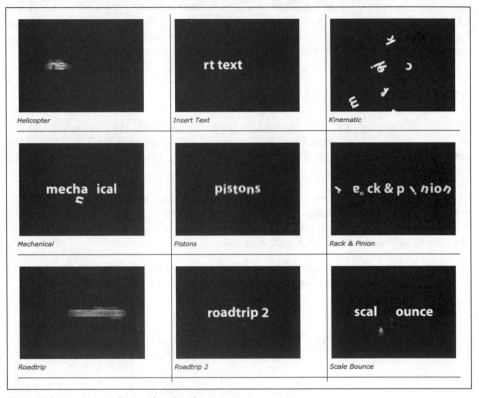

Figure 3-4. You can preview each animation preset.

Using an animation preset

So much for the overview; let's put some text in motion.

1. Open After Effects and, when the After Effects interface appears, either select Composition ➤ New Composition or click the New Composition button in the Project window to open the Composition Settings dialog box.

2. In the Composition Settings dialog box (see Figure 3-5) use the following settings:

   - Composition Name: Use your name.
   - Width: 320
   - Height: 240

- Pixel Aspect Ratio: Square Pixels
- Frame Rate: 24
- Duration: 0:00:10:00

When finished, click OK to close the dialog box. The new Comp will appear in the Project panel.

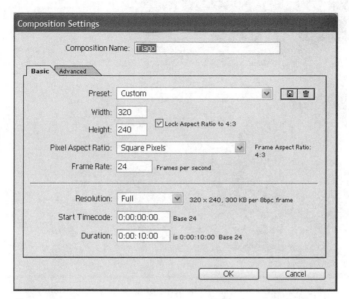

Figure 3-5. The composition settings that will be used to put your name in motion

3. Click the Text tool and click once in the Comp window. Enter your name.

Instead of clicking the Text *tool in the* Comp *window, you could also insert a* Text *layer by selecting* Layer ➤ New ➤ Text. *You can then enter the text directly into the new* Text

4. Select Window ➤ Character to open the Character panel. Select your name and change the font and point size used for your name. We chose 40-point Arial Black, but feel free to use any font.

5. With your name selected, click the Fill Color chip in the Character panel once to open the Color Picker (see Figure 3-6). Change the color at the bottom of the Color Picker to #FFFF00, which is a web-safe yellow. Click OK to close the Color Picker.

Figure 3-6. The After Effects Color Picker is the same one used by Photoshop.

As you have seen in this step, you get to choose from among three color spaces—HSB, RGB, and hexadecimal—when adding or changing the color of selected objects. These three spaces make sense because the display medium is the computer screen.

> *As of version 6.5 of After Effects, Adobe moved its* Color Picker *to one familiar to practically anybody in the digital media industry: the* Photoshop Color Picker. *You can enter color values directly into any of the fields, and the selected color will change. The two color swatches are the new color (top) and the original color (bottom).*
>
> *If you just can't wrap your head around the* Photoshop Color Picker, *you can change to your* System Color Picker *by select* Edit ➤ Preferences ➤ General *and selecting* Use System Color Picker.

6. If it isn't already open, open the Effects & Presets panel by selecting Window ➤ Effects & Presets.

7. Twirl down Animation Presets. And then twirl down the Text and Animate In folders.

8. Select the Center Spiral preset (see Figure 3-7) and drag it on top of your name.

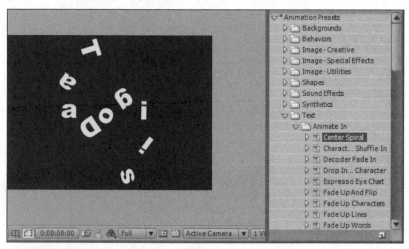

Figure 3-7. Drag and drop a preset onto a piece of text, and the text is swirling and twirling.

9. Click the Play button in the Time Controls panel, and your name will come swirling onto the screen.

As you can see, with little or no effort on your part, you can create an animated text effect that can be done in Flash only if you are prepared to invest a serious amount of time and aggravation to the project. The really neat thing about these presets is they can be readily exported to Flash . . . as vectors. Here's how:

1. Twirl down Text on the main timeline in order to see the keyframes. You may notice the animation occurs in less than three seconds.

2. Zoom in on the timeline and drag the timeline's Work End handle to the 3-second mark on the timeline as shown in Figure 3-8.

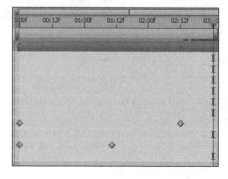

Figure 3-8.
Trimming a comp starts with reducing the length of the work area.

3. Select Composition ➤ Trim comp to work area. When you created the comp, you specified a duration of 10 seconds. Requiring a user to twiddle his or her thumbs for 7 seconds while staring at stationary text is not a best practice. By pulling the timeline's Work End handle to the 3-second mark and then trimming the Comp to that duration, you remove the section where the text just sits there.

4. Select File ➤ Export ➤ Macromedia Flash (SWF). The first thing you will be asked to do is to save the SWF file. Save it to the Exercise folder in the Chapter 3 code download.

5. When you click OK to save the SWF file, the SWF Settings dialog box (see Figure 3-9) will open. Don't worry about the JPG settings; just select Ignore from the Unsupported Features pull-down menu.

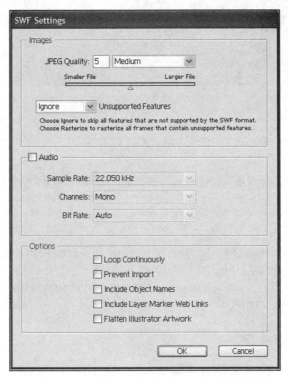

Figure 3-9. The most critical step of the process is telling the SWF file to ignore any unsupported features.

This dialog box is the key to successfully moving the animation from After Effects to Flash. By selecting Ignore from the Unsupported Features pull-down, any vectors in the project will not get flattened into bitmaps, which is a good thing because Flash is a vector-based application. This means the text, which is nothing more than vector artwork, moves into Flash in its common vector format.

6. Click OK. A dialog box will appear telling you that After Effects is exporting about 72 or so Flash frames, and you will also see a bar showing you the progress of the export process.

7. Save the project and quit After Effects.

Importing an After Effects SWF animation into Flash

Though you can import a SWF animation created in After Effects into Flash, you do need to be aware of a couple issues. The first is the contents of the SWF timeline are added to the Flash timeline, and Flash designers like to keep the main timeline as short as possible. The second is you can use ActionScript to import the SWF file at runtime, and, if you are new to Flash, this relatively simple process can be quite confusing. In this example, we are going to ignore both approaches and use a Flash movie clip instead.

1. Launch Flash 8 and, when the application opens, create a new Flash document and set the stage color to a medium gray—#666666—using the Color Picker in the Property inspector.

2. Select Insert ➤ New Symbol and when the New Symbol dialog box opens, name the new symbol Twirl, and select movie clip as its type. Click OK.

3. When you click OK in the New Symbol dialog box, the dialog box will close, and you will be looking at the timeline for the Twirl movie clip.

4. Select File ➤ Import ➤ Import to Stage. When the Import dialog box opens, navigate to the folder where you saved the SWF file from the previous exercise and double-click it to import the SWF file. Close the Import dialog box.

When the dialog box closes, you will see that the SWF file has arrived on the movie clip's stage as a series of keyframes (see Figure 3-10). Drag the playback head across the timeline, and you will see the animation.

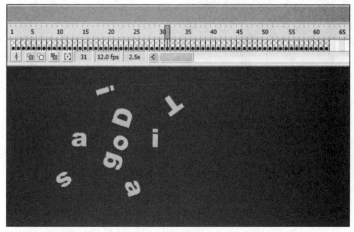

Figure 3-10. SWF animations from After Effects arrive on the Flash timeline as a series of keyframes.

> When the SWF animation is placed on the timeline, all of the symbols and graphics that make up the SWF file are also placed in the Library. Depending upon the complexity of the animation, this can result in a lot of stuff in the Library. In this case, the graphic symbols in the library are the letters in the animation. Click the folder icon at the bottom of the Library panel to add a folder to the Library. Name the folder Letters, and drag the graphic symbols, not the movie clip, into the folder.

5. Drag the playback head to Frame 60 of the movie clip. If you drag the playback head to the right, you will notice quite a few frames where nothing happens. Drag the playback head to the frame where the words stop moving. Select the next frame in the timeline. Press the Shift key and select the last frame in the animation. Right-click (PC) or Ctrl-click (Mac) and select Remove Frames from the context menu.

6. Click the Scene 1 link to return to the main timeline and drag the movie clip from the Library to the stage.

   You will see a blue box, the animation area of the movie clip, and a + sign, which marks the registration point of the movie clip. That + sign is the location of the similar sign in the movie clip.

7. With the movie clip still selected on the stage, set the movie clip's location to 76 on the X axis and 8 on the Y axis in the Property inspector.

8. Test the movie by pressing the Ctrl+Enter (PC) or Cmd+Return (Mac) keys. Your name should now be in motion as shown in Figure 3-11. If you wish, feel free to save this file.

Figure 3-11.
The name is in motion in the Flash Player.

Combining animation presets to create Flash animations

Now that you know how to use an animation preset to animate text in After Effects and use that animation in Flash, let's get into something a bit more complicated. You may have noticed that in the After Effects text animation presets there are two related folders: Animate In and Animate Out. These folders contain a series of preset animations that allow you to apply one effect to an animation and a different one, later in the timeline, to remove the animation from the screen. Let's have some more fun with your name.

1. Open After Effects and create a new Comp.

2. Click the Comp window once, select the Text tool, and enter your name.

3. Open the Effects & Presets panel and in Animation Presets select Text ➤ Animate In. Scroll down and drag the Twirl On Each Word preset onto your name.

4. Twirl down your name in the timeline and then twirl down the Text and Animator 1 categories.

> Animation presets, when applied to an object on the screen, will appear in the timeline as an **animator**. Each animation added to an object will create a separate animator in that object's timeline.

5. The animation is a bit too long for our purposes here. To shorten its duration to 2 seconds, drag the keyframe under the 3-second mark of the timeline to the 2-second mark as shown in Figure 3-12.

Figure 3-12. Reduce or increase the duration of an animation by moving keyframes.

That takes care of the first sequence in the animation. You are going to let your name remain static for about one-half second and then it will whirl off the stage. Here's how:

6. Drag the playback head to the 2:10 mark on the timeline.

7. Twirl down the Animate Out folder in Animation & Presets. Select Text ➤ Animate Out and drag the Twirl Off Each Word preset onto your name as shown in Figure 3-13.

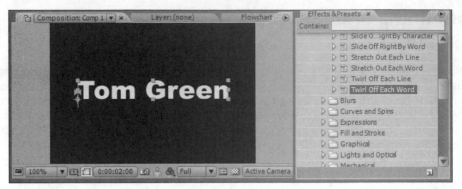

Figure 3-13. You use a simple drag-and-drop technique to apply animation presets to a selection.

8. If you go to the timeline and twirl down the Text strip, you will notice you now have an Animator 2 **category. Click the** Animator 2 **and the** Range Selector 1 **twirlies to see the keyframes, as shown in Figure 3-14.**

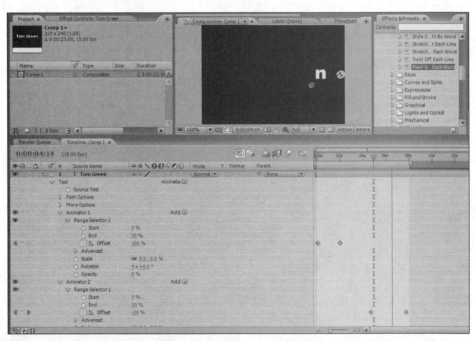

Figure 3-14. The Animate In and Animate Out sequences have their own animators in the timeline.

> *If you want to reduce the time between the two animations, simply Shift-click the two keyframes of the Animate Out sequence and drag them closer to the last keyframe of the Animate In sequence.*

9. Trim the work area to the 6-second mark and export as a Flash SWF file.

You may have noticed a few of the Animate In presets don't have an Animate Out counterpart. For example, you may or may not have noticed there is not a Center Spiral *preset, used in the first exercise in this chapter, in the* Animate Out *folder. Fear not. Flash to the rescue.*

If you double-click the movie clip in the Flash Library, you will open its timeline. When you see the keyframes, select them all on the timeline and select Modify ➤ Timeline ➤ Reverse Frames. If you press the Return/Enter key, you will see the animation now works in reverse. Press Cmd+Z (Mac) or Ctrl+Z (PC) to undo the change. With this invaluable nugget of information, we think you can see how to animate the sequence out. All you need to do is to select all of the keyframes and either right-click (PC) or Ctrl-click (Mac) to open the context menu. Select Copy Frames. Select Frame 62 on the timeline, open the context menu, and select Paste Frames. The range will be added to the timeline. To finish up, simply select the new frames added to the timeline and select Reverse Frames. Instant Animate Out effect.

Creating a rich media Flash Video with animated text

To this point in the chapter, you have discovered how easy it is to apply an animation preset to a single line of text. In this exercise, we deal with integrating the effect into an After Effects project.

The premise is rather simple: you will create a rich media ad that will promote the book you are reading. The project scope is such that the ad can't be more than 320 pixels high and 240 pixels deep. It must weigh in with a SWF file that is under 30K in size and contain user controls that allow the viewer to turn the video on and off.

If you have made it to this point in the book, you know how to meet the technical specifications. The Flash project will use a video object to stream the video, and you will use ActionScript to give the user control of the video stream. Both of these techniques were presented in the previous chapter, so it isn't necessary to add that to the exercise. What we will do, though, is show you a rather clever way of creating a very small FLV file that will load quickly and show you how to use Photoshop and Illustrator images in a Comp. Let's start building an ad.

1. Download the files for this chapter and unzip the Ad_01.zip file. Inside the AD_01 folder are an Illustrator image named clouds.ai and a Photoshop image named background.tif.

2. Open After Effects and create a new Comp using these settings:

   - Composition Name: MainComp
   - Preset: Web Video
   - Width: 320

- Height: 240
- Pixel Aspect Ratio: Square Pixels
- Frame Rate: 15
- Resolution: Full
- Duration: 0:00:14:00

3. Import the background.tif image and drag it from the Project panel to the timeline.

Importing and manipulating Illustrator images in After Effects

There is a lot you can do when you include Illustrator images in an After Effects project. Though this exercise just touches the surface, by the end of it, you will have a deeper appreciation of the creative possibilities open to you when these two applications team up.

1. Import the clouds.ai image from the AD_01 folder into the project. When you import an Illustrator image into an After Effects project, you will see a dialog box—as shown in Figure 3-15—that asks you how you want to treat the image. Your choices are as footage or as a Comp. Select Composition from the pull-down and click OK.

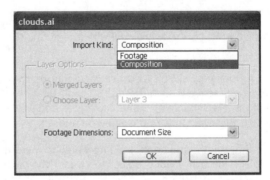

Figure 3-15. This dialog box starts the process of importing an Illustrator file into After Effects.

When the Illustrator file arrives in the Project panel, you will see that a new Comp, using the file name, has been added to the Project panel as well as a folder named CloudLayers. Inside this folder is a series of Illustrator images that really are nothing more than the images sitting on the six layers of the Illustrator document. If you double-click the Clouds Comp, you will also see each image in the folder has been placed onto its own layer in the Comp.

This is an important feature to note. By turning the clouds image into a Comp and placing each image on its own layer, you can animate or otherwise manipulate each image in the Comp, and those changes will appear when the Clouds Comp is placed on the main timeline. Let's do that right now . . .

2. Drag the Clouds Comp from the Project panel to the timeline. Drag the Clouds comp layer above the background.tif layer. The first thing you will notice is the Comp is seriously larger than the stage. This needs to be fixed.

3. Click the Clouds Comp once in the timeline to select it and press the S key. This will open the Scale properties for the Comp. Change the Scale value to 50%.

Even though you have scaled the clouds, they are still static. It is time to put them in motion. The neat thing about animating in After Effects is the application creates the motion based upon the values between the keyframes. Here's how:

4. Double-click the Clouds Comp in the Project panel to open the Comp in the time-line. The last layer, Layer 1, is the blue sky. The other layers are the clouds.

5. Select the first layer—Layer 3—and press the P key to open the Position properties.

> *You may have noticed the layers seem to be out of order. Not true. If you open the Illustrator document in Illustrator, you will see the layering order in After Effects is exactly the same as that in Illustrator.*
>
> *The After Effects timeline can become a pretty cluttered place when there are a lot of objects on the timeline. Though twirling down is one method of accessing properties, using the keyboard is a bit more efficient because only the property to be manipu-lated—in this case Position—appears under the strip.*

The plan for this animation is to have the cloud in Layer 3 move right and down and then up and to the right. The really cool thing we are going to do is to have the cloud look like it is moving in a 3D space. Here's how to do it by the numbers:

6. Click once in the 3D switch check box. You will see a small box appear in that layer. Now you can animate by the numbers.

7. Click the stopwatch in the Position property once. You will add a keyframe to the timeline. The three numbers are the X value, Y value, and the Z value. Use these settings:

- X: 151.5
- Y: 151.4
- Z: 0

8. Drag the playback head to the 2-second mark on the timeline and specify the fol-lowing values:

- X: 175.6
- Y: 141.3
- Z: 298

9. Drag the playback head to the 14-second mark on the timeline and specify the following values:

- X: 295.5
- Y: 91.4
- Z: 0

> *That's a lot of typing. Here's a really fast way of doing it. Right-click (PC) or Ctrl-click (Mac) and you will see an* Edit Value *menu. Click it and the dialog box shown in Figure 3-16 will appear. Enter the values and click* OK.

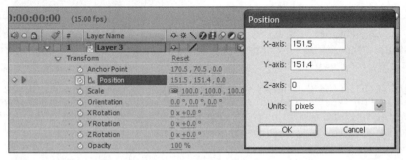

Figure 3-16. Layers can be positioned by the numbers by either changing the values on the timeline or using the Position dialog box.

10. Now that you know what to do, click the 3D switch for each layer containing a cloud and use these keyframe and position values:

Layer	Keyframe	Position
Layer 4	0 seconds	67.7, 173.7, 0
	14 seconds	493.5, 170.4, 0
Layer 5	0 seconds	493.5, 347.4, 0
	2 seconds	376.9, 351.2, 541.1
	14 seconds	191.5, 357.4, –267
Layer 6	0 seconds	457.5, 537.4, 0
	14 seconds	665.5, 534.4, 0
Layer 2	0 seconds	156, 507, 0
	14 seconds	420, 483, 0

If you drag the playback head across the timeline, you can see the clouds move. Those layers where there is a Z-axis value appear to grow and shrink depending upon whether they are approaching the viewer or moving away. Now that the clouds are done, let's fix the fact that they seem to cover the background image.

11. Close the clouds panel to return to the main timeline and select the Clouds comp layer.

12. Click the Modes pull-down in the Clouds comp layer and select Silhouette Luma. The sky disappears and the background image is faintly visible as shown in Figure 3-17.

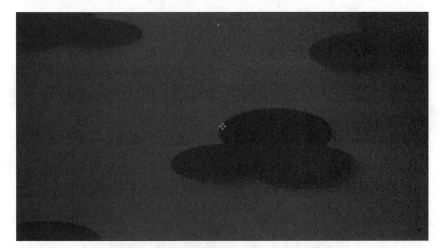

Figure 3-17. The Comp after the Silhouette Luma blend mode is applied to the Clouds comp layer

If you are a Photoshop, Flash 8, or Fireworks user, you are quite familiar with the blend modes. The one chosen here creates a silhouette over the background image by changing the luma values of the pixels in the Clouds comp *layer. You see the clouds because the lighter pixels become more transparent than the darker pixels in the*

Having completed the animation of the items in the background, we can now turn our attention to creating and animating the text that will appear over the background.

1. Click the Comp window once, select the Text tool, and enter the text a motion picture by. With the text selected, open the Character panel and use these settings:

- Font: Arial
- Style: Regular
- Size: 14 px
- Color: White

2. Change to the Selection tool and drag the text to a position just above the cloud in the bottom-left corner of the Comp window.

3. Open the Effects & Presets panel. Locate the Raining Characters Out preset in Text ➤ Animate Out and drag it onto the text.

4. Twirl down Text and Animator 1. Move the playback head to the 2-second mark on the timeline and drag the first keyframe to the playback head. Move the playback head to the 3-second mark and drag the second keyframe to the 3-second mark. The text will stay on screen for two seconds and then fall off of the bottom of the screen between seconds 2 and 3.

5. Select the Text tool and enter your name. When you open the Character panel, just change the size to 24 px. Drag your name to a point under the letter *p* in picture.

6. In the Animation & Presets panel locate the Evaporate preset—Text ➤ Blurs ➤ Evaporate—and drag it on top of your name.

Here's a quick way of hunting for a preset. Instead of opening a bunch of folders, just enter the name of the preset into the text input area at the top of the Animations Presets *panel. When you press the Enter/Return key, all of the presets containing that term will appear.*

7. Twirl down your name in the timeline and then twirl down Text ➤ Evaporate Animator ➤ Range Selector 1. Place the keyframes at the 2-second and 3-second marks, respectively. If you click the RAM Preview button and then drag the playback head across the timeline, you will see your name smudge out and evaporate (see Figure 3-18).

Figure 3-18. The Raining Characters Out and the Evaporate effects

8. Drag the Out points for both layers to the 7-second mark and drag your name layer under the other text layer. Save the file.

Combining animation effects

In this next part of the exercise, you create a rather interesting "Matrix-like" effect. The letters of the words pour in from the top of the screen, form a phrase, hold for two seconds, and then pour off of the bottom of the screen.

1. Click the Comp window, select the Text tool, and enter the text production assistant. In the Character panel, set the text size to 14 px. Drag this text layer under your name.

2. Set the In point for this layer to 3 seconds and set the Out point to 7 seconds.

3. In the Animation & Presets panel, twirl down Animation Presets ➤ Text ➤ Animate In. Locate the Raining Characters In preset and drag it on top of the text.

4. Twirl down the layer in the timeline and then twirl down Animator 1 ➤ Range Selector1. Drag the keyframes to the 3-second and 4-second marks.

5. Drag the playback head to the 6-second mark on the timeline and drag and drop the Raining Characters Out preset from the Animate Out folder onto the text.

6. In the timeline, twirl down its animator—Animator 2—and drag the second keyframe to the 7-second mark of the timeline. Twirl up the strip in the timeline.

7. Click the RAM Preview button and, when it passes the 7-second mark, click the Play button. The text, as shown in Figure 3-19, will rain into place, hold, and then rain out.

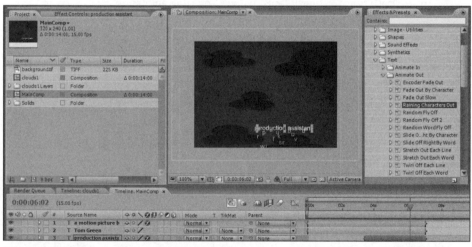

Figure 3-19. The exercise so far includes a number of effects including a Raining Characters Out effect.

8. Click the Comp window once, select the Text tool, and enter the text Tiago Dias. Set the size to 24 px in the Character panel and drag the text to a position just under the *t* in production.

9. In the timeline, set the In point for the new layer to 3 seconds and set the Out point to 7 seconds. Move the playback head to the In point and add the Evaporate effect to Tiago's name. Move the playback head to the 5-second mark and add another Evaporate effect to Tiago's name.

10. Open Animator 1 to see the keyframes of the animator's Offset property for the first Evaporate effect. Move the second keyframe to the 4-second mark on the timeline. Twirl down Animator 2 on the timeline and switch the positions of the two keyframes in Animator 2. This has the effect of reversing the Evaporate effect to a fade out. After you switch the positions of the keyframes in Animator 2, drag the first keyframe to the 5-second mark on the timeline and the second one to the 6-second mark. Save the project.

11. Move the playback head to the 7-second mark on the timeline, select the Text tool, and enter the text Poetry in Motion. Set the size to 24 px.

12. Open the Animation & Presets panel. Select Animation Presets ➤ Text ➤ Organic and drag the Drop Bounce effect from the Organic folder onto the text.

13. Switch back to the Text tool and enter friendsofED. Set the size for this text to 14 px and, in the timeline, drag the text's In point to the 8-second mark.

14. Drag the Boomerang effect from the Organic folder onto this text.

15. Rearrange your layers to match those in Figure 3-20 and save the project. If you do a RAM preview and click the Play button, you will see how carefully applying effects to text results in a rather interesting and engaging animation.

Figure 3-20. The layering and layer timing order so far

Now that the text is in motion, let's add a little bit more interest to the project.

1. Click the Comp window once and select Layer ➤ New ➤ Solid to open the Solid Settings dialog box shown in Figure 3-21. Specify these values:

- Name: Gray Solid 2
- Width: 320
- Height: 99
- Color: #666666

Figure 3-21. Creating the solid

2. Drag this layer under the Tiago Dias layer and set its blend mode to Color Dodge. The result of this mode will be to lighten the solid and make it look somewhat transparent.

3. The solid will move down and back up the video as it is playing. Drag the solid to a position just above the Comp window.

4. Move the playback head to the 1-second mark of the timeline and twirl down the Gray Solid 2 layer. Twirl down Transition and click the stopwatch once in the Position property to add a keyframe. Move the playback head to the 2-second mark and drag the solid to a point just under the bottom of the Comp window. This will result in a keyframe at this mark in the timeline and the motion is indicated by the dotted line running from the top to the bottom of the Comp.

5. Add a keyframe at the 5-second mark in the timeline.

6. Move the playback head to the 6-second mark of the timeline and drag the solid to a point just above the top of the Comp window.

7. Save the project.

8. With the project saved, add the Comp to the Render Queue by clicking the Comp once and selecting Composition ➤ Add to Render Queue.

9. Click the Render Queue tab and output the video using the following specifications:

- Format: QuickTime
- Compression Type: Video

10. Once you have rendered the QuickTime video, quit After Effects.

Creating the FLV file

The final step in this project is to create the FLV file that will be used in Flash. If you have been following this exercise rather closely, you may have noticed there is really no color in this video and there is no audio. This tells you that you can create a seriously small FLV file because you won't need to add an audio stream and that a low video data rate will have a minimal effect upon the quality of the video. The other important point to keep in mind is the user is only going to be able to turn the video off and on. There is no jog control. This means you can let the Flash 8 Video Encoder determine the keyframe placement. Remember the further apart the keyframes, the lower the final file size. Let's go to work:

1. Open the Flash 8 Video Encoder and add the video you just created to the queue. Click the Settings button to open the Flash Video Encoding Settings dialog box.

2. Click the Show Advanced Settings button to open the Advanced Settings area.

3. When the Advanced Settings area opens, specify the following values:

   - Output filename: Ad_01
   - Video codec: ON2VP6
   - Frame rate: 15
   - Key frame placement: Automatic
   - Quality: Custom
   - Max data rate: 175

When you have entered these values, click OK to return to the Render Queue. Click the Start Queue button to create the FLV file.

At this point all you need to do is to open Flash and create a custom player (Chapter 2) that uses only a play and a pause button. The complete FLA and SWF files (shown in Figure 3-22) can be found in the Chapter 3 Exercise folder if you want to explore the code.

Figure 3-22.
The project playing in the Flash Player

If you do explore the code, you may notice a new "chunk" of code that wasn't covered in the previous chapter. The code block is

```
ns.onStatus = function(info) {
  if (info.code == "NetStream.Play.Stop") {
    ns.seek(0);
    }
}
```

What this code does is to "loop" a video. When an FLV file plays through the Flash Player, it is sending status messages to the player. One of those messages essentially says, "I have reached the end of the FLV and the video is now stopped." When the player detects this message, you can capture it and tell Flash to go back to the start of the video— ns.seek(0)—and to start playing the video again.

> *The buttons used to control the video in the Flash movie are the* flat gray stop *and* flat gray play *buttons that can be found in* Window ➤ Common Libraries ➤ Buttons. *When the panel opens, the buttons can be found in the* playback flat *folder.*

Creating a motion graphics banner ad

In this exercise, you will create a rather "snazzy" banner ad that will promote this book. This one is going to be a bit different because you will be working in a rather limited space. The ad is 728 pixels wide and only 90 pixels deep. This means you must make effective use of the space and catch the viewer's attention.

You will be doing this using a number of the text animation presets and through the use of some **wiggles**.

Essentially a wiggle effect transforms the properties of the text it is applied to. The neat thing about this effect is it has certain randomness to it. It is both extremely powerful and effective. It is also able to produce effects that Flash can only do through the use of brute-force ActionScript. The bottom line: judicious use of wiggles is more effective than over-use. Let's sell a book.

   1. Open the Banner.aep file found in the AD_02 folder in your Chapter 3 Exercise folder.

As you can see in Figure 3-23, the interface has been somewhat constructed for you. The Actionscript_txt layer is animated, the other text layers and graphics are in place, and the layering order and In and Out points for the layers have been set. All you need to do is to add the effects.

Figure 3-23. The project is ready for you to finish.

To start, turn off the visibility of all of the layers above the NO ACTIONSCRIPT KNOWLEDGE layer.

2. Select the text in the Comp window and open the Effects & Presets panel.

3. Twirl down Animation Presets ➤ Text ➤ Miscellaneous and drag the Chaotic preset onto the text. When you release the mouse, the words will look like they have "exploded" as shown in Figure 3-24.

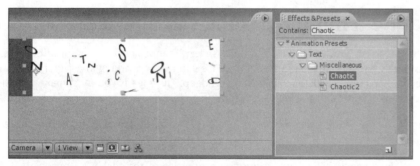

Figure 3-24. The Chaotic effect tends to explode text.

If you twirl down the layer and then twirl down Text, you will see how this effect works. The Position, Scale, Skew, and Rotation properties of the text have all had a wiggle applied to them. To see how a wiggle works, twirl down Wiggle Position and then Wiggly Selector 1.

Essentially you can have text bend, move, blur, spin, and so on by simply giving it some parameters for the effect. Where the randomness comes in is how the effect is applied. The parameter is the outer limit, which means the effect can be applied to any letter in the group and it will change using any value up to the parameter value.

For example, the phrase "NO ACTIONSCRIPT KNOWLEDGE" contains 23 letters. They are in a fixed position, but the Position parameter says the maximum distance each of the 23 letters can move is 50% of the start position. When the wiggle is applied, each letter will move any distance from 1% to 50% of its starting position, meaning one letter may move a short distance while the one beside it moves to the other side of the screen. The result is the explosion of letters that you see on the screen.

4. If it isn't already open, twirl down Wiggly Selector 1 under Wiggle Position.

5. Drag the keyframes in the Max Amount and Min Amount areas to the 1- and 2-second marks on the timeline. This keeps the animation confined to a second.

6. To clear the phrase off of the screen, move the playback head to the 3-second mark on the timeline, select the text in the Comp window and apply the Raining Characters Out preset to the text.

7. Twirl down Animator 1 and Range Selector 1. Drag the last keyframe in the Position property to the 4-second mark. Lock the layer and save the project.

8. Turn on the visibility of the JUST YOUR CREATIVITY layer.

9. Select the text and drag the Boomerang preset—Animation Presets ➤ Text ➤ Organic—onto the selected text.

10. Save the project. If you click the RAM Preview button, you will see that the Boomerang effect has your text come flying in from the front of the screen, move to the back of the screen, and then return to the front of the screen to form the words.

Applying effects to images

To this point in the chapter, we have been whirling and twirling text all over the screen. It isn't only text that benefits from special effects. The next layer in the exercise contains the image of a lightbulb. The plan is to have the bulb light up.

Here you will learn how to **key** a background color to remove it from an image and how to animate a Glow effect.

1. Turn on the visibility of the Lightbulb.tif layer. You can't help but notice the image is sitting on a green background and that the bulb shown in Figure 3-25 looks somewhat dull.

Figure 3-25.
A dull lightbulb is not exactly what we want.

2. Select the image on the stage and open the Effects & Presets panel.

3. Twirl down the Keying presets and drag the Color Key preset onto the image. When you release the mouse, this preset will appear in the Effect Controls panel.

4. This preset will be used to remove the green background of the image. In the Effect Controls panel, click the eyedropper tool in the Key Color area.

5. Roll the cursor onto the green area of the image in the Comp window and click the mouse. The green color, except for a thin edge around the object, will disappear and will also appear in the Color chip beside the eyedropper.

6. To remove the edge, twirl down Color Tolerance and drag the slider that appears to the right until you see a value of 60. As you drag the slider, the green glow will start to disappear.

7. Twirl down Edge Thin and move the slider all the way to the right. What you have just done here is to enlarge the mask that is hiding the green color and increasing the transparent area.

8. If your settings and image resemble those shown in Figure 3-26, twirl up Color Key.

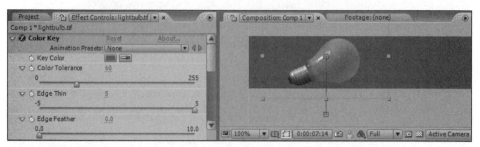

Figure 3-26. Color Key effects can be used to remove color backgrounds from images.

With the green color "keyed" out of the image, we can now concentrate on turning on the lightbulb.

1. In the Effects & Presets panel, twirl down the Stylize folder and drag the Glow preset onto the lightbulb.

The first thing you will notice is the bulb has changed color. This is due to the default value for this effect which, if you look in the Effect Controls panel, is set to Color Channels. This isn't exactly the effect we were hoping to obtain, but the default value gives us a clue as to how we can achieve our goal. When you are keying out the color of an image, you aren't removing the color, you are **masking** it. If you are familiar at all with masking in Photoshop, you know that the mask is applied to the image through the use an alpha channel, which is a channel that essentially "sits under" the image. It is no different in After Effects, and understanding this opens up a huge world of possibilities in Flash Video that utilizes an alpha channel. (We are going to dig deeper into this whole area in the next chapter.)

2. Click the Glow Based On pull-down in the Effect Controls panel and select Alpha Channel. You will notice there is a bit of a glow that appears around the bulb.

3. Twirl down Glow Radius and drag the slider all the way to the right. The maximum value of 100 is acceptable but still doesn't really do the job. The interesting thing about many of the maximum values you can apply to the various effect properties is that you can ignore them. Double-click the value in the Glow Radius area and change it from 100 to 164. The light, as shown in Figure 3-27, turns on! This is still not exactly what we are looking for. We want the bulb to light up in front of the viewer.

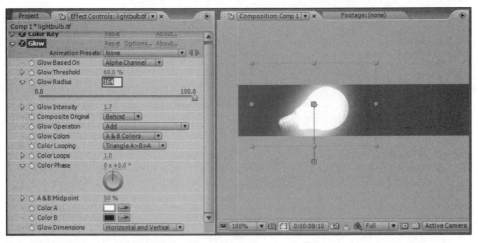

Figure 3-27. Turning on a light with the Glow effect

4. On the timeline, twirl down Lightbulb.tif ➤ Effects ➤ Glow.

5. Drag the playback head to the 7-second mark on the timeline and add keyframes for Glow Radius and Glow Intensity. Set the Glow Radius value to 0.

6. Move the playback head to the 7.5-second mark and change the Glow Radius value to 164 and the Glow Intensity value to 1.7.

7. Save the project and click the RAM Preview button. You should see your lightbulb turn on.

> *If you want to turn effects on and off, click the icon beside the effect in the visibility area of the timeline. You can also turn effects on and off by clicking the* Effects *icon beside the effect in the* Effect Controls *panel.*

8. Turn on the visibility of the POETRY IN MOTION layer.

9. Select the text and drop the Evaporate effect onto it.

10. Twirl down to Range Selector 1 for this layer and place the Offset keyframe at the In point of the layer and a second one at the 9-second mark.

11. Save the project.

From here you should render out the video as a QuickTime movie using the Video codec. This file can then be converted to an FLV file using the Flash 8 Video Encoder. To keep the size of the Flash SWF file manageable, set the stage size of the Flash document to match the 728×90 dimensions of the video. Place a video object on the stage, resize it to fit the dimensions of the video, and add the ActionScript that makes it play. Don't forget to use the looping code presented earlier in the chapter to keep the video playing. The SWF animation can then be placed in an HTML page and uploaded to your web server as shown in Figure 3-28.

Figure 3-28. The project is playing through a browser.

The QuickTime video, FLA, FLV, and the SWF files can all be found in the Ad_02 folder inside the Completed folder of the Chapter 3 download.

After Effects motion graphics used as loaders for Flash movies

Up to this point in the chapter, all of the examples have been used as video ads and so on. In this final section of the chapter, we answer a question that we commonly encounter: "Is that all they can be used for?" Based on the subhead for this section, the answer is, "Not really."

No matter how you approach it, a Flash movie sits on a straight line called the timeline, and all of the content in the movie has to load before the movie plays. That is a simplistic description of the linear basis of animation, but it is fairly close to the mark. Add navigation to the mix—either through buttons or ActionScript—and these movies become non-linear. Instead of going to Frame 3 from Frame 2, the Flash playback head may be sent to Frame 15 and, when that frame finishes, the user is taken to Frame 3. The problem with that is one we have all encountered: a pause in the playback as the content loads into the frame, and the viewer has to sit and wait for that to occur.

To avoid this nastiness, Flash developers will add loaders to their Flash movies that ensure the content is ready to play. These loaders can be anything from a graphic to a movie clip and, at their heart, they are a graphic indication that something really is happening when the movie first appears on the screen. This can take the form of a simple progress bar that grows to an After Effects motion graphic that plays and replays for as long as it takes to get the content loaded.

Obviously, there are as many approaches to the subject of creating a loader as there are Flash developers. In this section, we give you a taste of what we mean by presenting three different ways of using a simple motion graphic that plays while a really large image loads into a Flash movie. Each of the authors will present one approach, and the third one has been prepared by a colleague, Joseph Balderson, who is a Flash developer based in Toronto, Canada. The bottom line here is no one cares how you create your loader. They only care that it works.

Before we dig into using an After Effects motion graphic as a loader, let's create a very simple load bar that will familiarize you with the subject.

1. In Flash, open the Loader_01.fla file, which can be found in the Loaders folder of the Chapter 3 Exercise folder.

2. If you look at the timeline (as shown in Figure 3-29), you will see the movie is composed of three frames. Frames 1 and 2 have a white bar in them, and Frame 3 contains an overly large JPG image of an architectural detail from a Las Vegas hotel. The white bar, which is the Loader movie clip in the library, will be used as the loading progress indicator. Frames 1 and 2 will actually be the frames used to create the loader. The playback head will move between them until the JPG image in Frame 3 loads. When it loads, the playback head will jump from Frame 1 to Frame 3 and the image will appear.

Figure 3-29. The project requires only three frames, a movie clip, and one big, fat JPG image.

> *Why is the loader bar a movie clip? When manipulating objects on the Flash stage using ActionScript, an object's properties, such as its width, height, and color, can be manipulated using code. The only objects that can be manipulated in this manner are movie clips.*

Now that you know how the movie is constructed, let's discuss how the whole thing works.

Let's assume the amount of data in the JPG that has to load is 100 bytes and that the length of the loader bar is 200 pixels. What has to happen when 50 bytes of the JPG have loaded is the bar must be 100 pixels long. What we need to do, therefore, is to keep an eye on how much of the data in the JPG has loaded and have the length of the bar equal the percentage of the amount of data that has loaded so far. When the percentage equals 100%, the playback head is told to scoot over to Frame 3 and show us the JPG.

How this loader works is not terribly complicated. Frame 1 is where the movie asks how much of the JPG has loaded, and Frame 2 is where the bar's length is set to equal the percentage amount of data loaded so far.

3. Click once in Frame 1 of the Actions layer and open the ActionScript Editor by either selecting Window ➤ Actions or pressing the F9 key (PC) or Option+F9 (Mac).

4. Click once in the Script pane and enter the following code:

```
if (getBytesLoaded() > 0 && getBytesLoaded() ➡
>= getBytesTotal()) gotoAndStop(3);
```

In plain English, this line simply checks the number of bytes currently loaded for the movie (getBytesLoaded) and, if that value is greater than 0 and also greater than or equal to the bytes loaded so far (getBytesTotal), scoots the playback head over to Frame 3 and stays put (gotoAndStop(3)).

This line of code, or a variation of it, is at the heart of the vast majority of the loaders in use today, and you will see it used throughout this book and other ActionScript sources.

5. Close the Script pane to return to the main timeline. Select Frame 2 of the Actions layer and enter the following code:

```
mcLoader._xscale = (getBytesLoaded()/getBytesTotal()) * 100;
gotoAndPlay(1);
```

The first line is how the bar is sized. Let's use real numbers from the explanation given earlier. We know the size of the movie is 100 bytes and that the width of the loader movie clip (mcLoader) is 200 pixels. Let's also assume only a quarter of the movie has loaded at this point. Toss in those numbers and the code becomes

```
mcLoader._xscale = (25/100) * 100
mcLoader._xscale = .25 *100
mcLoader._xscale = 25
```

At this point the loader bar is scaled to 25% of its width (._xscale), and the playback head is sent back to Frame 1 to start the process all over again. When the getBytesLoaded() value is 200 bytes or more, the playback head is sent to Frame 3 instead of Frame 2.

6. Save the movie and press Ctrl+Enter (PC) or Cmd+Return (Mac) to test the movie.

Testing locally is a bit of a tricky process. If you test the movie and immediately see the JPG image, press the Ctrl+Enter or Cmd+Return keys once more. You should now see the loading process shown in Figure 3-30. Remember, your hard drive is not exactly a web connection, and things happen a lot faster on a computer. Pressing the keys again actually simulates the loading progress you would see in a dial-up modem.

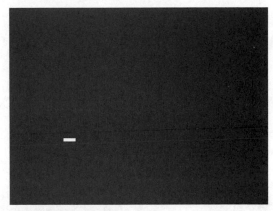

Figure 3-30. The loader in action

A frame-based loader

Now that you understand how a loader works, let's look at a couple of ways of using the After Effects animation presets to add a bit more zip to your movie than a simple bar growing on the screen.

In this example, you won't be checking to see how many bytes have loaded. Instead you will be telling Flash to keep an eye on how many *frames* have loaded.

1. Open the Loader_02.fla file in your Chapter 3 Exercise folder.

2. Click the first frame of the Actions layer and open the ActionScript Editor.

3. Click once in the Script pane and enter the following code:

```
onEnterFrame = function () {
  if  (_framesloaded <_totalframes) {
    gotoAndPlay(1);
  }else{
    gotoAndPlay (2);
    }
}
```

This code uses an onEnterFrame event rather than a stop() action to hold the playback head on Frame 1. When the playback head enters Frame 1, it checks to see whether all of the frames in the Flash movie have been loaded. If they haven't, the playback head stays put in Frame 1. If the frames have loaded, the playback head is sent over to Frame 2, and the JPG image displays.

4. Save the movie and test it.

The effect used is the Drop Bounce *effect from the* Organic *presets in After Effects. The AEP file (*LoadJPG.aep*) and the SWF file exported from After Effects (*Load.swf*) can be found in the* Loader_02 *folder in the* Completed *folder in the* Chapter 3 *code download.*

If it seems like the preloader plays for an inordinate amount of time before the image appears, you can speed things up. When the Flash Player opens to test the SWF file, select View ➤ Download Settings *and select* 56K (4.7 KB/s) *or* DSL (32.6 KB/s) *from the*

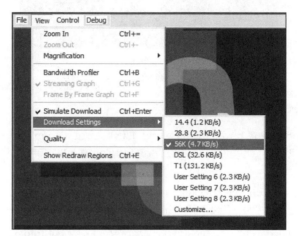

Figure 3-31. You can change the modem setting when you test your SWF animation.

A clip event used as a loader

In the previous exercise, you simply placed a movie clip on the timeline and used Action-Script to keep an eye on what was going on in the frames after Frame 1. In this example, we are going to assign that task to the movie clip on the stage. This will be accomplished through the use of an onClipEvent handler that is attached to the movie clip.

This handler was introduced to ActionScript when Flash 5 was released. Up until that point the only event handlers that could be used in ActionScript were found in keyframes and buttons. The onClipEvent handler is rather interesting in that you can apply the event to the wrapper of the movie clip's instance on the stage. By that, we mean the actions to be performed are attached to the movie clip. They are not added to the keyframe of a movie clip.

1. Open the Loader_03.fla file found in your Chapter 3 Exercise folder.

2. Click the first frame in the Content layer once to locate the movie clip on the stage.

3. Click the movie clip on the stage and open the ActionScript editor.

4. Click once in the Script pane and add the following code:

```
onClipEvent(enterFrame) {
    var bytes:Number = _root.getBytesTotal();
    var bytes_loaded:Number = _root.getBytesLoaded();
    if (bytes_loaded == bytes) {
        _root.nextFrame();
    } else {
        _root.gotoAndStop(1);
    }
}
```

The first thing you should notice is that the parameter being used for the onClipEvent is enterFrame. In this case, it is referring to Frame 1 of the timeline, not Frame 1 of the movie clip. The next two lines create variables—bytes and bytes_loaded—that will "hold" the values of the bytes loading into the main timeline (_root) and the total number of bytes that need to be loaded. The remainder of the script is fairly self-explanatory. If the value of the bytes_loaded variable equals the value of bytes, scoot the playback head to the next frame on the timeline. If they aren't equal, the playback head is instructed to stay put.

> *The keyword* if *indicates what is known as a **conditional statement**. These statements can only have one of two values:* True *or* False. *This sort of value is referred to by the code geeks as a **Boolean value**. The keyword* else *actually means "then." In the preceding code, if the values are not equal, "then" the animation is to stay put on Frame 1 of the main timeline.*

5. Save the movie and test it. The movie clip spins (see Figure 3-32) while the JPG file loads.

Figure 3-32.
The loading code can be attached to a movie clip instead of a frame.

If you have been using ActionScript for a while, you are probably looking at this approach with a bit of surprise. Attaching code directly to a button or a movie clip is not in the realm of current best practices. We are showing you this simply to give you another perspective on how a loader can be constructed. If this project were to follow current best practices, the code in Frame 1 of the Actions *layer would be*

```
this.onEnterFrame = function () {
var bytes:Number = _root.getBytesTotal();
    var bytes_loaded:Number = _root.getBytesLoaded();
    if (bytes_loaded == bytes) {
        _root.nextFrame();
    } else {
        _root.gotoAndStop(1);
    }
}
```

Using a movie clip and a ProgressBar component

In certain Flash circles, Toronto, Canada, is regarded as a major Flash center. In fact, one of the more influential annual Flash conferences, **FlashintheCan**—and Flash user groups—**FlashinTO**—are located in Toronto. Due to the fact one of the authors lives in Toronto, he didn't have to look far to find someone to contribute the final exercise in this chapter.

Joseph Balderson, more affectionately known as "Joeflash" (it's a long story, but has to do with his personal website named www.joeflash.ca), has been a fixture on the Flash scene in Toronto since 2001. Traditionally a generalist web/graphic designer since 1997, Joseph has in recent years undergone a renaissance as a Flash developer, expanding his interests to include teaching and writing about all things Flash at the college level and writing about Flash for Community MX (www.communitymx.com). Lately he has been spending a lot of time thinking and writing about the subject of loaders in Flash, and when we saw this loader—www.cmcforgings.ca—which makes extensive use of some very advanced ActionScript, it didn't take us long to contact him and ask for a contribution to this chapter. As you are about to discover, loaders in the hands of a master can be elegant and simple as well as technically sophisticated.

1. Open the Loader_04.fla file located in your Chapter 3 Exercise folder.

When the file opens, the first thing you will notice is the timeline is a bit different from what has been presented so far. We'll get deeper into that in a minute.

If you open the Library (see Figure 3-33), you will see how a pro sets up a Flash Library. Joe has set up a series of folders designed to contain all of the asset types that would be placed into a typical Flash movie. Even though many of the folders are empty, this is an extremely good habit to develop. The Library can be an extremely cluttered and messy place. Using folders to contain the content used in the movie brings order to that chaos.

Figure 3-33.
The Flash Library, in the hands of a pro,
can be a place of order and calm.

You will notice the timeline is composed of four layers:

- Labels: The little flags are the labels or names given to the frames. Labels are mostly used for navigation and are added by clicking a frame and entering a name for the label in the Property inspector.

- Actions: It is now common practice to put all ActionScript on the main timeline.

- Content: This layer holds the JPG image.

- Loader: This layer holds the movie clip, with the instance name of loaderani_mc, that will appear while the JPG image loads.

2. Click once in Frame 2 of the Actions layer and enter the following code:

```
stop();
import mx.controls.ProgressBar;
import mx.utils.Delegate;
this.attachMovie("ProgressBar", "pb_cp", 10);
pb_cp._visible = false;
pb_cp.mode = "polled";
pb_cp.source = this;
```

This codes sets up the loader. The first line stops the playback on Frame 2 to enable the movie to wait for the code to be executed before continuing.

The rest of the preceding code adds a ProgressBar component to the stage, hides it, and sets up the component's load monitoring parameters. Let's carefully go through this so you understand what is going on.

The first and most important thing you need to understand about the ProgressBar component—found in the User Interface section of the Components panel—is that it can't simply be yanked from the Components panel, placed on the stage, and be expected to go to work. In the case of this project, the component isn't placed on the stage by you. It is "pulled" from the Library to the stage using ActionScript. If you look in the 05 - components folder in the Library, you'll notice that the component is there.

Components are their own self-contained MovieClip class objects with their own methods and properties. In order to make them work, we need to tell Flash where to find the code for that particular component class. The second line of the code does just that. It "loads" the ProgressBar class code so you don't have to type in the full class path of mx.controls.ProgressBar every time you want to refer to the component. It is an abbreviation, a bookmark if you will, to the full **classpath**, or class location.

The other thing to understand about components is that, despite their ease of use, they are stone cold stupid. They need to be told what to do, what to listen for, and where things are. The third line tells Flash where to find the Delegate class. Later on in this example, we will look at how the Delegate class makes it easier for us to "tell the component" where the loader code is.

Having "loaded in" the ProgressBar and Delegate class files, you can now concentrate on making the component work.

The next line—this.attachMovie("ProgressBar", "pb_cp", 10);—pulls the ProgressBar component out of the components folder in the Library, gives it the instance name of pb_cp, and places it at a depth of 10. The keyword this refers to the root timeline of your main movie, and the component is added to the root timeline of the stage using the attachMovie() method.

This component is being used in a slightly different way than you may first assume. It will be used to monitor the load progress not as a load indicator. This explains why the component is made invisible: pb_cp._visible = false;. The final two lines tell the component how to monitor the load progress on the main timeline.

The first line—pb_cp.mode = "polled";—is the key. The mode property can have one of three values: event, polled, and manual. If the event mode is used, the component pays attention to progress and complete events emitted by the load source itself, which usually requires additional logic such as a Loader component. In polled mode, the component uses the source's getBytesLoaded() and getBytesTotal() methods to "drive" the progress and complete events, both of which are quite familiar to you by now. The manual mode would be used if the component were employed simply as a progress indicator, where the load is monitored by something other than the ProgressBar component—which is actually the complete opposite to how you are now using it.

The last line simply tells the component that the instance to be loaded and monitored—pb_cp.source—is the main or root timeline: this.

3. Press the Return/Enter key twice and enter the following code:

```
function loadProgress() {
   var frame:Number=Math.ceil(((pb_cp.percentComplete)*➡
loaderani_mc._totalframes)/100);
loaderani_mc.gotoAndStop(frame);
};
```

This function, though it looks complicated, is actually a variation of the code we have been using prior to this exercise. It simply determines which frame to send the playback head of your animation, located in the loaderani_mc movie clip instance. The equation within the Math.ceil() method takes the load progress, a number out of 100 (percentComplete), and converts it into a number in relation to the total number of frames in the animation (_totalframes). The Math.ceil() method then rounds up the result of that equation to the nearest whole number. If the method wasn't used and the result was 3.629, Flash would have a huge amount of trouble finding that frame number.

Notice that the loaderani_mc movie clip has an Actions layer with a stop() action spanning all frames of that timeline. This is present so that your animation will not play on its own, requiring that the loader control the timeline playback itself.

4. Press the Return/Enter key twice and enter the following code:

```
function loadComplete() {
    this.gotoAndStop("main");
    pb_cp.removeListener(pbListener);
    pb_cp.removeMovieClip();
};
```

The previous function tells Flash what to do while the content is still loading. This one tells Flash what do when the content has finished loading. The first thing it does is send the main timeline to the frame containing the frame label main. Having left the frame labeled loader, the component's job is done. The next line stops it from listening for load updates, and the last line removes the component from the stage.

5. Press the Return/Enter key twice and enter the following code:

```
var pbListener:Object = new Object();
pb_cp.addEventListener("progress", Delegate.create(this,loadProgress));
pb_cp.addEventListener("complete", Delegate.create(this,loadComplete));
```

As we stated earlier, components are not exactly the brightest candle on the tree. They need to be told what to do and, in the case of this code, the component is being told what to listen for and where the resulting code is located.

The first line creates what is called a **listener object** and gives it the name of pbListener.

The next two lines, using the addEventListener() method, tells the component what two events to listen for—progress and complete—and what to do when it "hears" it. Listeners can only react to events like a mouse click or, in the case of this example, a progress or complete event. In the first case, if the event is progress, which fires every time the load is updated, then our Delegate class "tells the listener" to execute the loadProgress function. In the second case, if the event is complete, which fires once the source (the main timeline) has finished loading, then our Delegate class "tells the listener" to execute the loadComplete function.

6. Save and test the movie.

A fully commented version of this exercise can be found in the Load_04 folder in the Chapter 3 Completed *folder.*

Summary

This has been quite the chapter, and we have only completed 25% of our dragon hunt. As you have discovered, there is quite an intimate relation between Flash and After Effects when it comes to putting text in motion and using it in Flash.

We started off by showing you how to apply an animation preset to a line of text in After Effects and how to get the swirling text from After Effects and into Flash as a movie clip. From there our "hunt" took us from applying a single effect to some text to applying a combination of effects to create a rather interesting effect for the entry and exit of text from the stage.

The next project kicked up the complexity level by a notch and showed you how to create a rich media ad using Illustrator content. As you discovered, Illustrator images, when imported into After Effects, not only arrive as a Comp, but that Comp also contains the layers used in the Illustrator image. You then discovered that you can actually animate or otherwise manipulate those Illustrator layers in the Comp. Among the effects we explore in this exercise were the Raining Characters In and Raining Characters Out, Drop Bounce, and Boomerang presets. We also showed a rather nifty way of making an extremely small FLV file using the Flash 8 Video Encoder and how to loop a Flash video using ActionScript.

The next project was the creation of a banner ad that was only 90 pixels high. In this exercise, we showed you how to use a wiggle effect thanks to the Chaotic preset. We also showed you how to "key" an image from Photoshop in After Effects and how to use a Glow effect to turn a lightbulb on and off.

The chapter wound up by answering the question, "What else can you do with these things?" We showed you three ways of using your After Effects animations as loaders in a Flash movie. The section started off by showing you how a loading progress bar is created by explaining how to keep an eye on the data loading into the SWF file. From there you were shown how to use an effect as a frame-based loader, and the next exercise showed you how to use the actual clip as the loader. The chapter finished with a somewhat advanced loader from our friend Joe Balderson, which was a slightly different take on the use of the ProgressBar component in Flash.

In the next chapter, we explore one of the hottest features of Flash Video, which is the introduction of the ability to use alpha channel video in Flash. You are about to discover that the After Effects/Flash 8 combination were made for each other when it comes to this technique. See you there.

When Flash Professional 8 was released in late 2005, Flash developers were rocked back on their heels when they learned they could incorporate video with an alpha channel into their work. Up until that point, that sort of thing was left to After Effects, and we took what we received from the video guys.

With Flash 8, not only could we create our own alpha channel video, but we discovered we could do our own compositing and even add special effects to the video. Sports companies such as Nike and Adidas took to this like ducks to water. This was not exactly unexpected, but we were curious to see how hard-core Flash developers would use this feature. It didn't take long to find out.

In early spring of 2006, Thierry Loa (www.deekons.com) launched two commercial sites that make extensive use of alpha video. The first piece—www.johnst.com/, shown in Figure 4-1—employs a traditional approach to the use of alpha video to promote the services of an advertising agency. One feature of the site immediately caught our attention. The section named "Book of John" uses an interactive video to turn the pages of a book and, when you click the book, the pages in the video fill the screen.

Figure 4-1. Welcome to John Street

The next piece that Thierry demonstrated was for a company named MIJO Corporation (www.mijo.ca). This company is a production shop for the creative industry, and Thierry created a video intro to that site that shows what happens when a powerful technique is placed into the hands of someone who knows what they are doing. When you enter the site by clicking the General link, a woman walks out of the clouds (see Figure 4-2) to welcome you to the site and to give you an overview of the company's services. When the welcome video finishes, the woman is transported to a hyper-modern environment where she invites you to navigate the site using a series of graphics that have been created in Flash.

Figure 4-2. Welcome to MIJO Corporation. Note the closed caption under the video.

The other thing that caught our eye was the attention to detail. For example, in the opening video, the narration also appears as captions, for the hearing impaired, under the video. In the main navigation video, the areas of the site appear above the video layer in Flash, and, as you roll over one of the navigation links, the woman's eyes follow the mouse as shown in Figure 4-3. As you are starting to guess, talking heads are no longer boring when it comes to Flash video.

Figure 4-3. The mouse is over the INSIDE MIJO link and her eyes are following the mouse.

In this chapter, we are going to show you how to create an alpha channel video in After Effects, demonstrate how to incorporate and manipulate that video in Flash, and finish off the chapter with a couple of rather interesting exercises that will introduce you to the possibilities of how Flash and After Effects can create some deep and engaging video experiences. It all starts with knowing how to create an alpha channel video in After Effects.

Keying video in After Effects

In the early summer of 2005, the company formerly known as Macromedia yanked one of the authors into the company's head office, sat him down in front of a video camera, and asked him to talk about what impressed him the most about the new Studio 8 release. The set was rather basic. He sat on a stool in front of a green screen, faced a camera, and answered the questions that were fired at him. When the Studio 8 release was announced, a clip from the session appeared on the Dreamweaver site (see Figure 4-4) and the green background was gone. It was replaced with a brownish, textured background instead. As well, his name appeared over his image and a set of video controls appeared on the screen.

Figure 4-4.
It is a sad day when a writer is reduced to a talking head.

In this exercise, you will work with an outtake from that session. We are going to approach it from two different perspectives. The first will be to use a variety of keying tools to remove the background and "pull" a mask. The second will show you how to use the Keylight filter for the same task. We are sure that once you understand how to use the Keylight filter, you will use it religiously. Still there are other tools in the toolbox, and a familiarity with them won't hurt you.

Before we start, it is important that you understand what you are doing. You will not be "removing" a green background from behind a talking head. What you will be doing is creating an alpha channel mask that will hide the background. This distinction is critical because, in Flash, an alpha channel mask can be read by the application. This means you can treat this form of video in much the same way you would treat a red square in a Flash movie clip. You can just as easily add a drop shadow or glow or other effect to a talking head as you can to a red box. The process starts with a video clip in After Effects.

1. Download the Chapter 4 source code material if you haven't already, access the Exercise folder, and open the GS_01.aep file in After Effects 7.

2. Select Window ➤ Effects & Presets. When the window opens, twirl down the Keying category and drag the Color Key filter from the Effects & Presets panel onto the Comp. When you release the mouse, the settings will appear in the Effect Controls panel as shown in Figure 4-5.

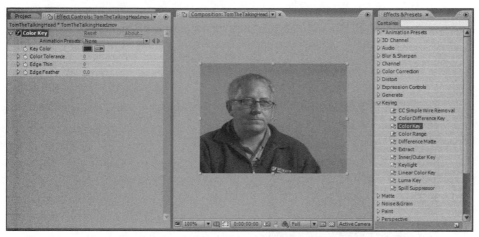

Figure 4-5. Dropping the Color Key effect on the Comp opens the controls for the filter.

3. Click the eyedropper beside the Key Color Color chip and click the green area in the Comp. Depending on where you click, the green color will be replaced with splotches of black. This indicates the background was not uniformly lit. Let's fix that.

4. Twirl down Color Tolerance in the Effect Controls panel. The slider you see when you twirl down will "expand" the selection.

5. Drag the slider to the right to increase the selection. Be careful here because you can give people some really bad haircuts if you get too aggressive. We have found a tolerance level of about 80 to be just about right.

You don't have to use the slider. You can click the value, and, as you drag the mouse to the left or right, the value will change and the mask will either expand or contract.

When you are "keying" a video, a good habit to develop is to toggle the transparency on and off by clicking the Toggle Transparency Grid *button in the* Comp *window. This is the button in the lower-right corner of the window immediately to the left of the* Active Camera *pull-down. Toggling the transparency allows you to closely monitor the edges of the subject. Another technique is to create a new solid using a bright color and to slide that under the subject. This will give you a really good view of the edges of the subject as well.*

If you look at the edges of the image, you will notice they are quite pixilated. This needs to be addressed.

6. Twirl down Edge Feather and move the slider. As you move it closer to the right, the subject seems to develop a halo. As it is in Photoshop, resist the urge to be aggressive with this slider. A small value—between .3 and .6—will quite nicely smooth out the edge of the mask.

You may now notice there is a bit of a green edge to the subject. If you zoom in to a 400% view, you can really see the green edge as shown in Figure 4-6. This edge is called **spill**. Spill is an artifact created when the foreground pixels are contaminated by reflected color from the background. The process of removing this artifact is called **despilling**, and it is the prudent Flash or After Effects designer who always looks for spill and removes it.

Figure 4-6.
Spill occurs when the backround color "spills" into the foreground colors.

7. In the Effects & Presets panel, twirl down the Keying category and drag the Spill Suppressor filter onto the Comp. When you release the mouse, the Spill Suppressor controls will appear in the Effect Controls panel.

8. If it isn't open, twirl down Spill Suppressor in the Effect Controls panel. When it opens, you will notice the controls are remarkably similar to those for the Color Key filter. You use the eyedropper to select the color to be suppressed, and the Color Accuracy and Suppression controls allow you to control the accuracy of the suppression.

9. Zoom in to an 800% or higher view of the subject and use the grabber hand—press the spacebar—to drag the image in the Comp until you can see the edge colors. Click the eyedropper once and click a medium green pixel on the edge. The green will disappear. If you zoom out to 100%, you will see a marked improvement in the Comp window (as shown in Figure 4-7).

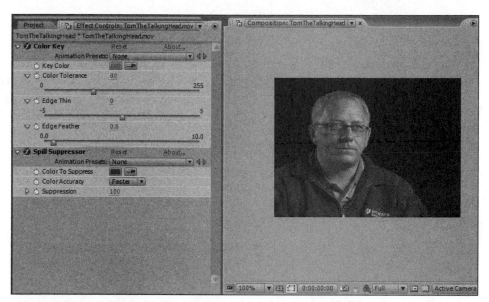

Figure 4-7. The settings so far

If you look at the edges, especially along the right edge of the subject, you will notice that there is still a bit of a jagged edge. There is another filter in your arsenal that will permit you to address this issue.

What you are going to do is to shrink the alpha channel by a couple of pixels to remove that edge. This is a common technique in Photoshop, and in After Effects it is called **matte choking**.

10. In the Effects & Presets panel, twirl down Matte Effects and drag a copy of the Matte Choker filter onto the Comp. When you release the mouse, the pixelization is reduced and the settings for the Matte Choker filter will appear in the Effect Controls panel.

At this point of the process, your job is done. Save the project and let's look at an even more powerful filter that can be used to create an alpha channel video: Keylight.

Using the Keylight filter

Talk to any After Effects user who has any sort of history with the application, and he or she will tell you the most valuable, industrial-strength keying tool in the arsenal is Keylight. This filter, which is available only in the Professional edition of After Effects 7, was introduced into version 6 of After Effects and is used for any number of tasks ranging from Hollywood films to Flash video. Just be aware that we are not going to explore a lot of what you can do with this filter. In fact, we will only be scratching the surface of its capabilities. Even so, you will be amazed at its power and ease of use.

The Keylight *filter is not automatically installed when you install After Effects 7 Professional. It is included in the third-party software option on the install disk.*

Follow these steps to create an alpha channel video using the Keylight filter:

1. Open the GS_02.aep file in your Chapter 4 Exercise folder. When the file opens, open the Effects & Presets panel, twirl down the Keying category, and drag a copy of the Keylight filter onto the Comp.

When you release the mouse, the Keylight controls—shown in Figure 4-8—will appear in the Effect Controls panel. If you examine them, the first thing that will occur to you is that all of the filters and controls used in the previous exercise are in the panel. We told you this filter was industrial strength!

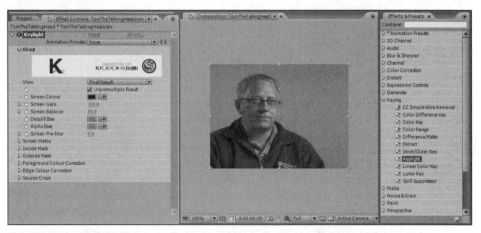

Figure 4-8. The Keylight filter is applied to the video in the Comp window, and the controls are ready to be used.

Another way of applying the filter is to click the Comp and then select Effect ➤ Keying ➤ Keylight.

2. Click the eyedropper and click the green background. The first thing you will notice is all the green disappears. If you toggle the transparency, you will see that the green is essentially gone. Unfortunately, it would be a huge mistake on your part to think "My job is done." Not quite. If you select Status from the View pull-down, you will see there is still a lot of work that needs to be done. The Status view, much like in Photoshop, shows you the mask. There is still a lot of gray in the Comp. The view should only have two colors: the subject should be pure white and the background should be pure black. Return to the Final Result view.

3. Twirl down the Screen Pre Blur control and set the Pre Blur value to 2. What this control does is to blur the matte. If you use DV footage, the pixels in the image can be rather blocky, and this control tends to give you a much smoother edge before you "pull" the key. You can see the effect by selecting the Combined Matte view and dragging the slider.

4. The next step in the process is to deal with those gray pixels you saw earlier. Switch to the Screen Matte view and twirl down the Screen Matte control. The controls you will be using are the Clip Black and Clip White controls. The Clip Black control functions very much like the Magic Wand tool in Photoshop and Fireworks. Moving the slider to the right increases the tolerance value and increases the size of the area covered in black pixels. Drag the Clip Black slider to a value of about 35. You will notice, as you drag this slider, a few gray artifacts appear in the white area of the mask. Twirl down the Clip White control and drag the slider to a value of 56. The gray pixels in the white, as shown in Figure 4-9, have disappeared, and you have a solid black-and-white mask.

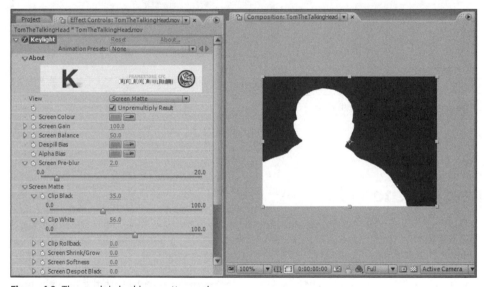

Figure 4-9. The mask is looking pretty good.

5. The next step is to shrink the mask a bit to ensure you don't have an odd-looking edge around the key. Twirl down the Screen Shrink/Grow control and set the value to -.5 to shrink the mask. You don't need a big value here. Remember, finesse is what counts when keying, not brute force.

6. The final step is to deal with the spill. The neat thing about Keylight is that it does manage this for you as you are working. It will find the spill and replace it with a default gray color. To see this at work, change the view to Intermediate Result and zoom in on an edge. You will see the spill. Change the view back to Final Result, and you will see the green is replaced with the gray. To refine this even more, twirl down the Screen Despot White control and change Replace Method to Hard Color. The result of this will be a softer blend of the green color being replaced.

7. Click in the Screen Despot White Color chip to open the Color Picker. Choose a green from the hue bar and when the color appears in the Color Picker, choose a green that is somewhere between full green and gray (see Figure 4-10).

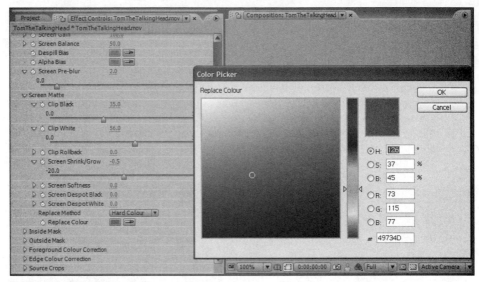

Figure 4-10. Dealing with spill suppression

8. Save the project.

Creating the video

If we had a Canadian Dollar or a Swiss Franc for every time we have heard someone say, "I did the keying but it doesn't work," we wouldn't be writing this book. We would be somewhere in a warmer climate and getting in a serious amount of "beach time." The alpha channel in a video is added when you render the video in After Effects. Even then you have to pay close attention to the choices you will make. Here's how to turn the Keylight project into a QuickTime movie with an alpha channel:

1. Click the Composition once and select Composition ➤ Add to Render Queue.

2. Open the Render Queue panel and click the Best Settings link to open the Render Settings dialog box. In the Time Sampling area, make sure the Field Renderer setting is set to Off. Click OK to close the dialog box.

3. Click the Lossless link in the Output Module to open the Output Module Settings dialog box. Make a mistake in this dialog box, and the project is doomed to failure.

4. Choose QuickTime Movie as the format and click the Format Options button to open the Compression Settings dialog box.

5. Choose Animation as the Compression and, in the Compressor pull-down, select Millions of Colors+. This color depth setting, shown in Figure 4-11, is the key. The **+** symbol indicates that the color with be 24-bit color **PLUS** an alpha channel.

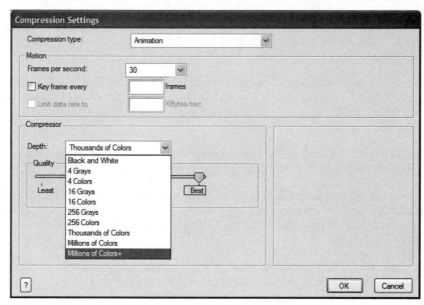

Figure 4-11. You must select Millions of Colors+ to include the alpha channel in the video.

6. Click OK to close the Compression Settings dialog box. You will be returned to the Output Module settings dialog box. Click the Audio Output check box. For some odd reason, the default setting in this dialog box is an unchecked Audio Output box. If you leave it unchecked, the audio will not be added to the video when the video is rendered.

7. Click OK to close the dialog box and return to the Render Queue.

8. Click the link in the Output To area to open the Output Movie To dialog box. Navigate to the folder where the video will be saved, name the video, and click the Save button to close the dialog box.

9. Click the Render button to create your video. When the process finishes, save the project and quit After Effects.

Creating an alpha channel FLV file

Before we create the FLV file for this project, compare the file size for the original video—20.8MB—to the size of the QuickTime movie you just created—59.8MB! That is one serious file size increase, and you may be asking two questions:

- How did it get so large?
- Isn't this going to "choke" the Flash Player?

Remember, you just output a video that contains 24-bit color **PLUS** an alpha channel using the Animation codec. Those three settings are the reason for the "jump" in file size. The color depth and the alpha channel have just as profound an effect upon a video as they do upon a Photoshop image. There is a lot of information here. The codec chosen, Animation, is a lossless codec, which means a lot of the information in the video is retained when it is compressed. Another major factor contributing to the file size is the audio setting. It is set to 44 kHz, 16-bit, stereo sound, which is comparable to the sound quality of a song purchased from your local record store.

The thing is, as we point out in Chapter 2, the file size is not an issue. The Flash 8 Video Encoder will apply the lossy ON2VP6 codec to the video portion of the file, and we are going to "knock" back the audio quality at the same time. The end result will be a file size that will surprise you.

1. Open the Flash 8 Video Encoder on your hard drive. When it opens, click the Add button and navigate to the video you have just created.

The first thing you will notice is that the default compression setting has already been applied to the file. This default is unacceptable for our purposes. The setting has a data rate more suited to a local area network (LAN) than the Internet. This will need to be changed.

2. Click the Settings button to open the Flash Video Encoding Settings dialog box. Name the file. We used TalkingHead, as you can see in Figure 4-12.

Figure 4-12. The basic encoding settings. Other than naming the file, they are quite useless for our purposes.

This dialog box actually contains two versions of the encoding settings. What you are currently looking at are the basic settings. Here you can choose a preset value from the encoding profile pull-down, trim the video by setting the In and the Out points, jog through the video, name the video, and open the Advanced Settings area for the Video Encoder.

If you open the encoding settings pull-down, you will notice there are settings for both Flash Player 7 and Flash Player 8. If you are using the ON2VP6 codec, plan to use the FLVPlayback component, or have a video with an alpha channel, you can only use the Flash 8 settings.

3. Click the Show Advanced Settings **button to open the** Advanced Settings **area shown in Figure 4-13. When the interface opens, specify these settings:**

- Video codec: On2VP6
- Encode alpha channel: **Checked**
- Frame rate: 15
- Key frame placement: Automatic
- Quality: Custom
- Max data rate: 175
- Data rate **(audio):** 48 kbps mono

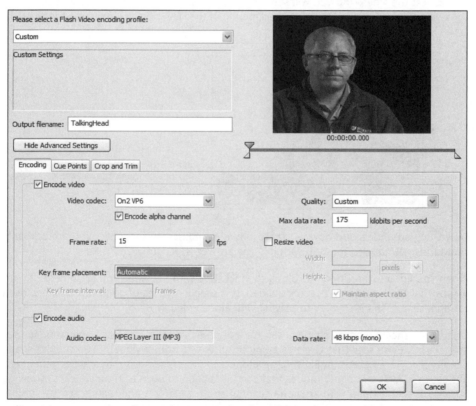

Figure 4-13. Alpha video can only be encoded using the Advanced Settings area of the Flash Video Encoding Settings dialog box.

If you are going to be encoding an alpha channel video, you must use the advanced encoding settings.

4. Click OK to close the Advanced Settings area of the Flash Video Encoding Settings dialog box. Click the Start Queue button to start the encoding process. When it finishes, quit the Video Encoder.

Adding and using alpha channel video in Flash

Adding alpha video to Flash is no different from adding any other video to the application; it is what you can do with it that moves it from "regular" to "cool" on the Flash technique scale.

1. Open a new Flash document, pull an FLVPlayback component from the Components panel to the stage, and link the FLV created in the previous exercise to the component.

2. Test the video, and you will see the black background you saw in the Video Encoder preview is gone and the white background of the Flash stage is visible (see Figure 4-14).

Figure 4-14.
An alpha channels removes the background in a video.

Now that you understand how to create, encode, and deploy the video, you are probably wondering, "What else can I do with it?" The answer is, "Quite a bit."

When you encode the video, the alpha channel stays with the video and Flash reads it. This means that Flash really isn't seeing a video, it is seeing a series of colored pixels enclosed within a shape. This is the key to playing with alpha video in Flash.

One of the most common shapes used for a Flash animator's first Flash animation is usually a circle. Flash sees that circle as being no different from a video. It is a circular shape filled with colored pixels. In Flash 8, developers and designers were handed a rather serious set of effects and blend modes that can be applied to objects in movie clips. Knowing how Flash sees a video with an alpha channel and that effects and blends can be applied to movie clips, it doesn't take a degree in rocket science to come to the realization that alpha video, placed in a movie clip, allows you to apply the Flash blends and effects to the video. Here's how:

1. With the Flash file open, right-click (PC) or Cmd-click (Mac) the component on the stage and select Convert To Symbol from the Context menu. When the Convert To Symbol dialog box opens, name the symbol Shadow, and select Movie Clip as its Type. Click OK.

2. Click the component on the stage to select it and click the Filters tab in the Property inspector.

3. Click the + sign once in the Filters tab to open the Filters pull-down menu. Select Drop Shadow.

4. Change the Quality setting to High and test the movie. The talking head now has a shadow (see Figure 4-15).

Figure 4-15.
You can apply effects, such as a drop shadow, to a video containing an alpha channel.

When you apply a filter or blend to the FLVPlayback component, don't get alarmed when you see the effect or blend applied to the entire component on the stage. The component is seen as the object until the Flash Player takes over.

In this next exercise, you will apply a blend mode to the video. That major difference here will be the use of a video object, not the component, in the movie clip. This way you can see that the blends and effects can be applied to video playing through the video object, not just the FLVPlayback component. The interesting area of intersection between both techniques is the use of a movie clip to stream the video.

1. Open the Blend.fla file found in the Blends_Filters folder of your Chapter 4 Exercise folder.

2. Select the video object on the stage and, in the Blend pull-down on the Property inspector select Screen (see Figure 4-16).

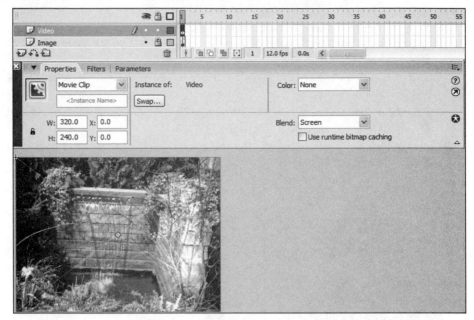

Figure 4-16. The blend mode can be applied directly to the movie clip containing the video.

3. Test the movie. The video looks somewhat ghostlike.

> *If you are wondering where the code that drives this video is located, double-click the video's movie clip in the Library.*

You don't need to use the Filters or Blend pull-down to apply these effects. They can just as easily be applied through the use of ActionScript. Let's apply the screen mode using code. Here's how:

1. Open the Blend_AS.fla file in your Chapter 4 Exercise folder. The only difference between it and the file you just used is the inclusion of an Actions layer, and the symbol on the stage has been given the name of mcMyVid.

2. Select the first frame in the Actions layer and open the ActionScript window. Click once in the Script pane and enter the following code:

```
mcMyVid.blendMode = "screen";
```

3. Save and test the movie.

As you can see, applying a blend mode is really quite simple. All you need to do is identify the movie clip to which the blend mode will apply, apply the blendMode property to each pixel of the movie clip, and then identify the mode. You can also use a number for the mode instead of the name. In this instance the code would be

```
mcMyVid.blendMode = 4;
```

Here is a list of the modes and their integer values:

- "normal" or 1
- "layer" or 2
- "multiply" or 3
- "screen" or 4
- "lighten" or 5
- "darken" or 6
- "difference" or 7
- "add" or 8
- "subtract" or 9
- "invert" or 10
- "alpha" or 11
- "erase" or 12
- "overlay" or 1
- "normal" or 13
- "hardlight" or 14

> *Be aware the order of the modes and the integers doesn't follow that in the* Blend *pull-down. If they did, the integer value for hardlight would be* 8, *not* 14.

Applying a filter using ActionScript is a bit more complicated than tossing a blend mode onto a movie clip. Filters have their own class in ActionScript, and, to apply a filter, you have to import the class and then apply the filter.

When you first apply the filter, you are going to be prompted to enter what seems like a confusing number of values as the parameters for the filter. They really aren't that confusing because they are exactly the same values you would enter in the Drop Shadow **filter** menu (see Figure 4-17). The only difference is the boxes requiring you to add a check mark will have a value of True or False in the code.

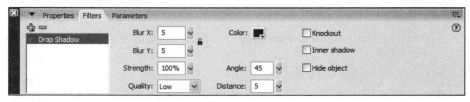

Figure 4-17. The parameters in ActionScript and the dialog box are an exact match.

> *If you are going to use a code-based approach to using a filter and are unsure what the final result will be, use the dialog box to set the values, and, if they are what you are looking for, write them down.*

Here's how to apply a Drop Shadow filter to the video using ActionScript:

1. Open the Shadow_AS.fla file in your Chapter 4 Exercise folder.

2. Select the first frame of the Actions layer and open the ActionScript Editor.

3. Enter the following code:

```
import flash.filters.*;
```

This line imports the entire filter package into the Flash Player. This leaves you the flexibility to apply multiple filters to a video without having to import each one, as you need it.

4. Press the Return/Enter key and add the following line of code:

```
var ds:DropShadowFilter= new DropShadowFilter(20,45,0x000000,.8,15,➥
15,1,3,false,false,false);
```

What you have done is to give the filter a name and created a new instance of the filter. Let's go through this to help you understand what you did.

The first thing you may have noticed is the tooltip (shown in Figure 4-18) that appeared when you pressed the bracket key. This tooltip gives you the order of the values to be entered and the type of value to be entered.

- distance: The distance for the shadow, in pixels.
- angle: The angle of the shadow; the values range from 0 to 360.
- color: The hexadecimal color of the shadow.
- alpha: The alpha transparency value of the shadow. Values are any number between 0 and 1. In this example, the .80 means the alpha value is 80% transparency.
- blurX/blurY: The horizontal and vertical blue values.
- strength: The strength of the shadow's spread. The higher the value, the more contrast there is. Valid values range between 0 and 255.
- quality: The quality of the shadow. 1 is low quality. 2 is medium quality. 3 is best quality.
- inner: Determines whether the shadow is an inner shadow. Values are either True or False.
- knockout: Applies a knockout effect if the value is True.
- hideObject: If set to True, the video is hidden, but the shadow isn't.

```
import flash.filters.DropShadowFilter;
var ds:DropShadowFilter= new DropShadowFilter(
new DropShadowFilter( distance:Number, angle:Number, color:Number, alpha:Number, blurX:Number, blurY:Number, strength:Number, quality:Number, inner:Boolean, knockout:Boolean, hideObject:Boolean )
```

Figure 4-18. The parameters you need to enter are contained in the tooltip.

5. Press the Return/Enter key and enter the following line of code:

```
mcMyVid.filters = [ds];
```

The filter is applied to the movie clip.

6. Save the movie and test it. Note the shadow as shown in Figure 4-19.

```
1 import flash.filters.*;
2 var ds:DropShadowFilter= new DropShadowFilter(20,45,0x000000,.8,15,15,1,3,false,false,false)
3 mcMyVid.filters = [ds];
4
```

Figure 4-19. Applying a filter using ActionScript

Create an iPod-style video

Up to this point in the chapter, you have pretty well mastered the basics of creating an alpha channel video, encoding it, and getting it to play in Flash. The balance of this chapter is designed to get you thinking about what you have learned and taking it to the next level.

The genesis for this exercise starts with a CD of video outtakes from the Studio 8 release. One of the authors had casually mentioned to a friend of his at Adobe that finding green screen material for a book was not exactly easy. About a week later, the CD arrived on his desk and a note with the CD simply said, "Think you will enjoy these. Have fun." Though there were a lot of hilarious clips of the actors "flubbing" their lines and generally cutting up, the one that caught his attention was a very short clip of one of the actors doing a "muscle man" routine.

Like most creatives, his first thought was, "What can I do with this?" A couple of nights later, an iPod ad appeared during a TV show he was watching and the proverbial lightbulb lit up.

1. Open the iPod.aep file in the iPodAd folder found in your Chapter 4 Exercise folder.

This clip is actually quite typical of the material that will be handed to you. Though it is a green screen video, there is an area on the left edge of the clip (see Figure 4-20) that shows the edge of the screen and some of the equipment on the set. This will have to be removed before you start.

Figure 4-20. You start with a "problematic" green screen video clip.

2. Click the Comp once, select the Pen tool, and draw a shape by clicking the mouse around the subject in the video. As you draw the shape, you will notice anything outside of the vector disappears from the Comp. The Pen tool is also a masking tool, and what you have just done is to create a **garbage matte** to get rid of anything on the screen you don't need.

3. Click the RAM Preview button or scrub across the timeline, and pay careful attention to the subject as the video plays. What you don't want to do is to have the matte cut off any part of the subject. If, for example, you notice the top of his hat is cut off, click the vector point once and select the Covert Vertex tool in the Pen tool pull-down menu. Click-drag the point to add a curve that goes above his hat (see Figure 4-21) and do another RAM preview or scrub through the timeline to be sure this solves your problem.

Figure 4-21.
Use the Pen tool to create a garbage matte.

4. Drag the Keylight filter onto the Comp and, using the eyedropper tool, select the green area behind the actor.

5. When the green disappears, use these Keylight settings to clean up the mask:

- Screen Pre-blur: .5
- Screen Matte—Clip Black: 42
- Screen Matte—Clip White: 52
- Screen Shrink/Gro: -.5

6. Select Screen Matte from the View pull-down, and you will see you have a clean mask (as shown in Figure 4-22). The next step is to turn the subject black.

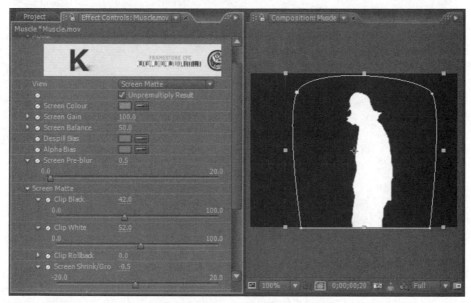

Figure 4-22. The masks and the Keylight settings in the Effect Controls panel

Working with color in After Effects is, unsurprisingly, similar to using the color control features of Photoshop. In fact, if you twirl down the Color Correction area of the Effects & Presets panel, you will see that many of the plug-ins are the same features found in Photoshop. To turn the subject black, all we have to do is put on our "Photoshop hats" for a moment. A rather common method to bring up the blacks (shadows) or the whites (highlights) in a Photoshop image is to open the Levels dialog box in Photoshop and adjust the white or the black point of the histogram. It really is no different here.

7. Drag the Levels filter from the Color Correction list onto the Comp. When you release the mouse, you will see a similar dialog box to that found in Photoshop.

8. Twirl down the Input White category in the Effect Controls panel and drag the slider from its current value of 255 to 0. The figure in the image will turn black. What you have just done is to tell After Effects, "All pixels with a value between 1 and 255 now have a value of 0," which is black.

> *If you are a Photoshop purist, you can also get the same effect by dragging the* White Point *slider under the histogram all the way to the left.*

9. Click the Toggle Transparency Grid button in the Comp window to see the effect (as shown in Figure 4-23). To get the "muscle man" moving, click the RAM Preview button.

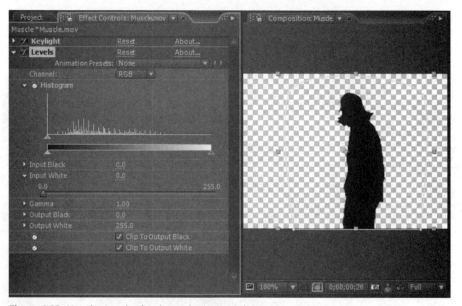

Figure 4-23. Use the Levels plug-in to change to color.

To finish up this project, render the video out as a QuickTime movie using the Animation codec with Millions of Colors+. Save the project and encode the video in Flash. When the video is encoded, open Flash and set the stage color of a new Flash file to a rather vibrant solid color. (We used a bright red, FF0000.) Add an FLVPlayback component to the stage or create and code up a video object. Link the iPod.flv file to the component and test the video. As you can see in Figure 4-24, you, too, can create an iPod-style ad.

Figure 4-24.
The final product playing in the Flash Player

Trimming Flash video and using cue points to trigger Flash events

In this exercise, you are going to learn how to use **cue points** embedded in an alpha channel FLV file to trigger events on the Flash stage. The plan is to have a young woman walk across the Flash stage, and, when she stops to look at the massive TV behind her, a video starts to play on the TV screen. She will then continue her walk, look at another TV, and trigger a second video.

There is an issue that will have to be dealt with before she takes her walk. The video containing the woman is over 700 pixels wide and just over 200 pixels high. The Flash stage is only 400 pixels wide. This means the FLV file will have to be trimmed.

The next aspect of this exercise deals with a feature that is new to Flash Video: the ability to add cue points to a video. The neat thing about cue points is they can be used to trigger events—a video starts playing when the cue point is reached—in the Flash movie. Like any new feature of an application, it has its good points and its bad points.

Cue points can be regarded as being either **destructive** or **nondestructive**. By destructive, we mean the cue point is hardwired into the FLV file and can't be changed or removed from it. If the timing is out, you will have to add another cue point, and if that one is wrong . . . yet another. The other method of using cue points is to use ActionScript. This is the nondestructive method. If a cue point is out of synch, you open the code and change the time for the cue point. We are going to show you both methods and let you decide which one best fits your needs.

Finally, this exercise answers a very common question: "Can I play multiple videos in a Flash movie?" The answer is obviously yes. For example, Microsoft is starting the buzz around their new Vista operating system and has hired the actor Tom Skerritt to be their spokesperson. When you arrive at the Vista page—www.seewindowsvista.com/—Skerritt stands in the middle of the screen, and behind him seven small videos play while seemingly hovering in space—check it out!

If you have been following this chapter so far, you know how the video for the actor on this site was created and how to create the shadows under the videos. What we haven't told you is how each of the small videos plays.

The answer requires you once again to think a bit differently about video. Remember, when you place a video into Flash, you aren't controlling the "video," you are controlling its data stream into the Flash 8 Player. This stream is turned on and off by using the NetStream class in ActionScript. What you may not realize about this class is it can control only one video per stream. Thus the Flash movie on this site is not one big Flash video. It is a collection of eight Flash videos, each having its own NetStream object. Pull the videos out of the image and replace them with eight separate pipes, and you will get the idea.

The other aspect of this piece is the actual size and length of the small videos. They are about 90 pixels wide and 60 pixels high for a reason: performance in the user's browser.

If you step away from the project and just consider it from a technical point of view, you need to understand the Flash Player 8 is doing a huge amount of work. It is managing the overall data stream into the user's browser and simultaneously managing the data stream of eight FLV files. As we have pointed out repeatedly to this point in the book, the physical dimensions of an FLV file and its length can have a profound impact upon smooth video playback. By reducing the physical size of the video to 90×60 and trimming its length to two or three seconds, the resulting FLV file size will be around 100K, requiring a minimum of processor resources to play in a browser.

So much for the theory; let's get our arms dirty with pixels right up to our elbows:

1. Open the CuePoint.fla file located in the Cue_Points folder of your Chapter 4 Exercise folder.

When the file opens, you will notice we have supplied you with the layers. There are two TVs on the stage, and, if you open the Library, you will see it contains a graphic symbol named Poster.

2. Select the Poster layer and drag a copy of the Poster graphic symbol from the Library to the stage. Place it behind the first TV by setting its X and Y values in the Property inspector to 97.4 and 88.8. As you may have guessed, the TV screen will be used to mask the video.

> You may be wondering how we created the "hole" in the TV. The image is one contained in the clip art that ships with Illustrator CS 2. The image was opened in Illustrator, and all of the pieces that compose the image were selected and then copied to the clipboard. The copy was pasted directly into the TV layer. The issue with vector art is that it maintains the vectors, which makes it difficult to cut a "hole" in an image. To solve this problem, we simply selected the entire image and "broke it apart." Breaking a bitmap or vector image apart—Modify ➤ Break Apart—reduces it to a collection of pixels. This allowed us to select the screen in the image and delete it.

3. Drag another copy of the Poster symbol to the stage and place it at 323.4 and 88.8. When you are finished, your stage should resemble the one shown in Figure 4-25. Lock the Poster layer.

Figure 4-25. The poster frames are in place.

*If you are familiar with digital video, traditionally, a video will show you the first frame of the piece. This frame is called a **poster frame**. Unfortunately the ability to display a poster frame in an FLV file is currently not doable without a serious amount of heavy ActionScript lifting. A workaround, as we have done, is to create a screenshot of the frame in the QuickTime or Windows Media Player and place it on the stage. Then you simply place a video object above the image. When the video plays, it will play "over" the poster frame, and when it finishes, the poster frame becomes visible.*

4. Create a new video object by selecting New Video from the Library pull-down menu. When the New Video dialog box appears, name the object and click OK to close the dialog box.

5. Hide the TV layer by clicking its visibility icon. Select the Video 1 layer, drag a copy of the video symbol from the library, and place it over the first Poster image. With the video object selected, enter these properties into the Property inspector:

- Instance name: myVideo
- W: 120
- H: 90
- X: 97.4
- Y: 88.8

6. Drag another copy of the video object to the stage and use the following settings in the Property inspector:

- Instance name: myVideo1
- W: 120
- H: 90
- X: 323.4
- Y: 88.8

7. Turn on the visibility of the TV layer and save the file.

With the assets in place, you can now turn your attention to adding the cue points to the alpha video.

Adding cue points and trimming video

If you play the betina.mov file in your Chapter 4 Exercise folder in the QuickTime player, you will notice it is quite wide. Select Window ➤ Show Movie Info, and you discover just how wide this video really is (see Figure 4-26). Considering the Flash stage is only 550 pixels wide, you are going to have to trim off about 206 pixels from the video's width, and, if you play the video, you notice there is a lot of white space above the subject, Betina. All of this space is not needed, and it, too, needs to be reduced.

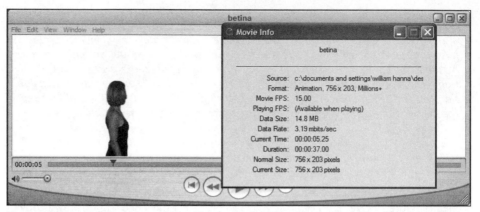

Figure 4-26. Get the dimensions of the video in the QuickTime Player. The Video Encoder won't give you this information.

Now turn your attention to the video as it plays. You will see that as Betina walks across the screen, she will stop, turn around to look at something, and then move on. The points in the video where she stops are where you are going to start the videos playing in the TV screens.

1. Open the Flash 8 Video Encoder and add the betina.mov file to the Encoder Queue.

2. Click the Settings button, and, when the Flash Video Encoding Settings window opens, name the video Betina. Click the Show Advanced Settings button to open the Advanced Settings area of the dialog box.

3. Use the following settings in the Advanced Settings area:

   - Video codec: On2VP6
   - Encode alpha channel: **Selected**
   - Frame rate: 15
   - Quality: Custom
   - Max data rate: 200

4. Click the Crop and Trim tab to open the Crop and Trim settings.

On the left side of the window are the sliders that will allow you to crop the video to a specific size. Be aware that the values that will appear in the slider input area represent the number of pixels being removed. The final size of the video will appear under the sliders in the Cropped video size area.

The slider at the top crops the video from the top. The left and right sliders crop the video from the right and left sides, and the bottom slider allows you to crop the bottom of the video.

5. Click the top slider and drag it downwards until you see a value of 63 in the input area. When you release the mouse, the Cropped video size value will change to 756 × 140.

6. Select the text in the right slider text input area and enter a value of 206. The values in the Cropped video size area will change to 550 × 140.

7. The final size of the FLV is indicated by the marquee in the Preview window. Drag the Out point in the Preview window until Betina is just outside of the selection (see Figure 4-27).

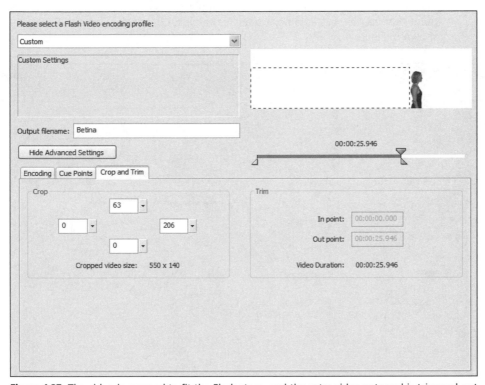

Figure 4-27. The video is cropped to fit the Flash stage, and the extra video not used is trimmed out by setting the Out point.

Having dealt with making the video fit the Flash stage, you can now turn your attention to creating the cue points that will "trigger" the videos to play in the TV sets.

1. Click the Cue Points tab to open the Cue Points window. In the Preview window, drag the jog controller to the start point of the video.

2. Drag the jog controller to the point where Betina first turns, which is somewhere around 00:00:05.701.

3. Click the + sign in the Cue Points area to add a cue point. You will notice the cue point that appears has a name, a time, and a type. Change the name to First.

The Type *pull-down gives you an idea of the power of cue points in an FLV video. They can be used to trigger other videos, movie clips, and so on while the Flash movie plays. These are known as* **events***. The other thing cue points can do is to* **navigate** *through the movie or other movie clips.*

4. Drag the jog controller to the point where Betina next turns, which is somewhere around 00:00:15.823.

5. Click the + sign in the Cue Points area to add a cue point. You will notice the cue point that appears has a name, a time, and a type. Change the name to Second as shown in Figure 4-28.

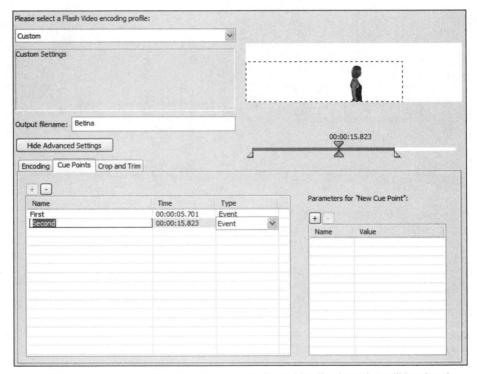

Figure 4-28. Cue points are set by using the jog controller to identify where they will be placed.

Remember, this method of adding cue points will hardwire them into the FLV meta-data. If you make a mistake and encode the video, you can't change or remove the cue point. If you need to make any changes, now is the time to make them.

To remove a cue point, select it and click the – button.

6. Click the OK button to return to the Video Encoder and click the Start Queue button to start the encoding process. When it finishes, quit the Video Encoder and return to your Flash movie.

> *Here's a little trick that will bail you out of a rather nasty cue point situation. Let's assume you discover, when testing the video in Flash, you have screwed up the timing for the first cue point. Relaunch the Video Encoder. You will notice that the video just encoded is still in the Encoder Queue. Select the video and then select* Edit ➤ Reset Status. *The settings will open, and you can then make the change in the* Cue Points *tab of the* Advanced Settings *area. Once the change is made, reencode the FLV file. If the video has been removed—you selected the video in the Video Encoder and clicked the* Remove *button—you are out of luck.*

7. When the Flash movie opens, select the Betina layer and drag a copy of the FLVPlayback component to the stage.

8. Link the component to the Betina.flv file you just created. When you close the contentPath dialog box, you should see the cue points you added now appear in the cuePoints area of the Parameters tab in the Component inspector (see Figure 4-29).

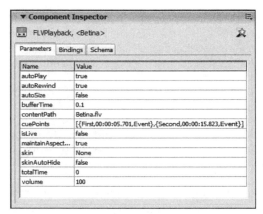

Figure 4-29. Cue points that are added to the FLV file will appear in the FLVPlayback component's parameters.

> *If you double-click* cuePoints, *you will open the* Flash Video Cue Points *dialog box. What you can't do here is remove a cue point or otherwise change it. What you can do, though, is to add a cue point or to change its type from* Event *to* Navigation.

9. Select the component on the stage and give it the instance name of Betina. Save the file.

Was that a cue point I just heard?

Just because the FLV has cue points embedded in it doesn't mean the videos in the video objects on the stage will play. You need to tell Flash, through ActionScript, what to do when a cue point is encountered. To do this, you need to tell the Flash Player what to listen for by creating what is called a **listener object**. This object will tell Flash what to listen for and what to do when it "hears" it.

In the case of this project, Flash is going to listen for a cue point named First and, when it detects the cue point, which is an event, to play an FLV in the video object named myVideo. It will then be told, "Hold on, there is another cue point named Second, and when you encounter that one, start playing an FLV in the video object named myVideo1."

Here's how to give Flash a pair of ears:

1. Select the first frame in the Actions layer and open the ActionScript panel. When the panel opens, click once in the Script pane and enter the following code:

```
var nc:NetConnection = new NetConnection;
nc.connect (null);
var ns:NetStream = new NetStream(nc);
var ns2:NetStream = new NetStream(nc);
```

Nothing new here other than there are two NetStreams created. If you flip back to the start of this exercise, we mentioned the fact that each video on the page requires its own NetStream object, because you can't play different videos on the stage through one stream. These two streams will feed into the video objects on the stage.

> You may have read that last sentence and wondered, "Hold on, guys, there are three videos playing on the stage." You are absolutely correct, but the third video—Betina.flv—will be fed into an FLVPlayback component. This component does all of this stuff automatically, so it isn't necessary to give it a stream.

2. Press the Return/Enter key twice and enter the following code:

```
var ourListener:Object = new Object();
ourListener.cuePoint = function( eventObject:Object ):Void {
  if( eventObject.info.name == "First" ) {
    ns.play("Nose.flv");
  }
  else if( eventObject.info.name == "Second" ) {
    ns2.play("Nose.flv");
  }
}
```

As you may have surmised, you have just written the code that gives Flash that pair of ears.

The first line creates an object named ourListener. By itself, this object is useless; it needs to be told what it represents. That is the purpose of the second line. It is going to "hold" the eventObject that results from the Flash Player finding a cuePoint event. If there is no cue point or one is found that isn't identified in the function, the Void operator is what tells the Flash Player to ignore the function.

The next two lines tell ourListener what to do when it encounters a cue point. The first thing it does is to check the name of the cue point. If it is named First, the Nose.flv file is dropped into the stream connected to the first video object on the stage. Those double equal signs mean "strict equality." If the event name in the code was entered as first, the video wouldn't be put in the stream.

Having written the function that tells Flash what to do when it detects a cue point, you still have to give Flash the ability to hear the event sent to the Flash Player when a cue point is reached and tell it where the event is coming from.

3. Press the Return/Enter key twice and enter the following line of code:

```
Betina.addEventListener( "cuePoint", ourListener );
```

This line of code is the other half of a common listener in Flash. The function you created earlier tells Flash what to do when it hears the event. This line tells Flash that the event will be generated by the Betina instance of the FLVPlayback component, and the addEventListener() method tells the Flash Player which object—ourListener—will receive the event notification message and what to do—execute the cuePoint function—when the message is received.

4. Press the Return/Enter key and add the final bit of code:

```
myVideo.attachVideo(ns);
myVideo1.attachVideo(ns2);
stop();
```

The first two lines connect the streams to the two video objects on the stage, and the last line simply holds the playback head in place.

5. Click the Check Syntax button to be sure you have no mistakes. If there are none, close the ActionScript window and save the movie.

6. Test the movie. As Betina walks across the stage, the videos start to play (see Figure 4-30) as she turns to look at the TV sets.

Figure 4-30. Note the different screens of the videos playing in the TV sets.

Using ActionScript to add cue points

In this exercise, you are not going to hardwire the cue points into the FLV. You are going to add them using ActionScript. As we pointed out earlier, this method of adding cue points is a lot more forgiving than adding them when the FLV is created. In fact, using ActionScript offers you a higher degree of precision and efficiency than the other method. The reason is you can adjust the location of a cue point by simply changing a number in code. This avoids constant trips back to the Video Encoder to change a cue point and the time wasted while you wait for the video to be reencoded.

> *There is a big heads-up with this technique. The code you will add only works with the FLVPlayback component. If the final size of the SWF file is a major production consideration, seriously consider hardwiring the cue points into the FLV file.*

1. Open the NoCuePoint.fla file located in your Chapter 4 Exercise folder.
2. Just to prove there is "nothing up our sleeves," click the FLVPlayback component once on the stage. Click the Parameters tab. You will notice the cuePoint parameters area has a value of None.
3. Select the first frame in the Actions panel and open the ActionScript Editor.

If you scroll through the code, you will see that, other than a comment in Line 20, the code is identical to the code used in the previous exercise.

4. Click once in Line 21 of the Script pane and enter the following code:

```
Betina.addASCuePoint(5.701,"First");
Betina. addASCuePoint(15.822,"Second");
```

The addASCuePoint() method is a part of the FLVPlayback class, and it requires only two parameters: the time of the cue point and the name of the cue point. When you name the cue point, be sure to put it between quotes.

The code for this project is as follows:

```
var nc:NetConnection = new NetConnection;
nc.connect (null);
var ns:NetStream = new NetStream(nc);
var ns2:NetStream = new NetStream(nc);
var ns3:NetStream = new NetStream(nc);

var ourListener:Object = new Object();
ourListener.cuePoint = function( eventObject:Object ):Void {
  if( eventObject.info.name == "First" ) {
    ns.play("Nose.flv");
  }
  else if( eventObject.info.name == "Second" ) {
    ns2.play("Nose.flv");
  }
}
```

```
Betina.addEventListener( "cuePoint", ourListener );
Betina.addASCuePoint(5.701,"First");
Betina. addASCuePoint(15.822,"Second");

myVideo.attachVideo(ns);
myVideo1.attachVideo(ns2);

Betina.attachVideo (ns3);
ns3.play("BetinaNoCue.flv");

stop();
```

5. Save and test the video.

You are probably sitting there thinking, "Gee guys, this is great stuff and all, but you haven't told me how to remove a cue point that is embedded into an FLV." That is a great question.

You have been told a few times that cue points embedded in an FLV file are there for life. We lied. Well not exactly; we didn't give you the full story. Let's look at a common scenario:

You have created the Betina.flv file and have a cue point in the FLV file, let's call it Third, that you discover really wasn't needed in the first place. You can use ActionScript to do the removal. The code to remove this cue point would be

```
var ourListener:Object = new Object();
ourListener.cuePoint = function( eventObject:Object ):Void {
  if( eventObject.info.name == "First" ) {
    ns.play("Nose.flv");
  }
  else if( eventObject.info.name == "Second" ) {
    Betina.removeASCuePoint("Third");
    ns2.play("Nose.flv");
  }
}
```

Summary

This chapter took our dragon hunt into the realm of alpha channel video. Talk to any serious Flash video developer about the new features of Flash Professional 8, and we can guarantee you the conversation will start here.

The chapter started with a brief discussion of some examples of well-done alpha channel video that is out there. If you need more inspiration, check out the Nike and Adidas sites. Both make extensive use of the techniques presented in this chapter.

We then moved into After Effects, and you were shown a number of ways of "keying" out the green screen (or blue screen) in a video. The first technique explored was the use of a combination of the Color Key, Matte Choker, and Despill filters to get a crisp edge around the subject. The next technique was an overview of the Keylight filter, and we think you will agree with us that once you use this one, "you ain't never going back."

Keying out the background is important, but even more important is how the final video is rendered out of After Effects as a QuickTime video. If you make a mistake here, your background will remain. The key is to use the Animation codec and to set the color depth to Millions of Colors+. The + is what tells the Animation codec to include the alpha channel.

From there, we explored how to use the Flash 8 Video Encoder to add the alpha channel to the FLV. The trick is to use the ON2VP6 codec and to select the Encode alpha channel option. Just be aware that if you are targeting the Flash 6 or Flash 7 Players, you can't use an alpha channel video in your Flash project.

Our travels then took us into Flash, and you discovered how to add the video to the FLVPlayback component and compile the SWF. That was interesting, but things really got intriguing when you discovered that by simply putting the FLVPlayback component or a video object into a movie clip, you can apply the new filters and blends to the video. In fact, you learned two ways of doing this: using the Property inspector and programmatically through ActionScript.

With the basics under your belt, we then moved into the creative uses of what you learned.

The first exercise was the creation of an iPod-style ad that used the Levels filter in After Effects to create the black subject common to these ads.

The final section showed you how to use a video with an alpha channel to "trigger" other events in Flash. This involved the addition of cue points to the FLV. We also showed you how to crop and trim a video.

The cue points exercise, which triggered two other videos on the stage, used a listener to capture the cue point events and play the videos. We also showed you how to add cue points using ActionScript, and we finished the chapter by showing you how to use ActionScript to remove a cue point that was hardwired into the FLV.

In the next chapter, the dragon hunt continues as we explore the creation of movie titling sequences, a few effects, and how to add closed captioning to video.

5 CREATING TEXT ANIMATIONS FOR FLASH

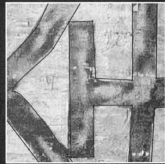
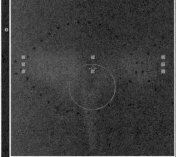

In Chapter 3, we showed you how to use the text animation presets to create some pretty amazing effects. The ability to drag and drop an effect onto a piece of text and then subsequently manipulate that text in a Flash SWF file is a pretty powerful technique to have at your fingertips. Still, an overreliance on what the application hands you can be more a hindrance to your creativity than an aid to the process.

In many respects, this is a chapter that will let you "play." By that we mean we are going to review a number of techniques ranging from captioning video to the creation of movie or video titling sequences. Individually, they are interesting, but together they are going to loosen the creative shackles a bit.

One of the hallmarks of this business is fearlessness around technology. Understanding what something does is necessary, but an artist's true creativity starts when he or she takes those fundamentals and "drives a truck through them" by playing "what if . . ." games. The iPod ad–mimicking animation from the previous chapter is a good example of this. We looked at the clip handed to us and asked, "What if we were to blow out the color in the video and create an iPod-like ad?" That process started us looking at the manipulation of color in After Effects and the discovery that the color correction skills we employ every day in Photoshop are easily transferable to the video field.

It will be no different in this chapter. We are going to play some "what if . . ." games:

- What if a deaf person were to see this video . . .
- What if we had a bunch of photos but wanted to do something a bit different as a lead-in to a Flash photo gallery . . .
- What if we had a poem handed to us and were told, "Do something with it . . ."

Closed captioning video

We thought we would start this chapter with one of the more important, noncreative uses of text in Flash video: the ability to use closed captions in video. Closed captioning simply doesn't have the sex appeal of, say, creating an iPod-like ad, but if you are going to be working with government or other organizations with accessibility standards, you will encounter closed captioning for the deaf.

A serious number of tools are available out there, and to review them all here would move us way out of the scope of this book. One tool, though, is worth a look: Captionate. It was designed expressly for Flash video—see www.buraks.com/captionate/.

We just love this business because you never know who is checking out your stuff and what will come sliding over the e-mail transom. Having just finished a book for friends of ED on the subject of web video (*Foundation Flash 8 Video, 2006*) one of the authors had been out yacking it up and showing people the "cool stuff" you can do with web video. Then the following e-mail arrives:

"I love your books and tutorials! They are very well explained. I have a question. Have you done any tutorials on how to add captions to videos? For example, there is CC button in your 'talking head video' box. I would love to learn how to write CC for that. I am deaf and would strongly advocate for all websites that have videos to have captions, but that won't happen right away due to $ and timing. I will be making a small 'talking head' video introducing myself in sign language, but I want to have captions for hearing people to know what I am saying :-) ."

This sort of stuck our feet back on the ground because it told us that in our "quest for cool" there are a whole bunch of people who would like to share in the fun. The other aspect of this e-mail that caught our attention was the intention of the author to go the other way: letting people who can hear see his video and understand what he is "saying."

To answer the question posed in the e-mail, "Yes, it can be done using cue points in Flash Professional 8."

The trick is to use an XML document to hold the times for the cue points and the captions. In this example, we use the "Tom the talking head" clip as the video. The file is opened up in QuickTime, the "words of wisdom" are jotted down, and their respective start points noted. From there we create a simple XML document in Dreamweaver 8 and save it to the folder CaptioningVideo (which you can find in the Exercise folder of the Chapter 5 code downloads). The XML from the captions.xml file in the CaptioningVideo folder is

```
<captions>`
  <caption start="1">Dreamweaver users now have access to Flash➥
    Video. Didn't have it before.</caption>
  <caption start="3">If you were to talk to a Dreamweaver user about➥
    three or four years ago</caption>
  <caption start="6">and ask, "Do you want to put video on a web➥
    page?"</caption>
  <caption start="8">They would look at you and go "Yeah. Dude. Yeah.➥
    Right. Uh Huh. Next."</caption>
</captions>
```

The numbers are the start times for the various bits in the video and the next node is the text. With just those two bits of information, you can start creating captioned video. Here's how:

1. Open Flash, create a new document, and add three layers named Video, Caption, and Actions. Save the file to the CaptionVideo folder in your Chapter 5 Exercise folder.

2. Select the Video layer and drag an FLVPlayback component to the stage. In the Parameters panel, set the skin to one that meets your needs. Ignore contentPath because you'll be adding the video to the ActionScript. Finally, select the component on the stage and give it the instance name of myVid. Lock the layer.

3. Select the Caption layer. Select the Text tool and draw out a text box. Set its property to Dynamic and select Multiline from the Line Type pull-down menu in the Property inspector. Finally, give the text block the instance name of txtCaption (see Figure 5-1).

5

Figure 5-1. The stage is ready to go.

4. Select the Actions layer, open the ActionScript Editor, and add the following code:

```
import mx.video.*;

myVid.autoPlay = false;
myVid.contentPath = "Captions.flv";
myVid.autoRewind = true;

var captions:Array;

var captionsXML:XML = new XML();
captionsXML.ignoreWhite = true;

captionsXML.onLoad = function():Void {
  captions = this.firstChild.childNodes;

  for(var i:Number = 0; i < captions.length; i++) {
    myVid.addASCuePoint(captions[i].attributes.start, ➥
captions[i].firstChild.nodeValue);
  };

};
```

```
captionsXML.load("captions.xml");

myVid.addEventListener("cuePoint", onCuePoint);

function onCuePoint(evntObj:Object):Void {
  txtCaption.text = evntObj.info.name;
};
```

The first line of the code brings in the video package because you will need its methods and properties of its class file to control the component. The next three lines access the autoplay, autoRewind, and contentPath properties from the Class file that would otherwise be used in the Parameters panel. The final line simply resets the video back to the start when it finishes.

An array is then created to hold the captions. With the housekeeping out of the way, we create a new XML object to hold the XML and tell the object to ignore any white space in the XML document that will be used by the XML object.

The onLoad() method is used to bring the XML document into Flash and the variable—captions—is set to be equal to the number of child nodes in the XML doc. The for loop uses the length of the caption array to set how many times the loop iterates. From there the times and the captions are pulled out of the XML document.

At the same time a number of cue points, equal to the number of items in the list, are created and the values in the XML document are used as the parameters for the cue point.

The next two lines simply load the XML document and add an eventListener that tells Flash what to listen for which—surprise, surprise—is a cuePoint. The last function tells Flash that, every time a cue point is encountered, it must stick the text associated with the cue point in the text box.

5. Save and test the video. The captions from the XML document will appear below the video, as shown in Figure 5-2.

Figure 5-2.
The captions appear under the talking head.

Playing with text

We are going to start this section of the chapter not by digging into some of the more complex things you can do with text. Instead we are going to give you the chance to familiarize yourself with the tools and a couple of techniques that will be used for the balance of the chapter.

Obviously the first tool available to you is the Text tool on the After Effects toolbar.

1. Start After Effects and create a new Comp using these settings:

- Composition Name: Text1
- Width: 320
- Height: 240
- Pixel Aspect Ratio: Square Pixels
- Frame Rate: 15
- Duration: 0:00:05:00

2. Select the Text tool, click once in the Comp, and enter Poetry in motion.

3. If the Character panel isn't open, select Window ➤ Character. Select the text in the Comp window and use these settings:

- Font: Times New Roman
- Style: Regular
- Size: 40 pixels

Before you start playing with the Character panel, it is important that you understand the importance of text. It is not the gray stuff you whirl, twirl, and blur. It is an information element on the screen. This means the text needs to be both readable and legible. By readability, we mean words are easy to read, and each character in each word is distinct. In motion graphics, this is especially important because, in many cases, the number of words on the screen are such that they can just as easily appear on a T-shirt as they can in a Flash animation. Though there are a lot of cool fonts out there, the characters are simply treated as graphics and are impossible to read.

Legibility is another important consideration in motion graphics. Words can be distorted to the point where they are no longer legible, meaning the information contained in those words is lost to the viewer. A classic example of this is the "Miniml-phase" that swept the Flash industry a few years ago. For some odd reason, "Flashies" thought the Miniml font using a light gray text that was 6 pixels high and on a dark gray background was cool. It was, but the phase ended when they discovered nobody could read the text.

The final point is the choice of font. The font you choose can either support your creative goal or conflict with it, because each font has a different look and thereby conveys a different message. For example, in Figure 5-3, the only difference between each of the four lines of text is the font. From top to bottom, the fonts used are

- Times New Roman
- Bodoni
- Geometric
- Confidential

Figure 5-3.
Same words. Different fonts.
Different meanings.

Notice how each font changes the "meaning" of the text block and, in many respects, determines the look of the piece. For example, if you are designing an animation that appeals to the extreme sports crowd, Geometric would be totally out of place, whereas Confidential, with its distressed look, will fit in quite nicely.

4. Select Window ➤ Paragraph to open the Paragraph panel. Click the Center Text button.

> *When animating text, be aware that the animation will be based on the center point of the text. The default alignment is* Left Align. *This means if you were to spin the text, it would spin around the letter* P. *Clicking* Center Align *ensures that spins and so on occur around the word* in.

Figure 5-4 shows the Character panel, where you can choose your font, its style, color, and so on. This figure also shows the Paragraph panel, where you can choose the alignment and the indent amount for the text block.

Figure 5-4.
Text is formatted and aligned in these two panels.

5. Open the Effects & Presets panel and twirl down Blur and Sharpen. Drag a copy of the Fast Blur Effect onto the text block.

6. Click the Effect Controls panel once and set the Blurriness value to 15.

7. In the timeline, twirl down the Text layer and twirl down the Effects area.

> *Another way of opening only the* Effects *area on the timeline is to select the layer and press the* E *key on your keyboard.*

8. Move the playback head to the 2-second mark on the timeline and add a keyframe. Move the playback head to the 4-second mark on the timeline and change the Blurriness value to 0, which will also create a new keyframe. Press the spacebar to test the animation. The blur is removed over the last two seconds of the animation.

That's all well and good, but is there more to this? Let's add a little bit more interest to the animation and have the text fade in over two seconds.

1. Press the Home key to move the playback head to the start of the timeline.

2. Press the T key to open the Opacity settings. Add a keyframe and change the Opacity value to 0.

3. Move the playback head to the 2-second mark on the timeline and change the Opacity value to 100%. When you press the spacebar, the text will fade in, blur, and then unblur.

So far so good, but surely there must be something "cool" you can do? How about rotating the text in a 3D space while it fades into legibility?

1. Pull the playback head back to the start of the timeline. Click the 3D switch in the timeline.

2. If you twirl down Poetry in motion ➤ Transform, you will see that a Z axis has been added to all of the Transform properties except for Opacity.

3. Add a keyframe in the Scale property and click the link icon (officially called the Constrain Proportions icon). This will allow you to set different values for the X, Y, and Z scales. Set the X and Y scale values to –40% and the Z scale value to 21%.

4. Add a keyframe to the ZRotation property and set its value to 35 degrees.

5. Drag the playback head to the 2-second mark and use the following values:

   - Scale: 19, 590, 43%
   - ZRotation: +90

6. Drag the playback head to the 4-second mark on the timeline and use these values:

   - Scale: 100, 100, 100%
   - ZRotation: +0.0

7. Press the spacebar to preview the animation. The text, as shown in Figure 5-5, is doing some rather interesting stuff.

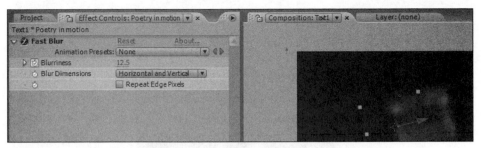

Figure 5-5. Tranforming text in a 3D space results in some rather interesting animations.

So there you have it—here you have achieved something with After Effects pretty easily, which is quite difficult to do in Flash—putting text on a Z axis and animating it. As with most of the other examples in the book, this demonstrates the value of the Flash/After Effects marriage rather nicely. These examples should not be looked at as After Effects exercises, but as effects that can be applied to objects in After Effects and subsequently placed into Flash. This exercise can now be rendered and, for example, used in a preloader for a Flash movie or as a separate piece of content on the Flash stage.

Lens flare

In this next exercise, you are going to do something that really can't be accomplished in Flash without a lot of complicated ActionScript. You are going to create an animated lens flare. Once you finish this exercise, you will put what you have learned to good use and couple the effect with a blur. From there, these two effects will be used to create an animated poem that incorporates audio and some rather fascinating, yet simple to accomplish, special effects.

This Lens Flare effect mimics what happens when a bright light is shining directly on the camera lens and creates reflections of itself through the barrel of the lens. Like all effects, this one is very effective and, staying with the theme, should not be overused.

1. Open After Effects and create a new Comp using these settings:
   - Composition Name: Comp1
   - Preset: Web Video, 320×240
   - Pixel Aspect Ratio: Square Pixels
   - Duration: 0:00:05:00

2. Create a new black solid by selecting Layer ➤ New ➤ Solid and setting the color to black when the Solid Settings dialog box opens. When you close the dialog box, the solid appears on the timeline.

3. Open the Effects & Presets panel and select Generate ➤ Lens Flare.

4. Drag the Lens Flare filter from the panel onto the solid. The effect, shown in Figure 5-6, will appear in the middle of the Comp.

161

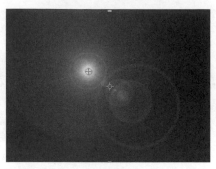

Figure 5-6. A lens flare

Obviously a static lens flare is right up there with counting the needles on a pine tree. Let's put it in motion. The plan is to have it rotate around the screen, brighten, and then fade out as it comes to its final resting position.

5. In the timeline, twirl down Solid ➤ Effects ➤ Lens Flare. You are going to work with the Flare Center and Flare Brightness properties of Effects.

6. In the Flare Center property, add the following keyframes and values:

- 0 seconds: 0.0, 0.0
- 1 second: 213, 36
- 2.13 seconds: 254, 196
- 4.1 seconds: 88, 204

7. In the Flare Brightness property, add the following keyframes and values:

- 0 seconds: 100%
- 1 second: 100%
- 1.17 seconds: 171%
- 2.13 seconds: 100%

Do a RAM preview of the movie. The flare brightens, as shown in Figure 5-7, as it moves around the Comp window and dims at the 2.13-second mark.

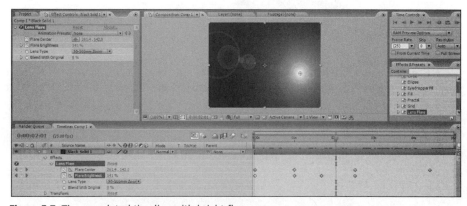

Figure 5-7. The completed timeline with bright flare

At this point you may want to save the project and render it as a QuickTime movie using the Animation codec.

What never ceases to fascinate us is how the lines are blurring, in Flash, between what is a video on the Flash stage and what is a Flash animation. This will be your next exploration. In Flash, you are going to play the lens flare video you have just created in After Effects and have some text blur on the Flash stage as the full intensity of the flare hits the text.

1. Open the Flash 8 Video Encoder and encode your lens flare video using the following settings:

   - Output filename: Flare
   - Video codec: ON2VP6
   - Frame rate: 15
   - Key frame placement: Automatic
   - Quality: Custom
   - Max data rate: 200

2. When the FLV file is created, open up a new Flash document and set the stage size to 320X240 and the stage color to black (#000000). Save this file to the same folder as the FLV file created in the previous step.

3. Add two new layers. Name the layers, from the bottom up, Video, Text, and Actions.

4. Select the Video layer and add a new video object to the Library. Drag this object onto the stage and, using the Property inspector, set the dimensions to 320X240 and set its X and Y coordinates to 0, 0. Select the video object on the stage and give it the instance name of myVid.

5. Select the Text layer. Select the Text tool, click the stage, and enter Flare it up!. In the Property inspector, set the text to 48 point _sans and set its color to yellow (#FFFF00). Click the text block on the stage once and convert it to a movie clip named Text.

6. Open the Text movie clip by double-clicking it in the Library. Add keyframes at Frames 30 and 60 of this movie clip. Drag the playback head to Frame 30, select the text on the stage, and apply a Blur filter (see Figure 5-8) using the following settings:

   - Blur X: 9
   - Blur Y: 9
   - Quality: High

   Apply motion tweens between the keyframes from Frames 1 to 30 and from Frames 30 to 60. Click the Scene 1 link to return to the main timeline.

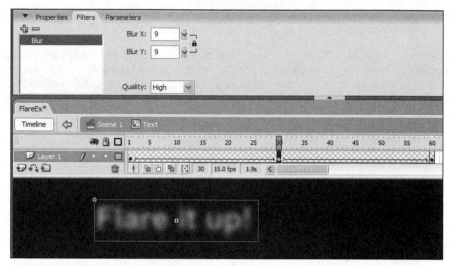

Figure 5-8. The Blur filter is applied to the movie clip.

Though you can apply filters, in Flash, to both text and movie clips, the blur won't tween if you just use text. This explains why the text block was placed in another movie clip.

7. Select the Actions layer, open the Actions panel, and enter the following code:

```
var nc: NetConnection = new NetConnection();
nc.connect(null);
var ns: NetStream = new NetStream(nc);
myVid.attachVideo (ns);
ns.play("Flare.flv");

ns.onStatus = function(info) {
   if (info.code == "NetStream.Play.Stop") {
      ns.seek(0);
   }
}
```

8. Save and test the movie (see Figure 5-9).

Figure 5-9.
Flash text, After Effects video

Now that you have seen how to have Flash content interact with After Effects content, a world of new possibilities has opened up for you. The Lens Flare effect can be used for explosions on the Flash stage, camera flash strobes, and many other places where a bright light needs to be animated.

A photo gallery intro

One of the more common uses for Flash is to display a gallery of photographs. There are some amazing photography sites out there but, in our humble opinion, one of the best sites of this genre is the Magnum Photos site at www.magnumphotos.com/c/Home_MAG.aspx. It is a showcase for the photographers this company represents, and, every now and then, Magnum will present an essay, called "Magnum in Motion," in which a photographer explains his or her work.

If you have ever produced a photo gallery, you know that this can result in a bit of a delay as the photos are downloaded into the SWF file. Your choices are to add a preloader to the project or expect the viewer to wait until everything pulls together.

In this exercise, we show you a slightly different approach. You are going to produce a video that will be used as a preloader. The difference is you are going to step outside of the size constraints you have dealt with so far in the exercises in this book. You are going to produce a physically large video—500 × 400—and still have it play smoothly in the browser.

The genesis for this project came about during a walk through the Factory 789 Art District in Beijing, China.

One of the authors was recently there and took a few photos of things that were hanging or painted on walls or words in signs that caught his attention. These images ranged from signs with "Chinglish"—literal translations from Chinese to English that make no sense—to Maoist slogans, such as in Figure 5-10, painted on the ceiling of an old tank factory.

Figure 5-10. "May Mao live 10,000 years and 10,000 and 10,000 more years."

The plan is to have a melodic Chinese folk tune playing in the background while two Chinese characters move across the screen revealing just pieces of the underlying images. The context for the characters becomes evident at the end of the video when they meld back into the image in which they originally appear.

> *This project will be taken to the point where it is output as an FLV file and placed in Flash. We covered how to use video as a preloader in the previous chapter. The slide show can use any one of a number of templates out there. Another very interesting slide show project appears in the book* AdvancED Flash Interface Design, *by Michael Kemper et al. (friends of ED, 2006).*
>
> *If you don't have Illustrator or are unfamiliar with how to use it, skip this section. We have included the final Illustrator file—*Symbol.ai—*in the* WallArt *folder found in the* Chapter 5 Exercise *folder.*

1. The first step in the process is to open a new document in Illustrator CS2 and import the Final.jpg image into the document.
2. Add a new layer to the document, select the layer, and select the Magnifying Glass tool. Zoom in on the wall characters in the image.

3. Select the Pen tool, turn off the fill color, and roughly trace each of the characters in the image (see Figure 5-11).

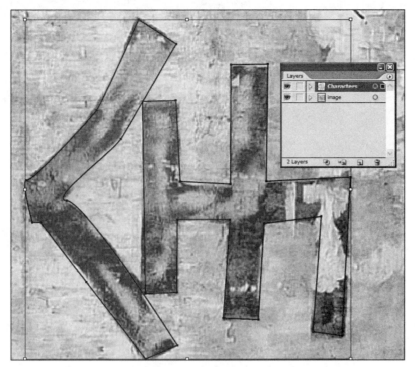

Figure 5-11. Trace the characters to a separate Illustrator layer.

4. When the two characters are drawn as separate closed paths, select them, fill them with black, and turn off the stroke.

5. With both filled objects selected, press Shift+Ctrl+F9 (PC) or Cmd+Shift+F9 (Mac) to open the Pathfinder panel. Click the Merge button to convert the two shapes to a single path (see Figure 5-12). With the merged path selected, press Shift+F9 to swap the fill color with a stroke color.

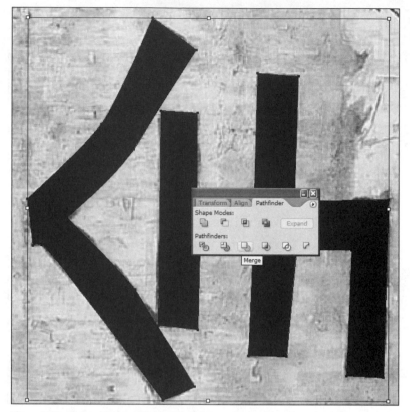

Figure 5-12. Merge the two filled objects into a single object by using the Pathfinder panel.

6. Select the layer containing the image and delete it.

7. Select the new object and copy it to the Clipboard. Save the Illustrator file and quit Illustrator.

The object sitting on the Clipboard will be used as a moving mask in After Effects. Here's how:

1. Open the WallArt_Masked.aep file in your Chapter 5 Exercise folder.

2. Create a new Comp using these settings:

- Composition Name: WallArtMasked
- Width: 500
- Height: 400
- Pixel Aspect Ratio: Square Pixels
- Frame Rate: 25
- Duration: 0:01:45:00

3. Click OK to close the Comp window, double-click your new Comp to open it, and drag the WallArtContent Comp to the main timeline.

4. Click the Comp window once and select Edit ➤ Paste. The Illustrator content on the Clipboard will appear in the Comp window.

5. Twirl down the WallArtContent layer and then twirl down the Masks property. Select Add from the blend mode pull-down and drag the playback head across the timeline. You can see the images through the mask (as shown in Figure 5-13).

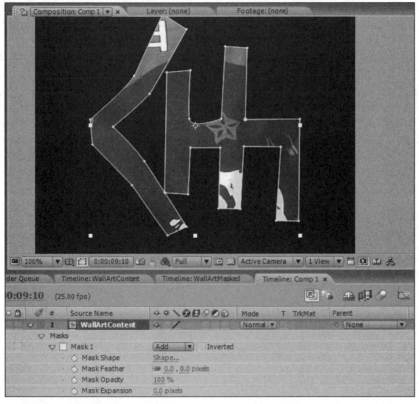

Figure 5-13. The mask is creating by selecting the Add blend mode in the Mask layer.

This is software you are dealing with and it doesn't hurt to be a bit suspicious. Though the Add *mode is the default blend mode for a mask, you really should give it a quick check to see that it has been applied.*

5

Having created the mask, now all you need to do is to move the mask around the stage.

1. Drag the playback head back to the start position on the timeline. An easy method of doing this is to simply press the Home key on your keyboard.

2. In the Comp window, click the Mask Shape property name to select the mask and drag the mask to a point just to the right of the stage.

3. Drag the playback to the 2-second mark of the timeline, add a keyframe, and drag the mask until the left edge of the mask is touching the left edge of the stage.

4. Go to various times on the timeline and move the mask (which will also add keyframes). When you reach the 0:01:38:00 point of the timeline, add a keyframe and stop there.

5. At the 0:01:38:00 mark of the timeline, the mask should be over its original shape. Drag the playback head to the 0:01:40:23 mark on the timeline.

6. Click the mask to reveal the nodes in the shape. Drag the nodes to positions that match the shape of the symbol on the wall (see Figure 5-14). If you drag the playback head between these two keyframes, you will see the mask shrink to fit the shape.

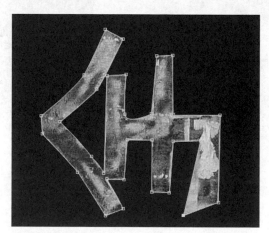

Figure 5-14. Move the nodes to their corresponding location on the image.

The final task is to have the mask expand to reveal the entire image. Here's how to do that:

1. Press the Home key to return to the start of the timeline. Add a keyframe in the Mask Expansion property.

2. Drag the playback head to the 0:01:38:00 mark of the timeline and add another keyframe.

3. Drag the playback head to the 0:01:42:00 mark of the timeline and change the Mask Expansion value to 313.0 pixels.

If you scrub the playback head between these two keyframes, you will see the mask grow outwards until it disappears and reveals the underlying image, as shown in Figure 5-15.

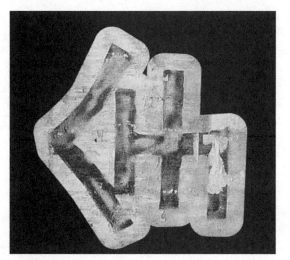

Figure 5-15. Change the Mask Expansion value to expand the "size" of the mask.

At this stage of the process, it would be a good time to save the project.

Finally, render the project as a QuickTime video using the Video codec. Don't forget to select the Audio check box in the Output Module Settings dialog box. Forgetting to do this will result in the loss of the audio soundtrack that has been added to the Comp. When you have finished rendering the video, quit After Effects.

Creating the FLV file

To this point in the book, the FLV files you have created follow a standard aspect ratio of 4:3. All of the FLV files have dimensions of either 320×240, 240×180, or even 120×90. This exercise moves well outside of standard to a physical size of 500×400 pixels. That is a lot of information to be shooting down the data pipe into the Flash Player.

The solution to this problem is one we learned from a colleague, Lee Brimelow, at www.gotoandlearn.com. This site is a collection of Flash video tutorials that all have a size of 640×480. Realizing the playback of videos at this size is problematic, Lee discovered a rather ingenious solution: slow down the video.

If you study his video tutorials, you will notice there really isn't a lot of motion—pans, zooms, things zipping across the screen. The only things in motion are the cursor moving around the screen and the screen itself as the cursor moves out of the capture area. If you study the exercise you have just completed, you will discover you have a similar situation in front of you. The mask moves around the screen at a leisurely pace while the images under the mask remain immobile. This means you can get away with a lower data and frame rate than normal.

1. Open the Flash 8 Video Encoder and add the video you just rendered in After Effects to the Render Queue.

2. Click the Settings button and, when the Flash Video Encoding Settings dialog box opens, name the file and click the Advanced Settings button.

3. Select the ON2VP6 codec and set the frame rate to 10 fps.

4. Select Custom from the Quality pull-down menu and set the Max data rate value to 200 kilobits per second.

5. Click the Encode audio check box and select 48 kbps (mono), as shown in Figure 5-16, from the Data rate pull-down.

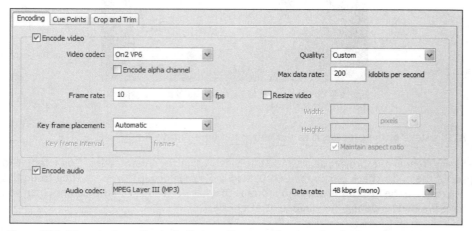

Figure 5-16. When dealing with physically large files, consider dropping the frame rate if there is not a lot of motion.

6. Click OK to close the Advanced Settings area and return to the Render Queue. Click the Start Queue button to start the render process.

> You are probably wondering what frame rate Lee uses for tutorials that are 640×480. The answer is 5 fps.

As we stated at the start of this exercise, the FLV file can then be used as a preloader for a Flash slide show. In addition to that, you also learned how to add and animate Illustrator content treated as a mask in After Effects.

Creating an animated poem

Ever since Hillman Curtis introduced one of the authors to *Born Magazine* (www.bornmagazine.com/) a few years back, he has been hooked on the site. Every now and then Flash needs to stretch its artistic wings and function as a purely creative (as opposed to functional or commercial) medium. *Born Magazine* is a great source for inspiration for this. As it says right on the front page of the site: "Born Magazine is an experimental venue marrying literary arts and interactive media. Original projects are brought to life every three months through creative collaboration between writers and artists."

It never ceases to amaze us how the collaboration between a Flash artist and a poet can result in some truly stunning work. One of our personal favorites at *Born Magazine* is "Flesh of a mango" by Nathan Barnett (www.bornmagazine.com/projects/mango/#). It is a moody, somewhat passionate piece that we regard as a classic example of the power of motion graphics. Using nothing more than images, sound, and text (see Figure 5-17), this piece manages to capture the tone of the poem in a manner that is both captivating and engaging.

Figure 5-17. A line from "Flesh of a mango"

In this exercise, you will discover that you can create a similar mood using nothing more than text, solids, and an audio track in After Effects.

> *Speaking of the audio track, the authors would like thank Claudio Cappellari at Toscano Records (www.toscanorecords.com) in Zurich, Switzerland, for the soundtrack for this and other exercises in the book.*

This exercise will also be a bit different from others presented so far. We have given you the completed file in order to let you "dissect" or "reverse engineer" the project with an eye to variations on the question "How did they do that?" What follows, therefore, is a series of short tutorials highlighting various aspects of the piece and answering these questions:

- How are things in an After Effects movie timed to a soundtrack?
- How was that gradient created?
- How can the Lens Flare effect be toned down?
- How is a sine wave animation created?
- How does the title blink and then melt?
- How are those pulsing circles that move across the screen created?
- How can text be highlighted while a video is playing?

173

A quick heads-up about the project file. You may notice the font used in the QuickTime movie for this project differs significantly from that in the AEP file in the Chapter 5 Exercise folder. The font used in the QuickTime movie is named AlphaMack AOE and was chosen because its look and feel evokes the mood of the poem. You probably don't have that font. In order to avoid a nasty "Font Missing" message when you open the AEP file in After Effects and the inevitable nasty e-mails that will follow, the font used in the AEP file was changed to Arial.

Synching animation to sound in After Effects

As we have pointed out in this book and in other publications to which we have contributed, regarding audio as the redheaded child in a family of blondes would be a huge mistake. It is the audio in this piece that contributes to the mood and feel of the production, and it is the deep sub-bass sound that contributes to the timing of the animations in the video.

If you open the sound file—track02.wav—in Adobe Audition or other sound editor, you can get a more detailed graphical representation of the sound track than you can in After Effects. As you can see in Figure 5-18, the deep bass sound is represented by the long spikes that stretch down from the middle of the graph. Another thing to notice is how regularly spaced the spikes are and that the first one appears at the 12-second mark.

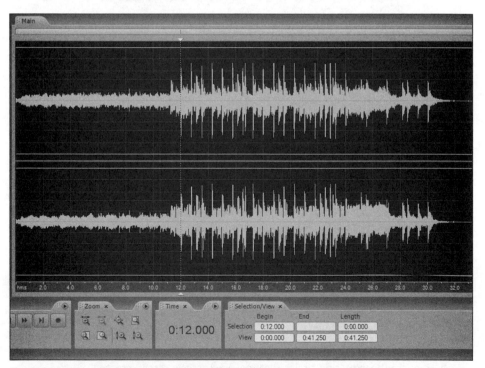

Figure 5-18. The audio track as viewed in Adobe Audition 2

Logging those times and somehow using them in After Effects can be a rather tedious process. There is another way: use Comp markers.

1. Open the Poem.aep file in the Poem folder found in your Chapter 5 Exercise folder.

2. Twirl down Layer 18 ➤ Audio ➤ Waveform to reveal the audio waveform (see Figure 5-19) for the soundtrack. Notice how closely it matches that shown in Figure 5-18.

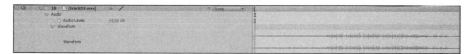

Figure 5-19. Showing the audio waveform in After Effects

3. Open the Info panel by selecting Window ➤ Info. On the right side of the timeline is a Comp Marker icon. Click and drag a marker onto the timeline. As you drag the marker across the timeline, its time in the Info panel will change. When the time shows 0:00:11:12, release the marker. This marker identifies the approximate location of the first sub-bass sound; this lets you see graphically where to start an animation based on the sound. Add four more markers at the following times:

- 0:00:14:12
- 0:00:17:05
- 0:00:20:00
- 0:00:24:00

What you should see are a series of numbered markers that look like little traffic signs above the timeline. Markers function much like frame labels in Flash. They allow you to reference specific frames in the timeline. In fact, you can jump to specific markers by simply pressing the marker number on the main keyboard . . . not the number pad. For example, if you were to move the playback head to any place on the timeline and then press 5 on the keyboard, the playback head, as shown in Figure 5-20, jumps to that marker.

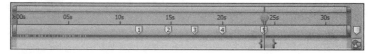

Figure 5-20. Use markers to identify key times in the movie.

To remove a marker, just drag the marker to be removed on top of the Comp Marker icon.

Creating a gradient background

Unlike in Flash, Photoshop, Fireworks, and Illustrator, in After Effects there really is no way to create a gradient using a Color Picker or other traditional method used by the drawing and imaging applications. Instead, After Effects uses the Ramp filter to create gradients and applies the gradient to a solid. Here's how:

1. Create a new Comp and set its dimensions to 720×280.

2. When the Comp opens, drag a copy of the Medium Gray-Orange Solid 1 to the timeline.

3. Click the solid in the Comp window to select it.

4. Open the Effects & Presets panel. Twirl down the Generate folder and drag a copy of the Ramp filter onto the solid. You will see that the gradient applied is grayscale and uses a default shape of Linear, as shown in Figure 5-21.

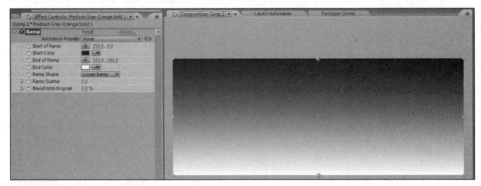

Figure 5-21. The default values used in the Ramp filter

5. Click the Effect Controls tab and use the following settings:

- Start of Ramp: Set X to 30 and Y to 186.
- Start Color: 142, 115, 73 (RGB values).
- End of Ramp: Set X to 350 and Y to 675.
- End Color: 66, 50, 25 (RGB values).
- Ramp Shape: Radial Ramp.

You can also use the crosshairs, shown in Figure 5-22, in the Start *and* End *areas of the* Ramp *filter. This allows you to drag the cursor across the screen and click where you think the start and end point of the gradient should be. Another method is to drag the crosshairs on the Comp to their final positions.*

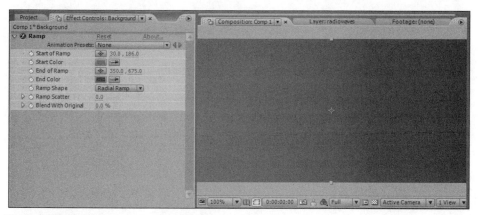

Figure 5-22. Gradients are created using the Ramp filter.

"Toning down" a lens flare

As you discovered in an earlier technique in this chapter, the Lens Flare effect can be quite overpowering. If you click the Timeline-Comp 1 tab, select your layer, and drag the playback head to the start of the solid, you will see the Lens Flare effect appears in the Comp window, but it is quite a bit more subtle than the one used in the earlier exercise. Here's how we did it:

1. Click the Timeline-Comp 2 tab and when the gradient appears, drag a copy of the Medium Gray-Orange Solid 5 onto the timeline. Drag the right edge of the Comp strip to the 40-second mark on the timeline to shorten its duration.

2. Apply a Lens Flare effect to the solid in the Comp window. As you can see from Figure 5-23, the effect is quite overpowering.

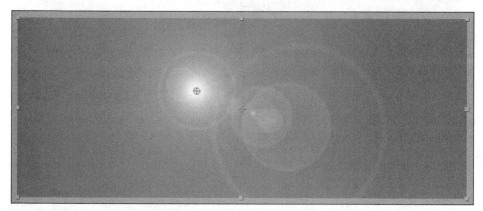

Figure 5-23. The Lens Flare effect is too strong for the piece.

3. Drag the playback head to the start of the layer strip or press the Home key on your keyboard, and twirl down Layer name ➤ Effect. Add a keyframe in the Flare Center property. Change the setting to 96, 33.

4. Drag the playback head to the end of the strip or press the End key, add a keyframe in the Flare Center property, and change the Flare Center to 425.1, 22.9.

5. Twirl up Layer and press the T key to open the Opacity properties for the layer. What you are going to do is to add four keyframes and change the opacity value for each frame. Use these times and values for the keyframes and the Opacity value:

Time	Opacity Value
0:00:10:00	8%
0:00:20:00	25%
0:00:30:00	25%
0:00:40:00	0%

As you can see in Figure 5-24, if you scrub the playback head across the timeline, reducing the opacity of the solid has the effect of toning down a very powerful effect.

Figure 5-24.
Reducing the layer opacity also reduces the strength of the effect.

Creating a sine wave animation

If there is one fact of life involved in being a Flash designer, it is this: we are, by nature, inherently lazy. This is not intended to be disrespectful but, as designers, if there is a faster, easier, and just as accurate way of doing something, we are going to use it.

When it comes to making geometric shapes or using geometry to animate objects in Flash, there is that moment when you discover using the sine method of the Math class in ActionScript—Math.sin(angle)—gives you the regular undulating motion of a sine wave. Upon discovering that a sine wave requires a basic knowledge of trigonometry, the average Flash developer will throw up his or her hands and sigh, "There has to be an easier way!" There is. It is the Write On filter in After Effects.

> *OK, maybe you aren't "lazy" and are simply curious as to how it can be done in Flash. friends of ED, our beloved publisher, has a couple of tremendous books that explore the relationship of mathematics and art in Flash. The first is* Foundation ActionScript Animation: Making Things Move! *by Keith Peters (friends of ED, 2005). His third chapter, "Trigonometry for Animation," is an excellent primer for "lazy" designers. The other book, once you grasp the concepts that Peters presents, is* Flash Math Creativity, Second Edition *by David Hirmes et al. (friends of ED, 2004). It moves right into hardcore math and the stunning work you can produce with just a few equations.*

5

If you play the Poem.mov file in the Complete folder of the Chapter 5 code download, you will notice that there is a small animation at the beginning of the piece composed of a series of dots that form a sine wave; the dots gently undulate, mimicking the waves at the seashore. Not only that, there are two lines of them that intersect as they form the waves. The dots are the result of the application of the Write–on effect to the solid. What this filter does is allow you to paint on a solid in a Comp. Here is how we did that:

1. Click the Timeline-Comp 2 **tab and drag a copy of the** Medium Gray-Orange Solid 3 to the timeline.

2. Twirl down Effects & Presets ➤ Generate and drag a copy of the Write On filter onto the solid in the Comp window.

You are probably looking at the properties of this filter (as shown in Figure 5-25) and wondering, "Huh?" Here is what they mean:

- Brush Position: Specifies the starting location of the brush on the solid
- Color: Specifies the color of the paint
- Brush Size: Specifies the circumference of the paint brush
- Brush Hardness: Specifies how strongly the paint is applied to the solid
- Stroke Length (secs): Specifies the length, in seconds, of the stroke at any point in time
- Brush Spacing (secs): Specifies the amount of time that will elapse between dabs of paint
- Paint Time Properties: Specifies whether paint properties (color and opacity) are applied to each stroke segment or to the entire stroke
- Brush Time Properties: Specifies whether brush properties (size and hardness) are applied to each stroke segment or to the entire stroke
- Paint Style: Specifies whether the stroke is applied to the solid or to a transparent layer over the solid

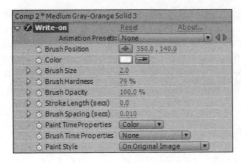

Figure 5-25.
The Write On filter lets you paint on a solid.

Naturally, there are some rules for using the Write On filter. The major ones are as follows:

- For this filter to do anything, the Brush Position needs to be animated between keyframes.
- The Brush Time Properties are used to animate the look of the stroke as it moves along the path.
- This filter does not draw lines. It draws a series of dots. A line is simulated by using a low number in the Brush Spacing parameter.
- You can't start to merrily scribble away. The Comp must be in edit mode.

Now that you have a better understanding of what this filter does, let's put it to work.

1. To put the Comp into edit mode, double-click the Comp name in the timeline. You will know you are in edit mode when the Comp appears in its own tab in the Comp window and there is a timeline under the Comp in the Comp window.

2. Twirl down Comp Name ➤ Effects ➤ Write On in the timeline. When the Write On properties appear, specify the following values:

   - Brush Size: 3.0
   - Brush Hardness: 51%
   - Brush Opacity: 48%
   - Stroke Length (secs): 0
   - Brush Spacing (secs): 0.068
   - Paint Time Properties: Opacity
   - Brush Time Properties: Size
   - Paint Style: On Transparent

You are now ready to start creating your sine wave. The properties you just set determine how the dots will appear and how far apart they will be when the wave animates. The key to animating a brush is the circle with the crosshairs that you see in the middle of the Comp window. It is the starting point of the animation.

3. Add a keyframe at the 0 point of the timeline in the Brush Position **property. Drag** the crosshairs to the upper-left corner of the Comp until the values in the Brush Position **area are** 24, 27. This will be the start point of the sine wave.

4. Drag the playback head to the 1-second mark, and change the Brush Position **to** 152, 224. When you release the mouse, you will see a dotted line. Use the following values for the remainder of the wave:

- 2 seconds: 372,71
- 3 seconds: 688,272
- 4 seconds: 707,286

If you look at the Comp window, you will see the dotted line appears, and there is a square where each of the keyframes is located. If you click one of those squares, you will discover that it has handles (similar to what you'd find in Illustrator or Fireworks) as shown in Figure 5-26. (The handles will appear as small dots on either side of the square you clicked.) This means you can move the locations of the keyframes and use the handles to adjust the path of the dots between the keyframes.

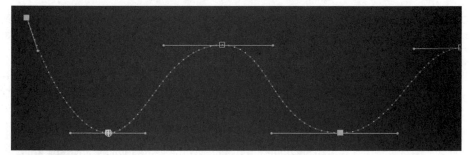

Figure 5-26. You can control the shape of the curve by adjusting the keyframe locations and moving the handles.

5. Click the Comp 2 tab in the Comp window. If you scrub the playback head across the Comp, you will see the dots create the curve shapes.

If you paid attention to the original animation, you may have noticed there are two waves that intersect each other. Does this mean you have to repeat these steps on a new layer? No. If you recall, we are inherently lazy, and here's a real neat way of duplicating the curve and flipping it with a simple drag of the mouse:

6. Select the layer in the timeline and press Ctrl+D (PC) or Cmd+D (Mac) to duplicate the layer.

7. Click the new layer once in the Comp window. Handles will appear around the edges of the Comp.

8. Drag the upper middle handle of the Comp to the bottom of the Comp. The animation "flips" as shown in Figure 5-27. Scrub across the timeline, and you have two waves of dots moving across the screen.

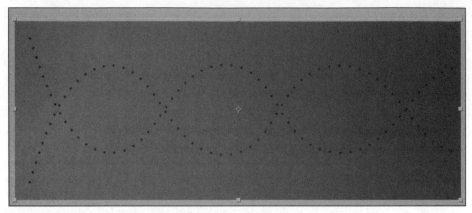

Figure 5-27. Duplicate the layer and "flip" it to create the second animation.

Blinking and melting text

During the opening sequence of our video, the text blinks a couple of times and then melts into some sort of liquid state and runs off the stage. This text effect is actually quite easy to accomplish. It only requires three filters.

1. Select the Text tool, click the Comp window that is open from the previous exercise, and enter inspiration in motion. Set the font to Arial, the size to 24 points, and the color to white (#FFFFFF).

2. Twirl down Effects & Presets ➤ Stylize and drag the Strobe Light filter onto the text.

The Strobe Light effect is actually quite interesting. As the name implies, anything affected by the Strobe Light filter will light up and disappear depending on how often the object is "lit up." This explains how the text "blinks." When you drag the filter onto the text, a number of properties will appear in the Effect Controls panel. Here is what they do:

- Strobe Color: Specifies the color of the light.
- Blend With Original: Indicates a percentage value that determines how strongly the effect is applied to the layer.
- Strobe Duration (secs): Specifies how long the object appears on the stage.
- Strobe Period (secs): Specifies how much time elapses between strobe blinks.
- Random Strobe Probability: Specifies the probability that any given frame of the layer will have the strobe effect, giving the appearance of a random effect.
- Strobe: Specifies how the effect is applied. Operates on Color Only performs the strobe operation on all color channels. Make Layer Transparent makes the layer transparent when a strobe effect occurs.
- Strobe Operator: Determines the blend mode to be applied to the subject. The default setting is Copy.

3. In the Effect Controls panel, apply these settings to the Strobe Light effect (see Figure 5-28):

- Strobe Color: #FFFFFF (white)
- Blend With Original: 0%
- Strobe Duration (secs): .8
- Strobe Period (secs): .2
- Random Strobe Probability: 23%
- Strobe: Makes Layer Transparent
- Strobe Operator: Screen

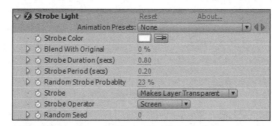

Figure 5-28. Applying a Strobe Light effect

If you drag the playback head across the timeline, the words will "blink."

The "melting" text is due to the interaction of two more filters: Gaussian Blur and Liquefy.

4. Twirl down Effects & Presets ➤ Blur & Sharpen and drag a copy of the Gaussian Blur filter onto the text.

5. In the timeline, twirl down Effects ➤ Gaussian Blur, add a keyframe in the Blurriness property at the 2-second mark, and change the Blurriness value to 2%.

6. Drag the playback head to the 4-second mark and change the Blurriness value to 25%.

7. Drag the playback head to the 2-second mark, open the Distort folder in Effects & Presets, and drag a copy of the Liquefy filter onto the text.

The amount of fun you can have with this filter should be illegal. If you open the Liquefy Settings in the Effect Controls panel, you will see a bunch of tools. These tools essentially allow you to "paint" with pixels and create some rather interesting effects as you distort the object. We really don't have the time to walk through each tool but, if you have some play time, take this filter for a highly entertaining test drive.

8. In the timeline, twirl down Effects ➤ Liquefy and, in the Distortion Mesh property, add keyframes at seconds 2 and 4.

9. Click the keyframe once at the 4-second mark, twirl down the Liquefy tools in the Effect Controls panel and select the Warp tool—we call it the "finger-painting tool"—and click and drag the "brush" from the top of the text to the bottom of the Comp. Notice how the pixels smear in the direction you drag the brush? Repeat this a couple times to give yourself an oozy bit of text as shown in Figure 5-29.

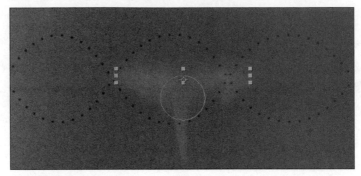

Figure 5-29. Liquifying text with the Warp tool to create an ooze effect

10. Do a RAM preview and click the Play button when the RAM preview finishes. The text will run off of the screen.

Creating pulsing circles

Remember those old black-and-white newsreels? There would be a radio tower at the start and a bunch of circles would radiate out from the top of the tower to indicate radio waves. If you watch the video for this exercise, you will see a similar effect occur in the upper-right corner of the stage: a circle seems to pulse out of that corner. Here's how we did it:

1. Drag a solid from the project pane to the timeline. Twirl down Effects & Presets ➤ Generate and drag a copy of the Radio Waves filter on top of the solid in the Comp window. When you release the mouse, blue "radio waves" will appear on the Comp (see Figure 5-30).

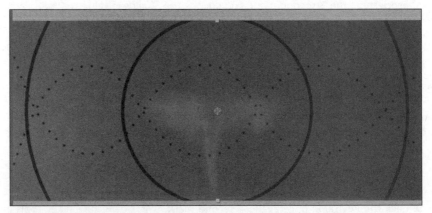

Figure 5-30. You start with blue waves.

The Radio Waves effect creates radiating waves from a stationary or animated effect point. It doesn't take a great deal of imagination to see how you can use this effect to generate pond ripples, sound waves, or intricate geometric patterns. Best of all, using the Effect Controls panel, you can control the shape of the wave and its width, color, speed, rotation, life span, fade rate, and other properties to create some rather interesting visual effects. In this exercise, you will create only one very light wave that pulses out of the upper-right corner of your Comp.

To clearly explain the features of this and many other effects presented throughout this book would require far more space than this book permits. If you select Help ➤ Effects Help, *you will open the* Effects Help *menu. To access the* Radio Wave *effect, click the* Generate *link and when the* Generate *effects appear, click the* Radio Wave *link. The page that opens gives you a full description of each control and property you see in the* Effect Controls *panel.*

2. Drag the crosshairs in the middle of the Comp window to the upper-right corner of the Comp to move the start point of the effect. Other ways of doing this are to open the Effect Controls panel and do it by the numbers or click the crosshairs in the Effect Controls panel and then click the Comp to indicate the start point.

3. Twirl down the Polygon property for the effect and change the Sides value to 128. The circle will appear larger as a result. Twirl up the Polygon property.

4. Twirl down the Wave Motion property and change the Frequency value to .35. The waves will now really spread out. Twirl up Wave Motion.

5. Twirl down the Stroke properties and specify the following settings:

- Profile: Sine
- Color: 7C643E
- Opacity: .07
- Start Width: 31.8

You will notice the pulse is fairly faint. If you do a RAM preview, you will see the circle pulse out of the upper-right corner and grow (see Figure 5-31) and fade as it moves across the screen.

Figure 5-31. Note the pulse in the right side of the Comp window.

Highlighting text

When you really think about the nature of our job, the new media artist is really no different from a magician. We use the art of illusion to trick the viewer into thinking something that really doesn't happen is happening. Near the end of the video, you will notice a couple of pieces of text seem to brighten to a highlight and then fade back into the text block. This is an illusion, and here is how to do it:

1. Click the Timeline: Comp 2 tab to open the Comp you have been playing with and drag a solid to the timeline.

2. Select the Text tool, click the Comp once, and type in a sentence of text. Use a font, font color, and point size of your choosing.

3. Highlight the first couple of words in the sentence, copy them to the Clipboard, click the Comp, and paste them into the Comp. You will now have two text layers. One is the sentence and the other (as shown in Figure 5-32) is the text you just pasted.

Figure 5-32. It starts with a solid and a couple of text layers.

4. Select the sentence, and, in the Effects & Presets panel, twirl down Animation Presets ➤ Text ➤ Blurs and drag a copy of the Blur By Word filter onto the sentence in the Comp.

If you do a RAM preview on this layer, you will see each word in the sentence start out as a blur and come into focus. This is not quite the effect you want.

5. Select the sentence in the timeline, twirl down Text ➤ Transform, and reduce the Opacity value to 20%. Now, if you do a RAM preview, the text is somewhat faint.

6. Select the layer containing the copied text and drag it into position on the text block.

> *For precise positioning, move the copied text into its position and then marquee the text with the* Magnifying Glass *tool. Use the arrow keys to nudge the text into position and zoom back out to the 100% view.*

7. Set the In point of this text block to the 2-second mark on the timeline and drag the Out point to the 8-second mark on the timeline. Now when you do a RAM preview, the text is faint, and when it all comes into focus, the pasted text lights up for six seconds (see Figure 5-33) and then disappears.

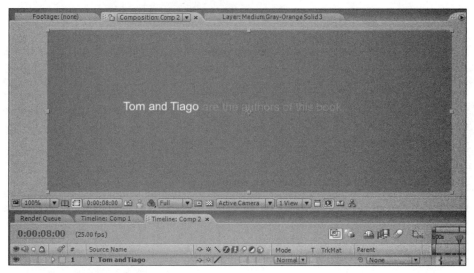

Figure 5-33. Ours is the art of illusion.

Summary

This chapter has been a rather extensive exploration of how judicious use of text and effects can produce some rather fascinating work. The subliminal message in this chapter has been it is becoming increasingly difficult to tell which element is video and which element is a movie clip on the Flash stage.

We started the chapter by showing you a method of creating closed captions for video. This technique works for short videos, but if you require more precision in the timing or a lot of captions, consider using a commercial product like Captionate.

From there, you started playing with text and getting somewhat familiar with both the Character and Paragraph panels. The exercise showed you how to create a short blurred animation of a text block and then showed you how to also use text in the 3D space. This is something unavailable to the Flash user.

We also showed you how to animate a Lens Flare effect and add it to a Flash animation where the effect interacted with a movie clip containing a blurred text animation. Without the FLV playback controls, it is quite difficult to dispassionately look at the SWF file and determine which effect was done in which application.

The next project was a photo gallery intro that used "text" created in Illustrator as a mask for the intro. As you discovered, a simple copy-and-paste job is all that is required to get a text outline, for example, from Illustrator into After Effects. The other part of that exercise was dealing with an offsize—500×400 pixels—FLV file. The key here is to reduce both the frame and the data rates.

The final exercise presented you with a variety of techniques used to create an animated poem.

You discovered how to use Comp markers to tie motion on the timeline to specific points in an audio track and how to create a gradient, using the Ramp filter on an After Effects solid. Among the remaining exercises were how to tone down a lens flare, create a sine wave animation using a Write On effect, make text blink and melt, create pulsating radio waves, and a rather interesting technique for attracting a viewer's attention to a piece of text.

This was a lot of information, but you also learned a lot of techniques that you can use to create visually creative motion graphics.

Speaking of visually creative, the next chapter digs into a serious number of special effects that can be added to your projects—transitions to smoke and clouds—as well as some really neat stuff you can do with video and the new filters in Flash Professional 8. See you there.

6 CREATING SPECIAL EFFECTS

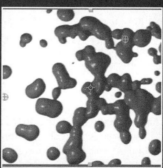

When we first started thinking about what to do with this chapter, one of the authors kept returning to a conversation with Josh Davis a couple of years ago. They were sitting in a restaurant, and Josh had mentioned that he was now doing some work for an automobile company. The problem, as only Josh could express it, was creating a site that presented a car that didn't look like every other site that presented a car. He and his partner, Brandon Hall, had been tossing ideas back and forth to no avail until it hit Josh: "Why not just blow up the car?" It was those two words—*blow up*—that kept resonating through the author's head. That phrase captures the intent of this chapter.

Though we are not going to show you how to "blow stuff up," we are going to show you how to create cool drop shadows, smoke, fire, and exploding fireworks; play with light; and generally add the element of mayhem to your Flash projects. We are also going to explore how to use the Flash filters and blend effects to add a bit more "jazz" to the stuff you will create in After Effects. In short, we are going to kick back and have a bit of fun.

Doing the drop shadow dance

We are going to start in a rather familiar place: adding a drop shadow to a video. A drop shadow tends to give the subject of the video a bit of depth and, in certain respects, makes the video a bit more realistic. In this exercise, we are going to look at the following techniques:

- Tossing a drop shadow onto a video in After Effects
- Adding the same drop shadow in Flash
- Creating a perspective drop shadow in Flash

1. Launch After Effects and open the Girl.aep file found in the DropShadow folder located in the Exercise folder of the Chapter 6 code download.

2. Open the Effects & Presets panel and twirl down the Perspective folder. Drag a copy of the Drop Shadow effect onto the Comp window and release the mouse. The Drop Shadow settings will appear in the Effects Controls panel.

3. As shown in Figure 6-1, use the following settings for the Drop Shadow effect:

- Shadow Color: #000000 (black)
- Opacity: 50%
- Direction: 0, 135
- Softness: 15

4. Do a RAM preview to see the shadow move. Now that you see how easy it is to apply a Drop Shadow effect in After Effects, you are now going to do the same thing in Flash. At this point, you can choose to save the file or render it as a video, being sure to use a lossless codec such as QuickTime's Video codec.

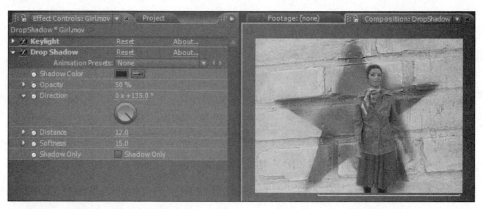

Figure 6-1. Applying a drop shadow

Applying a drop shadow in Flash

Flash Professional 8 gives you the opportunity to do the same thing in Flash; here's how:

1. Open the DropShadow_01.fla file, located in the DropShadow folder in your Chapter 6 Exercise folder.

2. Open the Library and add a new video object to the Library. When the Video Properties dialog box opens, don't bother naming the symbol. It will be the only video object used on the stage. Click OK to close the dialog box.

3. Create a new movie clip by selecting Insert ➤ New Symbol or pressing Ctrl+F8 (PC) or Cmd+F8 (Mac). When the New Symbol dialog box opens, name the symbol Video and select Movie Clip as its behavior.

4. Click OK in the New Symbol dialog box to open the Symbol Editor. With the video object selected, set its X and Y position in the Property inspector to 0, 0 and its size to 320✕240. Finally, give the selected video object the instance name of myVideo.

5. Add a new layer to the movie clip and name it Actions. Select the first frame in the Actions layer and press F9 (PC) or Option+F9 (Mac) to open the ActionScript Editor. Enter the following code:

```
var nc: NetConnection = new NetConnection();
nc.connect(null);
var ns: NetStream = new NetStream(nc);
myVideo.attachVideo(ns);
ns.play("Girl.flv");
```

6. Click the Check Syntax button to see whether you have made any mistakes and, if you haven't, close the ActionScript Editor. Click the Scene 1 link to return to the main timeline.

7. Drag a copy of the movie clip you just created from the Library to the Video layer.

6

8. Click the movie clip once on the stage and click the Filters tab in the Property inspector. Click the + sign to open the Filters pull-down menu and select Drop Shadow.

9. As shown in Figure 6-2, use these settings for the Drop Shadow filter:

- Blur X, Blur Y: 5
- Strength: 60%
- Quality: High
- Color: **Black** (#000000)
- Angle: 45
- Distance: 12

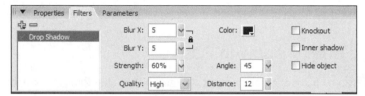

Figure 6-2. Applying a drop shadow in Flash

You may notice that the video object movie clip picks up the Drop Shadow settings. Don't be too alarmed by this. The video contains an alpha channel, which means the shadow will be applied to that channel, not to the movie clip. You also may be wondering why the video was put into a movie clip. The Flash filters can only be applied to movie clips and text.

10. Go ahead, test the video. You will see the shadow around the woman as shown in Figure 6-3.

Figure 6-3. Drop Shadow filter applied to a video

Now that you see how a drop shadow can be applied to a video, let's go a little further with this.

Select the video object on the stage and, in the Property inspector, apply the Multiply blend mode from the Blend pull-down menu in the Property inspector. The video changes completely. Instead of the woman interacting with the background image, the background image looks like it is projected onto the woman (see Figure 6-4).

Figure 6-4. Apply the Multiply blend mode, and the background image becomes part of the video.

This is due to the nature of the Multiply blend mode. Essentially, Flash looks at the color values of the pixels in the video and the pixels in the background image that are directly above each other. The values are multiplied and the result is divided by 256. The resulting pixel is always a darker pixel.

> The FLA and SWF files for this project are contained in the Blends_Filters folder found in the Chapter 6 Completed folder.

Applying a filter and blend using ActionScript

There is another way of adding the drop shadow and the blend mode to the video: do it using ActionScript. Here's how:

1. Open the Flash project you just created, select the movie clip on the stage, and click the Filters tab. Select the Drop Shadow filter and click the – sign to remove the filter. Also select the movie clip on the stage and set the blend mode in the Property inspector to Normal.

2. Select the movie clip on the stage and give it the instance name of myVid.

3. Add an Actions layer, select the first frame of the Actions layer, and open the ActionScript Editor.

4. Click the first line in the ActionScript Editor and enter the following code:

```
import flash.filters.DropShadowFilter;
var ds:DropShadowFilter = new DropShadowFilter(12,45,0x000000, ➥
.6,5,5,.6,3);
myVid.filters = [ds];
```

Let's go through this (you'll want to pay especially close attention if this is the first time you have ever written code for a filter).

You can't just jump in and tell Flash to apply a drop shadow to the movie clip on the stage. What you need to first do is tell Flash that it has to import the DropShadow class into the video. That is exactly what that first line of code does.

Now that the class is loaded, you have to tell Flash how to construct the drop shadow that will be applied to the video. That is the purpose of the second line of code. The filter is given an instance name—ds—and the filter properties are added as the parameters for the new DropShadowFilter(). Let's go through each of those numbers so you understand what they mean, and then we'll show you a really easy way of applying them. Here is what the values mean:

- **Distance**: 12
- **Shadow angle**: 45
- **Shadow color**: Black. When referring to hexadecimal colors in ActionScript, you need to use the 0x in front of the color value.
- **Shadow alpha**: .6. Percentages are always a value between 0 and 1.
- **Blur X**: 5
- **Blur Y**: 5
- **Strength**: .6. This corresponds to the 60% value added in the Filter dialog box.
- **Quality**: 3. There are three values in the Drop Shadow filter settings: Low, Medium, and High. ActionScript can't use those words and, instead, uses 1, 2, and 3. The value given, 3, is best quality.

That's obviously a lot to remember. Here's a little trick to help you enter the values. When you entered that second line of code, remember seeing a tooltip appear when you entered that first bracket? That tooltip shows the order for the values (see Figure 6-5). Instead of madly entering the values, enter each one followed by a comma. When you enter the comma, the tooltip will stay open and show you which parameter, indicated by bold text, has to be entered next. The tooltip will disappear when you enter that final bracket.

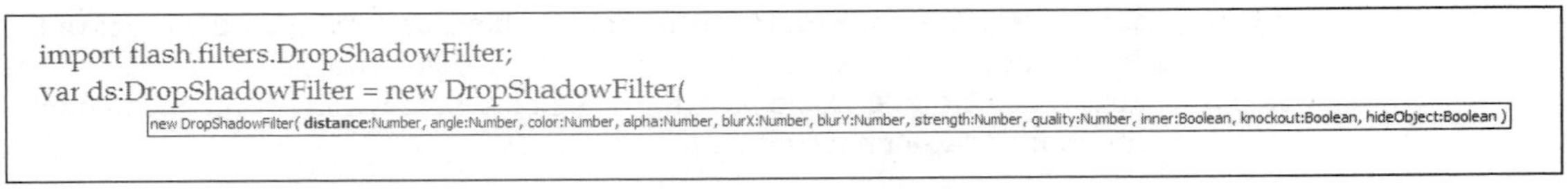

```
import flash.filters.DropShadowFilter;
var ds:DropShadowFilter = new DropShadowFilter(
```

new DropShadowFilter(**distance**:Number, angle:Number, color:Number, alpha:Number, blurX:Number, blurY:Number, strength:Number, quality:Number, inner:Boolean, knockout:Boolean, hideObject:Boolean)

Figure 6-5. Let the tooltip guide you. You are being prompted to enter a distance value.

The final line of code applies the Drop Shadow filter to the movie clip named myVid.

5. Check the syntax, close the ActionScript Editor, and test the video. The shadow, using the values entered, will appear as shown in Figure 6-6.

Figure 6-6. A programmatic drop shadow

> *The FLA and SWF files for this exercise can be found in your Chapter 6* Completed *folder. They are named* DropShadow_Code.fla *and* DropShadow_Code.swf.

Now that you have added a drop shadow using ActionScript, let's go a bit further and also add the Multiply blend mode.

Before you start, it is important you understand the blend modes are not, like the filters, in a class of their own. They are, in fact, a part of the ActionScript movieclip class. This makes it really easy to apply a blend mode to a movie clip. The syntax is

```
movieclipInstanceName.blendMode = blendModeNumber;
```

1. Open the ActionScript Editor for the current exercise and add the following line of code into Line 4 of the Script pane:

```
myVid.blendMode =3;
```

2. Save and test the movie. It is the same effect as the one you did earlier using filters and blend modes.

If you do decide to go the code route for this sort of thing, be aware that the order of the modes in the pull-down menu is not the same one used in ActionScript. If this was the case, the Multiply blend mode would have the value of 4. Here is a list of the blend modes and their corresponding ActionScript number:

- Normal: 1
- Layer: 2
- Multiply: 3
- Screen: 4
- Lighten: 5
- Darken: 6
- Difference: 7

- Add: 8
- Subtract: 9
- Invert: 10
- Alpha: 11
- Erase: 12
- Overlay: 13
- Hardlight: 14

This brings us to the obvious question: Which method—code or menu—is the most efficient? The debate that swirls around this one has been going on ever since ActionScript was introduced in the early days of Flash. We tend to side with the "codies" with this one because it is code, and computers love code. Still, when you really think about it, nobody cares how you did it. They just care that you did it.

Getting creative with a drop shadow in Flash

Here's a little trick we "swiped" from Chris Georgenes of Mudbubble fame. During the beta cycle for Flash Professional 8, Chris discovered that you could create perspective shadows and add them to movie clips. If you hit the home page for his site—www.mudbubble.com— you will see this technique in use. We saw it and thought, "Hey, that can be done with video as well." Here's how:

1. Open the DropShadow_02.fla file in your Chapter 6 Exercise folder.
2. Add a new layer above the Video layer and name it Video2.
3. Click the movie clip in the Video layer, copy it to the clipboard, and select the first frame of the Video2 layer. Select Edit ➤ Paste In Place. A copy of the movie clip will be placed over the one in the Video layer and will match its stage location. Having added the movie clip to the Video2 layer, turn off its visibility because you are going to use this copy of the movie clip in the Video layer as the shadow. Select the video movie clip on the stage and open the Drop Shadow filter.

The key to this technique is understanding the purpose of each of the parameters in the Drop Shadow dialog box. On the right side of the dialog box are three check boxes named Knockout, Inner Shadow, and Hide Object. Select Knockout, and the shadow is applied to the alpha channel, but the girl will be invisible. Select Inner Shadow, and a shadow is applied inside of the alpha channel. The last one simply shows the shadow and nothing else. It is a great trick for doing "ghosts" . . . or perspective drop shadows.

If you look at the background image, you can see it's somewhat cheesy, having a woman stand on a street and her shadow consisting of your standard drop shadow (see Figure 6-7). It just doesn't look real. It should fall along the sidewalk behind her.

Figure 6-7. A really cheesy drop shadow

6

4. Select the movie clip on the stage and apply the same Drop Shadow settings as you did earlier in this exercise, but this time click the Hide Object selection.

5. Click the movie clip on the stage and select Window ➤ Transform. When the Transform dialog box opens, distort the movie clip by deselecting Constrain and entering the values shown in Figure 6-8.

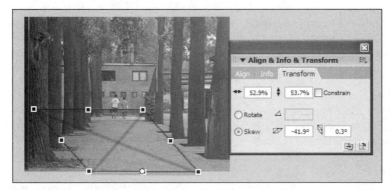

Figure 6-8. Distort the movie clip that contains the shadow.

If the clip still looks a little "off" (you want the bottom edge to closely follow the bottom of the stage), select the movie clip with the Autotransform tool and rotate a corner by clicking and dragging it. You also should move the movie clip to align its bottom edge with the bottom of the stage.

6. Turn on the visibility of the Video layer and save and test the movie. The shadow, shown in Figure 6-9, looks a lot more realistic.

Figure 6-9. A perspective shadow

Creating fire and smoke

There seems to be a fascination with destruction that comes about whenever we talk to Flash developers about using After Effects with Flash. Eventually the discussion gets around to setting something on fire or having something dissolve into a heap of smoking ashes on the Flash stage. Obviously, Flash isn't the tool for that job, but it can be done if you are prepared to do some heavy-duty lifting in ActionScript. As pointed out in the last chapter, being "lazy," we look at that stuff, pore through the scripts, and think, "There has to be an easier way." There is. It is the CC Particle Systems II effect from Cycore that you installed along with After Effects.

> *If you don't think you have installed the* Cycore *effects, fish out your After Effects Professional 7 installation disk or the Professional Studio Premium disk. These effects are found in the* Install Third Party Software *category.*

Before we dig into this subject, you need to clearly understand what you are dealing with. The CC Particle Systems II effect, at its core, does nothing more than create a particle (actually, regard the particle as a colored pixel) make it do something, and then the particle dies, or, in more simplistic terms, the pixel is turned off. A lot of particle generation and manipulation tools ship with After Effects or are available as third-party After Effects plug-ins. However, the CC Particle Systems II effect is one of the easiest to learn, so we'll review how to use it and let you use this as the springboard to future particle explorations in After Effects.

1. Open After Effects and create a new Comp that is 320×240 and is 10 seconds long. When the project is created, add a new black solid to the Comp and drag that solid onto the timeline, if it is not put there automatically.

2. Open the Effects & Presets panel. Twirl down the Simulation folder and drag the CC Particle Systems II effect onto the Comp.

You are looking at a black screen and probably wondering, "Uh, where are the particles?" What you need to know is this: "Particles are born." What you are looking at is the creation of the particles. Their point of origin is the crosshairs in the Comp window.

3. Open the Effect Controls panel and twirl down all of the properties. As you can see, there are a ton of properties that can have a direct effect upon the particle.

4. To see how these properties come into play, simply select Composition ➤ Preview ➤ RAM Preview. How about that? You didn't do a thing, and yet you have created a fireworks display (see Figure 6-10).

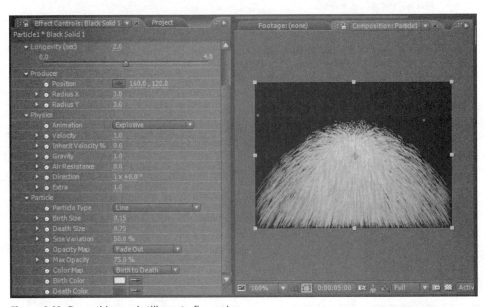

Figure 6-10. Do nothing and still create fireworks.

Now that you understand how the filter works, let's create some mayhem. You are going to create an explosion, using the particle effect you currently have open, that sets something on fire.

1. The first thing you are going to do is to make the background of the Comp white. Select Composition ➤ Background Color, click the Color chip, and select white, #FFFFFF, in the Color Picker. Close the Color Picker. Finally, the animation is going to have to occur from the bottom of the Comp upwards. Flip the solid by selecting the middle handle of the animation in the Comp window and dragging it to the bottom of the Comp window.

2. If you haven't already done so, twirl down the Producer, Physics, and Particle properties in the Effect Controls panel.

3. The first thing you are going to do is have a lot of particles appear on the stage. Double-click the Birth Rate value in the Effect Controls panel and change the value to 10.

4. Next up you are going to change the Physics properties of the particles to be created. You are going to tell After Effects how the animation will appear, how fast the particles are moving, how gravity affects that movement, and how the air they move through will affect their speed. Use the following Physics settings:

- Animation: Jet Sideways
- Velocity: 0.6
- Gravity: 0.3
- Air Resistance: 1.2
- Extra: 1.1

The Air Resistance setting essentially stops the animation from cutting off at the top of the Comp window. By increasing the air resistance, the particles slow down as they move up the Comp window. If you have ever lit a fire after a rain storm, you will actually see this. The air is so heavy with moisture that the smoke tends to flatten out rather than rise into the air because the smoke particles, as they rise, encounter the resistance of the moisture-laden air above the fire. The Extra setting allows you to add width to the effect.

5. The final step is to deal with the particles themselves. Specify these settings in the Particle area of the Effect Controls panel:

- Particle Type: Shaded Faded Sphere
- Birth Size: 0.06
- Death Size: 1.45
- Size Variation: 100%
- Opacity Map: Fade In and Out
- Max Opacity: 25%
- Color Map: Birth to Death
- Birth Color: #A90509 (dark red)
- Death Color: #000000 (black)

6. Drag a copy of the Levels effect from the Color Correction folder. Drag the white point to the left and, when the middle or gamma slider reaches the start of the histogram, release the mouse. The explosion looks a lot more real.

7. If your settings match those in Figure 6-11, do a RAM preview. The animation looks like a bomb hit something.

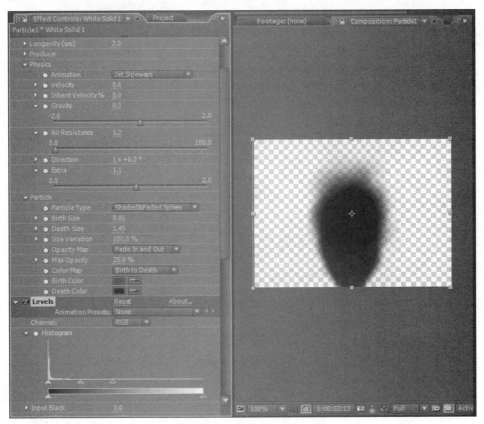

Figure 6-11. Fire and smoke at the click of a mouse button

At this point you have a rather interesting fire and smoke effect.

We looked at it and wondered what we could do with it in Flash. The decision was to have the effect spring out of one of the author's palms. The major consideration here was to have the fire be somewhat realistic. Before we rendered out the video, we keyed out the white background of the animation. This way the author's palm would appear in the video. The other consideration was we didn't want the fire to just suddenly appear on the palm of his hand. That, too, falls into the realm of "cheesy."

What we did was to open the image in Fireworks 8 and create a copy of the palm area of his hand. We copied and pasted the image into a new layer and moved it into position.

The neat thing about Fireworks is that it has always had a "drag-and-drop" relationship with Flash. We opened a new Flash document and, from the open Fireworks document, dragged the two layers onto the Flash stage. We put both images on separate layers and aligned them so they looked like one image.

The next step was to create a new movie clip and put an FLVPlayback component into it. The component was linked to the FLV file, the skin was set to None, and we turned off the Auto rewind property.

With the video handled, we added a layer between the two image layers and placed the video movie clip in that layer. We then selected the Autotransform tool and resized the animation. The stage, when we finished, resembled that shown in Figure 6-12.

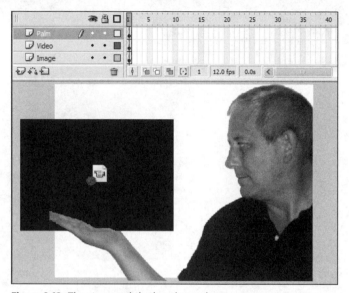

Figure 6-12. The stage and the layering order

> The FLVPlayback component is not exactly Autotransform tool–friendly. If you must scale the component, do what we did and place it in a movie clip.

You are looking at that image and probably wondering whether the end result will be another cheesy Flash project. Not quite. Remember, the video has an alpha channel, meaning the author's thumb, which is behind the component, will be visible when the video plays (see Figure 6-13).

> You can find the Flash and FLV files for this project in the Chapter 6 Completed folder. They are in the Fire_Smoke folder.

Now that you understand how to create a basic fire with corresponding smoke, let's put it to practical use and create a banner ad.

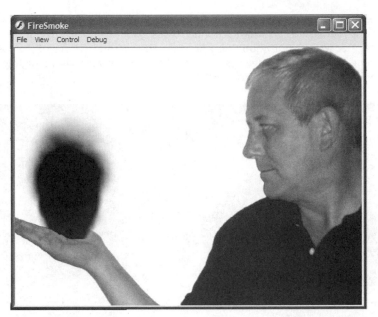

Figure 6-13. How to do a simple "magic trick"

Entering the inferno

Let's face it, the abyss, the netherworld or even hell are rather dark and forbidding places. Whether it be Dante writing about hell in the mid-fourteenth century or Stephen King or David Eddings writing about it in the twentieth century, the visions tend to include smoke and fire. The authors, intrigued with this concept, started playing "What if . . ." games that resulted with this exercise springing out of this scenario: "What if a Flash banner ad were to give the user the choice of visiting heaven or hell?"

The result is the `Banner06.swf` file found in the `BannerAd` folder inside the Chapter 6 `Completed\Fire_Smoke` folder. We are not going to provide you with a complete step-by-step tutorial here simply because it would be nothing more than a rehash of a lot of the techniques presented to this point in the book. Instead we are going to walk you through the techniques used to create the abyss in the piece.

> *Before we proceed, there are a couple of things about the project that need to be addressed. The first is the final file size of the banner is a bit bigger than the traditional 30K limit imposed on banner ads. This is due to our using the FLVPlayback component. Replace it with a video object from the Library, and the resulting SWF file will roll in at under 10K. Why did we use the component? Like we said in the previous chapter, we are "lazy." The second thing is all of the files used to create the banner are found in the* BannerAd *folder.*

If you open the hell.aep file, you first notice the piece was assembled using a series of compositions that all interact with each other (see Figure 6-14). The edge of the abyss is a simple image drawn in Photoshop CS2 and added to the bottom layer of the main Comp named Scene Hell. The fire is a series of four solids, each of which has a slightly different application of the CC Particle World effect.

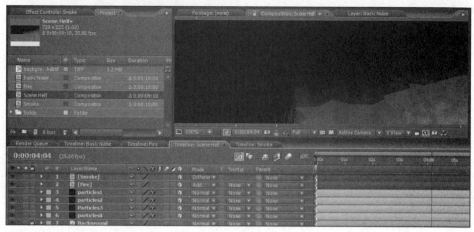

Figure 6-14. The main timeline for the Scene Hell comp

The reason we went with the CC Particle World effect is because fires usually have embers that spiral upwards out of the flames. In the case of this animation, we wanted stuff to shoot out of the cauldron and then fall back into it.

The CC Particle World effect is a bit more robust than the CC Particle Systems II effect in that it introduces a Z-axis to the animation, which means it works in a 3D space. If you select the Particle1 layer and open the Effect Controls panel, you will see how the flames were created (see Figure 6-15).

The important aspect of Figure 6-15 is the grid. It gives you a good idea of how the particles will interact with the Photoshop image. If you do use the grid in this effect, be sure to turn it off before you render the project. If you don't, the cube and the mesh will also be rendered, and you don't need that aggravation.

The remaining three solids are all variations of that first one. The main difference is the Birth Rate for the particles is different. The final tweak was to pull the opacity of each of the solid layers back to 40%. The reason is we wanted subtlety as opposed to an "in-your-face" approach to the effect.

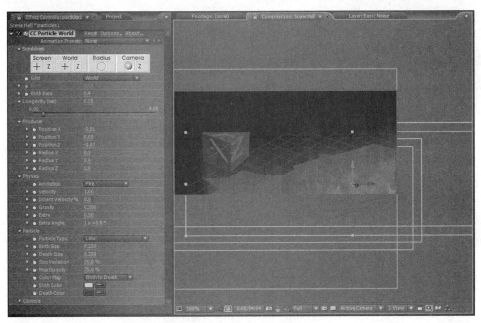

Figure 6-15. Using the CC Particle World effect to create flames

The actual fire effect started with the creation of a new Comp named Basic Noise. If you double-click the Comp in the Project window, you will see that it is composed of two black solids. The Basic Noise solid is what will give the flames their "roiling" action. The first solid is rather large—1400×500 pixels—because it will be put in motion across the screen. The actual "roiling" will be achieved through the Fractal Noise effect—Effects & Presets ➤ Noise & Grain ➤ Fractal Noise—which was dragged onto the solid. The Fractal Noise settings, shown in Figure 6-15, will be used to create to the roiling flames. The layer was then made to move in a gentle undulating motion as shown in Figure 6-16.

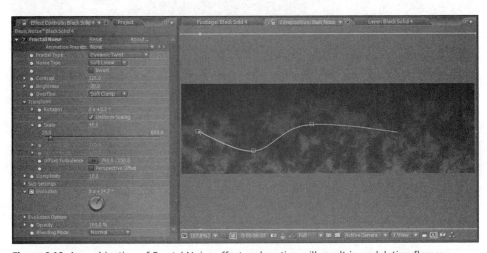

Figure 6-16. A combination of Fractal Noise effect and motion will result in undulating flames.

The other factor contributing to the motion is the Evolution property of the Fractal Noise effect. If you twirl it down in the timeline, you will see keyframes at the start and end of the timeline and that the evolution value for the last keyframe has changed from 0 x +0.0 degrees to 10 x +0.0 degrees. This causes the "noise" in the Comp to change its shape.

The next solid simply has a Ramp effect added to it, and the only change to it is changing the Blend with original property to 60%. This has the effect of adding a gradient mask to the effect, meaning the image fades from the bottom upwards.

Having created the basic effect, we can turn our attention to creating the Smoke and the Fire Comps.

These two are nothing more than further manipulations of the Basic Noise Comp. When the Smoke Comp was created, we added the Basic Noise Comp to a layer in the timeline. A Warp effect from the Distort folder was applied to this layer, and the properties of the effect were changed to give the fractal more of an up-and-down look. The layer was duplicated, and the only change to this layer was that its blend mode was set to Screen.

Having designed the flames, it was time to make them look like flames or some sort of lava. We added a new Adjustment layer to the Fire Comp and applied the Colorama effect to that layer. Adjustment layers are rather neat. Add one to the timeline, and any layers below it will be affected. The Colorama effect, found in Effects & Presets ➤ Color Correction, assigns a custom palette to an element in a layer and then cycles the palette. First you colorize an image with a specified palette, and then you cycle the colors in that palette— that is, change them smoothly around the Output Cycle palette or color wheel shown in Figure 6-17. This is how we got the flames or lava. Add the effect to the Adjustment layer, and the two Basic Noise layers beneath it have the color cycle through them.

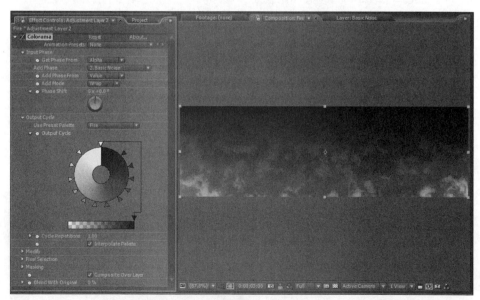

Figure 6-17. Colorama, applied to an Adjustment layer

The Smoke Comp is essentially the same as the Fire Comp with a couple differences. Rather than applying the Colorama effect, we applied the Minimax effect found in Effects & Presets ➤ Channel. The Minimax effect enlarges or reduces a matte for a specific channel or all channels. It assigns each pixel the minimum or maximum pixel value found within a specified radius. This explains why we applied this effect to the red channel and let it go out 8 pixels to increase the effect. This gave us a rather blotchy look, so we also applied the Fast Blur effect to the layer and the end result, shown in Figure 6-18, was "smoke wisps" that grow upwards.

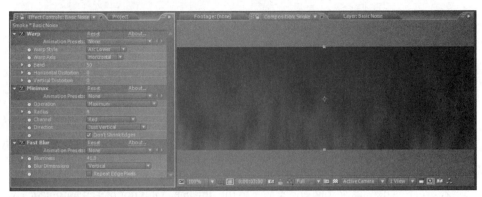

Figure 6-18. Another way of creating smoke

These two Comps were dragged onto the timeline and a mask applied in each one that would hide the edges of the layer. The final step was to apply a 3D layer by clicking the 3D switch in the timeline to all of the layers except the background image.

We rendered out the project using the Animation codec and linked the resulting FLV file to the FLVPlayback component. The final result, shown in Figure 6-19, is an exercise in sinister contrasts.

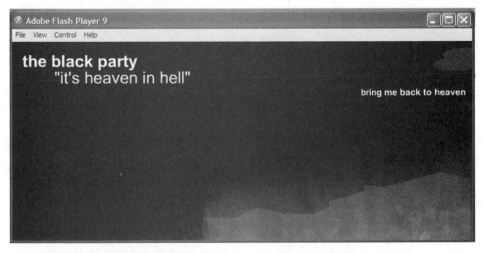

Figure 6-19. The final project in the Flash Player

Beware of the Blob

When we started thinking about the exercise in this section, we couldn't help but recall the 1958 horror flick named *The Blob*, and the heading for this section is the name of the Burt Bacharach theme song for the movie. The great thing about blobs is they can be either really gross looking or engaging. We are going to avoid the gross because we know, once you discover how it is done, that you will create your own gross versions of the one from this exercise.

In this exercise you are going to produce an animation of green blobs that appear on the stage. From there you are going to move over to Flash and explore how Flash content interacts with "blob" content. Let's create some blobs:

1. Launch After Effects and create a new Comp with the following settings:
   - Composition Name: Blob
   - Preset: Web Video, 320✕ 240
   - Pixel Aspect Ratio: Square Pixels
   - Frame Rate: 30
   - Duration: 0:00:10:00

2. Create a new black solid and drag it to the timeline, if it is not placed automatically. The blobs will be created using this solid and three filters.

3. Open Effects & Presets ➤ Generate and drag a copy of the Ramp effect onto the solid. In the Effect Controls panel, use these settings:
   - Start of Ramp: 159, 120 which are the X and Y coordinates for the start of the gradient
   - Start Color: #606060 (medium gray)
   - End of Ramp: 322, 293 which are the X and Y coordinates for the end of the gradient
   - End Color: #B7B7B7 (light gray)

The Ramp effect will be used in the same manner as an opacity mask is used in Fireworks or Photoshop. The nature of the Ramp effect is that it creates a color gradient that blends it with the original image contents—in this case, a series of blobs.

The next step is to create the blobs.

4. Open Effects & Presets ➤ Simulation and drag a copy of the CC Mr Mercury effect onto the solid. You may be looking at the Comp window and wondering, "OK, guys, where are my blobs?" The center point, or crosshairs, in the Comp window is the origin for the march of the blobs, and, if you scrub the timeline as shown in Figure 6-20, you will see gray blobs flooding out of that point. As you may have guessed, the effect simulates liquid mercury.

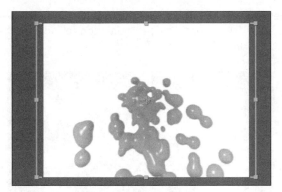

Figure 6-20. The blobs are on the march.

5. Twirl down the CC Mr Mercury settings in the Effect Controls panel and specify these values:

- X Radius: 57. The blobs move around the X-axis.

- Y Radius: 34. The blobs twirl around the Y-axis.

- Producer: 210,45. This is the point where the blobs will be growing out of the Comp. If you scrub through the values, you will see the blobs move up or down the screen.

- Animation: Twirl. The value in this pull-down determines how the blobs will move when they appear.

- Influence Map: Blob in & out. The choices in this pull-down allow you to determine how fat or how thin the blobs will be.

6. Twirl down the Light settings in the effect and specify these values:

- Intensity: 155. This defines how bright a light will shine on the blobs.

- Light Type: Point Light. This choice is similar to a focused spotlight.

- Position: 35,134. These two coordinates tell the effect where, on the Comp, the light will be pointing. You can also move this around by clicking the crosshairs in the effect and dragging them around the Comp.

7. Twirl down the Shading settings in the effect and specify these values:

- Ambient: 18. The blobs get really dark because the amount of "extra" light is low.

- Diffuse: 34

- Specular: 38

6

Adding those values makes the blobs look a little more real (see Figure 6-21). If you press the spacebar and wait a few seconds for the animation to move into RAM, you can see how the blobs wiggle around the screen.

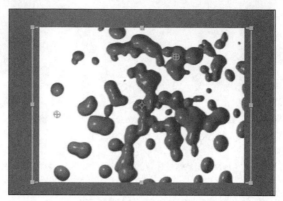

Figure 6-21. The blobs look a lot more real.

Obviously, there is something missing. The blobs look interesting, but they look like pieces of wiggling plastic. Let's give them some color:

8. Twirl down Effects & Presets ➤ Color Correction and drag the Colorama effect onto the Comp.

Holy smokes! The blobs look like mutant microbes under a microscope! In the previous exercise, we talked about the Colorama effect but didn't give you a chance to take it for a test drive. Remember, this effect adds color to anything it is added to, and what you are looking at are the default values for the effect. Let's turn the blobs a classic green color:

9. Twirl down the Colorama Output cycle in the Effect Controls panel. You will see a color wheel with a bunch of Color chips surrounding it. You really only need two colors: a bright green and a black.

10. Drag all of the color triangles, except for the green and the yellow colors, away from the wheel and release the mouse. This will remove those colors.

11. Double-click the yellow triangle to open the Color Picker. Select black and click OK. Drag the black triangle on top of the green triangle. The colors will revolve counterclockwise from green to black (see Figure 6-22), and the blobs take on a green color.

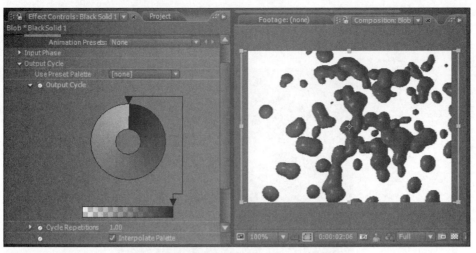

Figure 6-22. The blobs now have some color thanks to the Colorama effect.

12. To give the blobs a bit more of a "sinister" look, select Composition ➤ Background Color and set the background color to black.

In the original 1958 movie, little blobs combined to form one big blob and split apart again. You're going to make your blobs do the same. Here's how:

1. Open the timeline and twirl down the CC Mr. Mercury effect.

2. Drag the playback head to the 7-second mark on the timeline and add a keyframe to the Producer property. Change the Producer values to 210, 74.

3. Drag the playback head to the 8-second mark on the timeline and change the Producer values to 210, 970.

4. Scroll down to the Blob Death Size property. Add a keyframe. To grow the blob, add keyframes at the times shown and change the Blob Death Size property to the values given as well:

- 0:00:04:15: .75.
- 0:00:05:00: 7.89.
- 0:00:05:00: Add a keyframe.
- 0:00:06:15: .75.

If you scrub through the timeline, you will see the blobs coalesce into one big blob, as shown in Figure 6-23, and then split apart into the smaller blobs. At this point, you can save the project and render the video out using the QuickTime Animation codec.

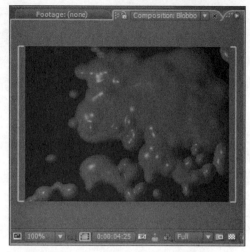

Figure 6-23. One great big, glowing, growing blob

Now that you have a QuickTime video, run it through the Flash 8 Video Encoder and use these settings:

- Output filename: Blob
- Video codec: ON2VP6
- Frame rate: 15
- Quality: Custom
- Max data rate: 275

With an FLV file waiting to be used, you'll now see what you can do with some blobs in Flash Professional 8:

1. Launch Flash Professional 8, and when the application opens, create a new document that is 320X240 and set the stage color to black.

2. Create two new layers on the timeline. From the bottom up, name the layers Video, Text, and Actions.

3. Open the Library and create a new video object. Drag it to the stage and give it the following values in the Property inspector:

   - Width: 320
   - Height: 240
   - X and Y positions: 0
   - Instance name: myVideo

   When you are finished, lock the layer.

4. Click the first frame in the Text layer, select the Text tool, and enter the following text: Beware of the Blob. Select the text and give it the following properties:

- Font: Arial or a font of your choosing
- Size: 30 pt
- Style: Bold
- Color: #FFFF00 (yellow)
- Type: Static

5. Click the text block on the stage and convert it to a movie clip.

6. Click once in the first frame of the Actions layer on the main timeline, open the ActionScript Editor, and add the following code:

```
var nc:NetConnection = new NetConnection;
nc.connect(null);
var ns:NetStream = new NetStream(nc);
myVideo.attachVideo(ns);
ns.play("Blob.flv");
```

The assets are in place, and, if you test the movie, you will see the text sitting over the blobs as they ooze across the stage. Interesting but, let's admit it, gosh is it boring. Let's jazz it up and have the text block interact with the blobs.

7. Select the text block and, in the Blend pull-down in the Property inspector, select Overlay. If you test the movie, the text, as shown in Figure 6-24, loses it yellow color and seems to run over the blobs as they move around the stage.

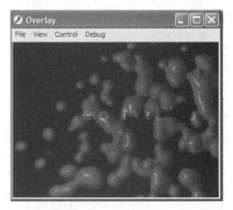

Figure 6-24. The text in Flash is interacting with the blobs from After Effects.

New to Flash Professional 8 are the blend modes. If you are a Photoshop or Fireworks user, these modes aren't exactly new, but their addition opens up a world of possibilities for the Flash designer. The blend mode we chose—Overlay—multiplies or screens the colors, depending on the base color, which, in this case, is the black background and the green in the blobs. Patterns or colors overlay existing pixels while preserving the highlights and shadows of the base color. The base color is not replaced—but is mixed with the blend color to reflect the relative lightness or darkness of the original color. This explains how the blobs retain their shape, color, and highlights while the text seems to slide "over" each blob.

Lights and flares

One aspect of After Effects that never ceases to amaze us is how we can do so much with so little. In this exercise, you will use one line of text, an Adjustment layer, and a solid to create a rather eye-catching "stinger" for this book.

1. Open the Lights&Flares.aep file in the Chapter 6 Exercise folder. When the project opens, you will see that all we have supplied you with are a Comp named RaysBlue, one solid layer, and one Adjustment layer.

2. Create a new Comp using these settings:
   - Composition Name: RaysRed
   - Width: 320
   - Height: 240
   - Pixel Aspect Ratio: Square Pixels
   - Frame Rate: 30
   - Duration: 0:00:10:00

   Click OK to close the dialog box.

3. When the RaysRed Comp opens, drag a copy of Black Solid 1 to the timeline. With the basic work done, the time has arrived to "jazz up" this layer.

4. Twirl down the Noise & Gain effect folder and drag a copy of the Fractal Noise effect onto the Comp. When you release the mouse, you will see what looks like a bunch of gray clouds. Let's fix this.

5. Open the Effect Controls panel and reduce the Brightness property to -50%.

Next, you want the "clouds" to become lines. Here's how:

6. Twirl down the effect's Transform property, deselect Uniform Scaling, and use these settings:
   - Scale Width: 15%
   - Scale Height: 5000%

> You may have noticed the sliders don't permit those values. The neat thing about After Effects is you can easily step outside of the edge of the "envelope." Double-click each of the existing values and enter the values given.

The Fractal Noise effect, once you enter these values, becomes a series of lines (see Figure 6-25) and not the "clouds" you started with.

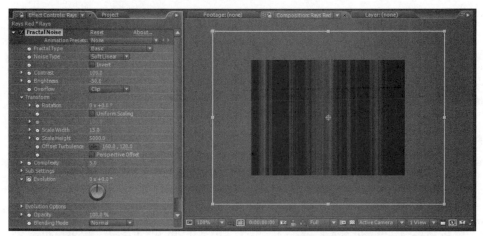

Figure 6-25. Using the Fractal Noise properties to change the look of the clouds in the solid.

Gray streaks are interesting, but they should have some color. Follow these steps to add some color:

1. Twirl down the Stylize presets and drag a copy of the Glow effect onto the Comp.

The Glow effect finds the brighter parts of an image and then brightens those and the surrounding pixels to create a diffuse, glowing look to the area affected. You can also use the effect to simulate overexposure of brightly lit objects. As well, you can base the glow on either the original colors of the image or its alpha channel. Right now, you aren't seeing much of a glow because there are really only two colors, black and white, in the image. Let's change that right now.

2. Twirl down the Glow filter in the Effect Controls panel and specify these values:

- Glow Threshold: 21.6
- Glow Radius: 24
- Glow Intensity: 3
- Glow Colors: A & B Colors

Notice that the bars really become quite distinct and almost have a fabric-like look to them.

3. Double-click the Color chip in the Color A property and change the color to #FFFF00 (yellow). The whites in the Comp are now yellow.

4. Double-click the Color chip in the Color B property and change the color to #FF0000 (red). The pattern takes on a brownish hue.

The Comp changes to almost look like a set of brownish curtains on a theater stage (see Figure 6-26). One more tweak and this Comp is just about ready for prime time.

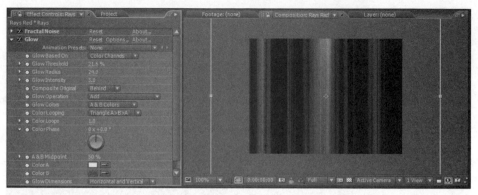

Figure 6-26. Adding a glow makes the lines look like stage curtains.

5. Drag a copy of the Polar Coordinates effect from the Distort folder onto the Comp. In the Type of Conversion pull-down in the Effect Controls panel, change the setting from Rect to Polar to Polar to Rect.

The Polar Coordinates *effect distorts a layer by transposing each pixel in the layer's (X,Y) coordinate system to the corresponding position in the polar coordinate system, or the reverse. The effect, in many respects, can be equated to taking an image, or solid in this case, and wrapping it around a cone. To see what we are talking about, drag the interpolation slider in the* Effect Controls *panel.*

Now that you have your solid in place, you'll put it to work.

1. In the timeline, twirl down the Fractal Noise effect. Press the Home key to scoot the playback head to the starting point of the timeline and add a keyframe in the Evolution property. Drag the playback head to the end point of the timeline and change the Evolution property to -5, 0.0 degrees. The -5 means the effect will move counterclockwise through the solid five times. If you scrub the timeline, you will see the colors move from right to left.

2. In the timeline, twirl down the Transform properties, return the playback head to the start point, turn on Uniform Scaling, and change the Scale value to 150%.

3. Click the stopwatch to add a keyframe in the Rotation property. Scrub to the end of the timeline and set the rotate value to 1, 0.0 degrees.

4. Scrub through the timeline and you will see the solid rotates once in a clockwise direction, and, as it rotates, the colors move through the solid (see Figure 6-27).

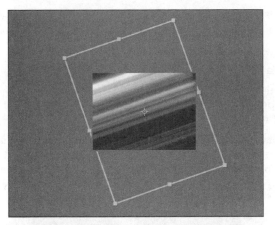

Figure 6-27. Changing the properties in the timeline puts both the Fractal Noise effect and the solid in motion.

Assembling the project

With two Comps created, you can now turn your attention to assembling the project.

1. Create a new Comp and name it Final Comp. Drag a copy of the RaysRed Comp to the timeline and then drag the RaysBlue Comp to the timeline. The RaysRed Comp should be on the bottom layer.

2. Select the Text tool, click once in the Comp window, and enter the text poetry in motion. This will add a new Text layer to the Comp. Change the In and Out points of this layer to 4 seconds and 9 seconds, respectively.

3. Select the text and set the text to 30-point Arial Black or Arial with a Bold style applied. Set the text color to white.

The plan is to have each letter light up, as though a spotlight were shining behind it, as it appears on the stage. Here's how:

4. Click the Selection tool in the Tools panel and click the text once to select it.

5. Twirl down the Generate effects and drag a copy of the CC Light Rays effect onto the text. Add the following values to the effect in the Effect Controls panel:

   - Intensity: 255
   - Radius: 41
   - Warp Softness: 32
   - Shape: Square
   - Transfer Mode: Screen

If you scrub the playback head across the timeline, you won't see anything light up. The reason is the center of the filter needs to be over the letters in the words. Here's how to fix that:

6. Drag the playback head to the In point of the Text layer.

7. In the timeline, twirl down Effects ➤ CC Light Rays and add a keyframe in the Center property. Drag the crosshairs for the effect to a point just to the left of the start of the text.

8. Drag the playback head to the 6-second mark on the timeline and drag the center point to a location just to the right of the last letter in the text block. As you drag the center point of the effect across the text, you will see the text "light up," as shown in Figure 6-28.

Figure 6-28. Lighting up text using the CC Light Rays effect

Now that the light rays are under control, you'll add a mask that reveals each letter in the words as they are lit.

9. Click the Rectangular Mask tool and draw a box over the text that just contains the letter *p*.

10. Drag the playback head to the 4-second mark on the timeline and twirl down Masks ➤ Mask 1 and add a keyframe to the Mask Shape property. Drag the playback head to the 6-second point of the Text layer. Holding down the Shift key, select the two right-corner points of the mask, and drag them until the words in the phrase are revealed. If you scrub across the text block, you will see the text appear, letter by letter, in the Comp window.

11. Finally, twirl down Transform ➤ Opacity. Drag the playback head to the 8-second mark on the timeline and add a keyframe. Drag the playback head to the 0:00:08:09 mark on the timeline and change the Opacity value to 0.

12. Select the RaysBlue layer, press the T key to open the Opacity properties, and add a keyframe at the 6.5-second mark. Drag the playback head to the 7-second mark and set the Opacity value to 0.

13. The RaysRed layer is going to be treated a bit differently. Select the RaysRed layer and press the S key to open the Scale properties. Drag the playback head to the 4-second mark and add a keyframe. Drag the playback head to the 5-second mark and change the Scale value to 1024, 1024.

14. With the RaysRed layer still selected, press the T key to open the Opacity properties. Add a keyframe at the 9-second mark. Drag the playback head to the 9.5-second mark and change the Opacity value to 0.

15. That finishes the layer. Twirl up the Text layer and do a RAM preview. The interplay of the solids and the CC Light Rays filter on the text, as shown in Figure 6-29, is quite striking.

Figure 6-29. The project so far

Some final "jazz"

We could stop here, but there is one final effect that will really make this project "pop."

1. Drag the Adjustment layer from the Solids folder to the timeline and place it under the Text layer.

2. With the Adjustment layer selected, drag a Lens Flare effect from Effects & Presets ➤ Generate onto the Comp window.

3. Use the following Lens Flare values in the Effect Controls panel:

- Flare Brightness: 117
- Lens Type: 105 mm Prime

4. Drag the lens flare's crosshairs in the Comp window to the middle of the Comp.

5. On the timeline, twirl down Lens Flare ➤ Effects ➤ Lens Flare. Drag the playback head to the 4-second mark on the timeline, add a keyframe in the Flare Center property, and set the center point of the effect to 0.0, 118.0. Drag the playback head to the 5-second mark and drag the flare's center point to the bottom-right corner of the Comp.

6. With the playback head still at the 5-second mark, add a keyframe to the Blend with Original property. Move the playback head to the 5.5-second mark and change the Blend with Original value to 100%.

7. Save the project and do a RAM preview. The addition of the Lens Flare effect, as shown in Figure 6-30, really does add some extra "bling" to this project.

Figure 6-30. The finalized project

A halftime break

This marks the halfway point of the book and of our dragon hunt. Let's head back to the locker room and take a break.

We suspect that, up to this point, you may either be a little overwhelmed with what you have done so far or you are starting to understand that there is more to the integration between Flash and After Effects than you had originally thought. This is understandable because, up until the start of 2006, Adobe and Macromedia were competitors. Adobe had After Effects. Macromedia had Flash. That was the reality of the market, and both apps essentially stayed within their solitudes.

With the merger of Adobe and Macromedia, those solitudes were shattered, and Flash developers started discovering that video was now an integral part of their development efforts. When Production Studio was released, the video and audio applications had a new best friend included in the installation CDs: Flash Professional 8. The upshot, as we said earlier in this chapter, was the lines between what is Flash and what is video on the Flash stage have been erased.

That's a rather radical statement, especially this early in the game, but rather than make the statement and move on, we asked a couple of our colleagues to participate in what turned out to be a rather fun challenge.

The challenge was this:

See what you can come up with in Flash using only a supplied FLV file, which was created using the default mode of the CC Particle Systems II *effect. The only rule was the video had to have no controls. It had to be played on the Flash stage and interact with the content on the stage.*

The results surprised even us.

> *All of the files, both the FLA and the SWF files for each project, can be found in the* Challenger *folder in the Chapter 6* Completed *file.*

First up was one of the authors, Tom Green. He has been doing a few training courses for FlashintheCan, and the image they used to promote the courses was a tight, grayscale crop of his eyes and glasses from his "Head and Shoulders" photo. His friends and students have been gently ribbing him about this photo, shown in Figure 6-31, claiming he looked even more sinister than normal.

Figure 6-31. Sinister? Nah!

Tom took this to heart and made it the theme of his project. He opened the image in Fireworks 8, zoomed in on the pupils of his eyes, and, using the Lasso tool, selected them, cut them out of the image, and then pasted them back into place. He then opened a new Flash document and dragged the image layer and the eyeballs layer from Fireworks to the Flash stage.

> *If you have never considered Fireworks as being an industrial-strength Flash imaging tool, think again. When you drag an image from Fireworks into Flash, it hits the Flash stage as a bitmap but, in the Flash Library, it arrives as a movie clip. To quote many a "Flasher": How cool is that?*

The layers were arranged and a video object pointing to the FLV file was placed into a movie clip. The movie clip was placed and resized under the face layer and keyframes were used to remove the pupils from his eyes. When the video plays, he looks normal, but a couple of seconds into the animation, his eyes light up as shown in Figure 6-32.

Figure 6-32. Now that is sinister.

Next up was David Stiller.

David Stiller—www.quip.net—is a partner at CommunityMX, runs his own multimedia development business, and, apart from being a Flash pro, also has a wicked sense of humor. David didn't even think twice when we floated the challenge by him, and his submission had us roaring with laughter.

Using a "JibJab" animation approach where parts of a bitmap are animated, Dave's submission is a great example of not being able to tell what is Flash and what is video. Dave took one look at the FLV file and instantly knew how it would fit into the project. We'll give you a hint: the file, shown in Figure 6-33, is named badhaircut.fla.

Figure 6-33. Preparing for a bad hair cut

Using a clever combination of tweens and short, embedded audio tracks, David managed to use the video in a manner that fits seamlessly into the Flash movie. The last thing we expected was to see a particle shower used as a metaphor for hair tonic gone wrong (see Figure 6-34).

Figure 6-34.
Now that really is bad hair.

Next up is Joseph Balderson who, under the moniker of "Joeflash," you met in Chapter 3. He showed you how to treat an FLV animation as a preloader for a Flash movie. In his submission, Joe sat on his balcony one evening, stared out at the stars, and got his inspiration.

When you ask Joe to get involved in something, you can expect it to be something you never would have considered in the first place. His project, shown in Figure 6-35, treats the FLV file as a comet. Of course, it isn't just a comet. There is a twist.

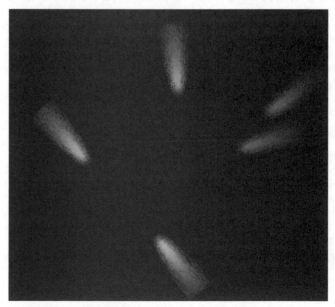

Figure 6-35. Comets in space

If you open the FLA file, you will see that Joe's approach is radically different from David's. The whole project is code driven. The comets are created on the fly, and they swarm around the mouse as you drag it around the screen. The neat thing about this one is it is interactive. Click the SWF animation once, and you can use the keyboard—press the spacebar—to add comets or press the X key to remove them.

Eerie eyeballs. Bad haircuts. Comets in space. They are nothing more than three simple treatments of an FLV video.

We think you now understand what we are getting at. Up until the introduction of Flash 8 and its video tools, video in Flash was just that: *video in Flash*. The projects shown demonstrate that observation is no longer valid. Video is now just another item on the Flash stage. Best of all, many of the advanced-level effects that are commonly done with rather extensive ActionScript driving them are now available to you, in many cases, at the click of an After Effects button.

Summary

OK, break's over, time to get back to work. Before we move on to the next chapter in the dragon hunt, let's review what you did in this chapter.

You started slowly by reviewing how to create drop shadows using After Effects, Flash filters, and even ActionScript to add the shadow and blend effect. From there you learned how to create smoke and fire using the CC Particle Systems II effect in After Effects. We then showed you how to set someone's hand on fire using the effect in Flash. From there you descended to the depths of the inferno. You saw how to create a Flash banner ad that includes an FLV file that takes you right to the edge of the abyss. This one used nothing more than a Photoshop image and a couple of solids and filters to create the illusion of roiling flames or lava.

The next technique appealed to the kid in all of us. You discovered how to make rather gross green blobs that slithered across the screen (using CC Mr Mercury), coalesced into one big blob, and then split apart yet again. We then showed you how to add text to this effect, in Flash, using the Overlay blend mode that caused the text to interact with the squirming green blobs.

The final effect showed you how to create a rather compelling animation using nothing more than a piece of text, one solid, and an Adjustment layer. Through a combination of filters and animation, you created an eye-catching animation of consisting of color and light.

The chapter finished with your heading for the locker room. The pep talk consisted of us reviewing a challenge that sprung out of this chapter. Convinced the lines between Flash and video are being erased, we asked a couple of associates to use an FLV file created from the default values for the CC Particle Systems II effect. The results were quite surprising and, hopefully, inspiring.

In the next chapter, you will really put text into motion and generally create mayhem as you get it to wiggle, jiggle, and move text around the stage. Should be fun. See you on the playing field.

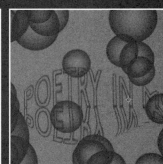

To this point in the book, we have treated text with a degree of reverence. Text has been both readable and legible and has pretty much been treated more as a communication element than a design element. In this chapter, we take text and make it shake, wiggle, jiggle, and otherwise bounce around the screen. In many respects, the treatment of text in this chapter reverses the order. Text starts as a design element and then comes to rest as a communication element.

Though we have covered the basics of working with text, this chapter digs even deeper into what you can do, including putting text on a path. Once you have those basic skills in place, we are going to "kick out the jams" and show you how to use text animators to add a rather high degree of control over the text put into motion. This will also include the use of range selectors, shapes, and one of the more fascinating tools in the arsenal: a Wiggly Selector that randomizes the properties that apply to the text.

This chapter consists of a number of rather interesting text effects that you can apply to your Flash projects. Each example in this chapter presents a specific effect or combination of effects you can use in your Flash efforts. They are in no way to be regarded as the definitive ways of accomplishing the effects we demonstrate. Instead, use the examples presented in this chapter as a creative spark.

Reviewing the After Effects and Flash text tools

Though Flash and After Effects have remarkably similar text capabilities, there are some major differences between them.

The After Effects Text panel (see Figure 7-1) is quite similar to the ones found in Photoshop or Illustrator, and it offers you a greater degree over the control of the appearance of the text than you have in Flash. One interesting aspect of the text controls in After Effects is that you can apply a variety of fonts and settings to the text in a text block. The thing is, you run the very real risk of making a mess of the block. If this happens to you, select the text block and choose Reset Character in the Character panel's Options pull-down.

The Flash text tools, shown in Figure 7-2, become visible in the Property inspector when you select the Text tool. The difference between the panel in Flash and its After Effects counterpart is how text is treated in Flash. Being a web tool, Flash can use **static text**, the text you see on the stage, or **dynamic text**, which is text added to a text box using ActionScript. This text can be added from an external source such as an XML document or added in the ActionScript code. Text can also be interactive in that you can assign a link to text that opens a web page when the text is clicked on the Flash stage.

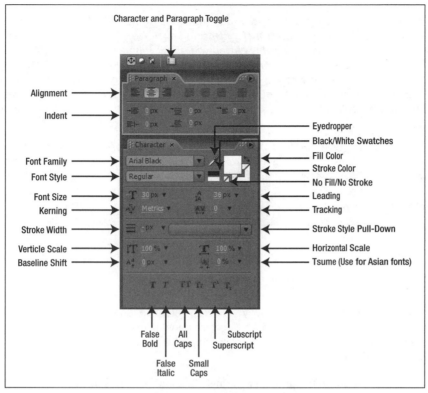

Figure 7-1. The After Effects Character and Paragraph panels. If you don't see them, simply click the Toggle button on the toolbar.

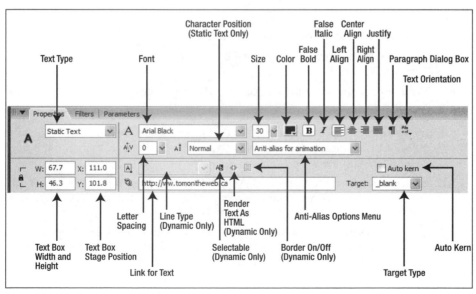

Figure 7-2. The Flash text tools

Dynamic text in Flash has an option not shown in Figure 7-2. When the Text Type *option is set to* Dynamic *in the Property inspector, an* Embed *button will appear beside the* Anti-Aliasing Options *menu. This button will allow you to embed an entire font or selected character from the font into the SWF file. This is a great feature to have available to you in situations where a client's corporate font has to be used. The downside to this is that embedding fonts also increases the final size of the SWF file. If you must embed a font, only embed the characters used. This way the file size increase is not as dramatic.*

What is the False Bold *and* False Italic *terminology that appears in both the Flash and After Effects menus? Essentially what this does is to simply add a stroke around the letters to "mimic" bold text or slant them to imitate italic text. If your font contains such terms as Italic, Oblique, Bold, Heavy, or Extra Bold as part of its name, then use these it in place of clicking the* False Bold *or* False Italic *button.*

Exploding Flash text

In this exercise, we are going to show you how to "blow up" some text on the Flash stage. Though Flash does not have the Effects & Presets panel contained in After Effects, you can still achieve some interesting text effects by simply, as we are fond of saying, "letting the software do the work."

In Flash, text inevitably hits the stage as a single block of text. This makes it rather difficult to scatter letters across the screen. A lesser-known feature of Flash is its ability to convert a complex object into a series of individual objects and then move each of those objects into its own layer. The amazing thing about this is there are really only two steps involved in the process:

- Break the object apart by pressing Ctrl+B (PC) or Cmd+B (Mac).
- Distribute the selected objects to their own layers by selecting Modify ➤ Timeline ➤ Distribute to Layers.

That's all you need to do. Once the objects are in their own layers, they can be animated off the stage in a manner of your choosing. Here's one way:

1. Open ExplodingText.fla in the ExplodingText folder found in the Exercise folder of the Chapter 7 code download. You will note the only things on the stage are an image and the word *Flash*.

2. Select the word on the stage by clicking it. Press the Cmd+B (Mac) or Ctrl+B (PC) keys. The word breaks apart into individual letters. Keep breaking the letters apart until they look like they are filled with pixels.

3. Select each letter on the stage and press the F8 key to convert each one to a symbol. When the Convert to Symbol dialog box opens, name each symbol for the letter selected and select Movie Clip as its type.

> *The Break Apart command converts letters from vectors to individual bitmaps. It is a handy command to know for text because once text is converted to a bitmap, those nasty font substitution issues tend to disappear. That is the good news. The bad news is the text is no longer editable.*

4. With the letters selected, select Modify ➤ Timeline ➤ Distribute to Layers. **The letters will appear on separate layers and, best of all, the layers have the same name as the letter in the layer (see Figure 7-3). Delete the original layer named** Flash **by selecting it and clicking the** Trash Can **in the** Timeline **panel.**

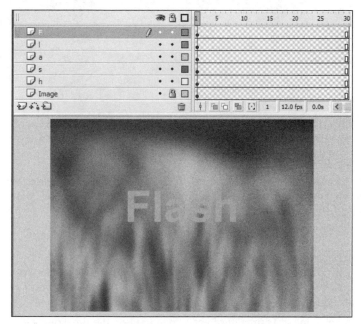

Figure 7-3. Selecting Distribute to Layers places the individual letters on their own layer.

5. Add keyframes at Frames 5 and 15 for each of the new layers. Add a motion tween, starting at Frame 5, between the keyframes just added.

6. Select each letter, starting with the keyframe at Frame 15, and move them into different positions. With each letter selected, choose the Free Transform **tool and** rotate the letter at its new position.

7. Select Modify ➤ Transform ➤ Scale and Rotate and scale each letter to 400% or 500%.

8. Add a keyframe for each layer at Frame 30. Move the letters completely off of the stage in Frame 30, and add a motion tween between Frames 15 and 30 for the layers.

7

9. When finished, drag the playback head to Frame 1 and press the Return/Enter key to start the animation. As shown in Figure 7-4, the letters will "explode" off of the screen.

Figure 7-4. The text seems to have, with apologies to *SCTV*, "blowed up really good."

Now that you have a basic Flash technique in your arsenal, you may be wondering, "That's nice, but surely there must be more I can do with it?" The answer: "Yes, there's a lot you can do with it." Here are a few ideas:

- Apply a blend mode to the clips on the stage. As the letters move, depending on the mode chosen, they will take on different colors.

- Apply a filter to the movie clips. For instance, apply a Bevel filter, and the letters will take on a 3D look. Couple that with a blend mode, and you can have some rather interesting results.

- Add a keyframe at Frame 20 of each animation on the timeline. Select each movie clip in Frame 30 and, in the Color pull-down in the Property inspector, set the alpha value to about 3%. As the letters move off of the stage, they fade out.

- Replace each letter in the movie clips with an FLV file using, say, the letters in the word acting as a mask, in After Effects, for the blobs from the previous chapter. The result is letter-shaped blobs in motion that change color as they move across the stage. Be careful with this one. Scaling up an FLV file is not suggested because of the "hit" on bandwidth. If you must scale, scale down.

Exploding text in After Effects

As you may have guessed by this point in the book, After Effects can do the job of "blowing up" text with a bit more "wow" than that obtainable in Flash. For example, you may want to use exploding text as a preloader for a Flash movie or have it "explode" into pieces when the user rolls the mouse over the text block in Flash.

There are a number of plug-ins that do quite a job in this area, and they range from the simple to use to the complex. Rather than dig into all of them, let's look at one effect—CC Pixel Polly by Cycore—that is quite easy to use and is a good way of figuring out how to use the more advanced effects like Shatter.

> *The Cycore plug-ins are included only with After Effects Professional and require you to install them separately from the application.*

CC Pixel Polly essentially breaks the layer it is being applied to into a series of squares or polygons and sends them spinning into infinity and beyond using a set of rather intuitive controls. Let's blow up some text:

1. Open the *Explode.aep* file in the ExplodingText folder found in your Chapter 7 Exercise folder. You will notice there is nothing more than a line of text in the Comp that is sitting over a black solid.

2. Open Effects & Presets ➤ Simulation and drag a copy of the CC Pixel Polly effect onto the text layer.

3. Do a RAM preview. The text, shown in Figure 7-5, breaks apart and flies off of the screen. Conclusion? The default settings for this effect aren't exactly the best. Let's fix that.

Figure 7-5. Interesting effect, but we can do better.

4. The first thing you may have noticed is the effect kicks off right at the start of the Comp. What if you want the text to explode after one second? If you twirl down the effect on the timeline, you will see there are no keyframes or other visible indicators that show when the effect starts. It starts as soon as the video starts playing.

   To fix this, the first thing to do is to open the Effect Controls panel and delete the effect. With the effect deleted, you have a "clean" text layer to work with. Drag the playback head to the 1-second mark on the timeline and select the Flash Rocks layer. Select Edit ➤ Split Layer and a second text layer appears.

   Set the In point of this new layer to the 1-second mark.

> *If you encounter situations where you need precise timing for an effect,* Split Layer *is the solution. It is also great for those effects, like* CC Pixel Polly*, where the effect starts immediately and you would like to have a bit of a delay.*

5. Select the Flash Rocks 2 layer and reapply CC Pixel Polly to the layer. If you were to do a RAM preview at this point, the text would be rather static and explode at the 1-second mark due to the effect being applied to the Flash Rocks 2 layer.

6. Now for some fun. How about you have the text explode into tiny pieces? Open the Effect Controls panel and specify these settings:

- Force: 150. The higher the number, the greater the "damage."

- Gravity: 0.61. How the pieces move. Higher numbers result in slower movement.

- Spinning: 1 X 150.0 degrees. The pieces will spin around once at an angle of 150 degrees.

- Force Center: 205, 123. Throw a rock through a window, and this is the point where the rock hits the window.

- Direction Randomness: 35%. Things explode outward, and higher randomness numbers will have some pieces appear to cross paths with each other.

- Speed Randomness: 10%. The pieces of the explosion will randomly fly out faster—up to 10% faster—creating a chaotic effect.

- Grid Spacing: 1. This is an imaginary grid that determines the size of the piece. A low number, such as this one, results in a lot of tiles and slower rendering when the file is output. Higher values create bigger chunks.

- Object: Textured Polygon. The choices in this pull-down describe the look of the pieces.

If you do a RAM preview, the text, after a delay of one second, will suddenly explode into a shower of pixels (see Figure 7-6).

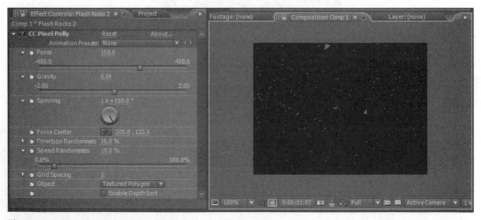

Figure 7-6. Text shattering into pixels

This effect is perfectly suited to situations in Flash where you don't want something to move off of the stage. Having text explode into a shower of pixels is something the viewer isn't expecting and will get his or her attention. Feel free to save this exercise. In the next exercise, we are going to show you how to get rid of an annoying talking head.

> *If you use the sliders for each of the effect's properties, the text on the screen changes to reflect the property setting. One thing you may have noticed is that setting the* Force *value to a negative value results in an implosion. The other thing you may have noticed is changing the* Grid Spacing *value makes the pieces larger. Finally, one drawback to this filter is the pieces all tend to be a uniform size. If you want the pieces to look even more irregular, apply a second version of the effect to the* Flash Rocks 2 *layer and use a different* Grid Spacing *value.*

Ending a video with a bang

It isn't only text that can be blown up. You can make your own version of *The Hitchhiker's Guide to the Galaxy*, or become Marvin the Martian from the *Looney Tunes* cartoons and actually succeed in blowing up the earth or, in the case of this exercise, an annoying talking head. Here's how:

1. Open the BlowUp.aep file found in the BlowUp folder located in the Chapter 7 Exercise folder. When the file opens, you will notice we have placed a copy of the TalkingHead.mov file on the timeline and applied a Keylight filter to the video to remove the green screen.

2. Select the TalkingHead.mov layer and select Edit ➤ Duplicate. This will duplicate the selected layer and put the duplicate in a separate layer on the timeline.

3. Drag the Duration strip of the video in Layer 1 so that its In point is at 0:00:04:00.

4. Drag a copy of the CC Pixel Polly effect onto the video in Layer 1 and specify these settings in the Effect Controls panel:

   - Force: –360
   - Gravity: 0.10
   - Spinning: 3 X 86.0 degrees
   - Force Center: 97.0, 62.5 (right on the tip of his nose)
   - Direction Randomness: 10%
   - Speed Randomness: 6%
   - Grid Spacing: 1
   - Object: Textured Polygon

7

If you do a RAM preview, you will see the talking head explode out into space, thanks to the really large Force value, as a shower of pixels (see Figure 7-7).

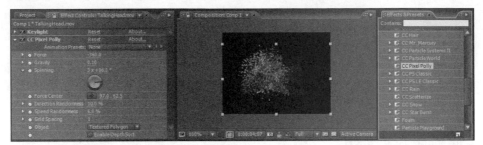

Figure 7-7. That talking head "blowed up real good."

As you may have guessed, using this effect in a Flash movie opens you up to all sorts of possibilities. The bottom line is it really is a great way of ending a video. If you create Flash games, this effect is also handy when objects on the screen need to be destroyed.

Names just flapping in the wind

Sometimes you just need something a little different from words that appear on the Flash screen and move around without your having to do a lot of coding in ActionScript. In this exercise, you will discover one of our favorite effects. It is Turbulent Displace, and it offers you a simple method of distorting a layer—in this case a Text layer, but it could be anything—in a relatively smooth manner that makes text look like it is flapping in the wind. Here's how:

1. Open a new After Effects project and create a new Comp using these settings:
   - Composition Name: Names
   - Width: 400
   - Height: 100
   - Pixel Aspect Ratio: Square Pixels
   - Duration: 0:00:04:00
   - Background Color: #02205C (dark blue)

> *Just a reminder: the background color for a Comp can be changed by selecting* Composition ➤ Background Color.

2. Select the Text tool, click the stage once, and enter your name. Select a font and size in the Character panel. Set the text color to white (#FFFFFF).

3. Open the Effects & Presets panel and twirl down Distort Effects. Drag a copy of the Turbulent Displace effect onto the text.

Like the CC Pixel Polly *effect, the best way of seeing what the various settings do is to open the* Effect Controls *panel and play with each control. The other thing you should do is to drag the center point of the effect across the text. Pay attention to how the text reacts to the center point, which has the official name of* Offset (Turbulence).

Right now the effect doesn't do much other than warp your name. The key to getting things in motion is to animate using the Evolution Options. Follow these steps to have your name flap in the wind:

1. Select the Text layer on the timeline and twirl down the Effects properties. Open the Effect Controls panel by either clicking the Effect Controls tab in the Project panel or pressing the F3 key.

2. Add a keyframe for each property by clicking the stopwatch and then enter the following values for the first frame of the Comp:

   - Displacement: Twist. This is the displacement map that will be used to manipulate the text. These things act in exactly the same manner as a displacement map in Photoshop.

   - Amount: 50. Higher values create more distortion.

   - Size: 176. The radius of the displacement of the text.

   - Complexity: 1.4. This is the detail value for the distortion. Higher values create smoother transitions between the pixels.

   - Evolution: 0 x +45 degrees.

   - Evolution Options: Cycle Evolution

   When you finish, the text should have a noticeable bulge as shown in Figure 7-8.

Figure 7-8. The text is starting to get a bit "turbulent."

3. Drag the playback head to the 2-second mark of the timeline and create keyframes by entering each of the following values:

   - Amount: 22

   - Size: 66

   - Offset Turbulence: 200, 26

   - Complexity: 2.5

   - Evolution: 0 x +113 degrees

   - Cycle (in revolutions): 2

   - Random Seed: 2

7

4. Drag the playback head to the 3-second mark of the timeline and enter the following values:

- Amount: 63
- Size: 162
- Offset Turbulence: 305, 46

5. Drag the playback head to the 4-second mark of the timeline and add a keyframe before entering each of the following values:

- Size: 160
- Offset Turbulence: 392, 71

Do a RAM preview and click the Play button in the Time Controls panel when the preview is completed. Your name should be flapping in the wind (see Figure 7-9).

Figure 7-9. The names are a bit windblown.

Again, this is another one of those effects that is more easily done in After Effects than in Flash. If you need a flag rippling in a breeze for your Flash project and only have a still photo, this effect will work in a pinch.

> *Don't forget, the* Turbulent Displace *effect can be applied to anything in an After Effects layer. That includes video, photos, and line art.*

The infamous "exploding P"

Having blown up the planet and set your name to flapping in the wind, let's look at another simple technique that involves an exploding letter. In certain respects, this one mimics the titling sequence of *Mission Impossible* where a fuse is lit and the text explodes. Though the flame on the fuse part of this exercise can be done in Flash by using a motion guide and a mask, the letter exploding into a series of shards can only be done using After Effects.

1. Open the explodingCap.aep folder in the Exploding Text folder of the Chapter 7 Exercise folder. If you open the Project panel, you will see that we have supplied you with the Comp and two solids that will be used in the project. We have also placed everything on the timeline. Your job is to make that large *P* explode.

2. Turn on the visibility of the Fuse layer and select it in the timeline. The *P* will disappear. Don't worry about it. You are going to fix that right now. Drag a copy of the CC Particle Systems II effect onto the layer. The *P* now appears. As you see in Figure 7-10, the letter is a mask.

Figure 7-10. Use the Pen tool to draw the object that will be used as the fuse.

Obviously a mask simply won't do because the lines won't be visible. As well, the shape we have drawn has to do "double duty." The first is to function as a path for the flame on the fuse, and the second is, as the flame moves along the path, for the line to become visible. For all of this to occur, you will need to use the nodes in the Bezier curve to determine how the flame will move on the path. You do this by using each node on the path as a position location for the effect. In this example, the fuse will be lit at the node at the bottom of the *P*, travel upwards to the node at the top of the *P*, travel around the curve, and end at the node to the left of the point where the lines intersect.

The After Effects Pen tool, as you have seen in Chapter 4, is a wonderful masking tool, but it can also be used as a drawing tool if you apply a stroke to the lines drawn. This is done through the application of the Stroke effect found in the Generate effects folder. The Stroke effect creates a stroke or border around a mask or along a Bezier path you may have drawn. Not only can you apply a stroke, but you can also manage such common stroke properties as stroke color, opacity, and spacing, as well as the characteristics of the brush being used to stroke the path.

3. Twirl down the Generate folder and drag a copy of the Stroke effect onto the Comp.

4. Open the Effect Controls panel, twirl down the Stroke effect, and use the following settings:

- Path: Mask 1. Providing the path is on the same layer as the effect, this will automatically appear.

- Color: #000000 (black). When you choose this color, the line comprising the *P* shape will turn black (see Figure 7-11).

- Brush Hardness: 66%. This will tend to "soften" the line from the default value.

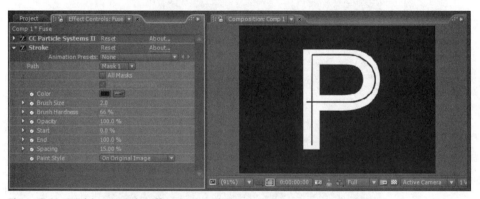

Figure 7-11. Applying a Stroke effect to a mask

5. Rewind the playback head by pressing the Home key. When you are at time 0, twirl down the End property of the Stroke effect and add a keyframe to the timeline. Change the value to 0%. What is going to happen here is that as the flame travels along the path, the path will turn black.

6. Add the following keyframes and end values to finish up:

- 2 seconds: 36.6%

- 3 seconds: 66.6%

- 5:23 seconds: 100%

Now that the path is drawn, you can turn your attention to creating the fire that will travel along the fuse and eventually result in the destruction of the letter in the Exploding P layer of the timeline.

The fire in the fuse, if you recall, is created through the use of the CC Particle Systems II effect that you applied earlier. Here's how:

1. With the Fuse layer selected, twirl down the CC Particle Systems II effect in the Effect Controls panel. Press the Home key to ensure the playback head is at the start of the timeline. For the flame to travel up and around the fuse, you are going to need to set a couple of keyframes and the color of the flame itself.

2. Select the CC Particle Systems II layer, twirl down the Producer, Physics, and Particle properties, and specify the following values:

   - Birth Rate: 1.8.

   - Longevity: 0.2.

   - Position: Add a keyframe and drag the crosshairs to the first node of the object located right at the bottom of the P. Alternatively, you can click the Crosshair button, move the cursor onto the Comp, and click the first node of the P object once. What you are doing here is setting the start position for the effect. It will travel up the P.

   - Radius X, Radius Y: 3.0.

   - Animation: Select Explosive from the pull-down menu.

   - Birth Size: .12.

   - Death Size: .27.

   - Max Opacity: 26%.

3. Drag the playback head to the 2-second mark of the timeline. Click the crosshairs in the Position property and move the cursor to the node at the top off the P. Click once. A keyframe will be added and the flame will move to the node just clicked.

4. Drag the playback head to the 2:08-second mark of the timeline. Click the crosshairs in the Position property and move the cursor to next node of the P. Click once.

5. Drag the playback head to the 2:18-second mark of the timeline. Click the crosshairs in the Position property and move the cursor to next node of the P. Click once.

6. Drag the playback head to the 3:00-second mark of the timeline. Click the crosshairs in the Position property and move the cursor to next node of the P. Click once.

7. Drag the playback head to the 4:00-second mark of the timeline. Click the crosshairs in the Position property and move the cursor to the point where it intersects the ascender of the P. Click once.

8. Drag the playback head to the 6:00-second mark of the timeline. Click the crosshairs in the Position property and move the cursor to the remaining node of the P. Click once. If you scrub the cursor across the timeline, you will see the flame travel along the path (see Figure 7-12), and, as it travels along the path, the path is revealed.

7

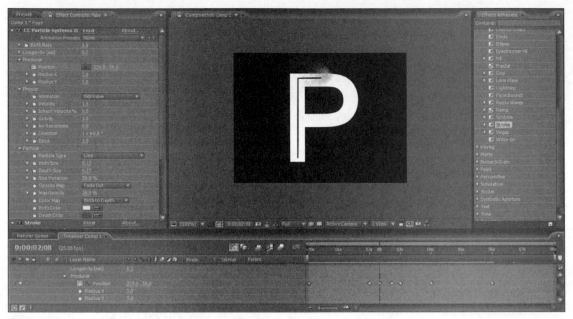

Figure 7-12. Using keyframes to move the flame along the fuse.

You may have noticed that the flame takes about two seconds to move between the last two keyframes. This is deliberate. The flame needs to use that time to grow and for the explosion to occur. Here's how:

1. Twirl down the Birth Rate property of the Particle System effect in the timeline and place the playback head at the 5:15-second mark. Add a keyframe in the Birth Rate property,

2. Place the playback head at the 6-second mark and change the Birth Rate property to 30.0. The flame gets quite a bit larger, and if you scrub the playback head between the keyframes, the flame will grow.

Now that the flame has finished its work, it is time to blow things up.

Earlier in this chapter you used the CC Pixel Polly effect to create some mayhem. In this exercise, you will use a real mayhem-inducing effect that is appropriately named Shatter. This effect, to be a bit technical, divides a layer into a variety of preset shapes or a custom map you can create, extrudes them, and then shoots them spinning off into a 3D space. If you have ever put a hammer through a piece of glass, you have an idea of the result of this effect. This effect is quite complex, and we have no intention of digging into the nuances of using it. For the purposes of this exercise, all you need is for the letter *P* to shatter into a bunch of pieces that will spin off the screen. When the effect is finished, all that will be left is the white solid in the Comp. Let's blow up a letter *P*:

1. Select the Exploding P layer on the timeline and drag the playback head to the 6-second mark, which is the In point of this layer.

2. In the Effects & Presets panel, twirl down the Simulation presets and drag a copy of the Shatter effect onto the Exploding P layer in the timeline. The Comp changes as shown in Figure 7-13.

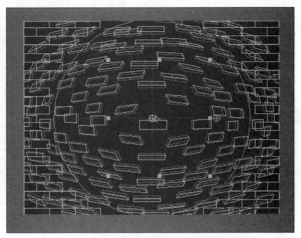

Figure 7-13. The Shatter effect takes a bit of getting used to.

What you are looking at is a wire frame view of the effect. This is quite a bit different from many of the effects you have used to this point in the book and, initially, it takes a bit of getting used to. If you scrub across the layer, you will see the squares in the circle spin out into 3D space, while those outside of the circle remain relatively unaffected. You move the center point, and the handles to change the force and direction of the effect.

3. To see the effect in all of its glory, click the Effect Controls tab and, in the View pull-down menu, select Rendered. The "grid" will disappear, and you will see the letter "shatter" into quite a few pieces as you scrub across the timeline.

4. There are quite a few properties that can be manipulated to create the shatter. Rather than get into each, you are going to make a few changes to the default values in the Effect Controls panel. Twirl down the Shape properties and make the following changes:

- Pattern: Glass
- Repetitions: 11
- Direction: 0 x +18 degrees
- Origin: 130, 180
- Extrusion: .4

What you have done here is to give the pieces that will be created the look of glass shattering, rather than a brick wall exploding outwards (see Figure 7-14). You can see this by simply changing the view to Wireframe Front View + Forces. Repetitions indicates how many times the pieces will be created and Direction indicates the direction, in degrees, the pieces will fly. Origin sets the start location for the effect, and Extrusion sets how thick the pieces created will be.

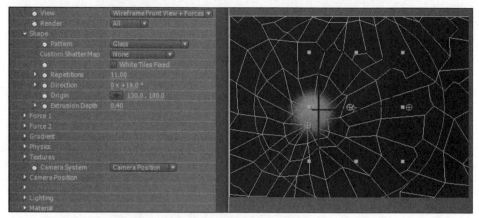

Figure 7-14. The Shape properties are set for the Shatter effect.

5. Twirl down the Force 1 property and change its Position to 131, 171. Twirl down the Force 2 property and change its Position to 140, 167. By changing these two locations, you are determining where the "force" that causes the letter to shatter will originate. These locations are the crosshairs on the Comp.

6. Twirl up the Force properties and twirl down the Physics properties. Make the following changes as shown in Figure 7-15:

- Rotation: .24. This value determines the rotation speed of the tiles.

- Randomness: .9. This specifies how randomly the tiles will fly out from the effect.

- Viscosity: .12. Higher values will cause the tiles to "stick" closer to each other.

- Mass Variance: 21%. This value defines the weight of the larger tiles as compared to the smaller ones.

- Gravity: 3.3. This determines the effect of applying 3G's of force to the objects in motion.

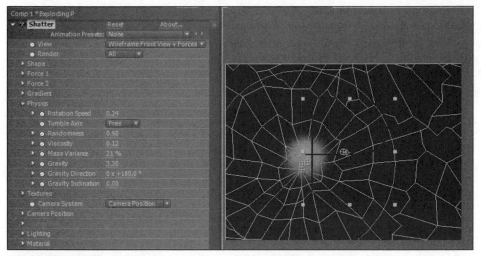

Figure 7-15. The Physics properties have been applied to the effect.

Having applied the Physics properties, the final step is to pay attention to the animation. This effect is a 3D effect, which means you can let the viewer ride through the explosion by changing the ZPosition and Focal Length properties in the Camera Position properties of the effect.

7. Twirl down the Camera Position properties in the timeline.

8. Place the playback head at the 6-second mark and, in the Exploding P layer, add keyframes to the ZPosition and Focal Length properties of the Camera Position property.

9. Move the cursor to the 6:20-second mark of the timeline and make the following changes:

- ZPosition: .13
- Focal Length: 192

10. Do a RAM preview, and you will see the letter explode across the screen (as shown in Figure 7-16).

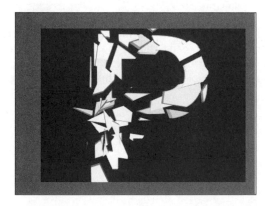

Figure 7-16.
The final animation

As you have seen, this is one powerful effect. Though we have used a rather large Comp size to demo it, you can easily create this effect in a much smaller space and use it to blast stuff out of existence on the Flash stage. Another use would be to apply the effect to an image and, when the user rolls over the image on the Flash stage, the image shatters. Only your imagination limits what you can do with this effect in Flash.

Something's fishy with Illustrator

In this exercise, we are going to turn a phrase into a fish, have it wave its tail, and then move that animation over to Flash. This will involve a slightly different workflow: Illustrator to After Effects to Flash.

The key here is not a "Fish" effect but using the tool best suited for the job at hand. To have text morph into a fish shape and then animate using Flash can be done, but there will be a lot of complex ActionScript and tweening involved. This is not to say it can't be done, but it strikes us that if an effect needed in Flash can be completed in less than an hour in After Effects, then it is the tool for the job at hand.

At its heart, text on the screen is nothing more than a PostScript drawing. Though it may not appear that way, PostScript and TrueType fonts are vectors. In fact, many people who create the fonts we use every day do the actual drawing of the characters in a font using Illustrator CS2. As such, it makes sense to use a vector tool—Illustrator CS2—that converts text to its original PostScript outlines.

1. Open a new document in Illustrator CS2.

2. Select the Type tool, click the page once, and enter the following text: POETRY IN MOTION. Set the text as 36-point Arial.

3. Change to the Selection tool (a quick way of doing this is to press the V key) and click the text.

4. Select Type ➤ Create Outlines—or press Shift+Ctrl+O (PC) or Shift+Cmd+O (Mac)—and the text will become a series of vectors.

5. With the converted text still selected, add a black stroke and remove the fill from the selection.

6. Save the document and quit Illustrator.

At this stage, the text has lost all of its "text" characteristics and is nothing more than a drawing on the screen (see Figure 7-17). You can't change the font or point size, or perform any other formatting tasks you can normally do with text. The advantage to using an outline is, for very short text blocks, you avoid the issue of the user not having the font installed on his or her system.

Text:

POETRY IN MOTION

Outline:

POETRY IN MOTION

Figure 7-17. Text can either be treated as text or be converted to PostScript outlines in Illustrator CS2.

> *If you don't have Illustrator, we have included a separate Illustrator document,* fishType.ai, *in the Chapter 7* Exercise *folder. In case you are curious, the font used and converted to an outline in the* fishType.ai *file is Chantilly. We will be using this document in After Effects, though you can use the one you just created.*
>
> *You can also use Flash to convert text to art. In this case, you would select the text block on the Flash stage and select* Modify ➤ Break Apart. *Once text is broken apart in Flash, it, too, becomes noneditable.*

Let's turn that outline into a fish in After Effects. Here's how:

1. Launch After Effects and import the Illustrator document you just created into the Project panel. Save the project as fishText.aep.

2. Create a new Comp using these settings:

- Composition Name: FishForm
- Width: 400
- Height: 300
- Frame Rate: 30
- Duration: 0:00:15:00

3. Select Composition ➤ Background Color and change the background color to #297699 (blue).

7

4. Drag two copies of the text from the Project panel to the timeline. Select the bottom layer on the timeline, and, using the down arrow key, move the artwork downwards until the top of the text block is just touching the bottom of the text block above it.

5. Select the top-middle handle of the text block you just moved and switch its position with the bottom-middle handle. When you release the mouse, the text will look like a reflection (as shown in Figure 7-18).

Figure 7-18. Text can be "flipped" by simply dragging the top-middle handle to the same position as the bottom-middle handle.

6. Select the layer containing the text reflection and rename the layer Bottom. Rename the other layer Top.

Renaming layers isn't difficult. Select the layer name, either press the Enter (PC) or Return (Mac) key, and then type in the new name.

To give the text its fish shape, you are going to use an effect that smoothly "bends" objects into a variety of shapes: the Bezier Warp effect found in Effects & Presets ➤ Distort. What this tool does is to use tangents and vertices to distort objects. **Tangents** control the curve and bend the object. **Vertices**, when moved, control the shape of the object. When the effect is applied to a layer, tangents are indicated by crosshairs and vertices are indicated by a handle (see Figure 7-19).

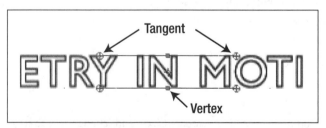

Figure 7-19. Drag a tangent to "bend" the object. Drag a vertex to change its shape.

You can assume from this explanation that the Bezier Warp tool is great for smoothly distorting objects to create such motion effects as turning objects into jiggling jelly or mimicking a flag blowing in the wind. Here's how to turn text into a fish:

1. Drag a copy of the Bezier Warp effect onto each of the objects in the Comp. Press the Home key to return the playback head to the 0 position on the timeline.

2. Select the Bottom layer and press the E key to open the Effects layer. Twirl down the Bezier Warp to open the effect's properties. You are going to change only a couple of them. Before you make the changes, be sure to add a keyframe:

- Top Left Tangent: 104.2, –118.9
- Top Right Tangent: 216.8, 73.7
- Right Top Vertex: 322, –6.3
- Bottom Right Tangent: 214.6, 39.7

3. Select the Top layer, press the E key, and add keyframes and make the following property changes:

- Top Left Tangent: 104.2, –118.9
- Top Right Tangent: 216.8, 73.7
- Right Top Vertex: 322, –6.3
- Bottom Right Tangent: 214.6, 39.7

Once you have made these changes, you will notice how the text, shown in Figure 7-20, takes on the shape of a fish.

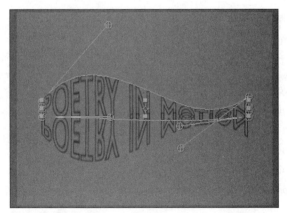

Figure 7-20. The Bezier Warp effect is used to turn text into a fish.

The next step in the process is to get the tail moving up and down. Here's how:

1. Create a new Comp and, when the New Composition dialog box opens, name the Comp FishAnimation and set the duration to 0:00:14:00.

2. Select Composition ➤ Background Color and change the background color to #297699 (blue).

3. Drag the FishForm Comp onto the timeline.

What you are going to do next is to mimic a fish swishing its tail up and down. You create a new Comp using the previous Comp because the "fish" will be regarded as a single object, not two objects, when you apply the next effect. The effect you will be applying is the CC BendIt effect. Here's how to apply and use it:

4. Drag the CC BendIt effect from the `Distort` folder onto the Comp.

When you drop the effect on the Comp, only the middle part of the fish will be visible. This is due to the location of the start and end points—the two sets of crosshairs above and below the fish. The bottom set of crosshairs is the start point and the top set of crosshairs is the end point.

5. Drag the start-point crosshairs to the point where the *P*s are touching—32, 163—at the front of the fish. Move the end-point crosshairs to the end of the fish—365, 165—where the *N*s are touching. Notice how, as you drag the crosshairs, more of the fish is revealed.

6. Open the Effect Controls panel, twirl down the Bend property, and move the slider to the right and to the left. The fish will move its tail up and down.

To see how the start point is the key to movement, drag the start point to the base of the *Y*s and drag the Bend slider. Notice how the front and the back of the fish move using the start point as a pivot. Before moving on to the next step, put the start point back in front of the *P*s.

7. Select the layer and press the E key to open the CC BendIt effect on the timeline. Twirl down the effect. Press the Home key to return to the start of the timeline, select the Bend property, and add a keyframe by clicking the stopwatch.

8. To put the animation in motion, you are going to add a keyframe every 2 seconds and change the Bend value. Use these times and values:

- 2 seconds: −14
- 4 seconds: 8
- 6 seconds: −13
- 8 seconds: 24
- 10 seconds: −8
- 12 seconds: 8
- 14 seconds: −0.6

9. Save the project and scrub through the timeline to see the animation as shown in Figure 7-21.

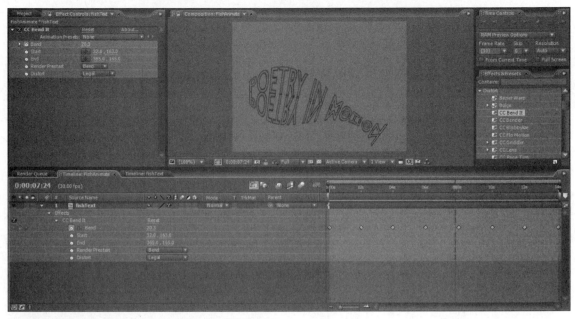

Figure 7-21. The Bend effect is what makes the fish swim.

So far you have created the fish and gotten its tail to swish. From an "eye-candy" point of view, this is interesting, but the fish just sits there. Let's add a bit of jazz to this project by having the text morph into the fish shape and then having the fish start swishing its tail. We will then finish the project by showing you a rather interesting and quick way of adding bubbles to the water.

1. Create a new Comp named TextMorph. Other than changing the name, you won't need to change any of the settings. Click OK to close the dialog box.

2. You aren't going to concern yourself with the background color. Instead, you are going to let a solid handle the duties. Select Layer ➤ New ➤ Solid, and, when the New Solid dialog box opens, name the solid Light Gray Solid 1 and set the color to #C9C9C9. Click OK, and the new solid will be added to the timeline.

3. Place two copies of the fishType.ai file in layers above the solid on the timeline. As you did earlier in this exercise, align them and flip the bottom copy of the text so it looks like a reflection. You don't need to rename these layers.

4. In the timeline, set the Out point for both of the fish layers—Layer1 and Layer 2— to 6 seconds.

5. Select the object in Layer 1 of the timeline and drag a copy of the Bezier Warp effect onto the Comp. Press the E key to reveal the effect and twirl it down to show the Bezier Warp properties. Add keyframes for all of the properties except the Quality property at the bottom.

To "morph" the text into the fish shape, you only need to change the values for a couple of the tangent and vertex properties. These changes will occur at the 6-second mark of the timeline.

6. Make the following changes using the times and values given:

Property	Time (seconds)	Value
Top Left Tangent	6	104.2, −118.9
Top Right Tangent	6	216.8, 73.7
Right Top Vertex	6	322, −6.3
Bottom Right Tangent	6	214.6, 39.7

7. Select the object in Layer 2 of the timeline, apply the Bezier Warp effect to the Comp, and use the same keyframe and property value settings as in the previous step to create the fish shape.

8. Scrub through the timeline, and you will see the text morph into the fish (as shown in Figure 7-22).

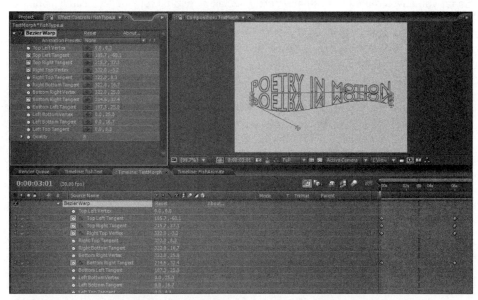

Figure 7-22. Using a Bezier Warp effect to morph an object into a fish shape

9. Twirl up the layer and drag a copy of the FishAnimation Comp to the timeline. Set its In point to the 6-second mark.

If you scrub through the timeline, you will see the words morph into a fish, and then the fish starts swishing its tail. The problem is the FishAnimation Comp has a blue background, but the solid covers it. There are a few ways of dealing with this. The first would be to simply set the Out point of the solid to 6 seconds. The problem with this approach is that the transition between the gray color of the solid and the blue background of the Comp will be far too abrupt. The second would be to place the solid under all of the layers. Another approach is to have the color of the solid change to the blue . . . over time. Here is how you do that:

1. Select the solid in the timeline and open the Effects & Presets panel. Twirl down the Color Correction folder and drag a copy of the Change to Color effect onto the layer in the timeline. Press the E key to open the effect in the timeline and twirl it down to reveal the properties.

2. Press the Home key to return to the start of the animation and add keyframes to the From and To properties of the effect. Also select Hue, Lightness, Saturation from the Change pull-down menu. Making that selection ensures the blue will eventually appear.

The effect doesn't immediately pick up the color of the solid. You need to tell the effect both the starting and the ending colors.

3. With the playback head at the 0 point of the timeline, click the eyedropper in the From property and click the gray color in the solid. Repeat this for the To property as well.

4. Move the playback head to the 3-second mark of the timeline and add keyframes to the To and the From properties. By adding these keyframes, you lock the color picked earlier into place.

5. Move the playback head to the 4-second mark of the timeline, click the Color chip in the To property, and, when the Color Picker opens, set the color to #297699 (blue). Close the Color Picker and scrub across the timeline. Notice how the Change to Color effect gently changes the color of the solid from the original gray to the blue used in the FishAnimate Comp (see Figure 7-23).

7

Figure 7-23. Using the Change to Color effect allows for a smooth transition between colors.

The final step is to add some "context" to the animation. Though the blue color does indicate a fish in water, having some bubbles run through the animation would serve to "seal the deal."

The bubbles are another area where using an effect in After Effects is a real time saver.

Bubbles, depending on how the developer or designer approaches the task, are created in Flash by first creating a movie clip and mimicking a bubble through the use of a circle with a gradient fill. The bubble is then animated either through the use of ActionScript in the movie clip to move it in the direction needed or by having the bubble, through the use of a tween, move along a wavy line that is used as a motion guide. The movie clip is then placed on the stage, and the clip is faded by reducing the movie clip's alpha value. Again, depending on how the movie clip is added to the Flash movie—physically or through the use of ActionScript—depth is added by either physically placing the bubbles on different layers and applying different scale and opacity values or using ActionScript to place the clips at various depths on the screen and using code to manage the scaling and opacity chores. Needless to say, it can be a time-consuming process.

> *If you want an idea of how the pros do it, the friends of ED titles* Flash Math Creativity Second Edition *by David Hirmes et al. (2004),* New Masters of Flash, Volume 3 *by Keith Peters et al. (2004), and* Foundation ActionScript for Flash 8 *by Kristian Besley et al. (2006) present a number of techniques that can easily be adapted to create bubbles using ActionScript in Flash.*

Follow these steps to add some bubbles to the animation:

1. Create a new black solid and add it to the timeline as Layer 1. Set the In point of the solid to the 4-second mark.

2. Open Effects & Presets ➤ Simulation and drag a copy of the CC Bubbles effect onto the solid.

3. Scrub across the timeline and you will see that a mass of black bubbles, as shown in Figure 7-24, rises from the bottom to the top of the Comp.

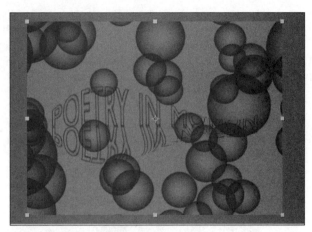

Figure 7-24. Did somebody request bubbles?

Obviously, there is a bit of a problem. First off, unless your fish is swimming in a tar pit, bubbles aren't black. The other problem is there are a lot of bubbles, and, unless there is an air hose under the fish, that isn't natural as well. The solution lies in the CC Bubbles Effect Controls.

If you click the Effect Controls tab, the various bubble properties will appear in the Effect Controls panel. The best way of seeing what each property does is to simply twirl down a property and drag the slider to the right or the left. For example, moving the Bubble Amount slider to the left removes bubbles, and moving it to the right fills the Comp with bubbles. The Speed slider controls how fast the bubbles move up the screen, and the Wobble Frequency and Wobble Amplitude sliders control the path the bubbles take to get from the bottom to the top of the screen.

4. Move the playback head to the 4-second mark on the timeline and specify the following values:

   - Bubble Amount: 68. This defines how many bubbles are created each second.

   - Bubble Speed: 0.9. Higher values make the bubbles move upward at a faster rate.

   - Wobble Amplitude: 7.9. This value and the next one determine how much the bubbles wobble and how often.

   - Wobble Frequency: 1.2.

- Bubble Size: 1.4.
- Reflection Type: Liquid. You choose liquid because liquid doesn't have as much of a reflection as does metal.
- Shading Type: Fade Inwards.

If you scrub the playback head across the animation, you will see that the bubbles act in a more natural manner, except for one thing: they still look like tar bubbles. Let's fix that right now:

5. Twirl up Layer and press the T key to open the layer's Opacity property. Place the playback head at the 4-second mark on the timeline and reduce the layer's opacity to 15%.

6. Do a RAM preview and you will see the bubbles gently rising from the bottom of the Comp to the top when you click the Play button (see Figure 7-25). Save the project.

Figure 7-25. The final animation showing the bubbles

Not all SWF files are created equally

This is an excellent place for you to learn just how true that assertion can be. Throughout this book, we have created Flash SWF files that are, for all intents and purposes, indistinguishable from their FLA counterparts. Actually, that isn't exactly true. If you think back throughout this book so far, we have told you when to create a SWF file. If you are new to either After Effects and/or Flash, you are in for a bit of a shock. This movie looks great in After Effects, but when converted to a SWF file, it looks terrible. In fact, it is beyond terrible; it looks like you didn't do a thing. No morph. No bubbles. No watercolor. To see what we are talking about, double-click the BadFish.SWF file in your Chapter 7 Exercise folder. When the SWF plays, as shown in Figure 7-26, all you really see is the words suddenly become a fish and the tail swishes. Other than that . . . nothing.

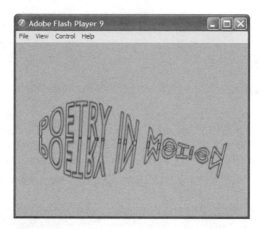

Figure 7-26. Ouch!

The reason behind this disaster actually has its roots in what we talked about right at the start of this exercise. Flash is a vector application, and several of the effects you applied only work with bitmaps. When you create a SWF animation from After Effects and don't rasterize it, all of the bitmap effects applied to the SWF file are ignored. That's the bad news. The good news is you can still import the BadFish.swf into a Flash movie clip—just like you did with the text animation presets—remove the frames where the words are static and still have a Flash movie clip where the fish swishes its tail.

If you do create the movie clip, remove the symbols and the bitmaps used to create the gray solids for the background. This way you can place the movie clip, as you see in Figure 7-27, over a background image or a solid stage color and not worry about it covering the image or any other elements on the stage.

Figure 7-27. A school of fish . . . real or otherwise

> *You can find the SWF and the Flash files for this example in the Chapter 7 Completed folder. The files are* FlashFish.fla *and* FlashFish.swf.

Follow these steps to create a SWF that contains all of the elements in the exercise:

1. With the TextMorph Comp open on the timeline, select File ➤ Export ➤ Macromedia Flash (SWF). When the Save File As dialog box opens, navigate to the folder where you will be saving the SWF file, enter a name for the file—we used TextMorph—and click the Save button. This will open the SWF Settings dialog box.

2. Select Rasterize from the Unsupported Features pull-down menu shown in Figure 7-28.

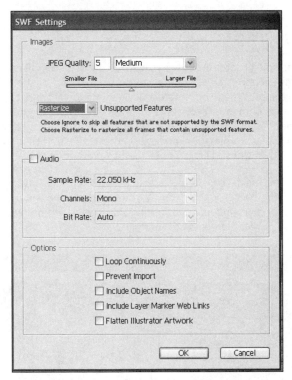

Figure 7-28. Select Raserize in the Unsupported Features pull-down to create the effects applied to the Comp.

This choice is the key. Selecting Ignore tells After Effects to ignore the bitmap effects you applied to the movie and the result is BadFish.SWF. Selecting Rasterize tells After Effects that anything in the SWF file that isn't a vector is to be flattened into a bitmap and rendered as such.

The options at the bottom of the dialog box are somewhat self-explanatory. If you want the SWF to loop, select Loop Continuously. The Prevent Import selection creates a SWF file that digital imaging or video editing applications can't import. We rarely select Include

Object Names, as this option includes all layers, masks, and effect names in the file. The end result is a seriously larger SWF file than is necessary. The Flatten Illustrator selection will flatten all overlapping objects into nonoverlapping pieces.

This is one of those options that works really well for simple artwork like that used in this file, but it actually has negative consequences for complex Illustrator art. In many instances, the file size of the SWF animation does not decrease but actually increases. As well, the flattening process may introduce objects Flash won't recognize and will ignore or will rasterize. You may also see white fringes around some objects. Though we aren't saying this feature should be ignored, it is important that you be aware of the implications of the selection. The best way of deciding whether you can live with it is to simply select it, create the SWF file, and check out the results. If they are unacceptable, you can always delete the SWF file and create another one with this feature unselected.

   3. Click OK and the Export dialog box will appear, showing you the progress of the export process and how many Flash frames make up the SWF file's timeline. If you think you have made a mistake, you can always click the Stop button. When the export process is complete, the dialog box will close, and you will be returned to After Effects. Save the project and quit After Effects.

If you navigate to the folder where the SWF file you just created has been placed, you will notice it is rather large. Our example, TextMorph in the Chapter 7 Completed folder, weighs in at a rather hefty 3.6 megabytes. This is a really large SWF file and, to be honest, even with a broadband connection, will take a serious amount of time to load into Flash. This file, therefore, is in need of a preloader if it is to be used as is in a Flash movie.

You can get around this by rendering the video out as a QuickTime movie using the Animation codec and creating an FLV using the ON2VP codec in the Flash 8 Video Encoder.

To keep the size of this sort of thing to a manageable level, the first thing to do is think small. This means a small stage, 320×240 max, and not the 400×300 size used in this exercise. Other ways of keeping it small are to reduce the time of the project, which will result in a corresponding reduction in the length of the various effects used in the project. For example, the duration of the morph could be cut from 6 to 3 seconds, and the fish animation in the Comp could also be reduced from its current 8 seconds to 4 or 5 seconds. This will result in the creation of fewer bitmaps and symbols in the SWF with a resulting file-size reduction.

Another trick would be to export out the bubbles and the fish, without the morph, as separate SWF files. You could then import the fish SWF file into a Flash movie clip and, using ActionScript, place it over an emptyMovieClip that uses the loadMovie() method to load the bubbles SWF file into the Flash movie at runtime.

Still, this example shows you a number of techniques and effects that simply are not available in Flash. We loaded the example with quite a few effects simply to give you a chance to take them out for a "spin." The subtext here, though, is that effects add weight to a SWF. The more effects, the larger the SWF.

7

Mixing Flash and After Effects

We are going to end this chapter with a rather important exercise and introduce you to an effect that is simply a lot of fun to use.

To this point, most of the exercises you have done treat the After Effects project as a stand-alone element on the Flash stage. That is, the After Effects project is there, but it really doesn't interact with what is going on in Flash. The reality of the situation is items on the Flash stage are rarely static. Things move around, menus pull down, and so on. As we pointed out in the last chapter, the line between what is Flash and what is video on the Flash stage has, for all intents and purposes, been erased. It makes sense, therefore, that when planning a Flash/After Effects project, that the stuff that moves, in either app, should be indistinguishable as to its source.

In this exercise, we are going to explore this concept. There is going to be motion on the Flash stage, and there is going to be text in motion in After Effects. The Flash movie will be prepared in such a way that the user can't tell which is video and which is a Flash object. Best of all, the resulting SWF file will be less than 5K in size, meaning it should play rather quickly.

Before you start the project, you'll have some fun and learn how to use the **Wiggler**.

As you have discovered in this chapter, text has certain properties in the timeline. What the Wiggler does is to add a degree of randomness to those properties. What you can do with this feature is have text bend, move, blur, shake, spin, and so on by changing the parameters for the effect. Where the randomness enters the picture is in how the effect is applied.

The parameters are the outer limit. This means the effect can be applied to text, and it will change using any value up to the limit you set. For example, you can enter your name into a text layer and use the Wiggler to set the maximum distance the letters in your name to be 50% of the start position. When the movie plays, each letter in your name will move any distance from 1% to 50%. This means the first letter in your name may move only a short distance while the third letter moves to the top of the Comp.

Let's have some fun:

1. Launch After Effects and create a new Comp named MyName that is 320X240 pixels in size, uses Square Pixels, has a frame rate of 30 fps, and has a duration of 0:00:10:00.

2. Set the background color to #FFFFFF (white).

3. Select the Text tool, click the Comp once, and enter your name. Use a font, size, and font color of your choosing.

4. Twirl down the Text layer on the timeline and click the Animate button on the layer strip. A pull-down menu will appear and show you all of the properties than can be animated. Select All Transform Properties. When you release the mouse, a new animator named Animator 1 will appear on the timeline.

5. On the Animator 1 strip is a button named Add. When you click this button, you will see a pull-down menu asking you to choose between a Property or a Selector. Click Selector and choose Wiggly, as shown in Figure 7-29. When you make your selection, all of the properties that can be "wiggled" will be listed in the Wiggly Selector that appears on the timeline.

Figure 7-29. Adding a Wiggly Selector to a Comp

If you drag the playback head across the timeline, you are in for a bit of a disappointment. Nothing happens because all of the default properties for the Wiggly Selector are set to 0. Let's fix that and figure out what you can do with this effect:

- Click each of the Position values once and drag the mouse. The value on the left moves the letters on the X-axis, and the value on the right moves them on the Y-axis. What you are seeing is the start position for the effect, and the values you have in the Position area are the maximum values the letters can move. Drag the playback head across the timeline, and the letters in your name will bounce around the Comp. Reset the Position values to 0.

- Click-drag the Scale value. If you scrub across the timeline, the letters in your name will appear to pulsate. When you drag the mouse across the values, notice both values remained equal. This is due to the lock icon—it looks like a chain link—beside them. If you click the lock, you can change the scale values so they are independent of each other. When you have finished playing with this, click the lock and reset values to 100%.

- Click-drag the Skew value. When you scrub across the timeline, your name jiggles as though it were been made of jelly. Reset the value to 0.

- The Rotate and Skew Axis properties have two values: a number and a rotation degree value. The number determines how many rotations will occur, and the degree value determines how the text will rotate. Set the Rotation number value to 2 and the degree value to 45. If you scrub across the timeline, the letters in your name will, for want of a better description, appear to jitter. Reset the Rotation values to 0.

Now that you have played with the properties, let's take a look at the selections under the Wiggly Selector. Twirl it down, as shown in Figure 7-30, and you will see the following:

- Mode: This pull-down determines how the selector should be combined with the objects above it in the timeline. This one is rather complex, so we will leave it alone.

- Max Amount, Min Amount: These two options specify the range for the selector. For example, assume you change the Position property values to 40, 45. If you scrub the timeline, the letters in your name will bounce around the screen. Some letters will move up and down, while others move right and left. The Min Amount and Max Amount properties will move things down and to the right. The Min Amount will move them up and to the left and are the range for the movement.

7

- Based On: This pull-down applies the wiggle based on a variety of choices ranging from individual letters to text blocks.

- Wiggles/Second: High values speed things up. Low values slow them down.

- Correlation: In many respects, this control applies kerning to the letters in motion. A value of 0 applies different values to each letter, and a value of 100% applies the same amount to each letter. Smaller percentages will pull the letters closer to each other.

- Temporal Phase: The key word here is *temporal*. The value you set here changes the timing of the wiggles in the effect. The first number determines the number of revolutions per second that will be applied, and the second number is the degrees through which the selection will rotate.

- Spatial Phase: Functions in a similar manner to the temporal phase but moves each character. In many respects, it is similar to running a wave through the text.

- Lock Dimensions: Scales the wiggled selection's dimensions by the same value. This is useful when wiggling the Scale property and the values need to be uniform.

- Random Seed: Enter a value to change the starting time for the animation by that value. When the seed is left at 0, a default value is derived based on the layer index and stream path.

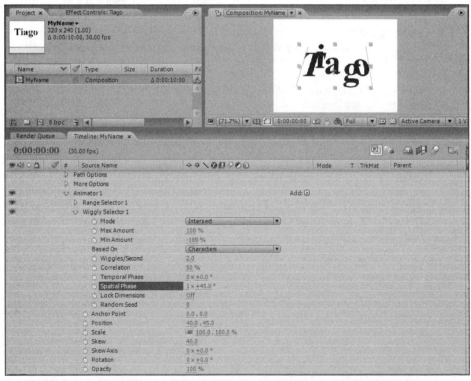

Figure 7-30. There is a lot more under the Wiggly Selector's hood than you might first assume.

6. Now that you understand what the controls can do, apply these Wiggly Selector values to your name:

- Max Amount: 100%
- Min Amount: –100%
- Based On: Characters
- Wiggles/Second: 2.5
- Position: 45, 45
- Scale: 50, 50%
- Rotation: 0 x +30 degrees

If you click the Play button in the Time Controls panel or press the spacebar, the letters of your name start to dance with each other. If the viewer needs to figure out what the dancing letters mean, the letters will have to come back into their proper order. This is not difficult to accomplish; remember, from the start of this exercise, nothing happens if the properties are reset to 0.

Let's turn this into a useful animation:

7. Add keyframes for each of the following properties at the 0 point on the timeline:

- Max Amount
- Min Amount
- Position
- Scale
- Rotation

8. Move the playback head to the 8-second mark on the timeline and set the values for each of the properties in the previous step to 0.

If you press the spacebar, you will see the letters in your name dancing with each other, and the dance slows down as the playback head approaches the 8-second mark on the timeline. Now that you have had a chance to explore how the Wiggly Selector works, we are going to show you a practical example.

> *A completed version of this exercise can be found in the Chapter 7 Completed folder. The file is named WiggleName.aep.*

The final exercise in this chapter is rather complex, and instead of spending a lot of time reviewing a lot of what you have already done, we are going to review how the project was assembled in both Flash and After effects, and we will also review a couple of new After Effects tricks that you may wish to add to your arsenal. You really don't need to do anything other than open the files and follow along with how the various bits and pieces of the project were assembled.

To get started, open the Wiggly.swf file located in the Wiggles folder found in the Chapter 7 Exercise folder. You will notice there are four colored squares on the stage, and both the squares and the text around them are in constant motion. The most important aspect of this SWF file is the fact that an After Effects video overlies the entire Flash stage. As well, the text that appears inside the moving blocks, shown in Figure 7-31, is prepared in After Effects. The implication here is you need a high degree of precision in After Effects to ensure those letters appear directly over the blocks.

Figure 7-31.
Precision placement of the effects in After Effects is called for if the effect is to appear over Flash content.

If you open the wiggly.fla file in the Chapter 7 Exercise folder, you will see how this precision was accomplished. The Flash stage is divided into precise areas through the use of guides. If you scrub through the timeline, you will see the squares stay within the grid on the Flash stage (see Figure 7-32). The right side of the stage is left essentially blank and will be used for a variety of After Effects text effects.

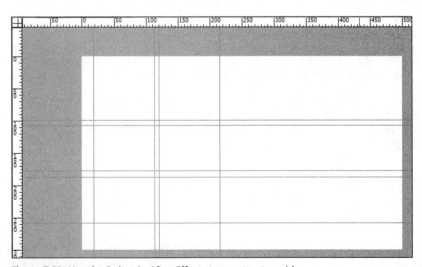

Figure 7-32. Use the Rulers in After Effects to construct a grid.

We carefully noted the positions of each of the various grid lines. These positions will be used to construct a similar grid in After Effects.

If you are lazy, like us, forget about writing down the position of the guides in Flash. The stage size used in After Effects will be the same as the Flash movie. Ensuring the Flash view is 100%, turn off the visibility of any of the objects on the Flash stage and take a screenshot of the stage and the guides. Import the screenshot into your After Effects document, and build the grid from the screenshot in an After Effects Comp.

Close the Flash document and let's examine how the project was assembled in After Effects.

Open the wiggly.aep file in your Exercise folder. When the project opens, you will see that we have constructed a grid that matches the one from Flash. Here's how we did it:

1. We selected View ➤ Show Rulers.

2. We zoomed out to a magnification level of 200% and, using the locations of the guides previously noted, dragged them from the horizontal and vertical rulers onto the Comp window. (If pixel precision were paramount, zooming out to an 800% view would set the rulers to single-pixel increments.)

3. To move around the Comp window, we held down the spacebar (if you are following along, you will see a Grabber Hand icon replace the cursor) and dragged the mouse.

4. Once we had the grid constructed, as shown in Figure 7-32, we selected View ➤ Lock Guides. By doing this, we prevented accidentally moving a grid line out of position. Note that you can also turn off the rulers by selecting View ➤ Hide Rulers or by pressing Ctrl+R (PC) or Cmd+R (Mac).

Be aware that zooming out to an 800% view will make it hard to read the numbers on the ruler. The numbers read down, not across.

Want a handy way of zooming without clicking? If you have a mouse with a wheel, rotating the wheel will zoom in and out on the Comp.

Let's now look at how many of the effects used in the video were created.

1. Twirl down the Poetry layer and scrub the playback head across the strip in the timeline. It fades in and out and tends to jiggle. We accomplished this by physically moving the text block from one location to the next and fading it in by tweening its opacity. Twirl up the Poetry layer.

2. Twirl down the In layer. If you scrub across its strip, you will see the blurred word zip in from the right and, as it bounces off of the guide, come into focus. We accomplished this through the addition of a Tracking animator and a Directional Blur effect.

    The Tracking animator was applied by selecting Tracking from the Animate pull-down. This animator adjusts the spacing between the characters in a word. We tweened the tracking by changing the tracking value from 0 to 232 in the Tracking Amount property. This is how the word splits apart at the end of the animation.

7

The Directional Blur, **found in** Effects & Presets ➤ Blur and Sharpen, **gives a layer the illusion of a motion blur**. In fact, in earlier versions of After Effects, this was the name of the effect. Note that we changed the blur length at various points in the timeline. Twirl up the In layer.

The other two In layers are nothing more than variations of the first one.

3. Twirl down the first Motion layer—Layer 11—and scrub across its strip. You will see the word *Motion* travel along the jagged line. We accomplished this by adding a solid to the layer, drawing the path, adding the text, and dragging the Path Text effect from the Text folder in the Effects & Presets panel onto the solid.

As you may have surmised, this is how you can do a "text on a path" animation effect in After Effects. You can define a path as a straight line, a circle of any diameter, or a Bezier curve. You can also import a path created in another application, such as Adobe Photoshop or Adobe Illustrator. In the case of our project, this didn't make sense, but it is something to be aware of if you need a more complex path. You can animate text on an existing layer or, for additional control over placement of text such as we have done, create a solid and animate the text on it.

You are probably wondering how the text moves from the top to the bottom. To move text along the path, create keyframes for the left margin or right margin and change the margin value in the keyframe. In our case, we used keyframes to adjust the Left Margin property of the effect as shown in Figure 7-33. In many respects, all you are doing as creating one seriously big indent in a paragraph.

Twirl up the Motion layer.

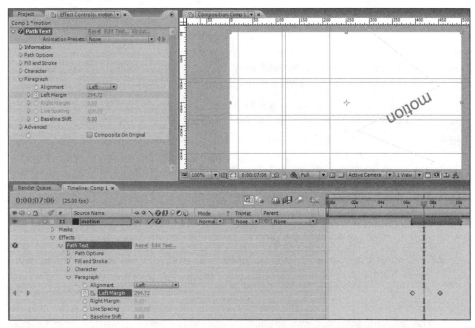

Figure 7-33. The margin properties are what move text along a path in the Path Text effect.

> *To change the text after closing the* Path Text *dialog box, click the* Edit Text *link at the top of the* Effect Controls *panel.*

The final "how to" involves how we created the series of letters that appear over each of the boxes in the Flash movie.

The effect is a classic example of our axiom: "Let the software do the work." In this case, we used a Unicode character table to change a letter into a series of disjointed characters and finish with the capital of the letter we started with.

1. Twirl down the F layer—Layer 4. Select the layer strip and twirl down Window ➤ Character. Change the text color from white to black. The text is white because it will reverse out of the solid color of the color block it is over on the Flash stage.

2. Scrub the playback head across the layer strip and you will see the text start as an *e*, cycle through a series of random characters, and finish as an uppercase F. How this is accomplished is by assigning a Character Value animator to the text and changing the value using a series of keyframes. If you twirl down the Animator 1 in the layer, you will see this property and the keyframes (as shown in Figure 7-34).

   Essentially what we did is to start with a lowercase *e* that has a Unicode value of 101 and finish the sequence with an upper case *F*, which has a Unicode value of *0*. By starting with one value and ending with another, you can change the character on the fly.

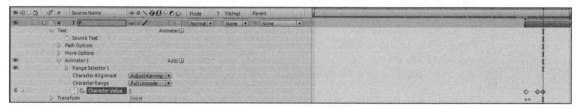

Figure 7-34. Tweening a Character Value property can result in a rather fascinating text effect.

> *This animator is also a great way of having a line of text display as a jumble of letters that appear to straighten out into a coherent sentence or word.*

3. With the text selected, reset the text color in the Character panel back to white.

> *If you can't be bothered with that last step here's a way of correcting a major mistake. Select* File ➤ Revert, *and the project will revert to the state it was in during the last time you saved the file.*

At this stage of the process, once we were satisfied with the piece, we saved the project and rendered it out as a QuickTime movie using the Animation codec with the color depth set to Millions of Colors+. These settings ensure the white background color for the Comp is ignored when the video is created. If it isn't, the FLV file will hide the Flash stage.

The FLV file was created using the Flash 8 Video Encoder and the ON2VP6 codec with Encode alpha channel selected. The frame rate was set to 15 fps and the data rate was set to 200 Kbps. The video was encoded, and we quit the Encoder.

In Flash, we added a video object to the Library and then added the object to its own layer on the Flash timeline. To ensure the video was properly positioned, we set its X and Y coordinates to 0, 0 in the Flash Property inspector, gave it the instance name of video, and then locked the video layer.

> *A quick note about the FLA file: you might be looking at its 500-frame timeline and thinking, "What a bunch of noobies!" This is just an exercise, so we took a few liberties. Still, if you kept an eye on the render in After Effects, you would have noticed the number of frames in the video is the same number of frames in the Flash movie. The important aspect of the exercise is not the Flash movie, but the interaction of the After Effects content with the Flash content.*

Finally, there is another way to approach this project that results in an even quicker-loading Flash file, and many developers and designers are now just discovering it. The technique involves approaching complexity from a position of simplicity.

This project involves an FLV file that is 500 pixels wide and 300 pixels high. Even though the FLV file is about 600K in size, the user will still face a delay as the FLV loads. As well, the After Effects timeline has a lot of layers, and the effects applied in each of the layers are quite sophisticated. In short, this is one very complex project.

If you look at the Flash stage, you see that it is, for all intents and purposes, based upon a grid design. All of the After Effects content plays within a defined section of the grid. This means that instead of one great big FLV file playing over the entire stage, you could have each of the animations contained in a separate FLV file. Suddenly one complex project is broken down into a series of rather simple pieces.

For example, the lettering effect that plays with the Character Values and is used in the boxes could be created in an After Effects Comp that matches the dimensions of the grid square it appears in. This would result in a series of four 4-second animations appearing in separate videos that are 96 pixels wide by 72 pixels high. The upshot here is a series of very small QuickTime movies and a series of FLV files that should come in well under 20K each.

Summary

This dragon hunt may be taking you to places you never explored as you turned your attention to text as art rather than communication. In this chapter, you have wiggled, jiggled, blown up, and bent text and, just to keep it interesting, reduced an annoying "talking head" to dust.

We started off by reviewing the Text tools in both applications and discussing the fact that text is nothing more than vectors, so that words and letters become a creative and a communications medium in your hands. The first exercise started in Flash and showed you a rather simple way of exploding text out of the stage.

From there we looked at a couple of other methods for creating text mayhem. You started with the CC Pixel Polly effect from Cycore and used it to break up some letters, reduce the letters to shards, and then used it to reduce the "talking head" to dust by having it implode and then explode.

The next effect we showed you was one of our favorites: Turbulent Displace. You used it to set your name flapping in the wind.

With a couple of rather simple exercises under your belt, we raised the intensity level by a notch and showed you how to light the fuse that explodes a letter. Through the use of the Stroke filter and the CC Particle Systems II effect, you were shown how to light a fuse and have it travel along a path. The explosion was brought to you courtesy of one of the neatest tools in the arsenal: the Shatter effect. We reviewed many of the features of this effect and how to use it to create the illusion of glass breaking.

From there we turned to the workflow that is developing between Illustrator, After Effects, and Flash. We created some text in Illustrator and converted it to outlines. This file was then imported into After Effects where, through the use of a couple of very interesting effects, it was made to morph into a fish that swishes its tail. The animation was then converted to a SWF file and it was at this point you discovered that not all SWF files are created equally. To manage this, we showed you a couple of ways of creating the SWF file. One method simply used the vectors and ignored the bitmap effects. This allowed you to place the SWF into a Flash movie clip and use it accordingly. The second method showed you how to output the SWF file in such a way as to include all of the effects and place it in a Flash movie.

The final exercise ratcheted down the intensity and complexity level and showed you how to use a Wiggly Selector animator to get text to wiggle, jiggle, and otherwise move around the screen without the use of an effect.

The chapter concluded with a "how-to" explanation that deeply explored the whole issue of how After Effects content and Flash content can interact with each other at runtime. The key, as we showed you, is precise placement of the After Effects objects in the Comp. To do this, we showed you how to duplicate a Flash grid in After Effects.

7

We also explained how to animate text on a path, and use a Directional Blue effect and the Character Offset animator to create a rather cool jumble of letters that form the letter or word you need.

With the production phase out of the way, we then told you how to render the final video out of After Effects—using the Animation codec with a color depth of Millions of Colors+—to remove the background color of the Comp. If you didn't do this, the video would hide the content on the Flash stage. We then explained how we "synched" the FLV video to the Flash content that moves around on the stage.

The example ended by our suggesting an alternative approach to the project that would have made the Flash project even more efficient. The key is to approach the complexity of the After Effects project from a position of simplicity.

Now that you have blown stuff up, bent it, twisted it, and generally added a degree of mayhem to your workflow, it might not be a bad idea to halt our dragon quest for a couple of minutes and take a break. Why? You want to look your best, because in the next chapter you meet the parents.

In 1999, the Flash community was all agog with a site designed to promote the Luc Besson movie *The Messenger*. It wasn't the design of the site that received the buzz. What was getting the buzz was a draggable movie clip that had a shield dangling from a horizontal post. If you dragged the post to the left, the shield would swing to the right and then sway, back and forth, once the post came to rest. It was the "sway" that caught all of the attention. It was among the earliest examples of work created by a Flash designer who actually paid attention to the physics of objects in motion.

Though the site is long gone, how that draggable movie clip worked is still valid. In fact, it was composed of two movie clips—one inside the other. If you moved the post, the shield moved with it, or, in "techie" terms, the shield assumed the position property of the post. This is a classic parent/child relationship.

When you work with Flash, you become quite familiar with grouping or nesting objects to create one object. The most common example of that is the almighty movie clip in Flash. When you put a movie clip on the main timeline or even into another movie clip, you can move it, resize it, and otherwise play with its properties, and the content in that movie clip will be affected. Though After Effects doesn't have movie clips, you can obtain somewhat similar functionality through the use of parenting.

The key to understanding parenting in After Effects is this: it allows one layer on the timeline to inherit the Transform properties of another layer. What this means is you can move a position point of one object (the post) called a **parent**, to a different position on the timeline, and all the objects attached to the parent (the shield), called **children**, will also move. The only Transform property that doesn't apply to children is the Opacity property.

In this chapter, you are going to explore how parenting works in After Effects and, in many ways, will make your life easier in Flash. Not to mention the fact that you can create some rather spectacular effects once you understand the basics of parenting in After Effects. With those skills under your belt, you can then sprinkle those amazing effects throughout your Flash movies.

Just be aware this chapter really has nothing to do with Flash. It is the point in the book where we step back and explain how rather complex animations can be created in After Effects by not only looking at parenting but how animations in After Effects really happen. A thorough understanding of these concepts will not only improve your After Effects skills, but also make your life easier in those situations where your client looks at you and says, "A spinning tire is really nice, but where's my branding on the wheel hub?"

Parenting 101

We are going to start with a very simple example that will show you how all of this works.

1. Open the Clock.aep file found in the Clock folder inside the Exercise folder in the Chapter 8 code download. When you open the file, you will see it is nothing more than a clock with layers for the clock face and hour and the minute hands.

The image is a multilayer Photoshop document. When you import a multilayer Photoshop document, you are given the option of importing either a flattened version of the image or each layer. For this example, import each layer.

2. Select the Minute layer on the timeline.

On the right side of the selected layer is a column named Parent. In that column is a pull-down menu with the word *None*. If you open the menu, you will see the three layers listed and the word *None*. The Minute layer is grayed out because you can't attach a layer to itself.

If you don't see the parent layer, right-click (PC) or Ctrl-click (Mac) any of the visible column names. When the context menu opens, select Parent from the choices presented. Another way of opening and closing the Parent column is to press Shift+F4.

3. Open the Parent pull-down menu and select Background. You have now made the Background layer the parent of the Minute layer.

4. To see how a parent/child relationship works, twirl down the Background layer and, in the Transform properties, click and drag the Scale value. The clock and the minute hand get bigger (as you see in Figure 8-1) and smaller, while the hour hand remains unaffected. This is a direct result of the parenting relationship you set up in the previous step. The child—the minute hand—takes on the properties of the parent—the background. This explains why the clock and the minute hand get bigger while the hour hand remains unaffected. The hour hand does not have a parent. Click the Reset link in the Background and Hour layers to revert back to the original size of the objects.

5. An interesting aspect of this relationship is that a child can transform without affecting its parent. Select the Minute layer, twirl down the Transform properties, and change the Position and Scale values. The minute hand will grow larger, get smaller, and move around the screen while the Background layer remains unaffected. When you finish, click Reset in the Minute layer.

6. There is no "one child per object" policy in place with After Effects. Parents can have as many children as you wish. Twirl up the Minute layer and select the Hour layer. To the left of the Parent pull-down is a little icon that looks like a coiled spring. This icon is called a Pick Whip tool. You can use it, instead of the menu, to establish a parent.

7. Click and drag the Pick Whip tool anywhere onto the Background layer strip in the timeline. When you release the mouse, the Background layer will appear in the Parent pull-down.

8. Twirl down the Background layer's Transform properties and change the scale value. All three layers scale in proportion.

8

Figure 8-1. The minute hand is a child of the parent, and when the parent gets larger so, too, does the child.

9. Select the Pick Whip tool on the Hour layer and drag it onto the Minute layer. Scrub the Scale value in the Background layer. Again, all three layers scale in proportion. Reset the scale value to 100% in the Background layer.

10. Twirl down the Transform properties for the Minute layer and scrub across the Scale value. This time only the hands get larger and smaller. The clock face is totally unaffected. Click the Reset link in the Minute layer.

What you did in those last four steps is to create an extended family. By making the Background layer the parent of the Hour and Minute layers, changing the parent layer affects them. When you change the parent of the Hour layer to the Minute layer, the Hour layer became a child of the Minute layer and the grandchild of the Background layer.

As we said earlier, parenting only affects Scale, Position, and Rotation. It does not affect Opacity. There is another aspect of this relationship that you need to know.

11. Open Effects & Presets ➤ Perspective. Drag a copy of the Drop Shadow effect onto the Minute layer.

12. Twirl down the Effect Controls panel and change the Distance for the Drop Shadow effect to 40.

When you do that, the minute hand develops a shadow (see Figure 8-2), but its child, the hour hand, doesn't. This is because effects are in the same boat as the Opacity property. They aren't a part of the parent/child relationship. If effects are going to be applied to a parent/child relationship, they have to be applied to each layer . . . individually.

Figure 8-2. Effects applied to parents don't apply to the children as well.

Let's wind up this discussion by "kicking the kids out of the house." To remove a child, you have a couple of choices:

- Select the layer and select None from the Parent pull-down.
- Cmd-click (Mac) or Ctrl-click (PC) the Pick Whip tool.

> *Either of these two methods to break the relationship can be applied to multiple or single layers. Another, more drastic, measure is to delete the parent layer. Do this, and the relationship will be severed.*

When you end the relationship, nothing should happen. The parent and the child layers should remain with the Position, Rotation, and Scale properties in effect when the relationship was severed.

What you also need to know is this: unparenting leaves the parents and children in place. It does not return them to their original starting values. If you really need to return to the original values, use keyframes for the parent and the child (children) in the Transform properties of their respective layers. Providing you don't change the values in those original keyframes, you can always return to them and remove the relationship.

Now that you know how to create families, extended families, and dysfunctional families, let's get a bit deeper into the technology behind parenting. You can close this project.

Parenting 201

You now know that when one layer is the parent of another, the child's Transform properties are changed relative to the parent's location. To understand this, open the Parenting202.aep file in the Chapter 7 Exercise folder's Clock folder. When the Comp opens, the minute hand is placed to the right of the clock face in the Comp.

Set the Background layer as the parent of the Minute layer and, if you move the clock 10 pixels to the left, the arm moves the same distance. If the relationship between the clock and the arm was an absolute relationship, the arm would move to the same location as the clock.

What happened there was After Effects calculated the change in position between the Anchor point of the child and Origin point of the parent. What you really need to understand is that the Origin point is not the same as the Anchor point. The Origin point is the upper-left corner of a layer. If you click the clock face on the Comp, the handle in the upper-left corner is the Origin point of the layer. The Origin point is the value of the Position point minus the Anchor point value. In the case of our clock, the Origin point is located at 200 – 250 and 200 – 335, or –50, –135. If you still have the clock face selected, this makes sense because the upper-left corner of layer is outside of the Comp area.

> *The Origin point for any Comp is always the upper-left corner, or the 0, 0 point.*

This relationship is extremely important to understand because sometimes, when a parent has multiple children, you may move the position of the parent, but the children don't appear to move in lockstep.

The reason is the Anchor point (the crosshairs in the center of the Comp) of any object is relative to the layer, while the Position property is relative to the Comp. In Figure 8-3, we have placed a solid that matches the 500×500 pixel size of the Comp. The Anchor point of the solid and its Position property are the same.

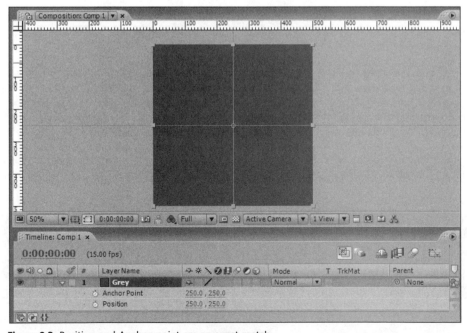

Figure 8-3. Position and Anchor point are an exact match.

In Figure 8-4, we change the position to 300, 300. Notice how the Position property changes but the Anchor Point property, the intersection of the guides, remains the same. What you can gather from this is the Anchor point is the pivot for all animation.

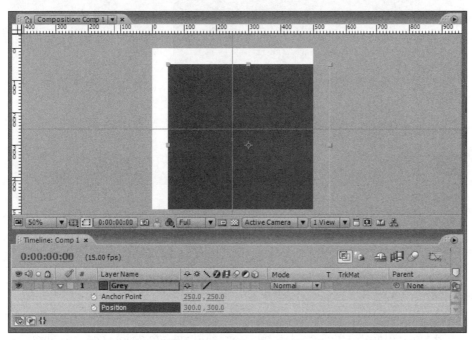

Figure 8-4. Changing the solid's position has no effect upon its Anchor point property.

When we change the Anchor Point property values to 350, 350, as shown in Figure 8-5, the gray solid moves up and to the left, but its Position property values remain unchanged. What we did was change the pivot point. We didn't change the Position point. Moving an Anchor point causes the object to move in the opposite direction in the Comp window. This is because the Position property is relatively clueless regarding the boundaries of a layer. It only keeps an eye on the position of the Anchor point relative to the layer . . . not the Comp.

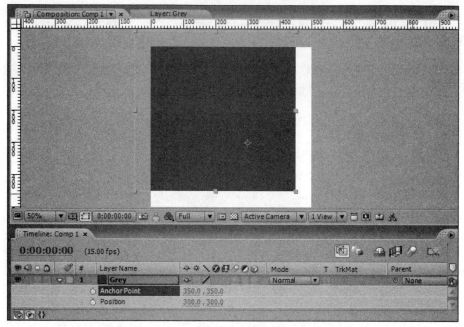

Figure 8-5. Changing the Anchor Point property has no effect upon an object's Position property. It simply moves the pivot point from one location to another in the layer, not the Comp.

> *Another way of changing the Anchor point position is to double-click any layer. This will open the* Layer *window. From there you can drag the Anchor point to any position in the Comp.*

Rotation also has a couple of gotchas you should be aware of. To see what we are talking about, let's go back to our clock.

The Background layer is the parent of the Minute layer. If you select both layers and press the R key, the Rotation properties for each layer will appear. Scrub through the degrees value of the Background layer and you will notice that as the values change in the Background layer's Rotation values, the Minute layer rotates, but there is no corresponding change to the Minute layer's Rotation property. How the Minute layer rotates is by subtracting the parent's Rotation value from the child's Rotation value (see Figure 8-6). The other thing to be aware of is changing the Rotation value of the parent can have an effect upon the child's Position property.

Figure 8-6. Rotate the parent and the child goes for a spin as well, but the child's Rotation property remains unchanged.

Finally, scaling is one those tasks that can get you into a world of hurt if you don't scale the parent uniformly.

To see what we are talking about, follow these steps:

1. Remove the parent from the Minute layer and set the Minute layer's Scale value to 50%.

2. Select the Background layer and set its Scale value to 75%.

3. Use the Pick Whip tool to make the Background layer parent to the Minute layer.

When you release the mouse, the Scale property values for the Minute layer change from 50% to 66.7%. Not only that, but the size of the minute hand in the Comp doesn't change to reflect the increased Scale value. If you remove the parent, the Scale property will return to 50%. What happened?

Again, it comes down to math. The child's original Scale value is divided by the parent's scale value: 50% divided by 75% is 66.7%. When it is time to render the Comp, the opposite occurs. The child's scale value is multiplied by the parent's scale value. In this case, 66.7% × 75% roughly equals 50%.

8

The world of hurt facing you involves nonuniform scaling of the parent.

4. Remove the parent from the Minute layer and select the Background layer.

5. Click the chain link icon in the Scale property of the Background layer to turn off uniform scaling.

6. Change one of the values from 75% to 50%. Reapply the parent to the Minute layer.

7. Open the Rotation values for the Background layer—you can press the R key—and scrub through it. As you change the value, the minute hand rotates, squashes, and stretches in unison with the Background layer.

8. Set the Rotation value for the Background layer to 0.

9. Open the Rotation property for the Minute layer and scrub through it. As the graphic rotates through the Background layer, notice how it squashes and stretches even though its parent is doing nothing (see Figure 8-7).

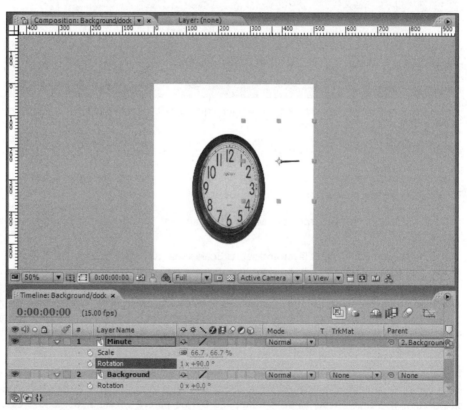

Figure 8-7. Nonuniform scaling of a parent can have unpredictable results when it comes to the children.

10. Close the Parenting202.aep file and, if prompted to save the changes, click No.

This is why applying nonuniform Scaling and Rotation values to a parent is not a good idea. The results for the child are unpredictable.

Enough theory and "techie talk." Let's put what we know to use.

The words on the rim go around and around

In this exercise, you will pull off what is, at best, extremely difficult to do in Flash. You are going to have text on a circular path rotate at the same rate as the circle that is its parent.

1. If it isn't open, launch After Effects and create a new project. Name the project Rims and save it to the Rims folder in your Chapter 7 Exercise folder.

2. Create a new Comp using the following settings:

- Composition Name: Rims
- Width: 320
- Height: 240
- Pixel Aspect Ratio: Square Pixels
- Duration: 0:00:12:00

3. Set the Background color to #000000 (black).

4. Import the Rim.tif file from the Rims folder into the project. Having assembled your assets, you can now concentrate on creating the animation.

To get started, you are going to put the rim into position on the stage and then enter a line of text that will be animated.

1. Drag the Rim.tif image to the timeline instead of the Comp window.

2. Press the P key to open the Position layer property and set the position of the image to 81, 122.

3. Select the Text tool, click the Comp once, and enter the text racing. Use the following settings in the Character panel:

- Font: Arial
- Style: Bold
- Color: #868712 (gold)
- Size: 28 px
- Tracking: 160

> *If you have a font named either Arial Bold or Arial Black, feel free to substitute the font. If you do have either one, don't change the style to* Bold. *If you have* Arial *but don't have* Bold *in the* Style *pull-down, click the* Faux Bold *button in the* Character *panel.*

8

4. Select the racing layer and press the P key to open the layer's Position property. Set the position of the text to 84, 135. If you use text with a different alignment, point size, or font, just position the text so it resembles Figure 8-8.

Figure 8-8. The words and image are positioned in the Comp.

Rotating the word

Here is the plan. The tire starts spinning and so does the word. At a certain point in time, the rim, along with the word, shrinks and rolls off of the right edge of the screen. Knowing how parenting works, this is not an insurmountable task. In fact, it is now dead simple to accomplish. Here's how:

1. Twirl down the Rim layer and, with the Shift key held down, press the P, S, and R keys to open the Position, Scale, and Rotation properties for the layer.

2. Select the Position strip and press the Home key to return to the starting point of the timeline.

3. Add the following keyframes and Position values at the times indicated:

- 0 seconds: 81, 122.
- 8 seconds: Add a keyframe.
- 10 seconds: 480, 125.

4. Select the Scale strip and press the Home key to return to the starting point of the timeline.

5. Add the following keyframes and Scale values at the times indicated:

- 0 seconds: 100%
- 6 seconds: 15%

6. Select the Rotation strip and press the Home key to return to the starting point of the timeline.

7. Add the following keyframes and position values at the times indicated:

- 0 seconds: 0 x +0.0
- 8 seconds: 4 x +0.0
- 12 seconds: 6 x +0.0

> *Rotation does not require you to enter an angle value if the object is only going to spin. That first number tells After Effects how many times the object is to rotate by that point in time.*

8. Select the Pick Whip tool in the Parent column of the racing layer and make the Rim layer the parent of the racing layer. If you scrub through the timeline, the word spins, resizes, and moves in lockstep with the Rim layer (see Figure 8-9).

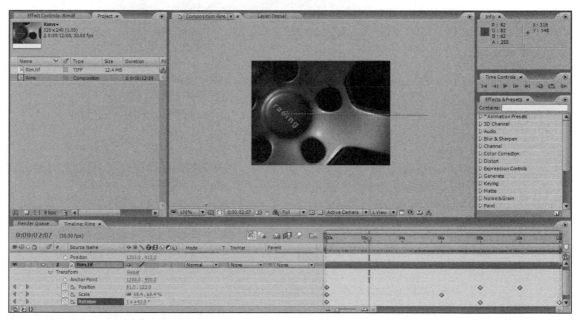

Figure 8-9. The timeline and the Comp so far

The client has looked at what we have done so far and is wondering, "Dudes, where is our branding? The company name is speedrims racing!" Let's keep the customer satisfied.

In the previous chapter, we showed you how to place text on a straight path, a curved path, and a jagged path. In this final part of the exercise, you put some text on a circular path. If you have never done this before in After Effects, you may find the process to be a bit confusing. It isn't, and, once you get the hang of it, you will wonder what all the fuss was about in the first place.

1. Create a new black solid by selecting Layer ➤ New ➤ Solid. When the New Solid dialog box opens, give the solid a name and set the color to #000000 (Black). Click OK to close the dialog box. The new solid will appear on the timeline.

2. Select the Elliptical mask tool and draw a circle on the solid. Adjust the size of the circle to fit over the hub of the rims as shown in Figure 8-10. This circle will serve as the path for the text.

Figure 8-10. You start by creating and positioning the path for the text.

Did you know you can choose the Elliptical Mask *tool by simply pressing the Q key on your keyboard? Press it again, and you switch to the* Rectangular Mask *tool.*

If you have ever done text on a circular path in Illustrator, Photoshop, or Fireworks, you are going to find how After Effects handles this chore to be quite different, yet oddly more intuitive than the workflow used in those applications. It is a three-step process:

- Add the Path Text effect to the solid.
- Enter the text to be placed on the path in a separate dialog box.
- Fiddle with the text formatting and placement in the Effect Controls panel.

Let's go to work:

1. Select the solid layer on the timeline. Open Presets & Effects ➤ Text and drag the Path Text effect on top of the solid in the Comp.

2. As soon as you release the mouse, the Path Text dialog box opens (see Figure 8-11). This is where the text used in the effects is entered. Select Arial from the Font pull-down and Bold from the Style pull-down. Click once in the text entry area and enter the word speedrims. Click OK to close the dialog box.

Figure 8-11.
The Text Path dialog box is how text is added to a circular path.

When you release the mouse, the text will appear in the Comp. Of course, it is totally inappropriate for our use, meaning the time has arrived to "fiddle" with the text in the Effect Controls panel.

The best way of learning to work with any new panel or dialog box is to work from the top to the bottom of the panel.

The Path Options determine the path the text will follow. There are a number of shape types—the default is Bezier—and, if you twirl down the Control Points, depending upon the shape chosen, you can adjust the start and end points and even the shape of the path. Thankfully, we aren't going to get that fancy.

3. Twirl down the Path Options in the Effect Controls panel. Select Mask 1 from the Custom Path pull-down. You will see the text curl up inside the circle as shown in Figure 8-12. No problem, you'll deal with that in a moment.

Figure 8-12.
Choose the mask as a Path Option, and the text curls up inside the mask.

The Fill and Stroke options allow you to choose the color for the font and the color of the stroke you may wish to add to it. Adding a stroke to a font is a really, really bad idea. It adds nothing to the text and has a negative effect upon its readability and its legibility. In fact, ask any professional graphic designer or anyone who works professionally with text or fonts about stroking text, and they will essentially tell you it would be no different from painting a moustache on the Mona Lisa. If you must use a stroke, then don't fill the text.

4. Twirl down the Fill and Stroke options, click the Fill Color chip, and change the fill color to #868717 to match the color of the word *racing*.

5. Twirl down the Character settings. This is where the text is "fiddled" with.

6. Scrub through the Size property to reduce the size of the text. We used 16 px, but you may find a different size to be more appealing.

7. Scrub the Tracking value to the right to spread out the letters in the word as shown in Figure 8-13. Try to keep the words contained between the top and the bottom Anchor points on the mask. Doing this ensures the text will not interfere with the word *racing* when you get around to moving the text above the mask. We found a value of +15 works for us, but depending on the font chosen, you may need a larger or smaller value.

Figure 8-13. Fiddling with the text

Now that you have the text looking the way you want it to, let's concentrate on getting it above the mask.

8. Twirl down the Paragraph settings. Scrub through the Left Margin settings to get the text into its proper position. We found scrubbing to the left and a value of –100 for the Left Margin served our needs.

9. All text sits on an imaginary baseline. To move the text above the path, simply apply a Baseline Shift value to the selection. Scrub through the Baseline Shift setting, and you will see, depending on the direction you move the mouse, the text move above the mask (a negative setting) or below the mask (a really big positive setting). You want the text to appear at the top, so use a value of –11.

10. Hold on, the text is backwards. We have saved the best for last. Click the Reverse Path check box in Path Options. The text pops above the mask and can now be read. Adjust the Baseline Shift, as shown in Figure 8-14, and you are finished.

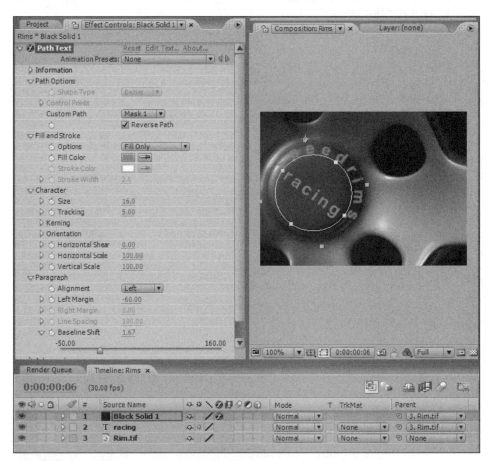

Figure 8-14. The text is set and its parent established.

11. Use the Pick Whip tool to set the Rims layer as its parent and scrub through the timeline. Everything rotates, moves across the Comp, and gets smaller as the tire rolls off of the screen.

12. Save the project.

Rendering the video and using it in Flash

There will be occasions, especially in situations involving high-definition video, where the Flash video, regardless of what you do, will drop frames . . . even if you are using the fastest processor on the planet. When this happens, a few developers have discovered that, with the addition of an audio track to the video—even if it is an empty track—the frame rate comes back into balance. In fact, the inclusion of an audio track in every video you create should now be a part of your normal workflow. Let's put that into practice:

1. Select Composition ➤ Add to Render Queue and click the Render Queue tab on the timeline to give it focus.

2. Click the Lossless link in the Output Module setting to open the Output Module Settings dialog box.

3. Select Quicktime Movie from the Format pull-down and then click the Format Options button.

4. When the Compression Settings dialog box opens, select the Animation codec. In the Compressor area, set the Depth to Millions of Colors and move the Quality slider to Best. Click OK to close the dialog box.

5. Click the Audio Output check box, as shown in Figure 8-15, to add an audio track to the video.

6. Click OK to accept the changes and close the dialog box.

> *Don't go getting "twitchy" about the inclusion of a CD-quality stereo soundtrack with nothing in it within the video. Remember, the final MOV file will be run through the Flash 8 Video Encoder, and you can deal with the issue there.*

7. Click the Rims.mov link in the Output To area and, when the Output Movie To dialog box opens, name the file and save it to your Exercise folder.

8. Click the Render button to create the video. When the render is complete, save the file and quit After Effects.

> *To this point in the book, we have been ignoring the File ➤ Export ➤ Flash Video (FLV) option. This is deliberate. Selecting this option in After Effects has resulted in, to be gentle, inconsistent results. Reports of computers crashing when selecting this export option are quite common. The odd thing is this crash is inconsistent. It doesn't happen 100% of the time to all users. One of the authors has his computer crash every time, and the other author has yet to experience it. Adobe is aware of this issue and tells us they will solve it for the next release of After Effects. The other thing to keep in mind is, at its heart, After Effects is a video tool. It only makes sense therefore to use the right tool for the right job at the right time. In this case, use After Effects to render a video and use the Flash Video Encoder to render the FLV file from the video.*

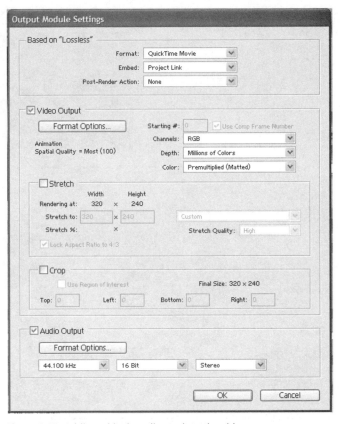

Figure 8-15. Adding a blank audio track to the video

Now that the video has been created, you can turn your attention to creating the FLV file you will use in Flash.

1. Launch the Flash 8 Video Encoder, add the MOV file you have just created to the Encoding Queue, and click the Settings button.

2. Click the Advanced Settings button in the Encoding Settings dialog box, shown in Figure 8-16, and specify the following values:

   - Output filename: Rims
   - Codec: ON2VP6
   - Frame rate: 15
   - Key frame placement: Automatic
   - Quality: Custom
   - Max data rate: 250
   - Encode audio: Selected
   - Data rate (audio): 32 kbps (mono)

8

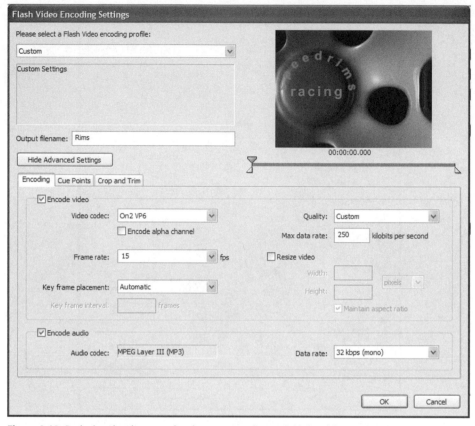

Figure 8-16. Reducing the data rate for the empty audio track in the video

> **3.** Click OK to return to the Encoding Queue, click the Start Queue button, and when the encoding is finished, quit the Flash Video Encoder.

A "down-and-dirty" poster frame

If you get into discussions with the Flash Video crew, one of their pet peeves is the fact that the FLV format, unlike QuickTime, does not easily allow for a poster frame. When the video hits the stage, it either starts playing immediately or there is nothing to indicate video is on the stage other than a blank space. Here is a relatively easy way of creating one:

> **1.** In After Effects, press the Home key to return the playback head to the 0 point of the timeline.
>
> **2.** Making sure nothing is selected in the Comp window, set the Comp window magnification to 100% and take a screenshot.

If you do a lot of screenshots, use a commercial product for the task. The authors, for example, on the PC side of the fence, use SnagIt 8 from TechSmith, or Snapz Pro X from Ambrosia Software on the Mac side of the divide. If the shot is destined for Flash, set the file format to JPG and the image resolution to 100 DPI in both applications.

3. Open the screenshot in Photoshop or Fireworks and crop the image to 320×240 or whatever dimensions are used for the video. Save the image as a JPG image and quit the imaging application.

One thing we do is to zoom in on the edges of the image to be cropped to ensure no pixels from the background are visible. Even a line that is 1-pixel wide will be visible in Flash.

4. Open the `Rims.fla` file located in the `Rims` folder found in your Chapter 8 Exercise folder. When the file opens, open the Flash Library. You will notice we have included the files you will need and have named the layers.

5. Drag the Rimshot movie clip from the library to the first frame of the Poster Frame layer. Set its location in the Property inspector to 180 on the X axis and 85 on the Y axis.

6. Select the movie clip on the stage, and in the Property inspector give it the instance name of mc_poster.

A good Flash habit to develop is to give instance names a prefix that indicates what they are. If you look at that image on the stage, you can't tell whether it is a graphic, button, or movie clip symbol. It also serves as a mental reminder as to what ActionScript events, methods, and properties can and can't be used when it comes time to do some coding.

7. Click once in Frame 2 of the Video layer and add a keyframe by pressing the F6 key. With the keyframe selected, drag the video object from the Library to the stage and, in the Property inspector, as shown in Figure 8-17, specify these values:

- Width: 320
- Height: 240
- X: 180
- Y: 80
- Instance name: myVideo

8

Figure 8-17. The movie is ready to be wired up with ActionScript.

With the assets assembled, it is time to "wire up" the movie with ActionScript. The plan is really simple: click the image and the video starts to play. Here's how:

1. Select Frame 1 of the Actions layer, open the ActionScript Editor, and enter the following code:

```
stop();
mc_poster.onRelease = function() {
  gotoAndPlay(2);
}
```

The first line stops the playback head on Frame 1. If it weren't there, the image would pop onto the screen and the video would start playing.

The function is how the playback head gets over to the second frame. When the movie clip named mc_poster is clicked, it sends the playback head to Frame 2 and plays whatever is in Frame 2. In this case, it is the video. Of course, if you have gotten this far in the book, you know you will need to write the code that plays the FLV video in the video object.

2. Select Frame 2 of the Actions layer, add a keyframe, open the ActionScript Editor, and enter the following code:

```
stop();

var nc: NetConnection = new NetConnection();
nc.connect(null);
var ns: NetStream = new NetStream(nc);
myVideo.attachVideo (ns);
ns.play("Rims.flv");
```

The first line is the key to this code. If it weren't there, the playback head would simply loop back to the first frame.

3. Save the file and test it.

Animating Photoshop layers: Can you dig it?

In this exercise, you will learn how to turn Photoshop layers into the bits and pieces of an animation. As you have learned earlier, Photoshop documents can be imported into After Effects in much the same way they can be brought into Flash. You can choose to import the individual layers or bring the image into After Effects as a single, flattened bitmap.

The Photoshop file you will be using for this exercise is the image of a large excavator, shown in Figure 8-18, that is composed of four layers. What you are going to do is to put the arm and shovel into motion in After Effects. The key aspect of this exercise is work-flow.

8

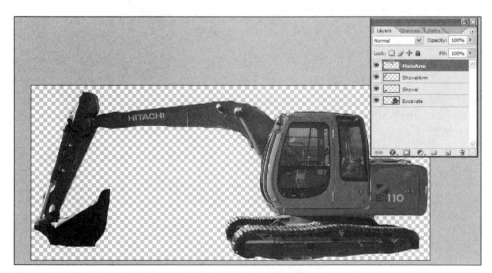

Figure 8-18. The Photoshop image and the layers that will be put into motion

297

It is not uncommon for a Flash developer or designer to be handed a multilayer Photoshop document and be asked whether the bits and pieces comprising the image can somehow be animated. Though the animation can be done in Flash, the problem with that approach is the amount of time that will be spent ensuring all the movie clips are properly aligned with each other and the tweens used in the animation are coordinated with each other. We aren't raising this point to discourage you from considering Flash to do the work. Instead, this exercise is here more to change your mindset from thinking every animation task handed to you can be done in Flash to using the "the right tool for the right job at the right time." The parenting feature of After Effects is the tool for the job at hand.

1. Open After Effects and create a new project.

2. Before you merrily bring the image into After Effects, consider this: the file contains four layers, and After Effects imports each layer into the project as an individual PSD document. If you were to import the file, you would have to select File ➤ Import ➤ File four times. This is rather inefficient and a waste of time. Instead, select File ➤ Import ➤ File and navigate to the Excavator.psd file, located in the Excavator folder found in the Chapter 8 Exercise folder.

3. When the Import File dialog box opens, navigate to the image, select it, and select Composition from the Import As pull-down menu shown in Figure 8-19. When you click Open, the image arrives in After Effects as a Comp and the images in the PSD document's layers are in a separate folder.

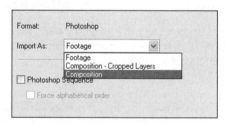

Figure 8-19.
Importing multilayer Photoshop documents as a Comp

4. Save the file using the name Excavator to the Excavator folder containing the file you just imported.

As it now stands, the image can be animated, but the Comp size is set to the size of the image imported into After Effects. This leaves absolutely no room for the arm to move. Let's fix that:

5. Select the Excavator Comp in the Project panel and select Composition ➤ Composition Settings. When the Composition Settings dialog box opens, change the Width value to 500, the Height value to 300, and click OK. When the dialog box closes, double-click the Excavator Comp in the Project panel to open it.

Now that there is room to move around, let's take a second and consider how this machine will animate. If you look at the Comp and relate the layers to real life, you realize that the MainArm doesn't move up and down. It pivots and, as it pivots, the ShovelArm and the Shovel will move. When the machine is digging, the motion for those two pieces changes because they pivot as well. If you carefully read the "Parenting 201" section of this chapter, you know that a pivot is nothing more than a rotation based upon the position of the Anchor point in the layer. The problem is the Anchor points for the two arms and the shovel are sitting in the middle of each layer. If you use their current locations, the animation will look, well . . . stupid. Here's how to fix that:

6. Select the MainArm layer and click the Pan Behind tool (it is directly to the left of the Rectangular Mask tool). When you select this tool, the Anchor point for the selected layer will become visible. Move the Anchor point to the position shown in Figure 8-20.

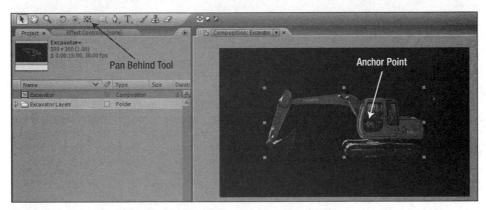

Figure 8-20. Using the Pan Behind tool to change Anchor points in a layer

7. Change the Anchor points for the ShovelArm and Shovel layers.

Here's a quick way of revealing only those layers to be worked on. Click the Solo Switch, *as shown in Figure 8-21, for the* MainArm *and* ShovelArm *layers, and everything else in the Comp is turned off.*

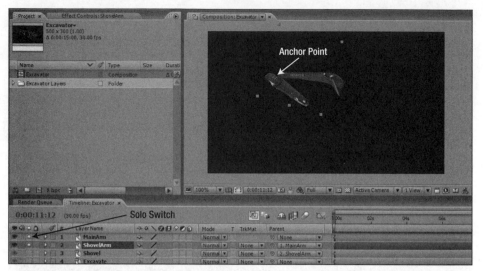

Figure 8-21. Clicking the Solo Switch turns off the visibility of only those layers you don't need to see. Note the location of the Anchor point for the ShovelArm layer.

8. With the Anchor points in place, hold down the Shift key and select the MainArm, ShovelArm, and Shovel layers. Press the R key to reveal the Rotation properties for the selected layers and scrub through the Rotation degrees to curl the arm up to a starting position as shown in Figure 8-21. We found a value of –5 degrees for the MainArm, –75 degrees for the Shovel Arm, and –93 degrees for the Shovel layers worked for us.

> *As you rotate the objects, they will move out of alignment with each other. Move them back into alignment before proceeding.*

With the assets in place in the Comp window, you can now turn your attention to putting this machine to work. In order to not drive yourself up the wall, across the ceiling, and down the other wall, you'll establish the parenting relationship before animating the arms and the shovel. If you don't do it now, the animations will be very, very disjointed, and you might be tempted to send us some nasty e-mails.

1. Use the Pick Whip tool to set the ShovelArm layer as the parent of the Shovel layer. Do the same thing to set the MainArm layer as the parent of the ShovelArm layer.

2. If the Rotation properties aren't visible, select the MainArm, ShovelArm, and Shovel layers and press the R key to open their Rotation properties.

3. Place the playback head at the 2-second mark of the timeline and add keyframes for each of the three selected layers. Use the following Rotation values:

- MainArm: 5
- ShovelArm: −80
- Shovel: −18

4. Place the playback head at the 4-second mark of the timeline and use the following Rotation values:

- MainArm: 22
- ShovelArm: 49
- Shovel: 106

5. Place the playback head at the 5-second mark of the timeline and use the following Rotation value:

- MainArm: 6

6. Place the playback head at the 5.5-second mark (the time will read 0:00:05:15) on the timeline and use the following Rotation values:

- ShovelArm: 40
- Shovel: 156

7. Place the playback head at the 6.5-second mark (the time will read 0:00:06:15) on the timeline and use the following Rotation values:

- ShovelArm: 20
- Shovel: 122

8. Place the playback head at the 7-second mark of the timeline and use the following Rotation values:

- MainArm: −10
- ShovelArm: 11
- Shovel: 73

9. Place the playback head at the 8-second mark of the timeline and use the following Rotation values:

- MainArm: 10
- ShovelArm: 11
- Shovel: 73

10. Place the playback head at the 9-second mark of the timeline and use the following Rotation values:

- MainArm: 5
- ShovelArm: −80
- Shovel: −18

11. Do a RAM preview, and you will see the machine at work, as you see in Figure 8-22. Save the file.

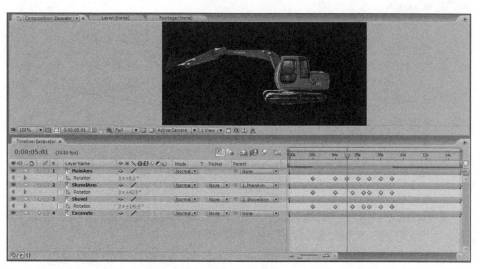

Figure 8-22. Animating the machine by changing the Rotation properties for the various layers

Now that we have the machine digging a hole in the screen, let's put the whole thing into motion. That means the machine will come onto the screen, dig a hole, and move off of the screen.

1. Create a new Comp named Final and drag the Excavator Comp onto the timeline. Drag the excavator down the Comp until its tracks are sitting on the bottom of the Comp window.

2. With the Shift key held down, drag the machine until it is just off of the right edge of the Comp window.

3. With the layer selected, press the P key to open the Position properties and add a keyframe.

4. Move the playback head to the 2-second mark of the timeline and, with the Shift key held down, drag the machine until the back edge of the machine is touching the right edge of the Comp window.

5. Place the playback head at the 10-second mark of the timeline and add a keyframe. Adding this keyframe without moving the machine ensures the machine stays in place during the digging process.

6. Place the playback head at the 12-second mark and, with the Shift key pressed, drag the machine to the left until the left edge of the machine touches the left edge of the Comp window.

7. Save the project and do a RAM preview. The machine will drive onto the screen, dig up a hunk of something, retract its arm, and drive to the edge of the Comp window (see Figure 8-23).

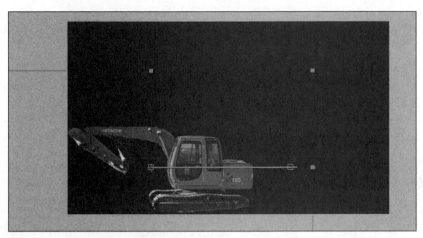

Figure 8-23. The machine is in motion.

The technique of animating Photoshop layers adds a rather powerful tool to the arsenal. Though this project was designed to demonstrate the technique, it has application ranging from banner ads that have to fit a small space to putting objects in motion without spending an inordinate amount of time in Flash getting it just right. It is the prudent Flash developer or designer who understands parenting in After Effects and uses it to his or her client's advantage. You dig?

When null is more than nothing

In this final exercise of the chapter, you will be using a Null object to affect movement in the Comp window. To Flash coders, this may be a rather odd concept to grasp because when null is used in ActionScript—nc.connect(null)—it tends to indicate values that may be missing or that don't have a predefined data type. It is actually quite remarkable, when we think about it, how similar the concepts are to each other. In After Effects, a null layer is a layer with an invisible object inside of it, meaning it, too, doesn't contain a predefined data type such as an image or text.

The decision to use a Null object is relatively easy to make. There will be occasions where you can't decide which object will be the parent or when you will need to edit the parent's properties without affecting those of its children. The neat thing about a Null object is its opacity is always 0, meaning it will never render and its Anchor point is always set to 0, 0— the upper-left corner of its layer. This means its Position and Origin are always the same, which makes the children's positioning also a bit more intuitive for you.

You'll do a simple exercise to learn how to use a null layer:

1. Open the `NullEx.aep` file, which is located in the `Null` folder inside the Chapter 8 Exercise folder.

2. When the project opens, scrub the playback head across the timeline. You will see that we have animated the layers from an Illustrator document to create a rather basic titling sequence.

> *Tired of constantly twirling down layers to reveal their Transform properties? Try this. Select all of the layers in the NullEx Comp and press the U key. All of the Transform properties for the layers, as shown in Figure 8-24, will appear. Press the U key again, and the layers collapse.*

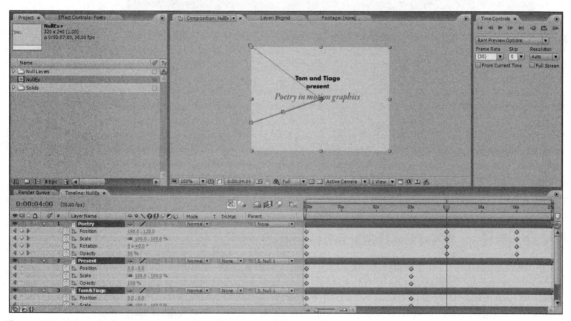

Figure 8-24. Select the layers and press the U key to reveal the Transform properties for the selected layers.

3. Select Layer ➤ New ➤ Null Object. What you will see is a new layer named Null1 appear on the timeline and an outlined box will appear in the Comp window. This is the Null object, and the only place it will appear is in the Comp window.

4. Use the Pick Whip tool to make the Null object the parent of the Tom&Tiago and Present layers.

5. Drag the Null object, as shown in Figure 8-25, to the top of the Comp window and add a Position keyframe. As you move the Null object, the two other layers attached to it will also move.

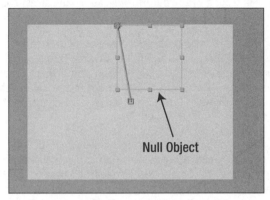

Figure 8-25. The Null object in the Comp window

6. Drag the playback head to the 4-second mark on the timeline and drag the Null object to the bottom of the screen. Pay attention to the two children that are following it. You want to make sure they appear just over the title in the Comp.

7. Save the file and do a RAM preview. The two layers will move from the top of the screen and shrink in size as they move into place.

> The animation is a bit long. It really should last only 4.5 seconds. Here's a fast way of doing that. Set the Out point for all of the layers to 0:00:04:15. When you finish, drag the Work End handle to the 0:00:04:15 point on the timeline and select Composition ➤ Trim Comp To Work Area.

As you have seen, the Null object allows you to create complex motion through the addition of yet another motion path to the animation. Again, this is a great technique to employ for the treatment of text in Flash banner ads, or motion or animation sequences where the motion of one object is required to be independent of the others.

Summary

As you may have gathered, parenting is one seriously powerful tool. For tasks that range from the movement of one object to the coordination of the movement of multiple objects, parenting provides you with an efficient method of undertaking tasks that are extremely complicated to accomplish in Flash and complete them in short order in After Effects.

8

You have learned how the parent/child relationship works and have really dug into some of the more important aspects of this feature in the "Parenting 201" section of the chapter. As you learned, parenting isn't as simple as it seems, and an awareness of the gotchas, such as nonproportional scaling of the parent, will reduce the stress factor when you really dig into this subject.

You saw how a simple parent/child relationship works by preparing the Rims project and discovered a couple of real time savers along the way. You also learned that the term "Pick Whip" is not as nasty as it sounds. We also showed you how to create a relatively easy poster frame for the video in Flash. You also learned how many developers are adding a blank sound channel to their After Effects rendering jobs to ensure their FLV files are as problem free as possible.

You then tackled a rather complex project that involved realistic animation of an excavator. The major aspect of that exercise was how you can actually import a PSD document composed of multiple layers as a Comp. You also learned how to use the Pan Behind tool to set pivot points and just how important a parent can be when objects need to rotate in different directions without distorting the animation.

We finished the chapter by showing you how to add a Null object to the timeline and how to use it as a parent object. As you discovered, a Null object is useful for situations where objects have to move, but nothing in the Comp will make a good parent.

This has been a rather complex and technical chapter, but an invaluable stop in our quest for dragons. In the next chapter, our dragon hunt takes us into the realm of masks. You have only been scratching the surface of this topic to this point in the book. Turn the page to find out more.

9 THE VIDEO BEHIND THE MASK

This chapter deals with masking video in Flash and in After Effects. It is an important chapter because knowing how to mask video, especially in the design area of the field, is a "must have" skill, not a "nice to know" skill. The reason is you are eventually going to receive footage for a clip that doesn't contain an alpha channel. In these situations, you will have to create one of your own. There will also be situations where the clip handed to you is to be used as the fill for letters in a word or for a shape. Again, a solid grasp of a variety of masking techniques is a good skill to have.

The most important skill is being able to determine which tool to use for the task at hand. For example, you are handed a photo of the pixel boards in Piccadilly Circus in London and told the client wants to have some fun and put one of his ads in one of the pixel boards. Both After Effects and Flash can do the job, but which one is best in this situation? It just might be Flash, because the video is going to play in a small area of the screen and an FLV file with a small physical footprint loads a lot faster than one with a large physical footprint. Then again, if perspective is important, then After Effects may be the tool. What if the client wants something cool like having the masked video rotate around the Y-axis? Flash isn't the tool for that job.

Regardless of how you approach the subject, masking video is a lot of fun and opens you up to a serious number of creative possibilities. In many respects, this chapter is designed to expose you to those possibilities. Once you see them and use them, you will most likely discover the same thing about masks that the authors have: the amount of fun you can have with them should be illegal.

Let's go for it.

A basic After Effects mask

You can create and edit masks directly in the Comp window. Like any task in After Effects, there are advantages and disadvantages to this. A major advantage of using the Comp window is the mask is applied in context with the other layers. By this, we mean you can see how the mask interacts with the content in the layers above and below the layer containing the mask. The disadvantage is it can be hard to see what you are doing with a mask if the layer has been transformed or has a lot of effects applied to it. In this case, working in the Layer window, not the Comp window, might be a better approach.

1. Open the Basic_01.aep file found in the BasicMask folder of the Exercise folder in the Chapter 9 code download.

2. Click the video in Layer 1 and select the Rectangular Mask tool. Draw a rectangle over the video in the Comp window. When you release the mouse, the area outside of the shape just drawn will turn black. Click the Toggle Transparency button in the Comp window, and the black area turns into the familiar checkerboard pattern you saw in Chapter 4's keying discussion.

3. Twirl down Layer 1 and you will see that a Masks strip has been added to the layer. Twirl down the Masks strip, and you will see the masking properties and parameters.

If you aren't in a "twirling mood" and want to see the masking parameters, select the layer and quickly press the M key twice to open the Masks properties.

4. Click the video in the Comp window and click the Toggle View Masks button—it is the button directly to the left of the Current Time Indicator (see Figure 9-1) in the Comp window—then click it again. What you will see is the color of the selection in the Comp window change. The yellow color around the video tells you that you are in Mask view and the color, which is the same color used in the Mask 1 layer, shows you the layer's boundaries.

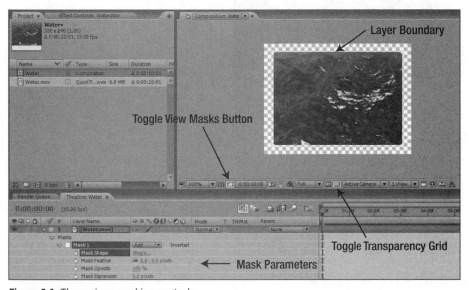

Figure 9-1. The various masking controls

5. Deselect the video in the Comp window and double-click the Water.mov layer instead. A new window—the Layer window—containing the video and the mask will appear. (Another way of making the Layer window appear is to double-click the Comp.) The neat thing about working in Layer view is that you can concentrate only on that layer and not have to worry about anything else. Changes made here will appear in the Comp window. Let's try that.

6. Change the Mask Feather value in the Mask 1 parameters to 50 pixels and click the Toggle Transparency Grid button in the Layer window. The video develops a seriously soft edge. Now click the Composition tab. Note how the feather hasn't changed between the two views. The Composition tab shows you the entire Comp with all of the layers, whereas the Layer view allows you to focus solely on the content in the layer.

7. You will notice that there is an Inverted switch in the Mask 1 layer on the timeline. Click the switch, and two things happen: a check mark appears in the switch, and the video develops a hole in the middle. What you did was to tell After Effects to put the mask inside the selection. Click the switch again, and the video changes.

8. What if you want the box or circle to change its shape? No problem. Press Ctrl+Alt (PC) or Cmd+Option (Mac), and the cursor changes from a solid arrow to the hollow arrow. With the keys held down, drag on one of the corner points. The point will transform from a corner point to a smooth point or vice versa. Drag the handle, and the mask changes its shape, as you see in Figure 9-2 (you might have to change to Layer view for this to work—although it should work in Composition view).

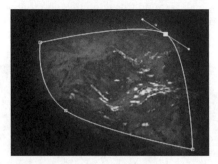

Figure 9-2.
Mask shapes can be manipulated.

> Here's a little trick: to convert all the curve points to corner points and vice versa, Ctrl+Alt-click or Cmd+Option-click one point in the mask. Don't drag.

So much for the basics in After Effects. Let's now turn our attention to masking video in Flash.

A basic Flash mask

As you saw in the previous exercise, when a mask is placed "over" an image or video, the things outside of the shape used as the mask will disappear. Though that is an overly simplistic explanation, it is a good way to envision a mask when it comes to Flash.

In Flash, masks can be applied either on the timeline or programmatically through ActionScript. Either way the object being used as the mask always sits on a layer above the object being masked. Let's look at both approaches.

> There is a lot more you can do with masks in Flash than what will be presented in this chapter. If you really want to dig into it, there is a whole chapter devoted to this subject in Foundation Flash 8 Video by Jordan L. Chilcott and Tom Green (friends of ED, 2006).

1. Inside the Chapter 9 Exercise folder is a BasicMask folder. Open it and then open the Basic.fla file in that folder.

2. Select the Video layer and add a new layer named Mask.

3. With the Mask layer selected, select the Circle tool, and, in the toolbar, turn off the stroke. Draw a rectangle with a width of 150 pixels and a height of 150 pixels over the video object on the Flash stage.

4. Right-click (PC) or Ctrl-click (Mac) on the Mask layer name on the timeline. A context menu will appear (see Figure 9-3). Select Mask. When you release the mouse, a couple of things will change on the screen. The first thing is the circle on the stage disappears and the video object on the stage is reduced to a big X on the screen. The second thing is the change to the Video and the Mask layers. They are both locked, the pencil with a line through it on the Mask layer says it can't be drawn on, and the name of the Video layer is indented on the timeline. Those changes to the layers indicate a mask has been applied.

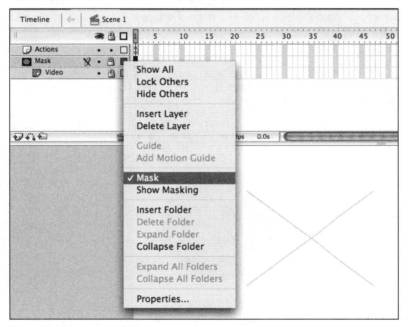

Figure 9-3. A layer mask in Flash

5. Test the movie and you will indeed see the mask has been applied.

To remove the mask, open the context menu for the Mask *layer and deselect* Mask. *Click the lock icons on the* Mask *and* Video *layers to make them editable again, and you are done.*

We won't be masking the FLVPlayback component in this chapter. It can be done, but the problem is you simply can't see the mask when it is applied. You can only see the mask at runtime.

You can also apply a mask programmatically by using the setMask method of the MovieClip class in ActionScript. This only works if one movie clip is masking another. Here is how:

1. Open the Basic1.fla file in the BasicMask folder. When it opens, you will notice a couple of changes to the previous exercise. The mask object and the video object are now movie clips in the Library, and the two movie clips are on the stage.

2. Select the Video movie clip on the stage and give it the instance name of mcVideo in the Property inspector.

3. Select the Mask movie clip on the stage and give it the instance name mcMask in the Property inspector.

4. With the Mask movie clip still selected, check Use runtime bitmap caching, if it is not already checked in the Property inspector (see Figure 9-4).

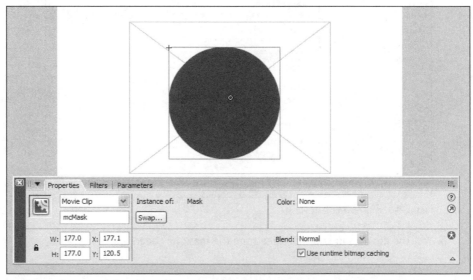

Figure 9-4. If the mask isn't in motion, select Use runtime bitmap caching in the Property inspector.

Bitmap caching is new to Flash 8. In previous versions of the application, all content—static and in motion—on the stage was constantly redrawn as the playback head moved through the movie. This tended to slow things down because the stuff that didn't move between frames was needlessly redrawn in each frame. The introduction of runtime bitmap caching in Flash 8 removes this drag on performance. The content to which it is applied is moved into a memory cache, which means Flash essentially ignores redrawing it as the playback head moves from frame to frame, unless it changes its look, of course. (Changing position doesn't mean the internal movie clip content has changed.) For this reason, you should be careful what you apply bitmap caching to—if the movie clip changes significantly during the course of the movie, it could actually reduce performance.

5. Select the keyframe in the Actions layer, open the ActionScript Editor, and enter the following line of code:

```
mcVideo.setmask(mcMask);
```

As you can see, all you need to remember is to use the movie clip used as the mask as the setMask method's parameter.

6. Test the movie, and you will see, as Figure 9-5 demonstrates, how one line of code applies a mask.

Figure 9-5. One line of code applies a mask if you use ActionScript instead of a mask layer.

What you have just done is use the two more common methods of masking an FLV file in Flash. We will be using them for the balance of this chapter. At this point, you can quit Flash and decide whether to save the files or not. You are going back to After Effects to put what you have learned to some really good use.

9

Using text masks in After Effects

There will be occasions when a shape just isn't what you need. The design calls for the text to act as a mask. In this exercise, we are going to show you how to do that in After Effects. Naturally, being the guys we are, a simple mask is boring beyond belief. Instead, along with showing how to create the mask, we are going to show you an interesting, eye-catching way of using a mask to create the illusion of speed.

What is going to happen is that the word used to mask the video will form, but the edges of the letters won't be hard edged. Instead, the edge will start out as a blur and gradually become hard edged.

Here's how:

1. In After Effects, create a new Comp that is 320X240, uses Square Pixels, and has a duration of 0:00:04:00 seconds.

Now that you have a Comp, let's take a second to review our plan of attack.

There is going to have to be something moving around behind the mask to give the illusion of speed. This tells you that a layer containing that animation has to be created. It also tells you that the mask is going to have to sit above the animation. You can approach this in a couple of ways. The first is the method we have been using throughout this book. We have been simply plunking the mask into the target layer by copying and pasting the mask artwork from Illustrator or Photoshop into the target layer. The second method, and the one we will be using here, is to put the mask into its own layer and manipulate the mask's parameters in that layer. The big advantage to this approach is the mask is not "wired into" the object it is masking as a masking property of the layer. It is just another piece of content in its own layer on the timeline. In many respects, the mask is quite similar to a layer mask in Flash in that it is an independent object that can be moved up and down in the timeline's layer order as needed.

The first step, therefore, is to create the object to be masked. What you are going to do is to create a rather colorful pattern. To create the background, follow these steps:

2. Create a new black solid. Select the name of the solid on the timeline, press the Enter/Return key, and change the name of the layer to FlowingBG.

3. Select Effects & Presets ➤ Noise&Grain and drag a copy of the Fractal Noise effect onto the Comp. When you release the mouse, you will see what looks like smoke on the Comp (see Figure 9-6). This is the default for the effect.

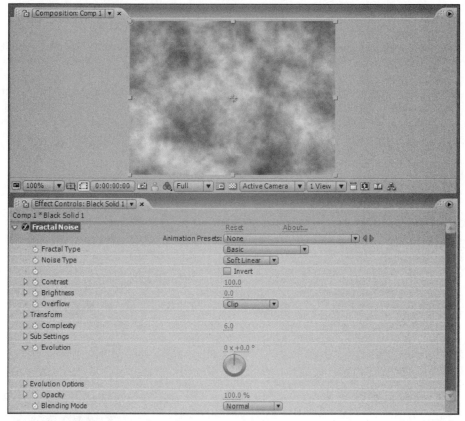

Figure 9-6. We start with smoke . . .

4. Obviously, you want something a bit different from the default values. Open the Effect Controls panel and use these values instead:

- Fractal Type: Turbulent Smooth. The smoke changes into what looks like a series of smudged cluster galaxies. Each selection in the pull-down results in a different look.

- Noise Type: Linear. The smudges become a bit more distinct. This is because the noise introduced won't be in the form of a random pattern. The pattern will be linear.

- Contrast: 645. You want black and white. Remember, double-click a value if you want to go beyond the scale of the slider which, in this case, is 400. By boosting the contrast to such a high level, you essentially remove practically everything that may have a gray value.

- Brightness: −158. Your clusters become quite distinct—the converse of the Contrast setting. By reducing the brightness, you bring up detail that is lost with such a high Contrast value.

- Transform: Twirl down this setting and deselect Uniform Scaling. By doing this, you can transform the clusters into lines.

- Scale Width: 500. The clusters stretch out.

- Scale Height: 1. You now have your lines, which look like streaks.

- Evolution: 0 x +292. The shape will change in a subtle manner. Evolution acts a bit differently from the controls that use Rotation and degrees. If you change the Rotation value, the pattern will change. Change the value to a different number, and the pattern will change to something completely different . . . it does not rotate. By not changing the Rotation value and instead changing the degrees, you can add a subtle change to the pattern and maintain its integrity as shown in Figure 9-7. In fact, you will be putting that change into motion in the next couple of steps.

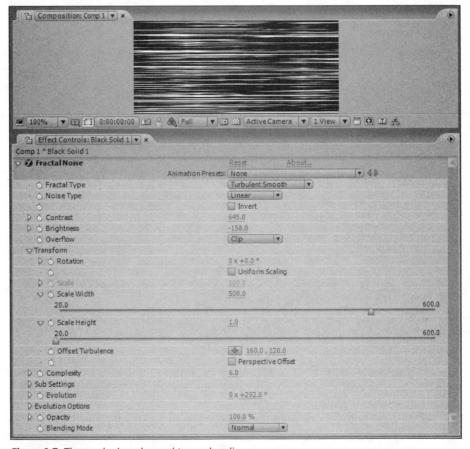

Figure 9-7. The smoke has changed to random lines.

5. Select the black solid layer and press the E key to open the Effects strip on the timeline. Twirl down Effects.

6. Select the Contrast parameter, add a keyframe, and change the Contrast value to 333. Move the playback head to the 1-second mark on the timeline and change the Contrast value to 656.

It may seem a bit odd to set a value in one place only to change it on the timeline as you just did with Contrast *parameter. The purpose of the* Effect Controls *panel in this case is to get the "look" you need and to then, using keyframes, have the solid animate to the final setting. Though you could stay with the original contrast value, we felt it needed to be a bit stronger.*

7. Return the playback head to the start of the animation. Click the stopwatch to add a keyframe to the Evolution parameter and change the value to 0 x +0.0 degrees. Press the End key to scoot the playback head to the 4-second mark and change the Evolution value to 3 x +128 degrees. If you scrub through the timeline, you will see the pattern gives the illusion of movement. Save the project.

The pattern is interesting, but the colors are a bit boring. Let's deal with changing the pattern from black and white to something with a bit more eye appeal. Here's how:

1. In the Effects & Presets panel, twirl down Stylize and drag the Glow effect from the folder onto the Comp. Nothing really seems to have changed because the colors for the effect are black and white.

2. Open the Effect Controls panel and twirl down the Glow effect. Use these settings:

- Glow Threshold: 23. A smaller value will allow the effect to be applied to a wider range of color values. Notice how, when you change the value, the streaks get larger, indicating the increased range.

- Glow Intensity: 2.1. Think of this as being a brightness control for the glow being applied.

- Glow Colors: A & B Colors. Nothing will happen just yet because you need to change the A and the B colors.

- Color A: #00CCFF (bright blue). Color A is the start color, and the glow will transform from Color A to Color B. You really didn't see a change here because you haven't set that second color.

- Color B: #0090FF.

The streaks now change color, and, if you scrub through the timeline, it sort of looks like that really scary TV screen from the movie *Poltergeist*.

3. Save the project (we used TextAE as its name) to your desktop or the Chapter 9 tEXT_ae folder.

With the animation completed, you can now turn your attention to creating the mask. Before you start, just be aware that you can't simply toss some text over a layer and expect it to act like a mask. What you need to do is to first create the text and then, as in Illustrator and Photoshop, convert the text to outlines and place those outlines in a separate mask layer. Though it may sound a little convoluted on the surface, you will see it really isn't complex and, in many respects, is quite intuitive. Follow these steps to mask the animation:

9

1. Click the Comp, select the Text tool, and enter the text got fluid?. Use these formatting values in the Character panel (see Figure 9-8):

- Font: Arial Black (Feel free to choose a different sans serif font.)
- Color: #FFFFFF (white)
- Size: 55 px
- Select Faux Bold (If you are using a sans serif font that has a Bold style, skip this setting and choose the Bold version of the font instead.)

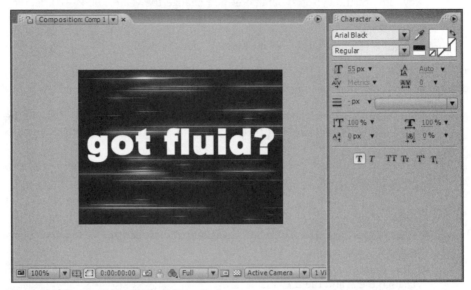

Figure 9-8. The text is created and formatted.

The text in the Comp is essentially a bitmap. The next step is how text is turned into PostScript outlines.

2. Select the layer with the text and select Layer ➤ Create Outlines. When you release the mouse, a new layer with the word outline in its name is created. Twirl down the Masks property of the new layer, and you will see that several masks have been created.

We are going to take a brief pause here to explain why there are so many masks.

If you were to look at the capital letter *P*, the chances are you would see it as a shape with a hole in it. That hole, in typographic terms, is called a **counter**. When a letter with a counter or a letter with a period over it (such as j or i) is created, the shapes aren't grouped. They are created as compound paths. In Illustrator, if you want to poke a hole through a solid, you would draw the hole and then turn both the solid shape and the circle into a compound path. This is exactly how counters are treated when the letters are drawn. This is an important concept to grasp because were you to convert the letter *P* into paths in Illustrator, the counter would be regarded as a separate shape, as in Figure 9-9, and thus become a separate mask layer.

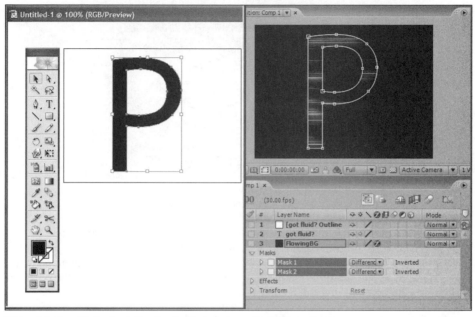

Figure 9-9. One Illustrator letter is actually two shapes in both applications.

The other thing you should notice about this layer is that it still isn't masking the background. This is because this layer's purpose is to create the paths, which are regarded as masks, and that is all. The contents of the layer are nothing more than a bunch of filled objects waiting to be put to work.

3. Twirl down the Outline layer, and, with the Shift key held down, select each of the masks. When they are selected, select Edit ➤ Copy. You are now finished with the Text and the Outline layers, so turn off their visibility.

4. Create a new black solid, select it in the Comp, and select Layer ➤ Mask ➤ New Mask. This will add a mask to the solid. Select the mask in the solid and select Edit ➤ Paste, and the letters will replace the single mask in the solid.

5. The letters all appear as black filled letters. Let's change that. Twirl down the Masks layer if it isn't open and change the blend mode of the g mask layer from Difference to Subtract. Scrub across the timeline, and you will see that the background animation shows through the letters (see Figure 9-10).

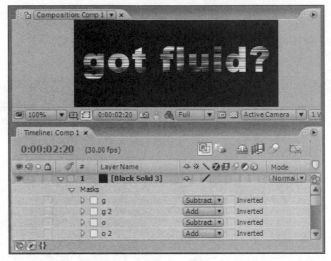

Figure 9-10. The mask is created by using the Add blend mode for the counters and the Subtract blend mode for the letter forms.

As we pointed out right at the start of this exercise, we don't want the animation to start with a defined edge on the mask. This edge is what makes each letter of the phrase distinct. Instead, the animation starts off with the letters blurring and then coming into focus. This is done by adding a blur or feather to the edge of each mask, except for the counters, and, using keyframes, having the feather value reduce to 0.

6. Twirl down each of the mask layers, except for the g2, o2, d2, and ?2 layers, and use the following for keyframe placement and Mask Feather values:

g	00:00 seconds, 85	01:11 seconds, 0	
o	00:15 seconds, 85	01:15 seconds, 0	
t	00:15 seconds, 90	01:19 seconds, 0	
f	01:00 seconds, 65	02:00 seconds, 0	
l	01:06 seconds, 70	02:06 seconds, 0	
u	01:10 seconds, 85	02:15 seconds, 0	
i	01:12 seconds, 60	02:18 seconds, 0	
d	01:20 seconds, 52	03:00 seconds, 0	
?	02:17 seconds, 85	02:20 seconds, 02:22 seconds, 196	03:00 seconds, 0

7. Do a RAM preview, and you will see a rather interesting text effect. Save the file.

8. Add the project to the Render Queue and create a QuickTime movie named TextAE that uses the Animation codec and includes an empty audio channel. When the render finishes, save the project and quit After Effects.

> *"Hold on," you might be thinking, "Aren't there two nonvisible layers that will get in the way of the render process?" No. In After Effects, layers with their visibility turned off are not rendered. If you are really paranoid, delete the two invisible layers before you render the video. Just be sure that before you do that you save the project under a different name. You may need to change the text.*

If you launch the video in QuickTime, you can't help but notice there is a lot of wasted space (see Figure 9-11). There will be occasions when you will need just the animation to appear in the FLV video. The next part of this exercise shows you how to trim an FLV video before placement in Flash.

Figure 9-11. The animation in the QuickTime Player. Note the wasted space.

Cropping an FLV video in the Flash 8 Video Encoder

1. Launch the Flash 8 Video Encoder and add the TextAE.mov file created in the previous exercise or use the file provided in the Exercise folder to the Render Queue.

2. Click the Settings button to open the Encoding Settings dialog box. Name the file FluidAE and click the Show Advanced Settings button.

3. When the Advanced Settings appear, use these values:

- Video codec: ON2VP6
- Frame rate: 15
- Quality: Custom
- Max data rate: 250
- Encode audio: **Selected**
- Data rate **(audio):** 48 kbps (mono)

Now that you have the encoding portion under control, let's crop out the dead space. Click the Crop and Trim **tab to open the** Crop and Trim **area.**

4. When the Crop and Trim area opens, scrub across the timeline to about the 3-second mark in the Preview area. This will show you all of the letters in the animation.

5. There are four sliders in the Crop area. As in Figure 9-12, they are, in clockwise order, top, right, bottom, and left. Click the top value and drag the slider downwards until the crop value is about 85. Notice how the dotted line in the preview moves down or up depending upon which direction you are dragging the slider.

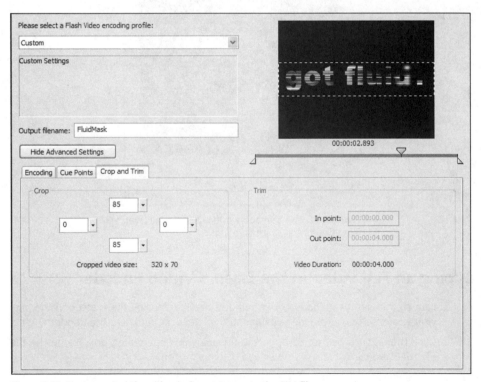

Figure 9-12. You can crop the video before you create the FLV file.

6. You can also do it by the numbers. Double-click the value in the bottom slider and enter 85. Again, a dotted line will show you the location of the crop, and at the bottom of the Crop area you will see the Cropped video size is now 320×70.

> *It would be a really good move on your part to write down the new dimensions of the FLV file. If you are using a video object in Flash, you are going to have to change it to the dimensions of the video playing in the video object. If you don't intend to use a video object and use the FLVPlayback component, it will resize to fit the dimensions of the FLV file.*

7. Click the OK button to return to the Render Queue.

8. Click the Start Queue button to create the FLV file. When it has finished, quit the Video Encoder. At this point, you can choose whether or not to place the FLV file in Flash or not.

Though we won't be using this FLV file again, it is important that you know how to crop a video. In the case of this file, there was a lot of black that served no purpose. By cropping the file, you are essentially reducing the final size of the FLV file, ensuring that it will quickly load and quickly play. When it comes to encoding video, the goal of the process is to have the smallest file size with the best quality you can get. These are subjective decisions, but little things like removing the dead space from an FLV file can have a profound impact on playback.

Creating a text mask in Flash

You have seen how to create a text mask in After Effects and are probably wondering if you can mask video with text in Flash. The answer is, Easily. Here's how to mask a video with text in Flash:

1. In the FlashTextMask folder found in the Chapter 9 Exercise file is a Flash file named Text.fla. Open it in Flash. When the file opens, you will see that we have placed a video object on the stage and wired it up with ActionScript to get the video to play. Test the movie to watch the video.

> *The video is called* Mamma Andretti's Pizza *and was produced by the students of the Film and TV program at the Humber Institute of Technology and Advanced Learning in Toronto.*

2. Click once in the first frame of the Mask layer. Select the Text tool, click the stage once, and enter the text Pizza.

3. With the text selected, use the Property inspector to apply these settings:

- Font: Arial. We used Arial Black simply because it takes up more room on the stage. Feel free to use any font of your choosing.
- Size: 120.
- Color: #000000 (black).
- Type: Static.

4. Select the Mask layer and turn the layer into a mask layer using the technique presented earlier in the chapter.

5. Test the movie. The pizza commercial, as shown in Figure 9-13, plays inside the text. Save the file and close it. We are now going to look at the Illustrator-to-Flash connection.

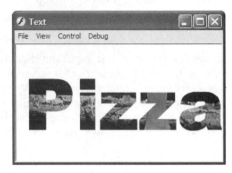

Figure 9-13. A text mask in Flash

Illustrator masks to Flash

You can use Illustrator to create masks for Flash video or other Flash objects on the stage. In fact, Illustrator CS2 gives you a lot more creative control over the shape of the mask than you get in Flash. In this exercise, you will learn how to bring Illustrator line art into Flash and use it as a mask. If you don't have Illustrator CS2, you can skip to step 4.

1. In Illustrator, open the Pizza.ai file found in the FlashTextMask mask folder of your Chapter 9 Exercise folder. Click the letter *P* with the Selection tool, and you will notice the document consists of the text Pizza, which has been converted to outlines.

2. Click the word to select it in Illustrator and copy the selection to the clipboard. Quit Illustrator.

3. Open the TextIll.fla file in the FlashTextMask folder.

4. Select the Mask layer and paste the contents of the Clipboard into the Flash document. You can paste the clipboard contents by either pressing Cmd+V (Mac) or Ctrl+V (PC) or selecting Edit ➤ Paste in Center. They both do the same thing.

> *The official method of importing Illustrator art into Flash is to use* File ➤ Import. *Flash developers and designers have found this to be a somewhat cumbersome practice and, in the case of simple line art such as this, prefer to use the copy-and-paste method demonstrated.*

5. Convert the Mask layer into a mask and test the movie. Holy smokes! Only the letter *P* is showing as a mask (see Figure 9-14). This is because each letter of the word is regarded as a separate piece of line art. You can only use one object in a mask layer, which explains why Flash is ignoring the remaining letters in the word. Let's fix that right now.

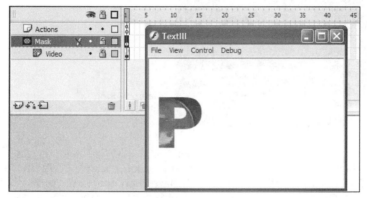

Figure 9-14. Only one masking object is permitted.

6. Remove the mask by right-clicking (PC) or Ctrl-clicking (Mac) the Mask layer and deselecting Mask from the context menu. Unlock the layers. Hold down the Shift key and click each of the letters in the layer. Convert the selection to a movie clip named Mask.

> *If you don't have Illustrator, drag the* Pizza *movie clip into the* Mask *layer.*

7. Apply the layer mask and test the movie. The video now shows through the letters. Even though there are multiple objects in the movie clip, Flash still regards the movie clip used as the mask as being a single object.

A gradient mask for a Flash video

Earlier in this chapter we showed you a technique for masking a Flash Video. It works fine for objects with a solid fill, but what about objects with a gradient fill? What if you are looking to have a video use the grayscale values in a gradient mask to fade out on the edges like the feathering you applied to the masks in After Effects? You will discover the technique doesn't work unless the video is embedded in the Flash timeline. If the video is a couple of seconds in length, this is a viable option; but embedded videos make for very large SWF files that will need an inordinate amount of time to load before the video plays.

The solution to this is a variation of a Flash technique that developers and designers use to create a Flashlight effect. In this effect, an image on a black background is "lit up" through the use of a mask with a hole in it. The object shows through the hole, as you see in Figure 9-15, and fades off in intensity from the edges of the mask. Here's a way to do the same thing with an FLV:

Figure 9-15.
The good old Flashlight effect

1. In the Chapter 9 Exercise folder, you will find another folder named FlashGradientMask. Open that folder and double-click the FLVMask.fla file in the folder to launch Flash. If you already have Flash open, use File ➤ Open to open the file. Other than our writing the ActionScript to play the video and supplying the video object in the Library, you are going to create the assets for this exercise.

2. Create a new movie clip named Mask. When the movie clip opens, select the Rectangle tool and draw a box on the stage that is 600 pixels wide by 500 pixels high. With the box selected, turn off the stroke in the Property inspector and change the color of the box to a bright color. We chose #00CCFF (blue). Set the box's X and Y position in the Property inspector to 0.

3. Select the Circle tool and change the fill color to a different color.

4. Click the Object Drawing mode button beside the horseshoe icon in the Options area of the toolbox (see Figure 9-16) and draw a circle on top of the box you just drew. Object drawing mode is new to Flash 8 and allows you to draw independent objects on top of each other. In previous versions of Flash, if you were to draw another box on top of the one you just drew, it would become a part of the blue box. It was a huge frustration for Flash designers. You can always tell when you are in this mode because the object drawn is inside a bounding box.

Figure 9-16.
Object drawing mode is turned on in the toolbox.

5. Set the circle's height and width dimensions to 200 in the Property inspector.

6. Select both objects and open the Align panel—Ctrl+K (PC) or Cmd+K (Mac). Making sure that Align to stage is not selected, click the Align to Vertical and the Align to Horizontal Center buttons. This will place the circle in the middle of the square.

7. Select both objects on the stage and press Ctrl+B (PC) or Cmd+B (Mac) to break apart the selection. This step essentially flattens the image. Click the circle and press the Delete key. The stage color will now show through the box.

8. Create a new movie clip named VideoMask. When the movie clip opens in the Symbol Editor, add a layer named Mask to the timeline. Change the name of Layer 1 to Video. Drag a copy of the video object from the Library and place it in the Video layer. In the Property inspector, change the size of the video object to 320×240 and give it the instance name of video.

> Be sure to spell the instance name of the video object exactly as we have. The ActionScript on the main timeline will be navigating to this clip.

9. Drag the Mask movie clip from the Library to the Mask layer and in the Property inspector set both its X and Y coordinates to 0.

10. Select both objects on the stage and align them vertically and horizontally with each other. You should see the video object through the hole in the mask.

11. Click the mask on the stage and click the Filters tab to open Filters. Click the + sign and select Blur from the pull-down list. Click the lock icon once to enable you to use differing blur values and use the following Blur filter properties:

- Blur X: 60
- Blur Y: 20
- Quality: High

This blur is the key to the mask. A blur essentially fades the edge of whatever object it is applied to by using changing alpha values from 100% to 0%. In many respects, this is quite similar to what happens when you applied a Mask Feather value to each of the masks in the last After Effects exercise.

12. Click the mask once, and in the Property inspector set its blend mode to Erase. What the Erase blend mode does is to "erase the background" based on the alpha value of the movie clip it is applied to. This blend mode does not work in isolation. It needs a Layer blend mode to be applied to its parent movie clip. Let's do that right now.

13. Click the Scene 1 link to return to the main timeline. When you arrive there, drag the VideoMask movie clip to the stage and give it the instance name of mcVideoMask in the Property inspector and set its blend mode to Layer.

14. With the movie clip selected, align the movie clip to the center of the stage.

15. Test the movie. The video has a gradient mask applied to it (see Figure 9-17).

Figure 9-17. Use blend modes to create a gradient mask for an FLV.

"Getting fluid" in Piccadilly Circus

Inevitably you are going to be asked to put a video in an area of a photograph. A couple of weeks ago a friend of one of the authors sent him an image of Piccadilly Circus in London. We looked at the image and thought, "Wouldn't it be neat if we put the 'got fluid?' animation from earlier in the chapter into the pixel board in the upper-right corner of the image?"

As Figure 9-18 illustrates, the problem with that is the area curves around the corner of the intersection. If the video was done right, it would follow the geometry of the area where it will be placed. The traditional approach to this problem is to place the image into Flash, draw a mask of the area that will contain the video, and then manipulate the video object with the Free Transform tool in Flash to get it to fit . . . somewhat.

Figure 9-18. The video is destined for the pixel board in the upper-right corner.

The issue is not one of getting it to fit. The video will need to have a bit of distortion added to it. Also, even though the video mask will give the illusion of a video wrapping around the pixel board, it will still look as though it is still "flat" (see Figure 9-19). It just won't look right because the Free Transform tool does not allow you to "bend" the lines to which it is applied. You can skew, scale, and rotate the video object, but you won't be able to bend the video to follow the curve.

Figure 9-19. Something just doesn't look quite right.

There is a solution. The answer lies in the word *bend*, and we have used a tool that will bend a video: the Bezier Warp effect in After Effects. Let's "get fluid" in Piccadilly Circus:

1. Inside the Chapter 9 Exercise folder is a folder named VideoMask. Open this folder and open the Warped.ae file to launch After Effects. When the file opens, you will see that we have included the image we will be using in Flash and a QuickTime movie rendered from the "got fluid?" exercise you did earlier in this chapter.

2. Select the TextAE layer and twirl down the Distort folder in the Effects & Presets panel. Drag a copy of the Bezier Warp effect in the Distort folder on top of the video in the Comp.

As you may recall, the Bezier Warp tool adds Anchor points, called **vertices**, and handles, called **tangents**, to the object in the Comp. What you are going to do is to manipulate the vertices to get the object to the proper size and then manipulate the tangents to "bend" it around the edge of the sign.

3. Drag the video and align its upper-left corner with the sign in the picture as shown in Figure 9-20. When the picture is aligned, drag the middle vertex at the bottom of the image upwards until the bottom-left corner of the video is roughly placed on the bottom-left corner of the pixel board. You may have to adjust the placement and size of the video because moving that vertex also moves the opposite edge inwards or outwards.

Figure 9-20. Drag a vertex to get the size to match the pixel board.

4. With the video into position, all you need to do now is to start fiddling with the tangents. Drag the bottom-right tangent point onto the bottom-right corner of the pixel board. Notice that when you move that point, it is almost as though you were manipulating a Bezier handle in Illustrator. In fact, it is the same process.

5. Move the upper-right tangent to the upper-right corner of the pixel board. In the Comp window, change the Magnification level to 200% and start fiddling with the handles. When you finish, the edge should resemble that shown in Figure 9-21.

Figure 9-21. The edge is pretty well complete.

6. Change the magnification level to 400% and move around the warp to fine-tune the placement of the handles and the edge of the video on the pixel board. You can move around the Comp window by pressing the spacebar and dragging the image.

7. When you finish, reduce the magnification to 100% and scrub through the timeline to see the effect. As you see in Figure 9-22, it looks a lot more natural than the one shown in Figure 9-19. Save the project.

Figure 9-22. The image looks more natural than the one in Figure 9-19.

Naturally, solving one problem raises another. Obviously this video is physically too large to be run through Flash. The Comp size matches the 550×400 dimensions of the Flash stage. A video of these dimensions, especially if the file is being streamed from a web server, will not give you smooth playback. There is a way of solving this problem, and it is to render out only the video portion, not the image, of the After Effects project. The result will be a very small video (physically and in file size) that will become even smaller when it is encoded as an FLV file. Here's how:

1. Select the Piccadilly.jpg layer and either turn off its visibility or delete it from the Comp.

2. To the left of the Toggle Alpha Transparency button in the Comp window is the Region of Interest button. Click it. A box with handles will appear in the Comp window.

3. Drag the handles, as shown in Figure 9-23, to adjust the size of the selection. What you have just done is to isolate the video on the screen.

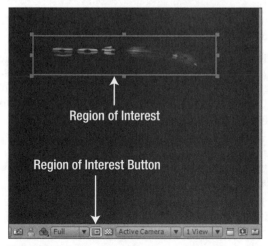

Figure 9-23. Set a region of interest to isolate the video.

333

> *What you might want to do is to scrub through the timeline to ensure the edges of the video in the Comp are within the region of interest.*

This region of interest not only isolates objects, it can also be used to crop a video to the size of the region you identify. Here's how:

4. Add the Comp to the Render Queue. Click the Lossless link and select QuickTime movie as the Format and use the Animation codec set to Millions of Colors as the compressor.

5. Click the Crop check box and then click the Use Region of Interest check box, shown in Figure 9-24. Selecting this crop option outputs the video to the dimensions of the bounding box used as the region of interest.

Figure 9-24. You can crop a video to the dimensions of the region of interest.

6. Select Audio Output and click OK to close the Output Module Settings dialog box.

7. Click the Output To link, navigate to your Exercise folder, and save the video as Warped.mov. Click OK to close the dialog box and click the Render button to create the video.

8. Save the project and quit After Effects.

The next step is to run the Warped.mov file through the Flash 8 Video Encoder to create the FLV file. To make life easier for you, we've done this already, and have included a copy of the two FLV files—Warped.flv and Looky04.flv—that are in the VideoMask folder and will be added in Flash.

Let's put some video up in Piccadilly Circus:

1. Open the VideoMask.fla file. You will notice that we have actually created the masks and the videos for you. The masks were created by selecting the Pen tool and drawing over the area of the image where the video will appear. We then switched to the Selection tool, clicked each object, and turned off the stroke in the Property inspector.

   The objects were then converted into movie clips named Warped and Tiago. Two layers were added to each movie clip. One was the Actions layer and the other contains the video object from the Library. The video object was lined up under its mask and the mask layer was created.

   If you zoom in on each of the movie clips, you will see how we used the X position from the masked video object to align each clip with its pixel board on the screen.

2. Save and test the movie. As shown in Figure 9-25, you will see Tiago looking around under the "fluid" animation. Don't quit Flash just yet. It is your turn to be a star.

Figure 9-25. Who can resist a cute puppy?

Before we move on, we want to remind you that rendering only a region of interest instead of an entire video is an extremely powerful tool. By cropping a video to the dimensions of a region of interest, you will produce a video that is close to the dimensions needed in the Flash movie. These physically small videos, which are inevitably destined for the Flash 8 Video Encoder, will be extremely small—the FLV file used in this exercise is just over 100K in size—meaning they will load and play almost immediately. In many respects, that is the ultimate goal of anything destined for Flash playback, and one way of achieving that goal is to remove anything that adds weight to a video.

> As you may have guessed, the Looky04.fly file contains an alpha channel. What you can gather from this is that both regular video and alpha channel video can be used in this sort of project.

What about you?

So far we have put an animation and a video into the pixel board. How would you like to wave at the crowds in Piccadilly Circus?

One of the great things about working with Flash Video is that it will also play a feed from a web cam. If you have one, connect it to your computer and let's put you in the TV screen beside the "got fluid?" animation. Here's how:

1. Select the Magnifying Glass tool and zoom in on the TV screen beside the "got fluid?" animation.
2. Select the Pen tool and draw over the image on the screen.
3. Switch to the Selection tool, click the object, and, in the Property inspector, set the stroke to None.
4. With the object still selected, convert it to a movie clip named Me.
5. Double-click the Me movie clip in the Library to open the Symbol Editor. Click the shape, and, in the Property inspector, ensure that its X and Y coordinates are set to 0.
6. Add two new layers to the movie clip timeline. Place them above and below the layer holding the object. Name the top layer Actions and the bottom layer Video.
7. Select the Video layer and drag the video object from the Library into the selected layer. Give it the instance name of myVideo in the Property inspector.
8. Select the Free Transform tool in the toolbox and click the video object on the stage. The white dot in the selection is the transform point. Drag it to the upper-left corner of the selection. With the Shift key held down, click the bottom-right corner of the object and drag the corner until the right edge of the video is just touching the right edge of the black object. What you want, as shown in Figure 9-26, is for the video object to be just a bit outside of the black object.

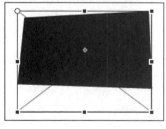

Figure 9-26.
Use the Free Transform tool to resize the video object.

9. Select the layer containing the object and turn it into a mask layer.
10. Select the first frame of the Actions layer and open the ActionScript Editor. When it opens, click once in the Script pane and enter the following two lines of code:

```
var myCamera:Camera = Camera.get();
myVideo.attach Video(mycamera);
```

The first line of code retrieves the camera object by using the Camera.get() method and gives the camera the name of myCamera. The second line simply attaches the feed from the video camera into the video object on the stage.

We wish we could say it is more difficult than that, but it isn't.

> *You may be wondering whether you can actually have a camera feed into this sort of Flash project on your website and broadcast it to anybody that may be looking at the site. The answer is a qualified yes. To do it properly, you will need to use a Flash Media Server. Needless to say, that is well out of the scope of this book. You can pick up a free copy of the server for use on your computer at* www.adobe.com/products/ flashmediaserver/. *While you are there, an excellent series of tutorials are available at* www.adobe.com/devnet/flashmediaserver/. *Another great site to learn about how to use the server is Stefan Richter's site at* www.flascomguru.com/tutorials/. *Finally, an open source "version" of the server, Red5, is available at* http://osflash. org/red5.

11. Click the Scene 1 link to return to the main timeline and add a new layer named Camera to the timeline. With the Camera layer selected, drag the Me movie clip onto the stage and put it into position over the image. Save the movie.

12. Test the movie. What you will see is a warning asking you about privacy. This warning simply allows the user, not you, to decide whether or not to permit the use of a microphone or a camera during the playback of the movie. Click the Allow button and you will be waving to the folks on the street as shown in Figure 9-27.

9

Figure 9-27. The finished product

If you aren't seeing a feed from your web cam, the odds are that Flash isn't using the proper driver for your web cam. To fix this, right-click (PC) or Ctrl-click (Mac) on the open SWF file. This will open the Flash Player context menu. Select Settings *to open the* Flash Player Settings *dialog box and click the* Camera *icon to open the* Camera *settings, shown in Figure 9-28. Select the driver from the pull-down list and click the* Close *button. Mac users may have a slightly different problem. If you use an iSight web cam, the iSight camera may not appear in the pull-down. Instead, select the* IIDC FireWire Video *option and then click the* Close *button.*

Figure 9-28.
Select your web cam in the SWF Settings dialog box.

Taking video for a spin

A couple of months ago the authors were asked to check out a website where a company named Freedom Interactive Design was in the middle of Times Square and other New York locations selling websites. The site, www.wouldyoulikeawebsite.com, featured people wearing sandwich boards asking people on the street if they would like to own a website. What caught our attention were the sandwich boards. They contained video of fully functioning websites and, as the subject wearing the board moved, the video as it played on the sandwich board, Figure 9-29, also moved and maintained its perspective.

Figure 9-29. Want a website?

Even though Freedom Interactive Design isn't telling how they did it, we thought we would show you one of the techniques used in the site. It involves rotating a masked video 360 degrees around the Y-axis, tilting it on the X-axis, and zooming it in using the Z-axis of a Comp. If you can make a video rotate and tilt in space and, at the same time, move along the Z-axis to give the illusion of depth, you are on your way to selling websites in New York.

1. Open the Spin.aep file located in the folder named Rotate. This folder can be found in your Chapter 9 Exercise folder. We have already created the Comp for you and added an Illustrator mask to the Water2.mov file on the timeline. If you scrub across the timeline, you will see water rising up and down through the key-hole mask.

2. Open the Perspective folder in the Effects & Presets panel and drag a copy of the Basic 3D effect onto the video in the Comp window.

3. Open the Effect Controls panel. This effect gives you a first peek at the power of 3D in this application. Instead of X-, Y-, and Z-axis controls, they are named Swivel, Tilt, and Distance to Image as shown in Figure 9-30. If you drag the Swivel handle, the keyhole video rotates on the Y-axis. Drag the Tilt handle, and the video rotates on the X-axis. Drag the Distance to Image slider, and the video recedes into space or returns to its original size depending upon the direction you dragged the slider. Click the Reset link at the top of the panel to return the effect to its default settings.

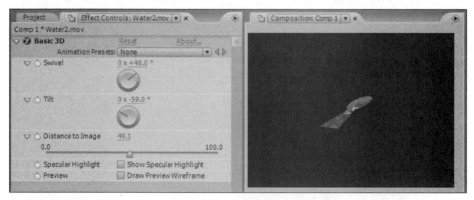

Figure 9-30. Water in space

> *Don't forget you can "go off of the page" with the* Distance to Image *value. The 0 setting assumes the distance is where you started, or the original size. This is a 3D effect, so double-clicking the value and entering a value of –50, for example, brings the object closer to the viewer and gives the illusion of a serious increase in size.*

4. To animate this effect, twirl up the layer on the timeline and then press the E key to open the Basic 3D effect. Twirl down the effect to reveal its parameters.

5. Press the Home key to return to the 0 point of the timeline and add keyframes at the 0 point to the Tilt, Swivel, and Distance to Image parameters.

6. Move the playback head to the 1:15-second mark and use the following values for the parameters:

- Swivel: +180
- Tilt: +180
- Distance to Image: 50

When you change the values, the video will spin around, turn upside down, and get smaller. If you scrub through the timeline, you will see this in motion.

7. Move the playback head to the 3-second mark and use the following values for the parameters:

- Swivel: +360
- Tilt: +360
- Distance to Image: 0

If you do a RAM preview at this point, you will see the video change and then return back to its starting state. At this point, you can save the project. The purpose of what you just did is to give you another creative tool to play with. This effect is rather interesting because it allows you to spin videos or other content on the Flash stage. If you were to simply Swivel or Tilt the video through a full 360-degree rotation, the video will become reversed at the midpoint and return to its proper orientation at the end point. For example, you can try playing with text in the same way—if you were to animate the word *Flash* using this effect, at the midpoint (see Figure 9-31) the word would look like you are trying to read it in a mirror.

Figure 9-31.
Even words can go for a spin.

Like all effects, use this one judiciously. Still, the ability to rotate video files, words, and objects in a 3D space is not something that can be done in Flash. Now, when you look at the wouldyoulikeawebsite video, you can start to see how they did it. The website content on the sandwich board was carefully masked, and, using Tilt and Swivel, the website videos were composited onto the boards. The use of the Basic 3D effect allows the video to move around in space in tandem with the movement of the board it is being composited on to.

If you are using this effect for video that tilts or swivels through a full 360 degrees, be sure to use a video that is smaller than the space allotted to it on the Flash stage. If this effect were to use a 320×240 video in an FLV file that is 320×240, there won't be enough room in the Comp for the full effect, and in Flash it will look rather disjointed. The video used in this exercise is 240×180 in size and *placed in a 320×240* Comp.

Happy birthday, Flash

Just as we were pulling this chapter together, Adobe launched a birthday celebration. Turns out that Flash first hit the street in August 1996. Having used Flash since version 2, the announcement gave the authors an opportunity to reflect on the long, strange trip the Flash journey has been through the years and to think of some of the brilliant artists and just plain characters that they have met who have had an impact on the Flash community over that time as well. It has been quite the journey where gradient-filled balls that moved across the screen were thought to be the pinnacle of the Flash art (if you remember Gabbocorp, you are a grizzled Flash vet), compared to the modern day, where examples like the ones featured in this book are within the grasp of anyone with the right tools and a creative spark. This brings us to the final exercise in the chapter.

We thought we would do our own little homage to Flash and, along the way, show you a couple of new tricks in After Effects and how to add a Flash movie clip to the Flash movie that plays at a later point in the FLV file. Also, because it is Flash's birthday, we aren't going to get you to do a lot of work. Instead, we are going to look at a couple of the highlights in the After Effects project and the Flash movie and explain to you how we did it. We'll get you to add a couple of effects that we haven't covered in this chapter.

Let's have a party:

1. To start, launch the bumper.swf file found in the Birthday folder. The folder can be found in the Chapter 9 Exercise folder. The project starts off with a timeline, some text that is wiped, some names, and then a rainstorm starts. The stylized *f* in Flash appears and explodes out of the screen. Close the SWF and let's look at how the movie was pulled together.

> For you trivia buffs, the official Adobe term for the stylized letters used for many of their products is **rune**.

2. Open the bumperEx.aep file located in the Birthday folder. If you open the Project panel, as shown in Figure 9-32, you will see that the assets found in the hBarLayers and flashLogoLayers folders were created in Illustrator. Those Illustrator files were imported into the project as Comps, which explains why there are Comps and folders with the same name. When you import a layered Illustrator file into After Effects as a composition, both the Comp and the folder containing the Illustrator assets—the Illustrator files are in the Birthday folder—take on the name of the Illustrator file being imported. There are also a couple of MP3 files and the usual collection of solids.

9

Figure 9-32. You don't need many assets to get started.

3. Let's walk through the timeline and examine how the project was assembled. The MP3 files in Layer 12 and Layer 13 were the first assets to be added, and everything else placed over them. You will notice that the background layer, Layer 11, is locked. This was done to ensure that once it was in position, the solid in the layer couldn't be accidentally moved. Click the lock on the background layer to unlock the layer and twirl down the layer.

4. Click the Solo switch in the background layer to hide everything but the selected layer. Twirl down the Effects strip in the background layer, and you will see that we have applied a Ramp effect to the solid. Select the effect and either twirl it down in the timeline or in the Effect Controls panel.

As you know, the Ramp effect is used to apply a gradient to a solid. The Start of Ramp parameter sets the start point of the gradient which, in this case, is the top-left corner of the Comp. The Start Color parameter is the first color in the gradient and the End of Ramp and End Color parameters are where the gradient ends—the bottom-left corner of the Comp—and the color used for the end of the gradient. We chose Radial Ramp as the Ramp Shape, which means nothing more than After Effects is told to create a radial gradient that runs from the upper-left corner of the Comp to the bottom-right corner of the Comp. The result was a smooth transition between subtle shades of gray in the background.

Click the Solo switch to turn the layers back on and lock the layer.

5. The TimeBar layer contains the hBar Comp from the Project panel. We found that name for a layer to be a bit unintuitive and changed it by selecting the layer name when the Comp was added to the timeline, pressing the Enter/Return key, and entering a more precise layer name.

Twirl down the Transform strip, and you can see that the animation of the dates was done by changing the Position and Scale properties of the Comp between the keyframes.

6. Click the Solo switches for the three text layers, Layer 7, Layer 8, and Layer 9, to isolate them. You may have noticed, when you watched the SWF, the text on these layers seems to have some sort of "wipe" transition effect applied to them as shown in Figure 9-33.

Figure 9-33.
The text in the SWF seems to have a
transition applied to it.

If you scrub through the timeline, you can see this is not exactly true. The transition is nothing more than a mask drawn using the Pen tool. The transition is the shape, which was pasted into each layer, being manipulated to hide the text. The text appears to be doing nothing more than changing its Opacity value from 10% to 100% between a couple of keyframes.

You may be looking at the Comp window, seeing the mask pass through the text, and yet the text outside of the edge of the mask is still visible (see Figure 9-34). A logical question when you see that is, What's with that?

The answer lies in the Mask Expansion property of the Mask1 layer. Rather than wasting a lot of time physically changing the mask's shape, we let the software do it between the keyframes. All this property does is to expand or contract the edge of a mask from the edge of the original mask, without physically altering the shape of the mask. In the case of Layer 9, the Mask Expansion values change from +20 to –16 pixels. All this means is the mask expands outwards from its original shape by 20 pixels and contracts inwards by 16 pixels.

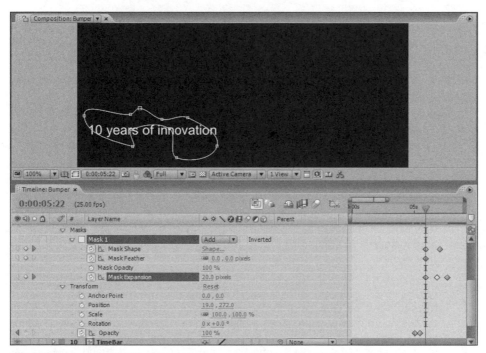

Figure 9-34. Tweening the Mask Expansion property lets the software do the work.

9

Sometimes it really is best not to overthink things and to just let the software do the work. In the case of this "transformation," playing with the shape of the mask, tweening Mask Expansion, and adjusting the Opacity values of the text is a lot easier than trying to get fancy with effects.

Turn off the Solo switches to reveal the content in the Comp.

7. The next two layers that we will look at, Layer 5 and Layer 6, are the animated squiggles. These were created using the Write On and Glow effects that you have used earlier in this book. Now it is your turn to participate in the project and to make it rain.

8. Twirl down the Rain layer and drag the playback head to the In point of the layer. Open the Effects & Presets ➤ Simulation folder and drag a copy of the CC Rain effect onto the Comp window. As soon as you release the mouse, you will see the effect on the solid, and, if you scrub the timeline, you will also see you have kicked off a rather nice rain shower.

9. Open the Effect Controls panel. We'll go through each of the parameters so you understand what they do, and you can give them the values we specify:

- Amount: Drag the slider to the right, and you have a hurricane on your hands. Drag it to the left, and you have a gentle shower. Set this amount to 170.

- Speed: This parameter is tied to the amount and how fast the drops are falling to the ground. Drag the slider to the right, and you have a downpour. Drag it to the left, and it is sprinkling. Set the Speed value to 0.9.

- Angle: Drag the slider, and the direction of the rain fall changes. Set the value to 13.2.

- Angle Variation: You will notice that the rain on the screen is not uniform. It moves from side to side. This slider determines that movement. We won't be changing this value, but, if you have moved the slider, use a value of 10.

- Drop Size: Moving this slider to the left makes for fatter rain drops. Moving it to the right makes them thinner. Use a value of 2.7.

- Opacity: Move this to the right, and the streaks become more distinct. Leave the value at the default setting of 20%.

- Source Depth: This is sort of like watching it rain through a window. Move the slider to the 100% mark, and the rain pattern is very distinct because you are close to the glass. Move it to 0%, and it is like trying to see the pattern from the back of the room. Use a value of 48%.

10. Twirl up the Rain layer and twirl down the FGlow layer. If you twirl down the Effects strip, you will see another application of the Glow filter, which you used to turn on a light bulb in Chapter 3. The purpose of the effect in this case is to have the rune—the stylized *f*—glow before it explodes.

The key to this effect is the keyframes used in the Glow Threshold, Glow Radius, and Glow Intensity properties. The Glow Threshold value, which starts at 45%, sets a threshold as a percentage of brightness to which the glow is not applied. A lower percentage produces more glow; a higher percentage produces less. At 45%, the effect starts out rather dark and increases in brightness until the Glow Threshold value reaches 27.7% at the second keyframe. The Glow Radius and Glow Intensity properties control how many pixels the glow extends out from the bright areas of the image and the brightness of the glow. The radius starts at 14 pixels, expands out to 56 pixels, and then contracts to 22 pixels. The keyframes for the Glow Intensity are pegged at a value of 2.1 to ensure the value remains constant even though the Threshold and Radius values are changing.

The Scale and Opacity properties in the Transform area have a series of keyframes that set how the rune grows and disappears.

Twirl up the layer strip and get set to get back to work.

Creating an exploding rune

In Chapter 7, we showed you how to blow up some text using the Shatter effect. In this final part of the exercise, we give you the opportunity to use the effect to blow up the Flash rune. Here's how:

1. Twirl down the flashLogo layer and click the Solo switch to turn off the other layers. Drag the playback head to the In point of the layer.

2. Open Effects & Presets ➤ Simulation and drag the Shatter effect onto the *f* in the Comp window. When you see the wireframe in the Comp window, open the Effect Controls panel (see Figure 9-35).

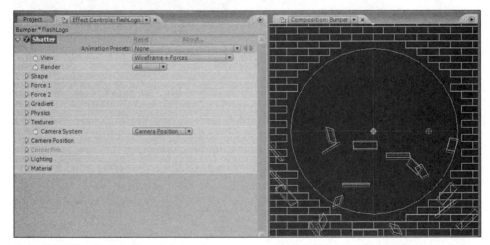

Figure 9-35. The Shatter effect default values. The size of the explosion is shown by the large circle in the Comp window.

3. Select Rendered in the View pull-down to see how the rune is affected by the effect and select Pieces from the Render pull-down to see the pieces of the shattered rune.

4. Twirl down the Shape properties to start working on the pieces of the rune. To start, you want a slightly different look from the bricks you see. Select Glass from the Pattern pull-down and leave the White Tile Fixed selection unchecked. You want all of the pieces to move.

You need more pieces than the default value. To do that, set the Repetitions value to 24.9. Set the Direction value to 37 degrees. This will change the orientation of the pieces in the Comp window. Leave the origin point alone. Changing this value will just move the contents of the Comp from one position to another in the Comp window. Finally, you want the pieces to be a bit thicker. To do this, change the Extrusion Depth value to 0.54. With the shape of the pieces determined (as shown in Figure 9-36), twirl up the Shape properties.

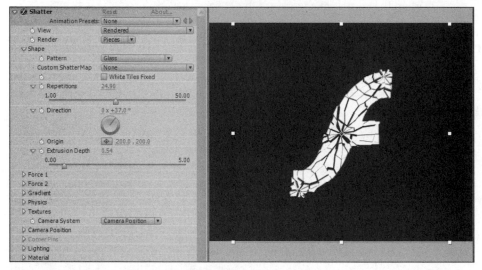

Figure 9-36. The shape of the pieces is determined.

5. Twirl down the Force 1 and Force 2 properties to use two forces to determine the blast area. Start with the Force 1 properties. Don't change the Position and Depth values, which set the center point for the force and the center point of the Z-axis, respectively. Change the Radius value to 1.23. The pieces will move further apart because you made the circle in the wireframe view larger. Don't change the Strength value. This property determines how fast the pieces move, and the default is fine for this exercise.

Next you set the properties for the second force, Force 2, which also causes the rune to shatter. Use these values:

- Position: 300, 200
- Depth: 0.10
- Radius: 0
- Strength: 5

The pieces, as shown in Figure 9-37, will shift position as you change the values. To see the effect in all of its glory, scrub across the timeline.

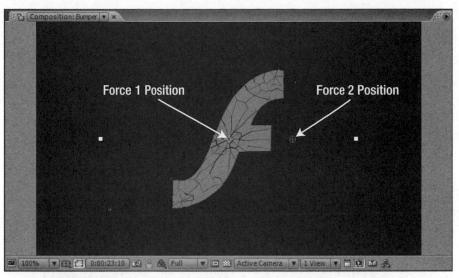

Figure 9-37. The position of the forces determines the size of the blast area.

6. The Gradient controls specify the gradient layer used to control the timing of an explosion and the pieces that are affected by the blast. You aren't going to make any changes here.

7. Having determined what the shatter pieces look like and the forces that caused the shatter, you can turn your attention to the physics of the effect. This is a fancy way of saying how the shatter pieces will move through space. Twirl down the Physics properties. You aren't going to change any of the values, but here is what they do:

- Rotation Speed: Drag the slider to the right to speed up how the pieces tumble and to the right to slow them down.

- Tumble Axis: The default value in this pull-down lets the pieces spin in any direction. The other choices lock the tumble to a variety of axes.

- Randomness: Increasing the value increases the spin and initial velocity of the pieces. A value of 0 shoots everything out of the blast's center point. Increasing the value adds a bit of disorder to the movement.

- Viscosity: This is nothing more than a fancy word for deceleration. Move the slider all the way to the left, and the explosion looks like it occurred in a tar pit. Move it to 0, and you can mimic a star exploding in space.

- Mass Variance: This determines the weight of the pieces. Small pieces will have a low mass. A value of 100% exaggerates the weight difference between the large pieces and the small pieces and spreads them out over a larger area of the Comp.

- The three Gravity settings determine the effect of gravity on the pieces as they move through space.

Twirl up the Physics values.

9

347

8. Twirl down the Lighting properties. These properties determine how the effect is lit. The only change you will make is the position of the light. Change the Light Position values to 200, 224. You will see the crosshairs, as shown in Figure 9-38, move and the shading of the pieces change.

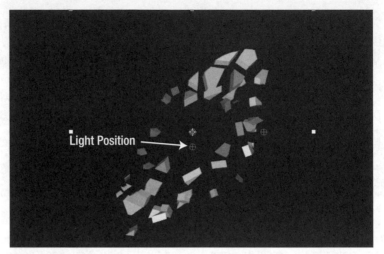

Figure 9-38. You can move the location of the light source by changing its position on the X-, Y-axis.

9. The final step to creating the explosion is to do a bit of color correction. Though the explosion is quite striking, it is really bright and needs to be "toned down." Twirl down Effects & Presets ➤ Color Correction and drag the Brightness and Contrast effect onto the Comp. Open the Effect Controls panel and set the Brightness value to –100 and the Contrast value to –2. The shards of the rune become a bit more defined (see Figure 9-39).

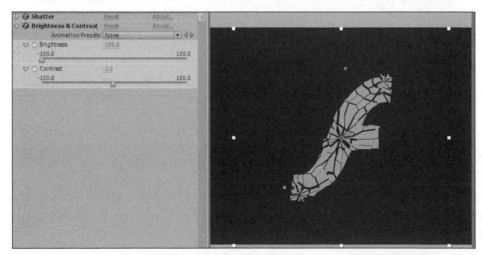

Figure 9-39. The pieces are a bit too bright. Tone them down by reducing the brightness and contrast.

At this point, you can turn off the Solo switch for the layer and save the project. The next step, of course, is to render the project and create the FLV file that will be used in Flash. We aren't going to cover this. The resulting FLV file can be found in the Birthday folder.

The power of the Shatter effect can't be understated, but we also must warn you against using it on a regular basis. Like getting rich in the stock market, the use of this effect comes down to timing. Use it at the right time and in the right place, and it is extremely effective. Overuse the effect, and you diminish its effectiveness. This exercise was a bit more thorough than the one presented in Chapter 7 because, in that chapter, we just wanted you to get comfortable with the effect. As you have seen, Shatter provides you with an awesome degree of control over how things blow up on the screen. Still, there is a lot more to this effect than what we covered here. The best ways of thoroughly understanding what you can do is to first carefully review the Effect Help files found in Help ➤ Effects Help. Each control and what it does is explained in rather minute detail in this document. The second method, in many respects, is the most fun. Start playing with controls and watch how they interact with each other.

Synchronizing Flash content to an FLV file

The final part of this project is to add the developer names to the project. Though we could have just as easily have added them in After Effects, we thought this would be a good opportunity to show you how to synchronize a movie clip in Flash to an FLV file.

If you look at the timeline in After Effects, you will see two Comp markers. Those markers are the points where the names are to come onto the stage and the point where the names will end. The first marker is located at 0:00:11:10 and the second one is at 0:00:18:05. This tells us the amount of time allocated to the animation is 6:25 seconds. That is a nice number to know, but not exactly useful because time in Flash is measured in frames per second. If you select Composition ➤ Composition Settings, you will see that the project is to play back at 30 fps. You now have a common factor between Flash and After Effects.

In Flash terms, the animation of the names should start at Frame 340 and end at Frame 545. How we arrived at those numbers is by multiplying the seconds in After Effects by the Flash frame rate—30—and adding the remaining frames to the result. For example, the start of the animation is at the 11-second and 10-frames mark of the After Effects timeline. This means the animation in Flash should start at Frame 340.

We also know the duration of the animation can be no more than 205 frames in Flash and that the maximum number of frames we can use in Flash is 545 frames.

The key number is the frame rate of the Comp. The frame rate of the Flash movie must match the frame rate of the After Effects project. In fact, when you create the FLV file, its frame rate must also match the one in After Effects.

9

1. Open the Bumper.fla file found in the Birthday folder. As you see in Figure 9-40, the movie consists of three layers, and the Library contains a video object that will hold the FLV file, a number of graphic symbols, and a movie clip named artists.

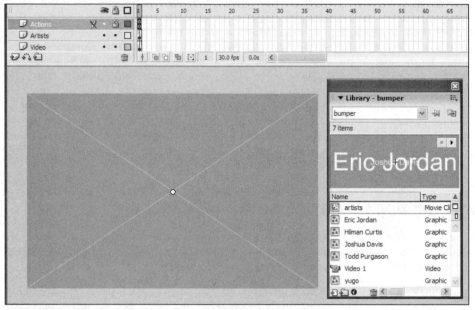

Figure 9-40. The Flash stage

You will notice that the frame rate for the Flash movie has been changed from the default value of 12 fps to 30 fps. How you do this is to select Document ➤ Modify *and when the* Document Properties *dialog box opens, change the* Frame rate *value. Other ways of doing this are to double-click the frame rate in the timeline or to click the* Size *button in the Property inspector.*

2. Double-click the artists movie clip to open it. Scroll to Frame 340. As you can see, the animations start where we determined they should. The blank dot at the end of each animation indicates a blank keyframe. A blank keyframe is nothing more than an empty keyframe (see Figure 9-41), but if it weren't there, the names would remain on the screen as a jumble of letters. To add a blank keyframe, right-click (PC) or Ctrl-click (Mac) and select Insert Blank Keyframe from the context menu.

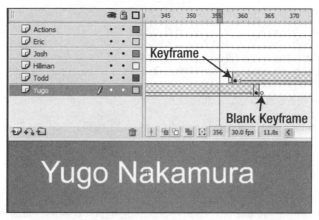

Figure 9-41. Use a blank keyframe to stop items from remaining on the Flash stage.

3. Scroll to the end of the animation. Even though our earlier calculations show the animation should end at frame 545 of the movieclip, this one ends at frame 455. Remember 540 is the maximum. As long as the animation starts at Frame 340, the movie will function as predicted.

> *Don't get hung up on precision when it comes to timing things in Flash. Depending on a number of factors, including bandwidth, open browser windows, and so on, the Flash movie may play at a slightly slower rate than 30 fps. If you are totally paranoid, there is enough of a "hole" in the video that starting the animation at Frame 345 or 350 won't have a major effect on the desired results.*

At this point, you can quit Flash and, if you wish, double-click the bumper.swf file in the Birthday folder to see how everything you have done throughout this exercise comes together.

Happy birthday, Flash.

Summary

Our dragon hunt started with a simple masking exercise in After Effects and ended at a birthday party where things were blown up, words disappeared, and Flash content was synchronized with an FLV file created from an After Effects movie. It was quite the journey.

What we hope you have learned from this chapter is that masking can be done in either Flash or After Effects and that each application has its limitations in this area. As we keep repeating throughout the book: "Use the tool best-suited for the job at hand."

The chapter started on the surface of an ocean as we showed you how to create a video mask in After Effects and in Flash. We also showed you how to use ActionScript to add a mask to the Flash stage. With the basics out of the way, our hunt led us to using text as a mask in both Flash and After Effects. Though it may on the surface appear to be relatively easy to accomplish this task in After Effects, it turns out the ability to add a mask layer to the timeline is a vital skill to have. We then showed you how to create a text mask in Flash and how to use text converted to Illustrator outlines as a mask in Flash.

Where After Effects and Flash part ways when it comes to masking is in Flash's lack of ability to "feather" a mask as can be done in After Effects. As we showed you, there is a way to do it using the blend modes and a Blur filter in Flash.

The next stop in our dragon hunt took us to, of all places, Piccadilly Circus in London, England. We looked at a pixel board collection from across the street and wondered, "Hmmm, how can we use them in Flash?" Using animation created earlier in the chapter, you learned how to "bend" a video to follow a curved surface and of the importance of the selecting a region of interest in an After Effects Comp. You also saw how to use a mask to place a video in a specific area of the Flash stage, and we even gave you the opportunity to wave at the people on the street by showing you how to add a feed from your web cam to the Flash stage.

From Piccadilly Circus, we moved to New York and watched a bunch of people wearing sandwich boards trying to sell websites in a variety of locations in the city. To understand the videos on the sandwich boards, we left New York and ventured into virtual space and showed you how to use the Basic 3D effect to spin video on the X-, Y-, and Z-axes of 3D space.

The chapter ended in the middle of a birthday party for Flash. This exercise showed you a couple of interesting masking techniques such as the Mask Expansion property, dug deeper into the Shatter effect, and finished with how Flash content can be synchronized to an FLV file.

. . . and we haven't finished with masks. In the next chapter, the dragon hunt shows you how a track matte in After Effects can be your friend. See you there.

10 TRACK MATTES ARE YOUR FRIEND

 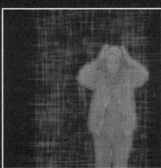 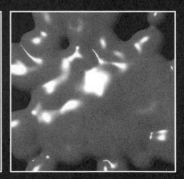

To this point in the book, we have tended to treat masks as somewhat static. They "poked holes" in solids, and the video or content below the solids was visible through the hole. We have also made it abundantly clear that an acute awareness of the power of transparency is the key to creating the composites that are the heart and soul of motion graphics.

In this chapter, we look at how track mattes can help you create some very effective motion graphics. You are most likely reading the term *track matte* and wondering, "Isn't that a fancy term for a mask?" The answer is an unqualified "sort of." You are probably aware that not all images or footage you will use come with transparency already built into them. Sometimes, as we have done with Illustrator images, you need to use a second image to add the transparency. This second image is called a **matte**.

Track mattes 101

In many respects, a matte is an alpha channel, and, if you are a Photoshop user, alpha channels are nothing new. What is new is adding an alpha channel to a video. To do this, you need to use the After Effects Track Matte feature. It really isn't as mysterious as it all sounds.

An alpha channel is a mask in a digital image. An image or digital video that contains an alpha channel is called a **32-bit image**. This means there are 8 bits each for the red, green, and blue channels plus a further 8 bits dedicated to the 256 shades of gray that make up the alpha channel. A 32-bit PNG image from Fireworks (see Figure 10-1), for example, usually contains a mask, and a similar image from Photoshop (see Figure 10-2), usually a PSD file, contains a separate channel for the mask. Both types of file can be used in After Effects.

> We have covered the use of Illustrator images as masks throughout this book. In this chapter, we are going to take a bit of a break and concentrate on alpha channels contained in images.

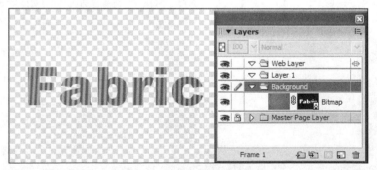

Figure 10-1. A Fireworks image containing an alpha mask

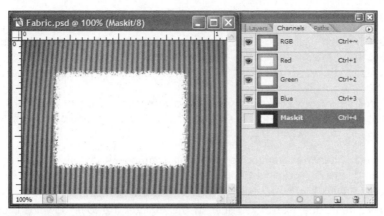

Figure 10-2. A Photoshop image with an alpha channel

The Track Matte feature of After Effects contains two options: Luma Matte and Alpha Matte. Your choice of which option to use rests on where the grayscale information in the image resides. If the image you are using as a matte is a grayscale image, it will get applied as a Luma Matte. If the information lives in an alpha channel, you get the Alpha Matte.

Regardless of the option chosen, there are some hard-and-fast rules regarding mattes in After Effects:

- The matte layer must be above the movie layer.
- The matte is applied to the movie layer, not the image being used as the matte.
- The matte layer's Video switch (the layer visibility icon) must be turned off.

To make all of this work, you must also have the Mode column appear in the timeline. You do this by clicking the Switches/Mode button at the bottom of the timeline as shown in Figure 10-3.

10

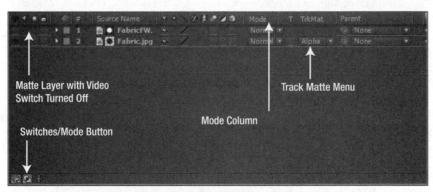

Figure 10-3. A track matte is in place in After Effects.

When you roll over the Switches/Mode *button in After Effects, you will see a tooltip that says* Expand or Collapse the Transfer Controls pane. *When talking about it, stay with the* "Switches/Mode *button" terminology, which everybody uses.*

So much for the theory. Let's do a small exercise that will help you to understand how 32-bit images are imported into After Effects and how to use their alpha channels. Follow these steps:

1. Launch After Effects and, when the application opens, double-click in the Content area of the Project panel to open the Import File dialog box. If you really are into using menus, File ➤ Import will open the dialog box as well.

2. Navigate to the Exercise folder in the Chapter 10 code download, open the Fabric folder, and select the FabricFW file. This file is the 32-bit PNG from Figure 10-1. When you select it, you will see that it is a PNG file in the Format area of the dialog box. Click the Open button to add the file to the Project panel.

3. Double-click the Project panel under the image you just imported. Select the FabricMask file. You will notice it is Photoshop file. Click Open.

4. Instead of the file appearing in the Project panel, the Interpret Footage dialog box, shown in Figure 10-4, opens.

   First off you didn't make a mistake. What is going on here is that After Effects has detected an alpha channel in the document and is asking you how you want to handle it. The choices are quite intuitive:

   - Ignore: Select this and you don't import the channel. Not a good choice.

   - Straight – Unmatted: Another really bad choice. The program that created the alpha channel must have built the straight alpha channel. If the footage is coming from a 3D application, feel free to select this one. Otherwise ignore it.

   - Premultiplied – Matted With Color: A Photoshop or Fireworks image creates a premultiplied alpha channel. All this means is the transparency information in the alpha channel is retained.

   - Guess: Actually this works quite well. It is just that clicking a button named Guess always makes us nervous. Ignore it.

Figure 10-4. The Interpret Footage dialog box asks you how you want to treat the alpha channel.

5. Select Premultiplied and click OK.

> *You may be wondering why the* Interpret Footage *dialog box appeared. This is an actual preference for After Effects. If you open the* Preferences *dialog box* (Edit ➤ Preferences *on a PC or* After Effects ➤ Preferences *on a Mac) and click the* Import *preference, you will see that the* Interpret Unlabeled Alpha As *preference is set to* Ask User *(see Figure 10-5). Thus the dialog box. If you click the pull-down menu, you see that you get to preselect the items in the* Interpret Footage *dialog box. To be honest, we like to be asked, so we leave this setting alone. If you do select* Premultiplied, *the two choices really aren't difficult to understand. The mask color is either white or black.*

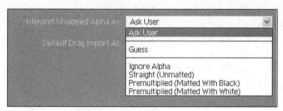

Figure 10-5. The Import preferences

6. Import the Words.psd document. This time a dialog box opens asking you how to handle the layers. This document is nothing more than the word *Fabric* in a transparent layer named Fabric in Photoshop. Select Fabric from the Choose Layer pull-down and click OK.

7. Finally, import the Fabric.jpg file into the Project panel.

What you have done is to import the most common forms of 32-bit images, and, as you discovered, each one is handled a bit differently from the others. Let's now use them. Here's how:

1. Drag the Fabric.jpg image from the Project panel into the timeline window. Make sure that you can see the Mode column; if you don't see the Mode column, click the Switches/Mode button (shown earlier in Figure 10-3) to make it visible.

2. Drag a copy of the Fabric/Words.psd file from the Project panel to the timeline. Drag the Words strip above the Fabric strip in the timeline.

3. Select the Fabric layer and select Alpha Matte "Fabric/Words.psd" from the Track Matte pull-down menu. The Words layer's Video icon is automatically turned off, and the fabric shows through the word *Fabric* as shown in Figure 10-6.

10

Figure 10-6. The track matte from Words.psd is applied.

4. Delete the Words layer in the timeline and replace it with the FabricFW.png image in the Project panel. Drag the FabricFW.png layer above the Fabric layer. A couple of things happen. First, the Alpha Matte was automatically applied to the Fabric layer. Second, the FabricFW.png layer's Video icon didn't turn off. Turn off the layer visibility for the FabricFW.png layer, and you will see the matte has, indeed, been applied.

5. Select Alpha Inverted Matte from the Matte pull-down and turn on the visibility of the FabricFW layer. The fabric becomes visible, and you can barely see the outline of the word. What happened is you essentially turned off the Fireworks mask. Delete the PNG layer.

The FabricMask.psd image is quite a bit different from the two images you have used so far in this exercise. The matte is contained in an alpha channel in the PSD document.

6. Drag the FabricMask.psd document onto the timeline and place it above the Fabric layer. Again, the mask is automatically applied to the Fabric image—a small mask icon appears beside the files type icon in the Fabric layer—but this time you only see the alpha channel. Turn off the Video switch for the FabricMask layer, and the matte, as shown in Figure 10-7, will be applied to the image.

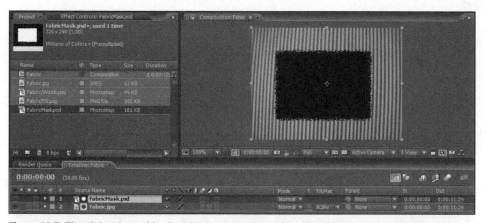

Figure 10-7. The alpha channel in the PSD document is used as a track matte.

So far in this exercise, you have worked with straight white and black mattes; you can create some amazing visual effects using gradient masks that can be done in Flash, if you know what you are doing, but which can be done in less than half the time in After Effects. In the previous chapter, we showed you how to apply a gradient mask to a video in Flash. It was a bit convoluted but quite effective. A little later on this chapter, we are going to show you another way of doing it that requires some rather hefty lifting by ActionScript. If ActionScript isn't your "thing," you can also apply a Gradient Track Matte to a video. Here's how:

1. Close the project that is currently open. We'll leave the decision whether to save it or not up to you.

2. Open the Waves.aep file found in the Fabric folder of your Chapter 10 Exercise folder. You will notice we have already added a video to the timeline for you.

3. Import the Water.psd file into the Project panel and select Premultiplied from the Interpret Footage dialog box that opens. This file is totally different from any that you have worked with so far in this exercise. It consists of nothing more than an alpha channel in a PSD document. The difference is a grayscale gradient runs through the word *Water* in the alpha channel.

4. This time, instead of dragging the image onto the timeline, press Cmd+/ (Mac) or Ctrl+/ (PC), and the image will be automatically added to the timeline—in the proper position above the video no less.

5. Select the Water.mov layer and select Alpha Matte from the Matte pull-down. Do a RAM preview, and the water fades out towards the bottom of the word as the water in the video undulates. To really have some fun with this, click the Toggle Transparency button in the Comp window to see the full effect (as shown in Figure 10-8).

10

Figure 10-8. A grayscale gradient in a Photoshop alpha channel is the key to this matte effect.

6. Decide whether you wish to save the project and then select File ➤ Close Project.

> *If you were to render this video with an alpha channel and convert it to an FLV file using the Flash 8 Video Encoder and the ON2VP6 code with* Include Alpha Channel *selected, you would have a video with a gradient mask without the heavy-duty ActionScript.*

Lighting it up with a Luma Matte

To this point in the chapter, we have been using shapes containing alpha channels as the matte for the video. One seriously cool aspect of track mattes is you can use the Luminance values of an image as the matte. This is a Luma Matte.

We'll help you understand this concept before you put it into practice.

When you add a footage item to the Project panel, After Effects sees it as consisting of 32 bits of information. There are the 24 bits assigned to the red, green, and blue channels, and the remaining 8 bits are assigned to managing transparency. There will be occasions when the image doesn't have a transparency channel. In this situation, After Effects gets rather sneaky. After Effects adds the alpha channel, but, because the assumption is everything is to be visible, the alpha channel is completely white. Drop a grayscale image into the Project panel, and After Effects will still give you four channels. A copy of the image is placed in each of the red, green, and blue channels, and the alpha channel is also white.

Drop a color image into the Project panel, and After Effects will quietly convert the channel color values to grayscale for you.

You may have noticed the word *grayscale* was liberally sprinkled through that last paragraph. The reason is the term *luminance* in After Effects refers to the grayscale values in the footage. The color values are irrelevant. This means an entire grayscale image, not just the channel, can be used as a track matte. Let's try it:

1. Open the AngelLuma.aep file found in the Matte folder of your Chapter 10 Exercise folder. When the project opens, you will see we have imported the Water.mov file into the Project panel and placed it on the timeline.

2. Import the AngelGray.jpg file into the Project panel. Select the image, drag the file to the timeline, and place it above the Water layer.

3. Select the Water layer and select Luma Matte in the Matte pull-down. Press the spacebar to play the video in the Comp window. Pay particular attention to how the grays in the angel act as a matte over the water video (see Figure 10-9).

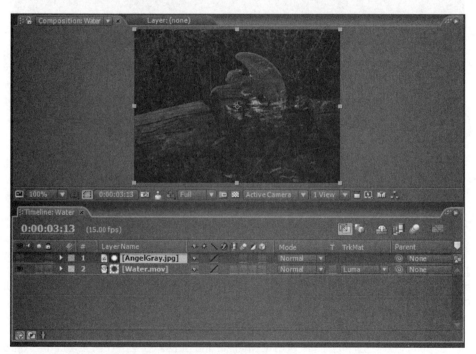

Figure 10-9. A grayscale image is used as a Luma Matte.

10

> *When we talk about a grayscale image, we aren't talking about a black-and-white photo with a single channel. After Effects needs the red, green, and blue channels for these things. If you are preparing these images in Photoshop or another imaging application, be sure they are RGB, not grayscale, images.*

Where this technique really rocks is when you use a grayscale image with an alpha channel. It is something that is virtually impossible to do in Flash but quite easy to accomplish in After Effects. Here's how:

1. Select the AngelGray.jpg image in the timeline and delete it to remove it from the timeline. Import the AngelAlpha.psd image into the Project panel.

2. Drag the AngelAlpha.psd image onto the timeline and place it above the Water layer.

3. Set the matte to Luma for the Water layer.

4. Press the spacebar to play the video in the Comp window. The water, shown in Figure 10-10, undulates in the angel, and the gray values in the image fade the video.

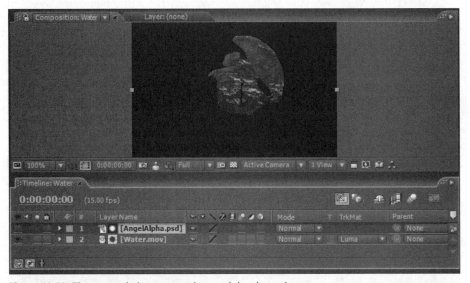

Figure 10-10. The grayscale image contains an alpha channel.

There will, of course, be occasions where either the Alpha Matte or the Luma Matte doesn't quite have the range of Luma values you need or the edges of the matte are not as well defined as you may like. Here's how to address that issue:

1. Select the AngelAlpha layer in the timeline.

2. Select Effects & Presets ➤ Color Correction and drag a copy of the Levels effect onto the Comp.

3. Select the Effect Controls tab in the Project panel to open the Levels controls as shown in Figure 10-11.

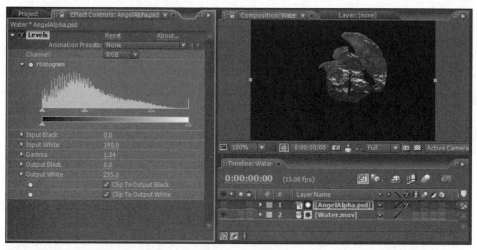

Figure 10-11. Use the Levels effect to increase the contrast in a matte. Compare this corrected image to the one in Figure 10-10 to see how adjusting the Levels properties can work to your advantage.

4. Drag the White, Mid, and Black point sliders under the histogram, and the image will become brighter or darker. The end result of this is sharper contrast and a more defined edge in the matte. Keep in mind that what you are not doing here is color correcting the angel. By moving the Black slider to the right, you are making even more pixels in the image black and thus filling in any holes you may see in the matte. Moving the White slider to the left increases the number of white pixels in the image, letting even more of the underlying image show through the matte. The Mid slider compresses or extends the grayscale range of the pixel values between the White and Black sliders and changes the opacity of the matte.

5. At this point, you can choose to save the project or close it.

> *If you are in a real pinch, you don't have to use the* Levels *effect. Instead, apply the* Brightness and Contrast *effect from the* Color Correction *folder. You can obtain some really interesting effects simply by moving the* Brightness *and* Contrast *sliders in the* Effect Controls *panel.*

Beam up the seal

In this exercise, you are going to use a Luma Matte with no external content and create an effect that looks suspiciously like someone using the transporter in *Star Trek*. How it will all come together is that a series of solids will provide the transporter effect while the actual video will be used to supply the Luma Matte. It's not as complicated as it first sounds. Follow these steps:

10

1. Inside the BeamUp folder in the Chapter 10 Exercise folder is a file named BeamUp.aep. Open the file. When the file opens, you will notice we have placed a video on the timeline and applied the Keylight filter to the video. If you twirl down the Transform properties, you will notice the opacity for this video is at 0% and rises to 100% at the 0:00:05:15 point. This gives us five-and-one-half seconds to have the beam-up effect occur.

2. Select the Nose layer on the timeline and select Layer ➤ Auto-trace. This will open the Auto-trace dialog box.

   What you are going to do is to trace around the guy in the video. The result will be a Bezier mask that you can subsequently use for the effect. The areas of the dialog box, shown in Figure 10-12, are not terribly complicated, and we'll explain them as you work your way through them. Enter these values:

   - Current Frame: Leave this radio button deselected. This will only draw the mask over the frame shown. This guy moves around.

   - Work Area: If not selected, click the radio button to select this in the Time Span area. This will create a mask that expands and contracts as the subject moves.

   - Preview: Deselect this option. If you select this, you can preview the mask results and the various values you will enter.

   - Channel: Alpha. This pull-down allows you to choose the channel to be traced. In this case, there is already an alpha channel. If one is not available, then use a color or a luminance channel that has the most defined edges for the mask. Preview the channels by clicking the Show Channel button at the bottom of the Comp window and selecting a channel from the pull-down menu.

   - Invert: Deselect this option.

   - Blur: Deselect this option. What this does is to blur the image before doing the trace. This way, small artifacts are removed and jagged edges are smoothed out. If the video is a high-contrast video, you can leave this option deselected. The radius value determines how far out the blur will occur.

   - Tolerance: 1. The value here, in pixels, specifies how far the traced edge is allowed to move away from the shape being traced.

   - Minimum Area: 10. This is the default value, in pixels, meaning any feature smaller than 10✕10 pixels will be ignored.

   - Threshold: 40%. Here's a quick way of wrapping your mind around this value. Any pixel on the edge being traced with a value less than 40% black (almost a medium gray) is mapped to black and is transparent.

   - Corner Roundness: 50%. This is the default value and specifies the roundness of the curve when the mask changes direction. Higher values yield smoother curves.

   - Apply to New Layer: Ensure this option is selected. This is how the mask will be applied to a solid. The solid will be the same size as the selected layer.

   When you click OK, you will have to wait for a few seconds for the mask to be created. When it finishes, a new solid will be added to the timeline, and you can see the mask by turning off the Video switch for the Auto-trace layer and scrubbing across the timeline. Set the matte for the video layer to Alpha Matte.

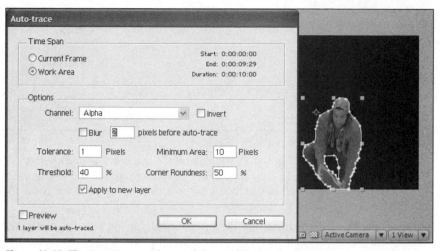

Figure 10-12. The Auto-trace settings and the resulting mask

> *Don't develop an unhealthy relationship with this tool. It is not perfect, but is a great starting point for the creation of complex masks. When the tool finishes tracing, you would be well advised to zoom in on the Comp and to scrub through the video looking for any stray points or shapes that should not be a part of the mask. Select the points on the artifacts and delete them to remove the shape.*

The mask is acceptable, but what you want to occur is for the shape to be a little less defined when it first appears. Here's how:

3. Select the solid layer just added and turn on the Video switch. Open Effects & Presets ➤ Matte and drag the Simple Choker effect onto the Auto-trace layer in the timeline. Set the Choke Matte value in the Effect Controls panel to –6.5. The matte will expand and make the mask look a bit puffy. Save the project.

Now that the shape is under control, let's create the transporter beam.

4. Add a new white solid to the Comp and set its In point to 0:00:02:29.

5. With the White Solid 1 layer selected, open Effects & Presets ➤ Noise and Grain and drag the Fractal Noise effect onto the Comp. When you release the mouse, you will see the familiar smoke pattern. As you may have noticed, this is a grayscale image. The plan, therefore, is to manipulate the pattern and use it as the Luma Matte for the Auto-trace layer below it. Move the playback head to the 0:00:03:00 mark on the timeline and twirl down Effects and Fractal Noise for the White Solid 1 layer and use these settings, adding keyframes at the times indicated:

10

Seconds	03:00	03:25	04:10	05:00	07:15	09:15
Contrast	145					
Brightness	−513	−89	−37	35	141	
Evolution	0 x +0.0					5 x +0.0

6. Press the E key to twirl up the Effects controls in the timeline and then press the T key to twirl down the Opacity control in the Transform properties. Move the playback head to 0:00:05:00 and add a keyframe. Move the playback head to the 0:00:05:15 mark of the timeline and reduce the Opacity to 0.

7. Scrub the playback head across the timeline, and you will see the mask interact with the Fractal Noise effect (as shown in Figure 10-13).

Figure 10-13. The Fractal Noise effect is added to a white solid.

8. Select the Mask layer and change its Track Matte setting to Luma Matte. If you scrub across the timeline, you will see the image in the mask fade in. Save the project.

Obviously, when you beam up in *Star Trek*, you don't magically appear out of a fog. Let's add the lights. What we are going to do here is to have the beam at its most intense during the opening seconds of the video. This is the section where the subject fades in.

1. Add a new black solid to the timeline and set its In point to 0:00:00:00 and the Out point to 0:00:05:09. Drag the playback head to a point in the timeline where the mask of the subject appears. Open the rulers and drag a vertical guide that runs downwards right through the middle of the subject. This guide is important because it will give you a visual reference point for the lights you will be adding.

2. Press the Home key to return to the start of the timeline. Open Effects & Presets ➤ Simulation and drag a copy of the CC Particle Systems II effect onto the Comp. Use these settings in the Effect Controls panel:

- Birth Rate: 11.2. **The shower gets thicker.**
- Longevity: 7.8: **The shower turns yellow because the particles are going to last longer and be slower to change color.**

Producer:

- Position: **Scrub the values until the crosshairs for this setting are over the guide.**
- Radius X: 0.
- Radius Y: 72. **The shower goes higher in the Comp.**

Physics:

- Animation: **Select** Fire **from the pull-down menu. The particles look like they are now shooting up from the bottom of the Comp.**
- Velocity: 0.
- Inherit Velocity %: –148.
- Gravity: 0.
- Extra: 0.5. **The particles look like a Roman candle.**

Particle:

- Particle Type: **Select** Star **from the pull-down menu. The stream of particles is starting to look transporter-like.**
- Birth Size: 0.
- Death Size: 0.67.
- Size Variation: 100%.
- Opacity Map: **Select** Fade In and Out **from the pull-down menu.**
- Birth Color: #00EAFF **(bright blue).**
- Death Color: #002AFF **(dark blue).**

3. If it is visible, twirl up the effect in the layer. Press the T key to open the Opacity properties of the layer, and change the Opacity value to 70%.

4. Scrub through the first few seconds of the timeline. You will see the particles start out looking somewhat tornado-like and swirling as the subject becomes more and more visible.

10

5. Now that you have the transporter beam working, it needs to move around a bit and disappear after a short period of visibility. Select the layer and press the E key to open the effect in the timeline. Twirl down Producer, add keyframes, and change the Position values at the following times:

Time	Value
0:00.02:00	Add a keyframe by clicking the stopwatch.
0:00:02:15	194, 202.
0:00:03:00	236.6, 105.
0:00:03:15	160, 115.

6. Twirl up Producer and twirl down Particle. Add keyframes and change the Max Opacity values at the following times:

Time	Value
0:00:01:20	Add a keyframe by clicking the stopwatch.
0:00:02:00	0%.

Obviously, that is a pretty lame transporter beam. To fix it, you simply add another solid and reapply the CC Particle Systems II effect and Opacity setting. To add some "sparkle" to the beam, you are also going to change its color.

If you are like us—lazy—and read that last sentence, your reaction was most likely, "Dudes, that's a lot of work!" We couldn't agree more. Let's work smart . . . not hard.

One of the neat features of After Effects is that you can duplicate a layer. When you do that, everything in the duplicate is a clone of the original. This means you only have to change a couple of settings in the CC Particle Systems II effect.

7. In the timeline, select the solid you just worked on and select Edit ➤ Duplicate. A new black solid layer is created. In order to avoid confusion, rename the layer to DupeSolid. Click the Effect Controls panel, and you will see the CC Particle Systems II effect.

8. Make the following changes to the CC Particle Systems II effect in the Effect Controls panel:

- Radius Y: 229
- Inherit Velocity: –104
- Birth Color: #00FF00 (bright green)
- Death Color: #387804 (dark green)

9. Select View ➤ Hide Guides to turn off the grid, save the project, and do a RAM preview to see your subject really "beam in" (as shown in Figure 10-14).

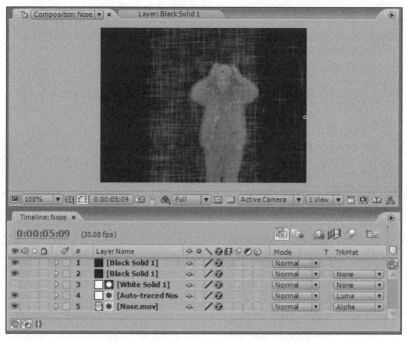

Figure 10-14. Beam me up, Scotty.

This exercise is a classic example of using the right tool for the job. Trying to create this effect in Flash simply can't be done without an expert level of knowledge regarding ActionScript and Flash, and, even then, the use of Luma Mattes in Flash is not a feature of the Flash application.

If you were to move this project, or one similar to it, into Flash, it would be a good idea on your part to use the Region of Interest button to crop out the wasted space on the Comp. Remember, Flash loves small, and removing space in the Comp that isn't used will result in a smaller FLV file and a faster load at runtime.

Who is that lady in the mirror?

In this exercise, you are essentially going to do the same thing twice. You are going create a reflection of a video in After Effects, and then you are going to create a similar effect in Flash. The difference will be in how Flash is used to create a reflection, and we are also going to show you how to use ActionScript to ensure that the videos on the Flash stage are synchronized with each other before they start playing.

Before you proceed, a bit of advice is called for. The video you will be using is physically quite large, and the Flash side of this project is best suited to playback from your computer. We are using a fairly large file—160✕210—simply to demonstrate the technique. If you do use this technique in your Flash projects, use small—120✕90—videos.

You start in After Effects. Here's how:

1. In the Reflect folder found in the Chapter 10 Code download folder is a file named Reflect.aep. Open it, and you will see we have already placed the video on the timeline.

2. Drag a second copy of the GirlMask.mov file from the Project panel to the timeline. Place the video so it is at the bottom of the Comp window below the first video. To avoid confusion, rename this layer Reflection.

3. Flip the bottom video by changing the position of the top-middle point with its counterpart at the bottom of the video as shown in Figure 10-15.

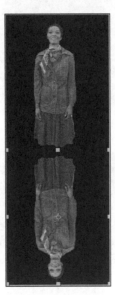

Figure 10-15.
The bottom video is flipped.

To give the illusion of something being reflected on a shiny surface, the bottom video should fade out towards the subject's head. Here's how:

4. Drag the Matte.psd file to the timeline above the Reflection layer.

5. Select the Reflection layer and change its Track Matte setting to Luma Matte. You may notice that the reflection is not exactly what you want. The bottom of the clip needs to fade out.

6. Select the Reflection layer and change the Luma Matte to Luma Inverted. The matte now runs in the opposite direction and the effect, as shown in Figure 10-16, is correct.

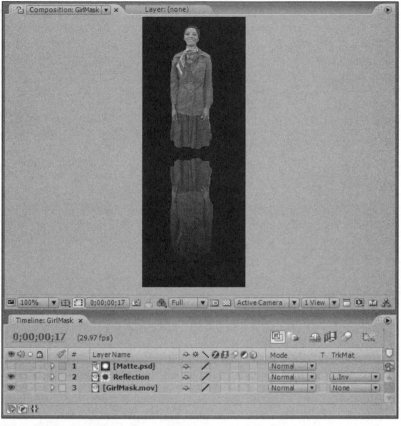

Figure 10-16. A reflection on a shiny surface

> *Sometimes you will be handed a gradient or you will create one that actually runs in the wrong direction. Using* Luma Inverted *saves you from having to redo the gradient.*

Reflections in Flash

As we mentioned at the outset of this section, Flash doesn't have a Luma Matte feature. Still, there is a way to reproduce what you just did in After Effects. You just have to approach the project from a different direction. Here's how:

1. Inside the Reflect folder of your Chapter 10 Exercise folder is a Flash file named Reflect.fla. Open it.
2. Open the Library and add a new video object to the Library.
3. Create a new movie clip named Video, and when the Symbol Editor opens, add a new layer to the timeline. Name the top layer Actions and the bottom layer Video.

4. Select the Video layer and drag the video object from the Library to the stage.

5. With the video object selected on the stage, enter the following values in the Property inspector:

- Width: 160
- Height: 210
- X: 0
- Y: 0
- Instance name: myVideo

The object is now the same dimensions as the FLV file that will be used, and the object is tucked up against the upper-left corner of the stage.

6. Select the first frame in the Actions layer, open the ActionScript Editor, and enter the following code:

```
var nc: NetConnection = new NetConnection();
nc.connect(null);
var ns: NetStream = new NetStream(nc);
myVideo.attachVideo(ns);
ns.play("Reflect.flv");
```

Nothing new here. You create the connection and the stream, hook the stream into the video object, and add the FLV file to the stream.

Now that you have the video in place, you can turn your attention to the "Luma Matte."

Even though Flash does not contain this feature, you can still apply a gradient mask to the video to achieve a similar result to that in After Effects. The thing you must keep in mind is you can't create a gradient, add it to a masking layer, and use it to mask the movie clip containing the video. Won't work.

For this effect to work, the gradient must be applied using the setMask() method of the MovieClip class and both the gradient movie clip and the movie clip containing the video to be masked must have their cacheAsBitmap properties set to true.

If you add a movie clip to the stage, you will see, in the Property inspector, a Use runtime bitmap caching check box option. Check this, and any vectors in the movie clip will be drawn to a bitmap rather than the Flash stage. The upshot is improved performance of the Flash movie. Though used primarily for content that doesn't move around the stage, in this case, it is a prerequisite. Both the movie clip being masked and the one containing the mask must use bitmap caching.

> *Like the Auto-trace feature of After Effects, don't get hooked on bitmap caching in Flash. If you have movie clips that change between frames or otherwise move, don't use the feature, because the time taken to draw the bitmaps in every frame can actually make the SWF file perform slower than had it not been applied.*

If you do use bitmap caching, be aware it can only be used in the Flash Player 8 or higher.

This option can be used in one of two ways: either by selecting the movie clip on the stage and selecting the Use runtime bitmap caching option in the Property inspector or through ActionScript.

To start, you are going to create the gradient that will be used as the "Luma Matte." Here's how:

1. Create new movie clip named Gradient.

2. When the Symbol Editor opens, select the Rectangle tool and draw a rectangle on the stage.

3. Click the rectangle once, and in the Property inspector turn off the stroke.

4. Set the Width property to 160 pixels and the Height to 210 pixels. Finally, set the location of the rectangle to 0, 0 in the Property inspector.

5. Select Window ➤ Color Mixer to open the Color Mixer panel. When it opens, click the rectangle on the stage to select it, and in the Color Mixer select Linear from the Type pull-down. The rectangle will fill with the gradient.

6. Click the Black crayon in the Color Mixer—the Black and White sliders you see above the gradient in the Color Mixer really are called crayons—and change the Alpha value to 50%. Do the same thing with the White crayon, but set its Alpha value to 0%. Don't worry about the Black crayon turning gray; it is only reflecting the Alpha value (see Figure 10-17).

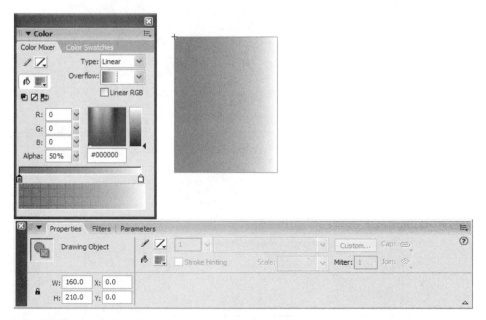

Figure 10-17. The gradient to be used in the mask is created.

10

7. Switch to the Gradient Transform tool and click the rectangle once on the stage. Drag the rotate handle in a clockwise direction, and release the mouse when the solid area of the gradient is at the top of the object.

8. Click the Scene 1 link to return to the main timeline. Save the file.

What you have done so far is to construct the elements to be used in the movie. The next step is to assemble the elements to create the effect.

1. Create a new movie clip named Reflect. When the Symbol Editor opens, add three new layers and name the layers, from the top down, Actions, Video, Mask, Reflect.

2. Select the Video layer and drag a copy of the Video movie clip from the Library to the stage. In the Property inspector, set its X and Y position to 0, 0. Give it the instance name of mcVideo and lock the layer.

3. Select the Reflect layer and drag a copy of the Video movie clip to the stage. In the Property inspector, set its X position to 0 and its Y position to 210. Give it the instance name of mcReflect.

4. Select the movie clip in the Reflect layer and select Modify ➤ Transform ➤ Flip Vertical. You won't see anything happen on the stage, but this selection essentially turns the movie clip upside down. Lock the layer.

5. Select the Mask layer and drag a copy of the Gradient movie clip to the stage. Set its position to 0, 210 and give it the instance name of mcGradient. If your screen resembles that shown in Figure 10-18, you are ready to "wire it up" with ActionScript.

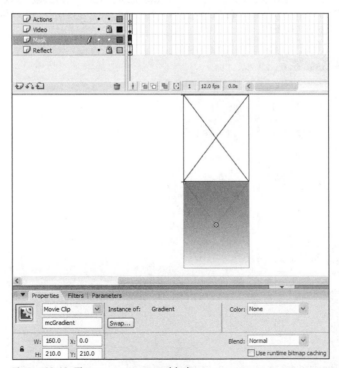

Figure 10-18. The assets are assembled.

Surprisingly, the ActionScript required to make this thing work is not complicated. In fact, it consists of three lines of code. You need two lines of code that set the cacheAsBitmap property for the gradient and the video under the gradient. The third line creates the mask.

6. Click once in the first frame of the Actions layer, open the ActionScript Editor, and enter the following code:

```
mcGradient.cacheAsBitmap = true;
mcReflect.cacheAsBitmap = true;
mcReflect.setMask(mcGradient);
```

The code is pretty well self-explanatory. The last line is where the "magic" happens. The setmask() method is applied to the movie clip under the gradient, and the mcGradient movie clip is the parameter for the method. The result is the mcGradient movie clip is used as the mask for the mcReflect movie clip.

Bitmap caching is new to Flash 8.The purpose of this feature is to "turbo charge" a SWF by taking a snapshot of the pixels in motion, and, instead of redrawing the stage every time something moves, it only redraws the pixels in the "snapshot" that have changed.

So why do you need bitmap caching in this exercise? It is needed to activate the alpha gradient inside the mask. This alpha gradient technique only works when both the mask and the object being masked are cached. If you didn't use the cache, you would be using the old way of doing things, which is to look for whether a pixel has been turned on or off. Shades of gray are simply not permitted.

When bitmap caching is turned on, you are using the bitmap rendering engine in the Flash Player 8 or Flash Player 9 and are able to use alpha masking in Flash.

> *There are a couple of things you need to know about using the setMask() method. The first thing is you can't have a movie clip mask itself. The second thing is if you use this method in a movie clip that is being used as the mask in a masking layer, the setMask() method takes priority over the layer mask. Finally, if you want to turn the mask off using the setMask() method, you would use a null parameter. For example, if you wished at some point to turn off the mask in this project, the code would be mcReflect.setMask(null);.*

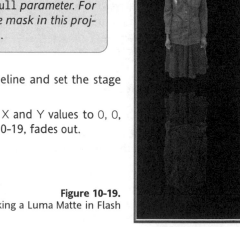

10

7. Click the Scene 1 link to return to the main timeline and set the stage color to #000000 (black).

8. Drag the Reflect movie clip to the stage, set the X and Y values to 0, 0, and test the movie. The girl, as shown in Figure 10-19, fades out.

Figure 10-19.
Faking a Luma Matte in Flash

Deep under the sea, a blob is waiting

The final exercise in this chapter is a lot of fun. You are going to create a 35-second animation, using text and effects, to promote a B movie. You will be using Luma Mattes for a couple of effects—we can't wait to show you how to use an effect called CC Blobbylize—and an Adjustment layer. The really interesting aspect of this animation is the effects and how they can interact with After Effects's Luma Mattes. The other thing to be aware of as you proceed through the exercise is that, as you pile on the effects, don't look at them in terms of After Effects. Instead, think of how each one can creatively be used alone or in combination with each other in your Flash projects. Let's have some fun:

1. Open After Effects and create a new Comp using these settings:

   - Composition Name: Blobbit
   - Preset: Web Video, 320 X 240
   - Duration: 0:00:35:00
   - Background Color: #000000 (black)

   Click OK.

2. Select the Text tool, click the Comp once and enter deep in the ocean. Open the Character panel and use these text formatting values:

   - Font: Arial
   - Style: Bold
   - Color: #FFFFFF (white)
   - Size: 30 px

3. Rename the layer to Deep. Move the playback head to 0:00:05:00 and set the Out point for the layer to that time.

> *Here's a quick way to set In and Out points by the numbers. Right-click (PC) or Cmd-Click (Mac) one of the column headings in the timeline to open the context menu. Select* Out *and a column named* Out *will be added. The time in the* Out *column is the end point of the duration strip. Click the time in the* Out *column to open the* Layer Out Time *dialog box. The value shown will be the current location of the playback head. Click* OK, *and the Out point is set to that time. Use this technique to set the In points for layers as well.*
>
> *You don't have to click a value in the* In *or* Out *columns; you can also scrub across the values.*

This text is the opening animation. The plan is to have it look like the viewer is underwater, and the text will start to jiggle. Here's how:

1. Duplicate the Deep layer and name it TextDupe. Open the TextDupe layer's Opacity strip and move the playback head to 0:00:04:00, add a keyframe, and set its Opacity to 33%. Move the playback head to 0:00:04:10 and reduce the Opacity to 0%. Lock this layer.

2. Create a new black solid and drag it between the two text layers. Set the solid's Out point to 5 seconds. Click the Solo switch for the unlocked Deep layer, and you can start on the first effect. By clicking the Solo switch, you ensure that the two layers above the text don't interfere with what you are doing.

3. Select the Deep layer. Open Effects & Presets ➤ Color Correction and drag a copy of the Colorama effect onto the Text layer strip. You have used this effect earlier in the book, so we aren't really going to explain each step other than to give you the values to use.

To review: the Colorama *effect assigns a custom palette to an element in a layer and then cycles the palette. Color cycling is a quick way to animate pulsing colors that follow a gradient path, colors that zoom out of a radial gradient, or in this case to give the illusion of sea water changing color. What you will notice immediately is the text changes color to a bright red. Don't let that bother you.*

4. Open the Effect Controls panel, twirl down Input Phase, and specify these values:

- Get Phase From: Value
- Add Phase: None
- Add Phase from: Hue
- Add Mode: Clamp
- Phase Shift: 0 x +12.0 degrees

Twirl up Input Phase.

5. Twirl down Output Cycle. This is where you create the colors that the effect will cycle through. In the Use Preset Palettes pull-down menu, select Deep Ocean. Twirl up Output Cycle.

6. Change the Blend with Original value to 33%. The text turns blue.

7. Twirl up the Colorama filter in the Effect Controls panel. Select Effects & Presets ➤ Stylize and drag a copy of the Glow effect onto the Deep layer. You have already applied a Colorama effect to the text, and this effect will add a bit of a glow to the text.

8. In the Effect Controls panel, twirl down the Glow effect and use these values:

- Glow Based On: Alpha Channel
- Glow Threshold: 50%
- Glow Radius: 5.0
- Glow Intensity: 5.0
- Glow Operation: Alpha Add
- Glow Dimensions: Vertical

When you finish, you will see that the text has developed a thin white outline around each letter. Let's work with that outline by changing its Radius and Intensity parameters. When you finish, the glow will look like the northern lights pulsing out of the letters.

9. Twirl up the Glow effect in the Effect Controls panel and twirl down the Glow effect in the Text layer.

10

10. Press the Home key to return the playback head to the start of the timeline. You are going to start with the Glow Radius values. Add keyframes and change the value at the following times:

Time	Value	Description
0:00:00:00	385	The glow seems to disappear.
0:00:01:00	102	You have the northern lights.
0:00:03:00	103	
0:00:04:00	354	The lights are gone.

11. Press the Home key to return the playback head to the start of the timeline. You are going to adjust the Glow Intensity values. Add keyframes and change the value at the following times:

Time	Value
0:00:04:00	5
0:00:05:00:	0

Scrub through the timeline and you will see, as Figure 10-20 demonstrates, that you have a nice little effect. Turn off the Solo switch for the Deep layer and save the project.

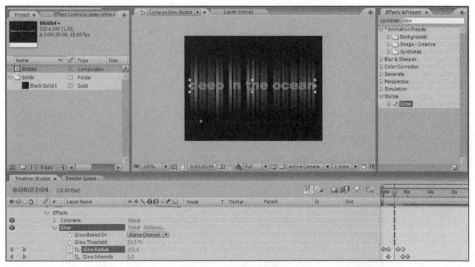

Figure 10-20. The text has a "glow on."

Now that the text is in place and the effect applied, you are now going to work on giving the text some texture by adding some fractal noise to it. Follow these steps:

1. Select the Black Solid 1 layer. Open the Noise and Grain folder in the Effects & Presets panel and drag a copy of the Fractal Noise effect onto the solid name in the timeline. The words appear over the familiar smoke pattern.

2. Open the Effect Controls, twirl down the Fractal Noise effect, and use these settings:

   - Fractal Type: Dynamic Twist. The smoke develops some swirls.

   - Contrast: 224. The swirls become black and white.

   - Brightness: −32. The background turns black, and the swirls become more distinct.

   Twirl down Transform and use these settings:

   - Uniform Scaling: Deselect. You are going to distort the swirls.

   - Scale Width: 260. The swirls appear to stretch.

   Twirl up Transform. Set Complexity to 7. The swirls become a bit more detailed.

3. Twirl up Fractal Noise in the Effect Controls panel. The next step is to hook the letters in the Deep layer to the effect you just applied to the solid.

4. Turn off the visibility of the TextDupe layer and change the Matte setting in the TrkMat column of the Deep layer from None to Luma Matte. You will see the colored text in Deep has some texture.

5. The effect is rather static. You'll give it some interest by adjusting the Brightness, Scale Width, and Evolution values at a couple of points in the timeline. Select the solid layer and press the E key to open Fractal Noise and twirl it down.

6. Move the playback head to the 0:00:01:00 point on the timeline and add a keyframe for the Brightness value. Move the playback head to 0:00:03:00 and change the Brightness value to 0.0. Move the playback head to the 0:00:05:00 mark and change the Brightness value to −44.

7. To give the illusion of motion, you will have the Scale Width property change from its current setting to a setting of 600% at the 0:00:04:00 mark. Twirl down the effect's Transform properties. Move the playback head to the 0:00:01:00 mark and add a keyframe to the Scale Width. Move the playback head to the 4-second mark on the timeline and change the Scale Width value to 600%.

8. With the growth of the noise pattern, you'll also have it look like the pattern is changing. You do that by adjusting the Evolution values. Add a keyframe to the Evolution value at the 1-second mark. Move the playback head to the 0:00:05:00 mark and change the Evolution value to 1 x +180 degrees. Scrub through the timeline, and you will see the pattern in the words has changed (as shown in Figure 10-21).

9. Save the project.

10

Figure 10-21.
The final effect

Another spotlight effect

Here's an interesting method of lighting up a short block of text. It is particularly effective for stationary text on the Flash stage.

1. In After Effects, select the Text tool, click the Comp window, and enter the following: is a danger. Name the layer Danger, and set the layer's In point to 0:00:05:00 and its Out point to 0:00:10:00.

2. Apply the Colorama effect to the text. In the Effect Controls panel, twirl down the Output Cycle and select Caribbean from the Use Preset Palette pull-down menu. The text turns blue. Drag the arrow that is pointing to the gradient in the Output Cycle to about the midpoint of the gradient. This will soften the blue color in the text.

3. Open the Project panel and drag a copy of the black solid to the timeline above the Danger layer. Set the solid layer's In and Out points to 5 and 10 seconds to match the duration of the text in the Danger layer. Open Effects & Presets ➤ Generate and drag a copy of the Beam effect onto the solid just added in the timeline. You will see a sort of red beam appear over the text. This beam will be used to create the spotlight effect.

4. Open the Effect Controls panel and make the following changes to the Beam effect:

   ■ Starting Point: 0.0, 120.0. The crosshairs move to the left side of the Comp.

   ■ Ending Point: 316, 120. The end point crosshairs move to the right edge of the Comp.

   ■ Length: 95%. The bar will stretch across the Comp.

   ■ Starting Thickness: 10. This value is the thickness of the beam at its start point.

   ■ Ending Thickness: 32. The beam thickens on the right side and pulls away from the right edge of the Comp.

5. Twirl up the Beam effect in the Effect Controls panel. Obviously, a red beam over the text is going to look a bit cheesy. Instead, you'll use the gradient in the beam to give the text a bit of depth.

6. Select the Danger layer and change its Track Matte setting to Luma Matte. If you scrub through the timeline, not much is happening. You'll put the beam in motion by changing its end point location at various times.

7. Select the solid on the timeline and press the E key to open the effect in the timeline. Twirl down Beam.

8. Move the playback head to 0:00:05:03, add a keyframe in the Ending Point property, and change the value to 285, 0.0. Move the playback head to 0:00:07:00 and change the Ending Point value to 303, 216. Move the playback head to 0:00:09:05 and change the value to 317, 119. Scrub the playback head across the timeline, and you will see the beam sweep, from the top to the bottom, across the text, thanks to the end point changes (see Figure 10-22). Save the project.

Figure 10-22.
Yet another way of calling the text to the viewer's attention

Creating wavy text

You don't always need to use a text animation preset to create text effects that can be used in Flash. Here's one technique:

1. In After Effects, select the Text tool, click once in the Comp window, and enter the text seeking you. Rename the layer to Seek and drag a copy of the black solid from the Project panel above the Seek layer on the timeline. Set the In point for both the Seek and solid layers to 0:00:10:00 and the Out point for both layers to 0:00:15:00.

2. Click the Solo switch for the Seek layer. Drag a copy of the CC Blobbylize effect from Effects & Presets ➤ Distort and drop it onto the text. You will see the text "flatten" and take on a wavy look.

3. In the Effect Controls panel, do the following:

Twirl down Blobbiness and change the property to Luminance. Set the following values:

- Softness: 12. The text appears to get smaller and look like it is dripping.
- Cut Away: 12.

Twirl up Blobbiness.

Twirl down Light and change the Intensity value to 354. You won't see a change because the text is white. You'll change that later.

Twirl up the CC Blobbylize effect in the Effect Controls panel.

The text is a bit flat. You want to stretch it out and wrap it around a sphere. Here's how:

4. Drag the Spherize effect from the open Distort folder and drop it onto the text. Use these values in the Effect Controls panel:

- Radius: 44. The center of the text develops a bump.
- Center of Sphere: 32, 123. The bump becomes less pronounced because the sphere has been moved away from the text.

5. The text is static. You'll put it into motion. Select the Seek layer and press the E key to open the effect in the timeline. Twirl down CC Blobbylize and move the playback head to 0:0010:00.

6. Twirl down Blobbiness, add a keyframe in the Softness value, and change the value to 11. Move the playback head to 0:00:14:00 and change the value to 80. The text suddenly takes on a very rounded appearance.

7. Twirl up CC Blobbylize and twirl down Spherize.

8. Place the playback head at 0:00:10:00 and add a keyframe to the Center of Sphere property. Move the playback head to 0:00:14:00 and change the Center of Sphere value to 289, 123. Scrub the playback head across the timeline, and you will see the text has become wavy. Turn off the Solo switch for the Seek layer.

We could stop here, but the white text color doesn't fit the feel of the piece so far. You are going to add a gradient to the text by applying a Ramp effect to the solid.

10

> *Remember, the* Ramp *effect creates a color gradient, blending it with the original image contents. In this case, it will be a simple grayscale gradient.*

9. Select the black solid above the Seek layer. Twirl down the Generate folder in the Effects & Presets panel and drag a copy of the Ramp effect onto the solid in the Comp window. When you release the mouse, the gradient will appear.

10. Open the Effect Controls panel and make the following changes to the Ramp effect:

- Start of Ramp: 14.6, 67.3
- End of Ramp: 316, 120

The gradient will now run from left to right rather than top to bottom.

11. The final step is to put the Ramp effect in motion by changing the Start of Ramp and End of Ramp values in the timeline. Select the solid layer and press the E key to open the Ramp effect. Twirl down Ramp.

12. Move the playback head to 0:00:10:01, add a keyframe, and change the Start of Ramp value to 0, 120. Change the values at the following times:

Time	Value
0:00:12:00	Add a keyframe.
0:00:13:05	0, 64.
0:00:14:05	298, 97.

13. Move the playback head to 0:00:10:01, add a keyframe to the End of Ramp property, and change the value to 47, 120. Change the values at the following times:

Time	Value
0:00:12:00	320, 120
0:00:14:05	310, 119

14. To "hook" the text into the changing gradient, set the Seek layer's Track Matte setting to Luma Matte. Scrub across the timeline, and you will see the gradient move through the letters as shown in Figure 10-23. Save the project.

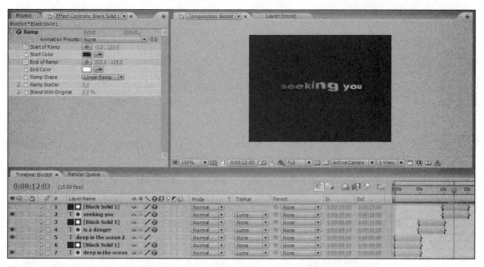

Figure 10-23. The project so far

This is yet another effective technique for grabbing a viewer's attention in Flash. Just keep in mind this technique uses the CC Blobbylize effect, which converts text to a bitmap if you are outputting the After effects file to a SWF file. If you do use this technique, output the file to a video and convert it to an FLV file using the Flash 8 Video Encoder.

Text with balls

Before you start giggling, this exercise uses the CC Ball Action effect to give the text a marble texture. Here's how:

1. Select the Text tool and enter the following text: waiting for you. This will create a new layer on the timeline.

2. Rename the new text layer to Waiting.

3. Drag a copy of the black solid from the Project panel and add it to the timeline above the text you just entered. Set the In point of both layers to 0:00:15:00 and the Out point to 0:00:20:00.

4. In the Effects & Presets panel, twirl down Simulation and drag a copy of the CC Ball Action effect onto the solid in the timeline. Open the Effect Controls panel and use these values:

   - Twist Angle: 0 x –75 degrees
   - Ball Size: 68
   - Instability State: 1 x +24 degrees

   If you scrub across the timeline, you aren't going to see much other than a couple of white dots. You'll fix that by playing with the Scatter, Twist Angle, and Ball Size properties on the timeline.

10

Before you proceed, it might be a good idea to review the settings:

- Scatter: Every ball is placed on an imaginary grid. The higher the number, the more the balls are spread all over the stage

- Rotation Axis: If the balls are spinning, use this pull-down to choose the spin axis. Just don't ask us what happens when you choose X15Z. We don't have a clue either.

- Rotation: The whole number is the number of rotations that will be applied to the entire effect, and the degree is the angle of the rotation.

- Twist Property: The selections in this pull-down determine which property of the balls will be used to distort them.

- Twist Angle: Same thing as the rotation but applied to the Twist property.

- Grid Spacing: How the balls are placed in the Comp. Lower values result in a tighter ball pattern. Think of a piece of graph paper and a ball being placed where the lines in the paper intersect. Really fine graph paper, lower grid spacing, results in more balls.

- Instability State: This only works if there is a Scatter value applied. This value determines how each ball in the grid moves in a random manner. If you are a control freak, the odds are you won't be using this feature all that often.

5. Open the effect on the timeline and twirl it down. Move the playback head to 0:00:15:00 and add a keyframe in the Scatter property. Move the playback head to 0:00:17:00 and change the Scatter value to 107.

6. Return the playback head to 0:00:15:00 and add a keyframe to the Twist Angle. Change the Twist Angle value to the one shown at the following times:

Time	Value
0:00:16:00	0 x +27
0:00:18:05	0 x +51

7. Return the playback head to 0:00:15:00 and add a keyframe to the Ball Size property. Change the Ball Size value to the one shown at the following times:

Time	Value
0:00:17:00	53
0:00:18:05	11
0:00:19:00	0
0:00:20:00	131

If you scrub through the effect, you will see little balls moving through the text. You are going to add a bit of "jazz" to the balls. You will notice they suddenly disappear because of their size increase. What you are going to do is to have those balls morph into streaks. To achieve that, you are going to add the CC Rain effect to the solid.

8. Twirl down the Simulation folder in the Effects & Presets panel and drag a copy of the CC Rain effect onto the solid layer in the Comp. If you scrub through the solid, you will see that yes, indeed, it is raining on the words and the entire solid. Not exactly the desired effect. You want to fix that.

9. Click the Waiting layer once and change its Track Matte setting to Alpha Matte. When you scrub through the layer, you will see the effect is restricted to the text but is only visible when the text disappears (as shown in Figure 10-24).

Figure 10-24. You get some interesting results when you use the effects in tandem.

This is a really interesting technique that demonstrates the interaction of a pair of effects and an Alpha Matte in After Effects. Though you could use this as an FLV video in Flash, another approach would be to do the effect in the solid, output that as a video, convert it to an FLV file, and use the text in Flash to mask the effect in the FLV file.

Blinking text

No spook film that is worthwhile doesn't have text that blinks on and off in such a way as to scare the bejabbers out of the audience. This will hold true for our B film after you complete these steps:

1. Click the Comp window and select the Text tool. Click once in the Comp window and enter the following text: WATCH OUT !!!. Rename the text layer Watch.

2. Drag the black solid from the Project panel to a new layer above the text layer just created.

3. Set the In point for both layers to 0:00:20:00 and the Out point to 0:00:25:00.

4. Drag the CC Rain effect onto the solid.

5. In the Effects & Presets panel, twirl down the Stylize folder and drag a copy of the Strobe Light effect onto the Comp. In the Effect Controls panel, twirl up the CC Rain effect and twirl down Strobe Light. The effect does exactly what the name implies, and the controls, listed here, allow you to do a lot with it:

   ■ Strobe Color: Pick a color for the light using the Color Picker.

   ■ Blend With Original: The percentage value you add here determines how the entire effect is applied to the layer.

   ■ Strobe Duration: Strobe lights turn and off. This value specifies, in seconds, how long the effect lasts.

10

- **Strobe Period:** The time between light bursts is called the **period**. For example, if the Strobe Duration is set to 0.1 second and the Strobe Period is set to 1.0 second, the layer will have the effect for 0.1 second and then be without the effect for 0.9 second. If this value is set lower than the Strobe Duration, the strobe effect is constant.

- **Random Strobe Probability:** Think of this as random flickering. Sort of like those street lights in spook films that can't seem to stay on and flicker on and off.

- **Strobe:** You have two choices in this pull-down menu that determine how the effect is applied. Operates on Color Only performs the strobe operation on all color channels. Make Layer Transparent makes the layer transparent when a strobe effect occurs.

- **Strobe Operator:** Here you specify the blend mode to use when Operates on Color Only is selected from the Strobe menu. The default setting is Copy.

6. Change the Random Strobe Probability value from 0% to 32%. Twirl up the Strobe Light effect in the Effect Controls panel.

7. Select the solid layer and press the E key to open Effects in the timeline. Twirl down CC Rain. The plan is to have the rain increase in intensity over a couple of seconds.

8. Drag the playback head to 0:00:20:00 and add a keyframe in the Amount setting. Drag the playback head to 0:00:22:00 and add another keyframe. Place the playback head at 0:00:24:00 and change the amount to 590.

9. Select the Watch layer and change its Track Matte setting to Luma Matte. If you scrub the playback head across the layer, as shown in Figure 10-25, you will see the words blink on and off. When the words are in the off state, the rain shows through. Save the project.

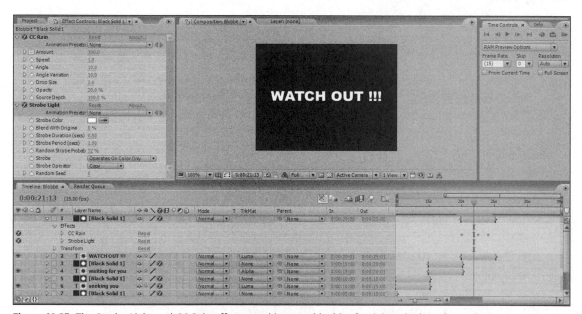

Figure 10-25. The Strobe Light and CC Rain effects combine to add a bit of a sinister look to the project.

This is another one of those techniques that you can "sneak" into Flash. You can create the effect of a lightbulb flickering on and off in a random manner and render just the bulb by cropping the video to the region of interest. The resulting FLV file placed into Flash will be physically small, and so too will its file size. Couple the Blink effect with a Glow effect, and you could have a flickering light on a foggy wharf at night. Really spooky.

Bring in the blobs

In this final effect of the project, you will be revisiting the CC Mr Mercury effect. This time, though, you are going to approach its use a bit differently. The blob will start out as a jiggling sphere and then ooze out to create the effect. There will, of course, be text masking the effect, and the oozing will occur within the lettering.

1. Click the Comp window, select the Text tool, and enter Beware of the Blob. Rename the layer Beware.

2. Click the Text tool between the words *of* and *the* and press the Return/Enter key to make a second line of text. Select all of the text, and in the Character panel set the size to 56 px and the Leading value to 44 px.

3. Create a new white solid. Set the In point for the solid and the Text layer to 0:00:25:00.

4. Select the white solid on the timeline, and select Effects & Presets ➤ Simulation. Drag a copy of CC Mr. Mercury onto the solid. Click the solid's Solo switch to turn off the other layers. If you scrub through the layer on the timeline, the blobs look more like a white splotch. Let's fix that.

5. In the Effect Controls panel, make the following changes to the CC Mr Mercury effect:

   - X Radius: 0. The blob rotates to the left.

   - Y Radius: 0. The blob rotates downwards.

   - Direction: 0 + 0 degrees. You don't need the blob to move around.

   - Velocity: 0.2. The blob needs to ooze, and changing this value slows it down to a gentle ooze.

   - Longevity: 3. Each blob is visible for 3 seconds, and the pattern on the solid will shrink by a small amount.

   - Gravity: 0. This is the force that pushes the blob out. Notice how the shape in the solid essentially transforms into what looks like a splat.

   - Animation: Select Jet Sideways from the pull-down. Notice how your blob starts to look "blob-like."

   - Blob Birth Size: 0. The blob becomes more rounded. This value determines the size of the blob when it is created.

   - Blob Death Size: 1. This value determines the size of the blob when it reaches the end of its Longevity value.

10

The Light and Shading settings of the CC Mr Mercury effect are what add the third dimension to the blobs. The Light settings determine how the object will be lit, the color of the light, intensity, and so on. You will be using the default values. The Shading settings are what give the object its form. Twirl down the Shading settings in the Effect Controls panel and bring this blob to life by using this setting:

- Ambient: 10. Notice how the blob suddenly looks like it has depth. Ambient light is a second source of natural light, not the main source.

If you scrub the playback head across the layer, the blob almost looks like something inside of it is trying to escape. Let's help it escape by making some changes to the Direction, Velocity, and Blob Birth Size on the timeline.

6. Select the White Solid 1 layer on the timeline and press the E key to open the effects. Twirl down CC Mr Mercury, move the playback head to 0:00:28:00, and add keyframes for the Direction, Velocity, and Blob Birth Size properties.

7. Move the playback head to 0:00:32:00 and make the following changes:

- Direction: 0 x +112 degrees.

- Velocity: 9.8. You have blobs because they had enough "speed" to break out of the initial shape.

- Blob Birth Size: 2. All those blobs coalesce into one massive blob on the screen (see Figure 10-26).

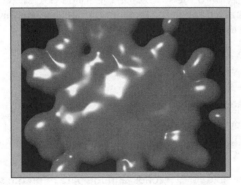

Figure 10-26.
That is one serious blob.

8. Turn off the Solo switch for the white solid and select the Beware layer. Change the Beware layer's Track Matte setting to Luma Matte. When you scrub across the layers, you will see the blob form and explode within the confines of the lettering. Save the project.

Plastic blobs are OK, but they don't quite fit the sinister theme of this exercise. You are going to give them some color, but instead of using a solid, you are going to apply it through the use of an Adjustment layer. The best way of thinking about an Adjustment layer is to regard it as a Null layer that has nothing but effects applied to it. Just keep in mind that anything that appears under the Adjustment layer will also have the effect applied to it. In the case of this project, you are going to have some color applied to the layer containing the Strobe Light effect and to the blobs. Here's how:

1. Select Layer ➤ New Adjustment Layer. A layer with that name will appear in Layer 1. Set the Adjustment layer's In point to 0:00:22:00.

2. Select the Adjustment layer and drag the Colorama effect onto the Comp.

3. Open the Effect Controls panel, twirl down the Colorama effect's Input Phase and Output Cycle, and make these settings:

   ■ In the Input Phase area, select Get Phase From. Select Alpha from the pull-down. If you scrub across the effect, the blobs look a bit psychedelic.

   ■ In the Output Cycle area, select Use Preset Palette. Select Fire from the pull-down. The blobs now look rather sinister.

4. Save the file.

In Chapter 6, we showed you how to have Flash text interact with a blob effect through the use of a Flash blend mode. Though the Luma Matte applied over the blobs effectively acts as a mask, you don't necessarily need the text layer. You could simply create the effect with the Adjustment layer and then output the blobs to a QuickTime movie, which is subsequently encoded into an FLV file. The text can be added as a mask layer in Flash; you get the same effect. Whether to do the whole thing in After Effects or to use a combination of Flash and After Effects is more a personal decision than anything else. Still, if you were to output only the blobs, you can change the text in the mask more readily than you could in After Effects or even have a series of phrases mask the blob in Flash.

Summary

This chapter has taken the dragon hunt in a rather interesting direction. Up this point, our journey has used Illustrator artwork and even masking layers to achieve some interesting visual effects. This chapter ignored all of that and showed you how a track matte offers you the same opportunity as other masking methods.

We started off the chapter by explaining what a track matte is and how you can use the alpha channels you create in Adobe Fireworks and Adobe Photoshop as masks. We also showed you a really cool technique where you can use an entire grayscale image and its alpha channel as a mask for a video.

Having shown you the fundamentals, we then moved into some really complicated techniques. In one of them, we used a video's Luma Matte, traced it, and used that to create the illusion of someone beaming up to the Starship Enterprise.

The next exercise was rather interesting. We explored the use of a Luma Matte to create a reflection of a video in After Effects. We then repeated the exercise in Flash and showed you that even though Flash does not have a Luma Matte feature, you can still create reflections. The key is understanding the new bitmap cache feature of Flash and how to apply a mask using ActionScript. We'll bet you were a bit surprised to discover it involved three simple lines of code.

10

The final project was presented as a series of techniques—rather than a long After Effects project—that you can use to support your Flash design efforts. You discovered how to use a few new effects—Beam, Spherize, CC Ball Action—to create a variety of effects from another spotlight effect to wavy text.

The next chapter takes our dragon hunt into territory that is the Holy Grail of Flash: how to integrate 3D content into a Flash movie.

11 ADDING A THIRD DIMENSION

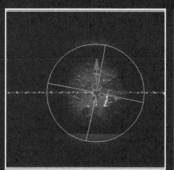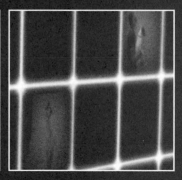

If anything in After Effects 7 is designed to give you a creative jolt, it is the inclusion of 3D layers. The ability to move objects around in a 3D space can't help but open a series of creative possibilities. The thing to keep in mind is that even though lighting, camera angles, and a Z-axis are available to you, After Effects is not a 3D modeling application. Still, 3D is the Holy Grail of Flash and After Effects that gets you into the game.

To understand 3D in After Effects, let's take it right back to the basics. You know that After Effects works in a flat space. Everything you have done to this point in the book has essentially involved working with objects that have length and width and nothing else. For example, you have faked objects moving closer to the viewer by tweening the object's size property between keyframes, and you have moved objects from "here" to "there" by changing the object's X and Y position. The X- and the Y-axis are the two dimensions of movement. When you faked growth, you created the illusion of the object moving closer to the viewer. In 3D, this is "depth" accomplished by moving the object along a third axis: the Z-axis.

What you need to have a clear understanding of at this point is that After Effects is a two-dimensional application that does not allow depth. When you activate a 3D layer in After Effects, you introduce depth and can create some amazing work using the 3D viewing and lighting tools. Even so, After Effects is not a 3D modeling application. You can't create a sphere, for instance, and turn it into Planet Earth. The best you can do is to take your 2D objects in the Comp and move them around in a 3D space.

You can see this in Figure 11-1. Notice how, when the number is rotated toward you, it flattens and, in the third panel, essentially disappears. This is because the object only has those two dimensions. You can easily reproduce this effect in Flash by simply using the Skew feature, shown in Figure 11-2, of the Transform panel.

Figure 11-1. Objects in the Comp can easily be rotated in After Effects.

Figure 11-2. Use the Transform panel in Flash if you need to rotate an object.

396

To move an After Effects object from 2D to 3D is rather simple. All you have to do is to click the 3D switch in the timeline (see Figure 11-3). Once you do so, the Anchor, Position, and Scale properties for the object develop a Z-axis. A new property—Orientation—is added to the properties and Rotation splits into separate X Rotation, Y Rotation, and Z Rotation properties. As well, the object in the Comp window sprouts three colored arrows. The red arrow is the X-axis, the green arrow is the Y-axis, and the blue arrow is the Z-axis. You can move an object in the Comp window by click-dragging an arrow. When you place the cursor over an arrow, the letter X, Y, or Z will appear beside the cursor.

Now that you understand what you will be looking at in After Effects, let's start using the tools.

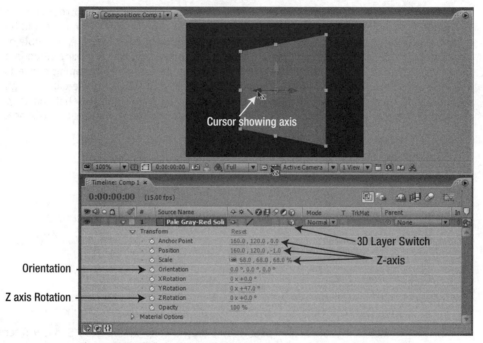

Figure 11-3. Click the 3D layer switch and the timeline and selected object in the Comp window develop a Z-axis.

11

Creating a 3D button animation for Flash

Throughout this book we have been concentrating upon the creation of QuickTime movies that are then subsequently converted into an FLV file and used on the Flash stage. This exercise is going to show a couple of different ways of using an animation created in After Effects.

Though we have been quite adamant throughout the pages of this book that embedding an FLV animation on the Flash timeline is evil, this is not necessarily true. Short animations of up to about 5 seconds can be embedded in Flash movies. The key, though, is to keep the physical size of the video as small as humanly possible.

The other technique is a throwback to the early days of Flash. Prior to the introduction of Flash video in Flash MX, video was essentially a hit or miss proposition. The video could be embedded into the timeline, but the result was one seriously bloated SWF file. A couple of developers, most notably Hillman Curtis, discovered a rather nifty way of faking video in a movie clip. Instead of embedding the video, rotoscope the video—**rotoscoping** converts a video to a series of still images—and import the images into a Flash movie clip. Though it sounds rather complex, you will discover Flash isn't as dumb as it looks when it comes to this technique. We start by creating a button that rotates in all three dimensions in space. Here's how:

1. Open After Effects and create a new Comp using these values:
   - Composition Name: Button
   - Width: 140
   - Height: 50
   - Frame Rate: 15
   - Duration: 0:00:03:15
   - Background Color: #FFFFFF (white)

2. Select the Text tool and enter the text Click me. In the Character panel, set the font to Arial Black or Arial Bold, the size to 20 pixels, and the color to #FF0000 (red).

3. Open Effects & Presets ➤ Perspective and drag a copy of the Drop Shadow filter onto the text in the Comp window.

4. Open the Effect Controls panel and set the Distance value for the Drop Shadow filter to 11 and the Softness value to 14.

> *Keep in mind that the effects are 2D effects that can be applied to 3D layers. That's the good news. The bad news is they can't be applied to light and camera layers.*

5. Click the 3D switch for the Text layer and twirl down the layer's Transform properties. You now have the stage set to put the button in motion (see Figure 11-4).

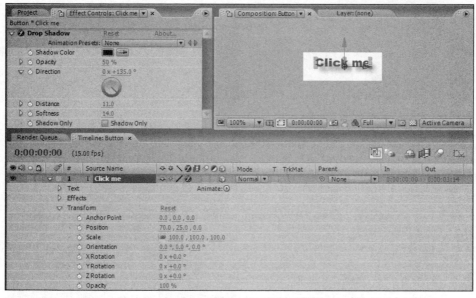

Figure 11-4. Combine a drop shadow with a 3D layer for a little extra jazz.

What we are going to do is spin the text around the X-axis and then around the Y-axis, and change the position to give the appearance of the text moving close to the viewer and receding into the distance. What we are not concentrating on is beauty. This whole exercise focuses on technique. Once you have that mastered, then you can start playing your own "what if . . ." games and experimenting.

1. Place the playback head at 0:00:00:00 and add a keyframe to the X Rotation property.

2. Move the playback head to 0:00:01:00 and change the X Rotation value to 1 x +0.0 degrees. If you scrub across the timeline, you will see the words rotate on the horizontal axis.

3. With the playback head still at 0:00:01:00, add a keyframe to the Y Rotation property.

4. Move the playback head to 0:00:02:00 and change the Y Rotation value to 1 x +0.0 degrees. Scrub the playback head across the timeline and the text rotates around the vertical axis.

5. With the playback head at 0:00:02:00, add a keyframe to the Position property. Change the Z value in the Position strip at the following times:

   ● 0:00:02:10: 250. Notice how a positive value pushes the image further away from the viewer.

   ● 0:00:03:05: −17. Negative values bring it closer.

   ● 0:00:03:14: 0. The words move back to their start position.

11

6. Click the Play button in the Time Controls panel to see your animation in action (as shown in Figure 11-5). Save the project and quit After Effects.

Figure 11-5.
Going for a spin on the Y-axis

We aren't going to ask you to render the video or produce the FLV file. It just doesn't make sense to have you do the same thing twice in the same exercise. Instead, if you check the FlashButton folder found inside the Chapter 11 Exercise folder, you will see we have already created an FLV file of the project. Let's put it to good use:

1. Launch Flash and open a new Flash document. When the document opens, change the stage size to 160X70 pixels.

2. Select Insert ➤ New Symbol and when the Create New Symbol dialog box opens, name the new symbol Button and select Movie Clip as its Type. Click OK to close the dialog box. When the dialog box closes, the Symbol Editor will open.

3. Add a new layer and name it Actions. Rename Layer 1 as Video.

The next couple of steps are going to walk you through the process of importing a video into the Flash timeline. You can import a number of formats such as QuickTime and AVI. If you do import these video formats, you will be walked through the conversion process using the Video Wizard. Our advice is don't use the Video Wizard if the file is in the QuickTime or AVI format; use the Video Encoder. Here, you'll go ahead and use the Video Wizard to import the FLV file into the movie clip.

> *If you must import video to a timeline, use a movie clip. Many Flash designers reserve the main timeline for the actual movie. Everything else gets put into symbols. Though there is no formal list of best practices in Flash, this is considered a best practice.*

4. Select Frame 1 of the Video layer and select File ➤ Import ➤ Import Video. When you release the mouse, the Video Wizard is launched (see Figure 11-6). Click the Browse button and navigate to the FlashButton folder in your Chapter 11 Exercise folder. Open it, select the Button.flv file, and click Open. The dialog box will close, and the path to the FLV file will appear in the File Path field.

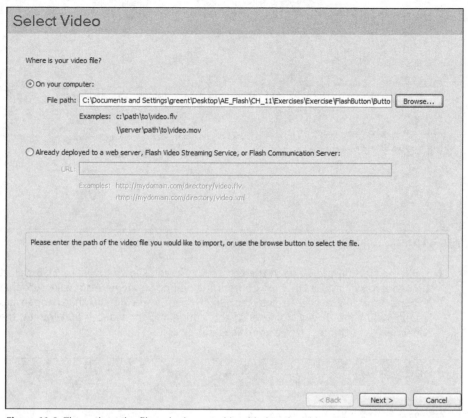

Figure 11-6. The path to the file to be imported is added to the Video Wizard.

5. Click the Next button to open the Deployment screen. You are going to be embedding the FLV file into the final SWF animation, meaning your only choice is Embed video in SWF and play in timeline. When you choose this option, the message shown in Figure 11-7 on the right side of the screen appears to warn you, like we have, of the evils of embedding video in the timeline.

11

The warning is dead on. The Flash timeline can contain up to a maximum of 16,000 frames. At 30 fps, a 9-minute video will require 16,200 frames. Do the math. If that video contains sound, the size of the SWF file will go through the roof. Also consider the fact that a SWF file needs to completely load before it will play in a browser. All these negatives are what contribute to really bad user experiences. In the case of this FLV file, we know it is 4 seconds long at a frame rate of 15 fps. This means the file, which doesn't contain an audio track, will only require 60 frames in the movie clip. That number is totally manageable.

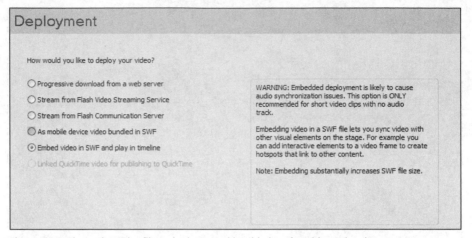

Figure 11-7. The path to the file to be imported is added to the Video Wizard.

6. Click the Next button to open the Embedding screen shown in Figure 11-8. Select Embedded video as the Symbol type from the pull-down menu. Also make sure that Expand Timeline if needed is selected. Right now the movie clip that is open has about 600 frames. If you don't select this option and the video is 900 frames, the video will get trimmed. Not a good scenario.

Figure 11-8. Always be sure that the "Expand timeline if needed" option is selected.

7. Click Next to be taken to the Finish Video Import screen. There really is nothing important here. Click the Finish button. The Video Wizard will close, the video will appear on the stage (as you see in Figure 11-9), the layer will contain the content across 60 frames, and the Embedded Video icon will appear in the Library. Select the video on the stage, and, in the Property inspector, change its X, Y location to 0, 0.

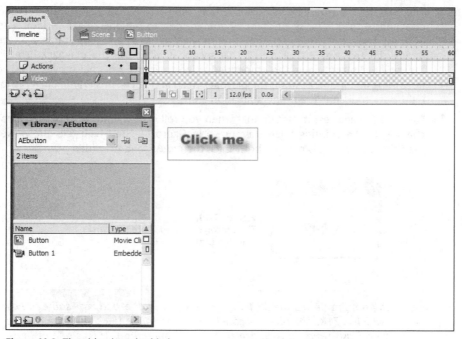

Figure 11-9. The video is embedded.

8. Select Frame 1 of the Actions layer, open the ActionScript Editor, and enter the following code:

```
stop()
```

9. Add a keyframe in Frame 60 of the Actions layer, and add the following code:

```
gotoAndStop(1);
```

The first line stops the playback head on Frame 1 of the movie clip. This means the user only sees the first frame of the video. The last line sends the playback head back to Frame 1 of the movie clip and, in many respects, acts like an auto-rewind button. The next step is what makes this movie clip act like a button.

10. Click the Scene 1 link to return to the main timeline and add an Actions layer. Drag the movie clip from the Library to the stage and give it the instance name of mcClick. Select the first frame in the Actions layer, open the ActionScript Editor, and enter the following code:

```
mcClick.onPress = function() {
  this.gotoAndPlay(2);
}
```

11

The first line is not new. You know that movie clips can have mouse events attached to them. The second line, if you are new to ActionScript, may look a bit odd. All it says is, "If the user clicks the movie clip, go to and play Frame 2 of the movie clip that was just clicked." That means it will move the playback head in the movie clip containing the embedded video to Frame 2 of that movie clip. The neat thing about that is, when the playback head in that clip hits Frame 60, it is shot right back to Frame 1, and the animation stops.

11. Save the file and test it. Notice that when you roll over the movie clip, the cursor changes to the pointing finger (as shown in Figure 11-10), which tells the viewer the thing the mouse is over is "hot." Click the mouse, and the video plays.

Figure 11-10.
The button is clicked. Note the cursor over the button.

If you were to publish this file, the SWF file would come in at exactly the same size as the FLV file, which is 71K. The obvious conclusion from this is the size of the FLV file embedded on a Flash timeline is added to the SWF animation. This is one of those techniques that should be used with caution. In the case of this exercise, reducing the effects, the physical size of the movie, and the time to 1 or 2 seconds will have a profound effect upon the final size of the SWF file.

Want to physically reduce the size of the After Effects Comp and resulting QuickTime movie from its current 140×50 size? Drop the point size of the text in the button to 12 or 14 pixels and remove the drop shadow. Always look for dead space or extraneous effects in the Comp, and, if you can, remove the space and lose the effects.

Rotoscoping a video

This technique, as we pointed out earlier, is how video was done in the early days of Flash. It is an extremely effective technique if used for very short—1 or 2 seconds—videos. Nothing gets people's attention more than discovering something they rolled over is a looping video. Here's how:

1. Open the After Effects project you have been working on so far.

If you didn't save it before heading off to Flash in the previous exercise, we have included a copy, FlashButton.aep, in the FlashButton folder.

2. Add the Comp to the Render Queue.

3. Click the Lossless link in the Output Module and open the Format pull-down menu shown in Figure 11-11.

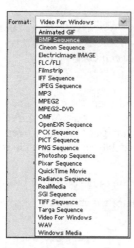

Figure 11-11.
Videos can be exported as a sequence of images.

If you take a look at the choices, you will notice there are a couple of choices that have the word *Sequence* in their name. What these choices do is to output the video as a series of images. The best way of visualizing the end result is to consider the images as the pages in a flip book. The choices are

- BMP Sequence: Outputs a series of BMP images. This is a PC imaging format.

- IFF Sequence: Flash won't recognize this format, so ignore it. IFF was originally developed in 1985 as a generic file format to allow data transfer between software products developed by different companies. AIFF, an audio format, and TIFF, an imaging format, are echoes of that history.

- JPEG Sequence: The images are output as JPG files. This is the one you should use.

- PCX Sequence: Another throwback to the good old days. Ignore this one because Flash doesn't recognize the format.

- PICT Sequence: Outputs a series of PICT images. This format had its origins on the Mac but works on both the Mac and the PC.

- PNG Sequence: If the video has an alpha channel, use this format. Though Flash recognizes the PNG format, the files tend to be a bit larger than their BMP, PICT, and JPG brethren.

- Pixar Sequence: Great for animations destined for a 3D modeling application.

- SGI Sequence: Another format best used in a 3D modeling environment.

- TIFF Sequence: This format has become more of a print than a digital media imaging standard because it can use either the CMYK or RGB color spaces. Not needed if you are heading to Flash.

4. Select JPEG Sequence and click OK in the Output Module Settings dialog box.

11

5. Click the Output to link and open the Roto folder found in the FlashButton folder. This is an empty folder and was included for this exercise.

> *You may notice the name of the file—Button_(#####)—is a bit odd. Don't change it. The # signs will actually be used when the individual images are output. If you must change anything, change the name, Button, but don't touch (#####).*

6. Click the Save button to close the dialog box and then click the Render button. When the render process finishes, save the project and quit After Effects. If you open the Roto folder, you will see there are 60 images that have been created. Don't move or delete any of the images. If you do delete or change a file name, the import into Flash will be, to be gentle, problematic.

7. Open Flash, create a new document, and change the Stage Size to 160×70 pixels.

8. Create a new movie clip and select the first frame of the movie clip in the Symbol Editor.

9. Select File ➤ Import ➤ Import to Stage. When the Import dialog box opens, navigate to the Roto folder found in the Chapter 11 Exercise folder.

10. When you navigate to this folder, you will see there are 60 JPG images in the folder. Your first reaction will be to import all of the images. Big mistake—don't do it. If you import the images, you will have to put them all in register with each other, which takes an inordinate amount of time. Instead, select the first file, Button_00000, and click Open.

11. As soon as you click the Open button, the dialog box closes, and an alert box appears (see Figure 11-12). This box is essentially telling you, "Dude, there are a whole bunch of images here that seem to be a sequence. Do you want me to put the sequence, in order, on the timeline?" Click Yes. A progress bar, depending on how many images need to be processed, will appear, and, when it disappears, all of the images are in individual frames on the timeline. Scrub across the timeline, and you discover the images are not only in sequence, they are in dead register with each other.

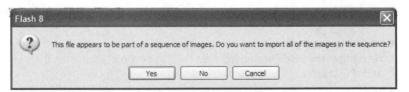

Figure 11-12. The software is offering to do the work for you.

12. Click the Scene 1 link to return to the main timeline and drag the movie clip from the Library to the stage. If you test the movie or publish the SWF and open it, the animation, as shown in Figure 11-13, will play.

Figure 11-13.
The SWF file, not a test SWF from the
FLA file, is playing.

Let's just take a second here and start looking at this in a rather dispassionate manner.

The size for the SWF file just created should come in around 143K, which is about twice the size of embedding the FLV file into the timeline. The reason for this is each JPG image is about 4K in size—we used a Quality setting of 8, which is about standard for JPG compression—and there are 60 of them in the Library. The assumption is that the SWF file should actually come in around 240K, but remember, Flash is applying JPG compression to the images as well. This should tell you that, in order to bring the SWF down to a more reasonable size, you need to work with smaller images—think about the size of a button on the Flash stage—and fewer images.

What about the other formats? Do they result in small files? In a nutshell, yes, they do.

If you open the FlashButton folder found in the Completed folder of the Chapter 11 Exercises folder, you will see we have reproduced this project using images in the BMP, PICT, and PNG formats. The BMP SWF file weighs in at 59K, the PICT SWF file is 61K, and the PNG SWF file is 60K. The reason is simple. Each of the images used is output in Flash as a JPG image. Bottom line: the three other formats result in a SWF file that is just under half the size of its JPG counterpart. Our suggestion is to go with the PNG format rather than the JPG format. Whether you choose to or not is up to you.

Viewing 3D layers

One of the issues regarding working with 3D layers in After Effects is figuring out what you are looking at when determining where in 3D space an object is located and how it interacts with other objects in the Comp that are located in that same 3D space. In this short exercise, we are going to give you a chance to get comfortable with the 3D views available to you in After Effects.

1. Open the Views folder found in the Chapter 11 Exercise folder and double-click the Views.aep file to launch After Effects.

2. When the file opens, you will see that we have placed a video over a solid, and when you look at the Comp window, as shown in Figure 11-14, your first observation is the video is almost as large as the solid. Not really.

11

Figure 11-14.
First impressions can be deceiving.

3. At the bottom of the Comp window is the Active Camera pull-down menu. Select Left from the menu (see Figure 11-15). The line you see at the right is the video, and the one behind it is the solid. What that tells you is the video isn't large, it is closer to the viewer than the solid.

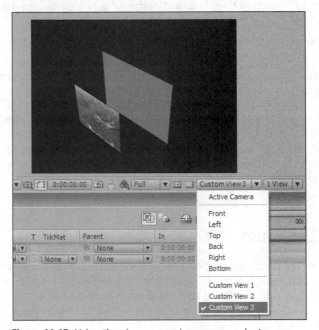

Figure 11-15. Using the view menu gives you a peek at your virtual world.

4. Select Custom View 3 from the pull-down menu, and you will see the video is indeed quite a distance away from the solid.

The Active Camera view, which is the default, is what the user sees when he or she views the video, and this is the view you should use when you are checking the file prior to rendering the video. The other views give you a great idea of positioning in the 3D space.

The first six views are called **orthogonal views**. They show you the position in space but don't give you any perspective. The three Custom Views add the perspective. Having nine views of the same space might seem like a bit of overkill, but once you start working with 3D layers, you will find yourself using them quite a bit. The orthogonal views are ideal for establishing relationships between objects in the 3D space as well as their size and positions. Get into the habit of using these views before using the Custom Views.

There is another way of viewing the Comp as follows:

5. Click the 1 View pull-down menu in the Comp window and select 4 Views – Right from the menu. The Comp window will split into four sections as shown in Figure 11-16. As you see, you get two orthogonal and two perspective views. Change the view to 2 Views – Horizontal, and you get one of each.

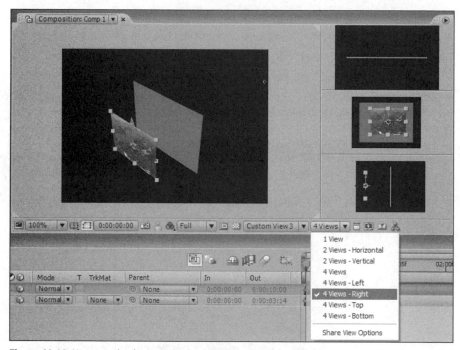

Figure 11-16. You can also have multiple views.

6. Click and drag the video in the Comp window. You will see that its position changes in each view.

The next technique is the addition of a Light layer. In Chapter 9, we showed a sort of flashlight effect—a gradient mask for Flash—you could add to an FLV file. This technique is an absolute snap to do in After Effects if you use an animated Light layer. The neat thing about a Light layer is that it shows up in the timeline, and that means it can be moved and otherwise manipulated. Let's reproduce the flashlight effect:

11

1. Switch back to the Active Camera view for the project that is open.

2. Select Layer ➤ New ➤ Light to open the Light Settings dialog box shown in Figure 1-17. Though you are going to go with the default settings, let's look at the features of the dialog box:

   - Light Type: There are four choices available. Parallel is a directional light from an infinitely distant location from the object being lit. This is best used if uniform lighting and a specific lighting direction are required. Spot is basically a cone of light and is the only one that allows you to have Cone Angle and Cone Feather options. Point is much like a lightbulb lighting up whatever is close, and Ambient has no source and can be treated as a secondary light.

   - Intensity: The values range from no light, 0%, to white hot bright, 100%.

   - Cone Angle: Used only by Spot, this sets the width of the light on the subject.

   - Cone Feather: How the light from Spot will fade out at the edges.

   - Color: This opens the Color Picker so you can choose a color for the light.

   - Casts Shadows: Select this, and the object being lit will have a shadow.

   - Shadow Darkness: How dark and ominous do you want the shadow to be?

   - Shadow Diffusion: This sets the softness of the shadow based on the distance of the light from the object. A large value creates soft shadows and vice versa.

Figure 11-17. The default light settings

3. Click OK, and the light appears in the Comp window. Switch to the 2 Views – Horizontal, and you can see that the light is fairly close to the video. Select the Left view in the Active Camera pull-down menu and change the Magnification Level in the Comp window to 100%. The orthogonal view changes, and you get a better look at the light in 3D space.

4. Select the Z-axis, the blue arrow, in the Left view, and drag the light to the right, as shown in Figure 11-18. The cone moves away from the video, and the lit area of the video, as expected, gets larger.

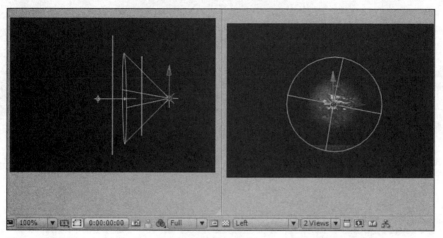

Figure 11-18. You can adjust the lighting angle and distance in the Comp window.

5. Twirl down Transform in the Light layer, and scrub the X-axis in the Position area to drag the light to the left side of the Comp. Add a keyframe in the Position and Point of Interest properties. Actually, you only need to add the one keyframe. When you change a light's Position setting, you also change its Point of Interest setting.

Point of interest? Take a look at the Left view in the Comp window. The crosshairs to which the line seems to be attached indicate the point of interest. It is the point where the light is aimed. The default point of interest is the center of the Comp.

11

6. Move the playback head to 0:00:02:00 and move the light on the X-axis to the right side of the Comp window. If you do a RAM preview, you will see you have created a flashlight effect with a couple of clicks of the mouse (as shown in Figure 11-19).

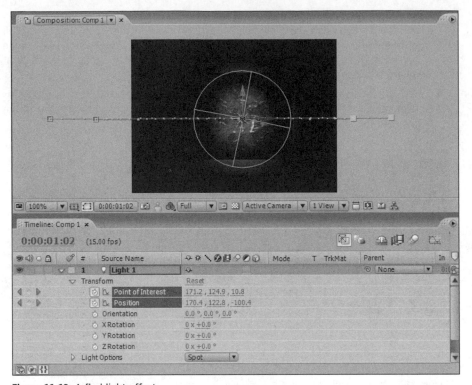

Figure 11-19. A flashlight effect

We have our lights. How about a camera?

If there is one feature of After Effects and 3D that seals the deal, it is the ability to add cameras and move them around. The reason is the Active Camera view is fairly static; you can't move the camera from "here" to "there." When you add a new camera layer, it contains properties that allow you to, for example, slowly pan a camera across a still image rather than move the image. Let's create a rather nifty little piece that uses camera movement:

1. In the Chapter 11 Exercise folder is a folder named Cameras. Open it and open the Camera.aep file in the folder. When the file opens, the Comp looks a little disjointed. Words overlap each other, and, if you scrub across the timeline, you will notice nothing moves. We have saved the file with the 2 View – Horizontal view—the orthogonal view is a Top view—and you can also see there are pieces of text in 3D space. You are going to put this whole thing in motion by moving a camera, not the text.

The use of a camera in After Effects is one great, big, fat subject, and we will admit we aren't even coming close to exploring what you can do with this feature. The purpose of this exercise is simply to get you going with a camera and to show you what you can do by simply moving it around in a 3D space and exploring what happens when you change the various properties of a camera layer and views.

2. Select Layer ➤ New ➤ Camera to bring up the Camera Settings dialog box (see Figure 11-20). Use the following values:

- Zoom: 374.1. Notice how the Angle of View value changes. Change the Angle of View value to 46.31.

- Enable Depth of Field: Selected.

- Focus Distance: 177.1.

- Lock to Zoom: Deselected.

- Aperture: 66. Notice how the F-Stop value changes as well. If you are a photographer and prefer to use f-stops, any change to the F-Stop value will also change the Aperture value.

Click OK to accept the values.

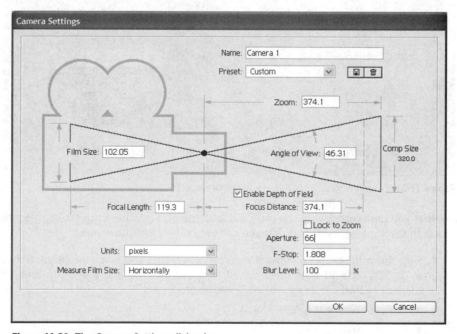

Figure 11-20. The Camera Settings dialog box

11

413

There is a lot to the Camera Settings *dialog box, and space simply doesn't permit us to get deep into it. There is a great overview of the dialog box in Chapter 9 of the After Effects User Guide or select* Help ➤ After Effects Help ➤ 3D Layers ➤ Cameras, lights, and points of interest ➤ Camera Settings.

3. When you close the dialog box, a Camera 1 layer appears on the timeline. Drag the Camera 1 layer between the motion and our layers. You will also see the camera in the orthogonal view. Press the spacebar and drag the orthogonal view pane upwards, if you can't see the whole diagram already. The little rectangle, as shown in Figure 11-21, is the camera position. Click the camera and drag the mouse, and you can see in the Active Camera view how it is creating the "shot."

Figure 11-21. The orthogonal view shows you the camera.

Now that you understand what you are looking at, the plan is to have the camera meander around the various pieces of text that you can see in the orthogonal view.

4. Twirl down the Camera 1 layer's Transform properties and place the playback head at 0:00:00:00. Add keyframes for all of the properties and make the following changes to the Point of Interest and Position properties:

- Point of Interest: 160, 120, −52
- Position: 160, 120, −350

> *As you start changing the properties, pay close attention to what happens in the Comp. For example, when you changed the* Position *value, the word* poetry *moved closer to the viewer.*

5. Move the playback head to 0:00:02:00 and make the following changes:

- Point of Interest: 160, 120, 270
- Position: 160, 120, –41

The camera moves through the word *poetry* and the words *in motion* become visible (see Figure 11-22).

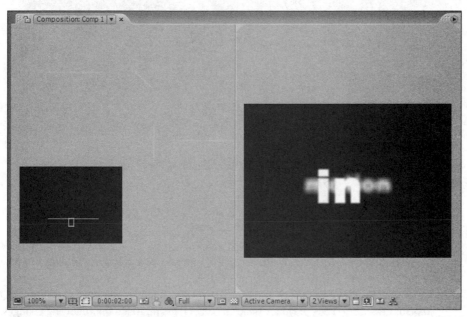

Figure 11-22. The camera Position and Point of Interest settings have changed.

6. Move the playback head to 0:00:03:15 and make the following changes:

- Point of Interest: 160, 120, 496
- Position: 160, 120, 185

The camera moves through the word *in*, and the word *motion* comes into focus.

7. Move the playback head to 0:00:05:00 and make the following changes:

- Point of Interest: 160, 120, 519
- Position: 160, 120, 207
- Y Rotation: 0 x +2.3 degrees

The word *motion* moves closer to the camera, moves to the left, and becomes a bit fuzzy.

11

8. Move the playback head to 0:00:07:10, add a keyframe to the X Rotation property by clicking the stopwatch, and change the Y Rotation value to 0 x +53 degrees.

The camera swings around to the right, and just a piece of the word *our*, as shown in Figure 11-23, becomes visible.

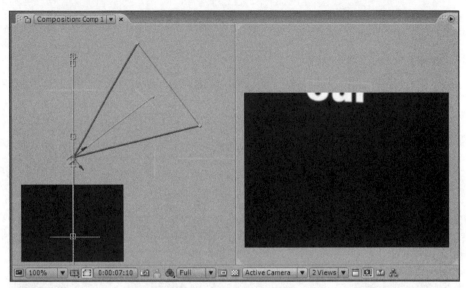

Figure 11-23. The word *our* is moving into the frame.

9. Move the playback head to 0:00:08:15 and change the X Rotation value to 0 x +21 degrees. The word *our* moves onto the Comp.

10. Move the playback head to 0:00:10:00 and change the X Rotation value to 0 x +44 degrees and the Y Rotation value to 0 x +92 degrees. The word *first* moves into the frame.

11. Now you need to prepare to move across the camera animation layer: move the www.osflash.org/red5 playback head to 0:00:11:15 and make the following changes:

- Point of Interest: Add a keyframe.
- Position: 160, 120, 208.
- Orientation: Add a keyframe.
- X Rotation: Add a keyframe.
- Y Rotation: Add a keyframe.
- Z Rotation: Add a keyframe.

12. Move the playback head to 0:00:13:15 and enter the following values:

- Point of Interest: 327, –21, 372
- Position: 327, 196, 62
- X Rotation: 0 x –46 degrees
- Y Rotation: 0 x +51 degrees

13. Move the playback head to 0:00:14:15 and enter the following values:

- Position: Add a keyframe.
- Z Rotation: 0 x +10 degrees.

14. Move the playback head to 0:00:15:25 and enter the following values:

- Position: 938, 196, 62

15. Scrub through the timeline and pay particular attention to the movement of the camera in the orthogonal view.

16. Change the view to 1 View, and do a RAM preview (see Figure 11-24). The camera does the moving, not the words. Save the project.

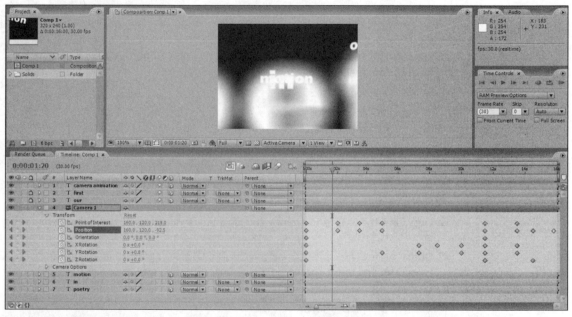

Figure 11-24. Let the camera do the work for a change.

Video in a box

In this exercise, you are going to try the opposite approach from that of the previous exercise. The camera is going to stay put, and the objects are going to be doing the moving. What you are going to do is to build a four-sided video cube and rotate it. Along the way, you will also discover a rather invaluable aid in getting stuff just right: the Orbit Camera tool.

This definitely falls into the category of "Stuff You Can't Do in Flash." As you know, Flash does not have a 3D capability, and to accomplish this in Flash would require a lot of skewing of movie clips. Though you will be using a single 320×240 video for this exercise, there is nothing that says you can't use four or even six different videos.

This technique may look rather cool, but it does have a definite use in Flash. You could put the cube on the Flash stage and use it as a lead-in to a frame in Flash where the user can pick the video to watch. Another approach would be to take a screen shot of the first frame of each video in the cube and use it as a button, in the same Flash frame as the cube, to launch the selected video. There are a lot of ways of playing multiple videos in Flash, and many of them are presented in *Foundation Flash 8 Video* by Jordan L. Chilcott and Tom Green (friends of ED, 2006). Let's build a box:

1. In the Chapter 11 Exercise folder is another folder named Box. Open this folder and double-click the Box.aep file in that folder.

2. When the file opens, notice we have already created the Comp for you and added the Water.mov file to the Project panel. The Comp size is 500 pixels wide by 400 pixels high because you need the extra space to accommodate the video cube spinning around. Drag the Water.mov file to the timeline and click the 3D layer switch.

3. Rename the layer to Back and twirl down the Transform properties. Add these settings to the layer:

   - Anchor Point: 160, 120, 160
   - Position: 250, 200, 0
   - Orientation: 180, 0, 180

   If you look at the Top view, you will see the video has moved to the top of the Comp window.

4. Duplicate the layer and change the Position value to 252, 200, 0. Change the Orientation value to 0, 270, 0. Rename the layer to Right.

5. Duplicate the layer and change the Orientation value to 180, 90, 180. Rename the layer to Left.

6. Duplicate the layer and change the Orientation value to 0, 0, 0. Rename the layer to Front. The end result should be a nice box in the Top view (see Figure 11-25).

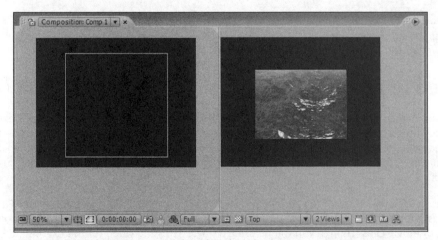

Figure 11-25. You have constructed the sides of a video box.

Though we have given you the numbers, if you want to do it using your eyes, here are a couple of tips:

- Build all layers with the Active Camera view set to Front. It makes it easier to orient in 3D space.

- When you position solids, video, or other content, you need to work with the Top view switched on.

- The anchor points for the objects in motion have to be positioned in the middle of the Comp. This explains why we have included guides in the Comp.

Putting a camera in orbit

The thing about 3D is that sometimes it lies. What looks great in one view is not exactly correct in another. Panels may actually not be butting up against each other or not aligned and so on. Though you have a number of views available to you, the odd thing is there aren't enough of them. This is what makes the Orbit Camera tool so invaluable. You can spin an object around, tilt it, and so on, looking for issues. You can also use it to position the camera in a camera layer in 3D space.

What this tool does is to rotate the current view around the point of interest. It only works when there is a camera layer. Let's try it out:

1. Add a new camera layer to the Comp. When the New Camera dialog box opens, select the 35 mm preset and click OK. Twirl down the Transform properties and change the Point of Interest value to 250, 200, –225 and the Position value to 250, 200, –712.

2. Select the Orbit Camera tool by either pressing the C key or clicking the tool as shown in Figure 11-26.

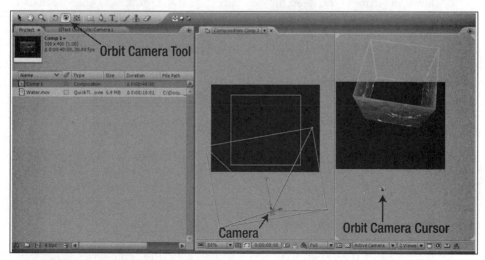

Figure 11-26. Using the Orbit Camera tool

11

3. The cursor will change. Click once in the Comp window—not the orthogonal view window—to select the window and click-drag the mouse. The cube in the Comp window and the camera in the Top view window will follow the mouse and rotate depending on where the mouse is dragged. Pay close attention to where the videos butt up against each other. When you finish, reset the Position value of the Camera 1 layer to that from step 1.

> *If you are working with a cube, get the sides in place and then marquee the corners in the* Top *view using the* Magnifying Glass *tool. This will zoom right in on a corner, and you can adjust the position of the edge that is out of alignment using the arrow keys.*

Preparing for parenthood

At first glance, rotating the cube may seem to be a rather daunting task. The sides have to remain perfectly aligned, but they need to rotate as a unit in 3D space. You could be in for a long spell of playing with the Transform properties of each layer, just getting things right. But the authors are just a lazy as you, and if there is a quick way of doing it, we'll find it and use it. The solution is simplicity in itself: why not group the layers and have them move as a unit? You can't group layers, but, as you may remember from meeting the parents in Chapter 8, you can change the properties for one layer and have its children follow the lead of the parent. Here's how:

1. Press the Home key to return the playback head to 0:00:00:00, twirl down the Transform properties for the Front layer, and add a keyframe to the Y Rotation value.

2. Right-click (PC) or Cmd-click (Mac) the keyframe just added and select Keyframe Velocity from the pull-down menu. This will open the Keyframe Velocity dialog box shown in Figure 11-27. Keep the degrees/sec at 0 and set the Influence to 16.67 in both the Incoming and Outgoing areas. Click Continuous to select it and click OK. The keyframe changes from its diamond shape to an hour glass shape, indicating keyframe velocity on both the incoming and outgoing aspects of the animation on the timeline.

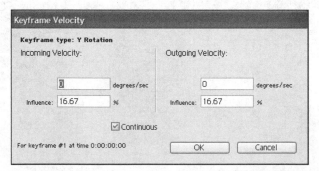

Figure 11-27. Keyframe velocity is familiar to the Flash community.

3. Move the playback head to 0:00:05:00 and change the Y Rotation value to 2 x +314 degrees. Notice how you have another velocity keyframe. Open the Keyframe Velocity dialog box. Deselect Continuous. Change the Incoming degrees/sec value to 21.84 and leave its Outgoing counterpart at 0. Change the Influence value for Incoming to 40.96 and Outgoing to 16.67. Click OK to close the dialog box.

4. Add a keyframe to the X Rotation and Z Rotation properties.

5. Move the playback head to 0:00:05:20 and change the Z Rotation value to 0 x +90 degrees. This tilts the layer.

6. Move the playback head to 0:00:06:15 and change the Z Rotation value to 1 x +0.0 degrees to spin the layer. As you make the changes, the video in the Front layer will move around in both the Top and Active Camera views in the Comp window.

7. Save the project.

If you are a Flash user, **keyframe velocity** may seem to be a bit of a mysterious term. It isn't. In the Flash world, it is known as **custom ease in** or **custom ease out**. The difference is, unlike in Flash, you can set the start and the end speeds for the effect. Where the two worlds intersect, though, is in their alternative method of setting this value: both use a graph. Being old school, we prefer to "do it by the numbers," so we aren't going to give you a full-bore overview of the graph feature. Still, it is there, and you should know where it is and how to change things.

To open the Graph Editor, click the Graph Editor button in the timeline, and the timeline changes to that shown in Figure 11-28. What you are looking at is called a **speed graph**, and the curve is showing you acceleration and deceleration.

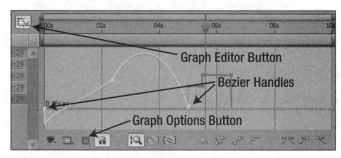

Figure 11-28. The Graph Editor

The curve can be manipulated by using the Bezier handles, those yellow dots, to change the shape of the curve or to move a point. You can also change the graph by clicking the Graph Options button and making a choice from the pull-down menu. The three buttons at the right are the Easy Ease, Easy Ease In, and Easy Ease Out buttons. Click them, and the handles will be adjusted automatically. To turn off the graph, simply click the Graph Editor button.

11

The Flash Custom Ease In/Ease Out Editor, shown in Figure 11-29, is remarkably similar. To use it, create a tween on the Flash timeline, click anywhere between the keyframes, and click the Edit button in the Property inspector. Make your changes, click OK, and the changes are made. This editor is ideal for creating bouncing balls, for example, that actually lose energy over time. Add a few curves for the bounces, and the ball will bounce lower each time it hits one of those points. If you deselect Use one setting for all properties, you can change the Position, Rotation, Scale, Colors, and Filters properties involved in the tween.

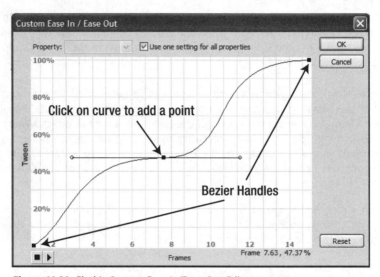

Figure 11-29. Flash's Custom Ease In/Ease Out Editor

Finishing up

Now that the Front view is moving around, let's get the rest of the layers moving in lockstep.

1. Select the Right, Left, and Back layers and set their parent to Front.

2. Scrub the playback head across the timeline, and you will see all four layers move together as shown in Figure 11-30.

422

Figure 11-30. How about that? Water on a box.

3. Change the view to 1 View and click the Play button in the Time Controls panel. The box will spin, twirl, and rotate.

Live . . . from your computer . . . it's the Fake TV Late Show!

TV show promo spots are a staple of our lives. Whether it be the promos for CNN or something "cheesy" for a local late night talk show, these spots are designed to get your attention. Our mythological channel—Fake TV—needs a promo for its Late Show, and in the final project of this chapter, you're going to make one; this is a good opportunity for you to pull together what you have learned in this chapter and use a couple of new effects along the way.

The plan is to have six short clips appear in a grid that moves through a 3D space. The piece finishes off with the name of the show. The key to this project is the ability to work in a big space—640X480—and then output to a smaller space—320X249. The reason is sometimes you just need the extra room to see whether the idea you have works. The more area you have to work with, the less you will be frustrated. If this were to be done at the final size of 320X240, you would be constantly zooming in on the videos and the grid. The problem with that is, as videos in the Comp window are magnified, they become fuzzy. Working at 100% size with everything keeps the frustration level to a minimum.

In order to keep this project relatively uncomplicated, we are going to start by having you construct a version of the interface used in the project. You will be constructing a grid, placing a really tiny video in a position on the grid, and using a camera to give the illusion the video is larger than it is. This way, when you head over to the project and you see six videos on the grid, you will understand how it was all put together. If you can do one video on the grid, you can do six. Let's get busy:

11

1. In the Chapter 11 Exercise folder is a folder named FakeTV. Open the folder and double-click the Grid.aep file. All we have done for you is to create a Comp and import the video to be used.

2. Create a new solid and set the color to #767676 (gray). Open the Comp in the Comp window.

3. Open Effects & Presets ➤ Generate and drag a copy of the Grid effect onto the Comp. The Comp is now filled with a grid. You can do two things with this grid: either use it as a graphic element in the Comp or use it as a mask. You are going to use this pattern as a graphic.

4. In the Effect Controls panel, apply these settings to the Grid effect:

   ■ Size From: Select Width Slider from the pull-down menu. This choice will use the width value to determine both the height and the width of the cells in the grid.

   ■ Width: 40. The cells will get larger.

   ■ Border: 2. The border around the cells shrinks to what looks like a hairline (see Figure 11-31).

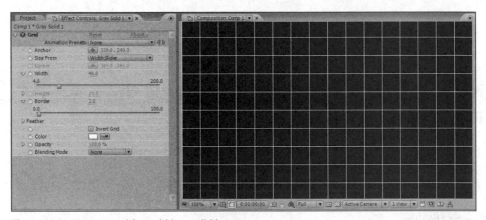

Figure 11-31. You start with a grid in a solid layer.

5. The grid is a bit boring. Add some "jazz" to it by feathering the intersection points of the grid. Open Effects & Presets ➤ Stylize and drag a copy of the Glow effect onto the Comp. Nothing really happens.

6. Twirl down the Glow effect in the Effect Controls panel and use these settings:

   ■ Glow Threshold: 0

   ■ Glow Radius: 4

   ■ Glow Intensity: 2

   ■ Glow Colors: A&B Colors

If you reduce the Magnification Value to 50%, you will see the glow is showing where the grid lines intersect.

7. Rename the layer to Grid and twirl down Transform. When the Transform properties open, set these values:

- Position: 50, 74. **The grid shifts to the left.**
- Scale: 200.

Twirl up the Grid layer.

8. Drag the video to the timeline and place it above the solid on the timeline.

9. Select the Video layer and twirl down its Transform properties. Use the following Transform values:

- Anchor Point: 320, 288. **The video will move up the screen.**
- Position: 502, 261.
- Scale: Deselect the link and set the scale value to 12, 14.8. Click the link.

The key to working with objects in a 3D space is to get them into position in a 2D space. This is exactly what you have done with the video and the grid. Even though the video looks really small, you are going to make it look fairly large through the use of a camera. Before you do that, you need to get the video and the grid positioned in a 3D space. Here's how:

1. Set the Grid layer as the parent of the Video layer and click the 3D switch for both layers.

2. Select the Grid layer, twirl down Transform, and change the Orientation value to 320, 30, 0. Change the Y value in the Position layer to 164. The grid and the video will, as shown in Figure 11-32, tilt downward to the left. Switch the view in the Comp window to 2 Views – Horizontal. Select the orthogonal view and change it to Top.

Figure 11-32. The grid and the video are ready for a camera.

11

425

3. Insert a new camera layer and use these settings in the New Camera dialog box:

- Zoom: 3178
- Angle of View: 11.5
- Enable Depth of Field: Selected
- Focus Distance: 755.1
- Lock to Zoom: Deselected
- Aperture: 35

You still aren't going to see much because the camera still isn't pointing at the video.

4. Twirl down the Camera I Transform settings and use these values:

- Point of Interest: Click and drag each of the values until the video appears in the Active Camera view. As you drag across the values, the point of interest will move. You can stop moving when it is over the video in the orthogonal view.

- Position: You want the camera to be below the grid as shown in Figure 11-33. Start with 313, –18, –887.

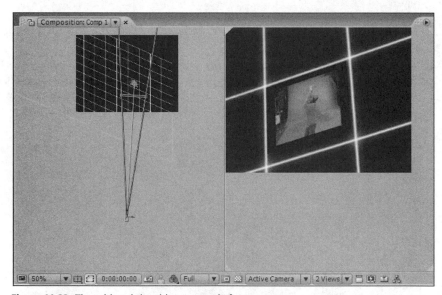

Figure 11-33. The grid and the video are ready for a camera.

5. Do a RAM preview, and you will see the video play in its grid square.

That may seem like an awful lot of work for one video. It is if you have never done it before, but once you get the hang of it, the time it takes gets a lot shorter. An obvious next question is, What does all of this have to do with Flash? The short answer is, Everything. Flash simply can't zoom in on an object without distorting it. Zooming in, in Flash, is nothing more than resizing. In the case of a video, this can result in your having a really bad day. A camera can zoom, and you have seen that in action. The short answer to the Flash question is, What you do with it in Flash is up to you. The creative possibilities are endless and, now that you know how to do this, check out this video: www.neave.tv/ #hexstatic_deadly_media. A lot of what we have covered in this one exercise and to this point in the chapter can be found in the piece.

Now that you understand how to zoom in on a video in a 3D space, let's put it to a practical use and create a lead-in to a TV show. At this point, you can save this project and close it. You won't be revisiting this one. Like we said at the start of the exercise, if you know how to use one video on a grid, you know how to use six videos on a grid.

Playing with a camera

To this point in the chapter, most of the camera work has involved moving a camera around in 3D space. We are going to continue with this theme but introduce another technique: you are going to change the camera properties as well. Remember, values in an object's properties are nothing more than data. That means the object can be manipulated by simply changing the numbers.

1. Open the TVopener.aep file in the Fake TV folder found in the Chapter 11 Exercise folder.

> You might want to take a minute and examine the project. You will see that we have placed the videos on the grid, and there is also a solid in Layer 11 that will provide the special effects at the end of the piece.

2. Twirl down Camera Options in the camera layer. As you can see in Figure 11-34, many of the properties from the New Camera dialog box are available to you.

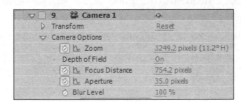

Figure 11-34. You can play with the properties of the camera itself.

11

Before we get going, let's quickly review each of those properties:

- Zoom: The distance in pixels from the position of the camera to the video on the solid.

- Depth of Field: The distance range at which an image is in focus. Images beyond the range are blurred.

- Focus Distance: The distance in pixels from the camera's position at which the object appears in focus.

- Aperture: The size of the lens. Changing this value will also change the depth of field blur and the f-stop.
- Blur Level: The Depth of Field blur value. Leaving it at 100% creates a natural blue based on the camera settings.

This is about to become one of the more complicated pieces you have worked on to this point. Don't let it intimidate you. If we didn't think you were ready, it wouldn't be here. What is going to happen is between times 0:00:00:00 and 0:00:12:15 you will be making changes to the camera's position, camera type, and the position of the grid in 3D space. Each video needs to appear in the Comp, and this can only be accomplished by moving the grid to the camera and then moving the camera to make the shot more interesting.

> *One final point: you are dealing with seconds and frames in this project and have no need for minutes or hours. We are going to shorten the time code to reflect this. This means, instead of asking you to go to time 0:00:12:15, we will ask you to go to time :12:15. Note the colon in front of the 12. Let's get busy.*

1. Twirl down the Transform properties for the Camera and the Grid layers. You should be seeing all of the Transform and Camera Option properties for the camera layer and all of the Transform properties for the Grid layer. You will also notice we have added the first keyframes.

> *If you have a second monitor attached to your computer, now would be a really good time to move the Comp window to that second monitor. As you change the values below, watch what happens to the video and the grid.*

2. Move the playback head to :01:26 and add a keyframe to the Camera 1 Focus Distance.

3. Move the playback head to :02:26 and enter the following values:

   Camera 1 layer:

   - Focal Distance: 562.2

   Grid layer:

   - Anchor Point: **Keyframe**
   - Orientation: 319, 30, 0 **(degrees)**
   - X Rotation: Keyframe
   - Y Rotation: 0 x +68 degrees
   - Z Rotation: **Keyframe**

4. Move the playback head to :04:00 and use these values in the Camera Options:

   - Zoom: 3468.2
   - Focus Distance: 467.2

5. Move the playback head to :04:14 and use this value in the Camera Options:

- Focus Distance: 964.2

6. Move the playback head to :04:24 and change the camera's Point of Interest **setting** to 200, 311, 0. Now move the playback head to :06:03 and change the Point of Interest setting to 429.5, 41, 0. If you scrub between these two keyframes, you will see the video change.

> *You may notice After Effects takes more time than you are used to as it moves between the keyframes. Remember, you are dealing with an immense Comp— 640×480—and an equally immense grid as shown in Figure 11-35. They take time to render.*

Figure 11-35. We are working an immense virtual space. This view is at 6.5% percent, and the grid still runs out of the Comp window.

7. Move the playback head to :06:10 and use these values in the Camera Options:

- Focus Distance: 634
- Aperture: **Keyframe**

8. Move the playback head to :06:20 and change the Grid's Y Rotation **value to** 0 x +3.0 degrees.

9. Move the playback head to :07:06 and enter the following Camera **values:**

- Point of Interest: 569, 43, 0
- Zoom: 2894.0
- Focus Distance: 501.2
- Aperture: 10

10. Move the playback head to :08:15 and enter the following Camera **values:**

- Point of Interest: 341, 241, 0
- Position: 389, 251, –807.2
- Zoom: 1894

11

11. Move the playback head to :09:22 and add a keyframe to the point of interest. Move the playback head to :10:09 and change the point of interest value to –32, 374, 0. You are finished with the Camera 1 layer. Twirl it up.

12. Move the playback head to :09:29, and, in the Grid layer, add a keyframe to the Anchor Point and Orientation properties.

13. Move the playback head to :10:29 in the Grid layer and change the Orientation value to 357, 30, 0.

14. Move the playback head to :11:15 and add a keyframe to the Position property. Right-click (PC) or Ctrl-click (Mac) the keyframe just created and select Keyframe Assistant ➤ Easy Ease In. The keyframe, as shown in Figure 11-36, changes to a right-pointing arrow.

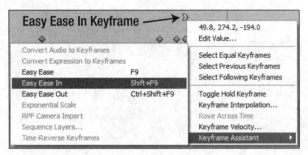

Figure 11-36. Use the Easy Ease assistants to control the easing of objects into and out of keyframes.

The three Easy Ease assistants have specific functions. Easy Ease *eases the speed coming into and out of a keyframe.* Easy Ease In *controls the ease speed coming into a keyframe, and* Easy Ease Out *controls the ease speed when the playback head moves out of the keyframe.*

15. With the playback head still at :11:15, add a keyframe to the Orientation value and change the Y Rotation value to 0 x –128.0 degrees.

16. Move the playback head to :12:14. Change the Position value to –457.6, 239.2, –483.3 and be sure to change the keyframe to Easy Ease In. Change the Orientation value to 357, 64, 0 and twirl up the Grid layer (make sure you changed the orientation on the grid layer, not the camera layer).

17. Save the project and click the Play button. The grid will move through space (see Figure 11-37), colors will appear in the background, and the text will appear at the end of the video.

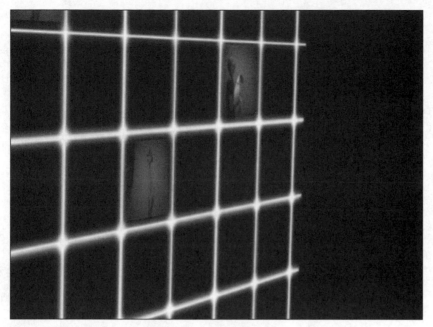

Figure 11-37. Welcome to the Fake TV Late Show.

Making the movie Flash Friendly

As it currently stands, this project will play in Flash if the user has a bandwidth pipe the size of the tunnel between France and the U.K. and has the most powerful PC in existence. Everyone else attempting to watch this in Flash can simply forget about it. The size of this video—640×480—will simply overwhelm the Flash Player. In many respects, it will be like trying to push a watermelon through a worm.

This isn't to say it can't be done. You can push a 640×480 FLV file through the Flash Player providing there isn't a lot of movement and that the frame rate for the FLV file is reduced to at least 5 frames per second. The problem here is there is a serious amount of movement. The grid is in motion, and the videos play while the grid moves. Toss in the fact the camera is swinging around to show the videos, and you can see that playing this video at its current size is simply not an option.

To make this movie Flash friendly, it needs to be resized. The hard way of doing it would be to simply start over with a Comp that is 320×240. The easy way is to let the software do the work. Here's how:

1. Click the Comp window and add the Comp to the Render Queue, which will open the Render Queue panel.

2. Click the Lossless link to open the Output Module Settings dialog box.

11

3. Select QuickTime movie from the Format pull-down menu and select None in the Embed pull-down menu.

4. Click the Format Options button in the Video Output area to open the Compression Settings dialog box. Select Video from the Compressor Type pull-down menu and move the Quality slider to Best in the Compressor area. Click OK to accept the changes and return to the Output Module Settings dialog box.

5. Select Stretch and change the Width and Height values to 320×240. Make sure the Stretch Quality is set to High and that the Lock Aspect Ratio option is selected as shown in Figure 11-38. These settings won't stretch the video. They will simply reduce its output size to a Flash-friendly one. Leave the Crop area deselected.

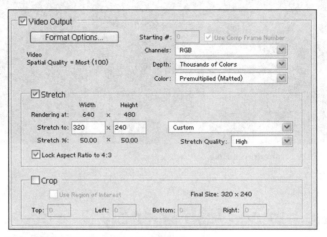

Figure 11-38. The key is the Stretch values.

6. Select Audio Output and click OK to close the dialog box.

> Yeah we know . . . there is no audio. Remember what we mentioned earlier in this book? Sometimes the timing and playback of an FLV file in Flash can be a little off. Flash video designers and developers have discovered including an audio track in the QuickTime movie and the FLV file solves this potential issue.

7. Click the Output to link and navigate to the folder where you have been working on this project. Click Save.

8. Click the Render button in the Render Queue. When the render finishes, save the project and quit After Effects. Play the rendered video in the QuickTime Player as shown in Figure 11-39. Not bad.

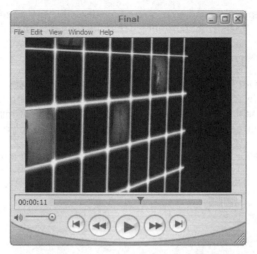

Figure 11-39. The resized video playing in QuickTime

We have included both the QuickTime and FLV versions of this project in the Chapter 11 Completed *folder found in the* Chapter 11 Exercise *folder.*

Summary

The dragon hunt has taken you into territory regarded as the Holy Grail of Flash . . . the third dimension. Even so, we showed you a number of ways ranging from rotoscoping to camera movement that allow you to add 3D works to Flash.

One of the major themes of this chapter has been that though After Effects has some industrial-strength 3D tools, the objects in 3D still remain flat. If you need to extrude a surface, use the tool for the job—a 3D modeling application—not After Effects.

We started looking for 3D dragons by creating a simple text-based button that spun on the X-, Y-, and Z-axes. We then showed you how to add the button to Flash by embedding it into the Flash timeline. We also showed a rather cool technique that allowed you to convert that After Effects button into a series of images and how to import the whole series into the Flash timeline at the click of a button.

The chapter then explained how 3D space works in After Effects and how to use the various view menus to get an accurate picture of where objects are in that 3D space. You also explored the lighting and the camera features of After Effects by creating a flashlight effect and creating an animation based on camera movement.

11

With those fundamentals in hand, you created a video cube that used a stationary camera and rotating videos, thanks to parenting. The final project pulled the entire chapter together by showing you how to work in a large 3D space and Comp and how to prepare the project for placement in Flash.

Make no mistake about it, though, the exercises in this chapter were designed to get you using 3D in After Effects. We covered just the fundamentals. There is a lot more to what you can do than presented here. Still, this chapter should get your mind working overtime looking for ways to incorporate even more complex 3D work into your Flash projects.

Our dragon hunt is about to end. It concludes with one of the more underrated aspects of any Flash or After Effects project: audio. Turn the page and we'll meet you there.

12 AUDIO, THE RED-HEADED KID IN A FAMILY OF BLONDES

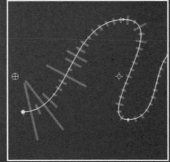

Sometimes we just don't "get" audio, and, to a great extent, our clients don't either. Why is it that audio is regarded as either an afterthought or a line item on the budget for the project? Yet when you really think about it, we are surrounded by sound, and people do tend to become a bit anxious when they encounter profound silence. Think back to your reaction when watching TV and suddenly the audio disappears. Your immediate reaction was probably, "What the . . . ?" Though we aren't psychiatrists or psychologists, we suspect that reaction came about because you were suddenly deprived of access to information.

Sound, whether in the form of a voice, music, or sound effect, is an important aspect of video and Flash work. It enriches the user experience because it adds an aural dimension to the piece and, if done properly, has a profound effect upon how the audience both reacts to and perceives the work. The film industry understands this so deeply, it is ingrained into their DNA. When the music in a sound track suddenly takes on a sinister edge, you just know someone is about to have a really bad day.

This chapter, which concludes this book, is not designed to turn you into an audio master. Our intention is to show you the fundamentals of working with audio in both After Effects and Flash. There are some fascinating things you can do with audio in both applications. What you need to understand, though, is how they each handle audio in their own unique manner.

To start that process, we are going to look at each application as a separate entity. We will start with importing, previewing, and generally manipulating audio in After Effects. Then we will head over to Flash and explore the fundamentals of audio in that application. We will then conclude the chapter with a couple of neat audio exercises that visualize audio in After Effects and conclude with an After Effects project that "Rocks Da House."

Download the files for Chapter 12, crank up your speakers or put on some "cans," and let's get busy.

The basics of audio in After Effects

Audio in After Effects is no different from an Illustrator drawing, Photoshop image, or video. It is content, and it goes on its own layer in the timeline and appears in the Project panel. The audio file formats that can be imported into After Effects are as follows:

- **AAC (Advanced Audio Coding)**: You might know this better as the MPEG-4 format. Designed as the successor to the MP3 format, it is a format used by iTunes.

- **AU**: Originally developed by Sun Microsystems, you commonly find files of this format buried in a Java applet. The sound quality is not good, which tends to explain why this might be the first time you are encountering this format.

- **AIFF (Audio Interchange File Format)**: This is the standard for the Mac. For you trivia buffs, here's a quick way to win a free dinner at your next conference or gathering: AIFF has a sample rate of 22,254.44 KHz. If you do trot this number out during your contest, you are going to be challenged on where it came from. That rate is the original Macintosh sample rate and was based on the horizontal scan rate of the monitor built into the original 128K Mac.

- **MP3**: The official name is Moving Pictures Expert Group Level—Layer-3 Audio, which sort of explains why "MP3" is used. All audio in Flash, regardless of original format, is output to MP3.

- **Video for Windows**: The AVI and WAV formats are used here:

  - **AVI (Audio Video Interleave)**: This format was developed by Microsoft as a container for both audio and video data.

  - **WAV (Waveform Audio Format)**: No, we don't have a clue where the *V* comes in. This format, until the rise of MP3, was "King of the Audio World" on the PC.

> *All audio files used in this chapter are available in WAV, AIFF, and MP3 formats. We will be adding the file extension to the file name when we ask you to import or export audio.*

1. Open After Effects and create a new Comp that is 44 seconds in duration.

2. Select File ➤ Import. Navigate to the Basic_AE folder in your Chapter 12 Exercise folder. Open it and import the track01.wav file into the Project window.

3. Drag the audio file to the timeline and twirl down Audio ➤ Waveform in the timeline. You will notice the only audio property available to you is the audio level and that you can see the audio waveform on the timeline, as shown in Figure 12-1.

Figure 12-1. The Audio layer on the timeline

> *Waveform too small? In the timeline, roll your cursor (don't click and drag) downward through the bottom waveform. When your cursor changes to a double arrow, drag downward, and the waveform will become wider.*

12

4. There are a number of ways of previewing the audio just added to the timeline. If you click the Play button in the Time Controls panel or press the spacebar, you won't hear a thing. The technique you choose to preview audio depends upon what you intend to accomplish. Try each of these:

  - **To scrub the audio**: Press the Ctrl (PC) or Cmd (Mac) key and drag the playback head across the timeline.

  - **To play a short piece of the sound**: Press the . (period) key on your numeric keypad or select one of the options under Composition ➤ Preview ➤ Audio Preview.

  - **To preview the sound in the work area**: Press Alt+. (PC) or Option+. (Mac).

5. You can extend the duration of the preview. Open the After Effects Preferences dialog box and select Previews. Change the Duration value to 0:00:08:00 in the Audio Preview section (see Figure 12-2).

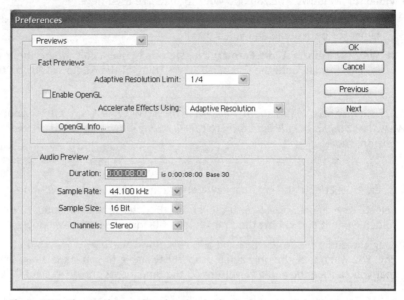

Figure 12-2. Change the preview duration in the Preferences dialog box.

6. After Effects also includes a VU meter that shows you **audio clipping**, which is a distortion that occurs when the audio signal exceeds the maximum allowed by the device and allows you to change the volume level of the audio track. If you don't see the Audio panel, select Window ➤ Audio.

The Audio panel, shown in Figure 12-3, contains level controls, the VU meter, and the level units. You can change the level by clicking the Audio Options button on the panel, selecting Options, and changing the Level Units setting to either decibel or percentage and setting the minimum values for the slider. Select the audio file on the timeline, press the 0 key on the numeric keypad, and move a slider up or down. You will notice that as soon as you click the Audio panel, the sound stops. Move the slider to another position and preview the sound again.

Deselect the audio track on the timeline, and you will see the sliders gray out.

Two things will also happen. The first is, if you dragged the slider downward, the volume will be reduced. The second is, if you look at the waveform, that, too, will be reduced toward the line running through the middle of the waveform. That line indicates silence. By moving toward the line, the sound gets fainter.

Move the slider upward, and the sound gets louder and the waveform moves away from the silence line.

The two sliders on either side of the Volume slider control the volume for the individual channel. Drag the right slider downward, and you will notice its waveform changes, the Volume slider moves down, and, if you preview the audio, the affected channel is fainter. You should also notice the Audio Levels properties in the timeline also change.

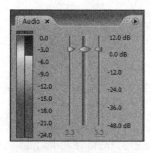

Figure 12-3.
The Audio panel

The numbers at the bottom of the VU meter are the actual Audio Levels properties in the timeline. Double-click one, make a change, and the audio is changed and the value is shown on the timeline.

If you own Production Studio Premium, which comes with the whole range of audio and video products, you also have Audition installed on your computer. If you want to edit the audio file in Audition right out of After Effects, select the audio file either in the Project panel or on the timeline and select Edit ➤ Edit in Adobe Audition. When you finish making your changes in Audition, save the file, and it will appear in After Effects.

Flash and audio

Before we start, clearly understand we are not going to cover all of the aspects of sound in Flash. It is a big subject. There is a whole chapter devoted to the subject in *Foundation ActionScript for Flash 8* by Kristian Besley et al. (friends of ED, 2006), Danny Franzreb has an amazing sound visualization tutorial in *New Masters of Flash, Volume 3* (friends of ED, 2004), and, speaking of masters, Craig Swann of CRASH!MEDIA (www.crashmedia.com/) is regarded by many in the industry as being the "Master Of All That Is Sound In Flash." Check out his site for tutorials and presentations that he has delivered at conferences around the world.

If you flip back to Chapter 2 in this book, there we showed you how to turn the sound in a video on and off through the use of the Sound class in ActionScript. What we did was to pull the sound out of the FLV file, toss it into an empty movie clip, and then used the setVolume() method to play the sound—setVolume(100)—or turn it off—setVolume(0). What we are going to do here is to show you a couple of other things you can do with

12

audio in Flash. Sometimes you may want to have Flash play the audio while an effect is playing in the background or being used as a preloader. You may also want to use the audio file elsewhere in Flash. For example, an audio file is added to an After Effects project that gets converted to an FLV. You realize the tune in the audio is really catchy and would like to have it play as a sort of background music in the Flash project as well.

> *Do not try to synch Flash audio with FLV video. It will never be exact, so get that idea out of your mind. If audio is to play in synch with video, use After Effects.*

If you are going to be adding audio to your Flash project, try to stay within standards. That means AIFF, WAV, or MP3 files should be used. If the file is to be embedded into the SWF file, feel free to import any of the three formats into the Flash Library. If the file is to be kept external to the SWF file and streamed in using the loadSound() method, you can only use the MP3 format. The other thing to keep in mind is audio files can be just as massive as video files. Though audio files, just like their video brethren, can be embedded on the Flash timeline, don't do it. Here's how to stream an audio file into Flash:

1. Open Flash, create a new movie, and save the Flash file (name it whatever you wish) to the Basic_Flash folder in your Chapter 12 Exercise folder.

2. Select the first frame of the movie, open the ActionScript Editor, and add the following code:

```
var mySound:Sound= new Sound();
mySound.loadSound("track01.mp3" , true);
mySound.onLoad = function() {
  mySound.start();
}
```

The first line creates a Sound object with the instance name of mySound. The audio file is loaded into the object using the next line of code. The loadSound() method has two parameters: the first is the name of the audio file, and the second is a Boolean value to tell Flash the audio file is streaming off of the web server into the SWF file. The function turns on the sound when it has loaded.

3. Save the file and test it. The audio plays.

An audio controller

In this exercise, you will be building on what you did earlier. This time though, you are going to stream in a sound and use buttons to turn it on and off. We are also going to show you how to build a simple slider that controls the volume of a sound that may be playing. In fact, we will be doing this exercise a second time to show you how the controller can be used to control the volume in an FLV file as well. Let's start with a simple audio controller:

1. Open the Controller.fla file in the Basic_Flash folder. When the movie opens, you will see we have given you the basic elements for the control—two movie clips and two buttons. It is your job to "wire them up" with ActionScript. Still, there are a couple of tasks to perform before you start.

2. Double-click the Ball movie clip in the Library to open it in the Symbol Editor. You will notice there is a small text box just above and to the right of the ball (see Figure 12-4). This text box is going to show the user the volume level of the sound as the ball is dragged from one side of the bar to the other. Select the text box in the Text layer, change its text type from Static Text to Dynamic Text, and give it the instance name of VolText.

The reason for these settings is the text (actually it will be a number) in the box will constantly change. By changing the text type, the numbers will be able to update. Before you finish, there is one more task to perform. Flash doesn't have a clue there is a dynamic text box on the stage. If ActionScript is going to change the numbers, give the text box the instance name of volText. When you change the text type, note how the text box is surrounded by dots—another visual clue that the text is dynamic.

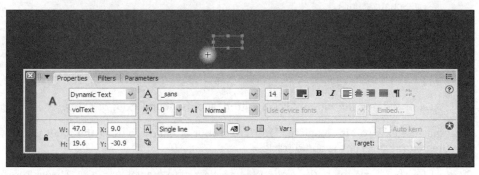

Figure 12-4. Creating a dynamic text box and giving it an instance name

3. Double-click the Bar movie clip in the Library to open it in the Symbol Editor. Select the Ball on the stage and give it the instance name of volBall. Click the Scene 1 link to return to the main timeline.

4. Click the Play Sound button on the stage and give it the instance name of btnPlay. Click the Stop Sound button and give it the instance name of btnStop. Finally, select the slider on the stage, and, as shown in Figure 12-5, give it the instance name of mcVolSlider. You are now ready to start writing the ActionScript.

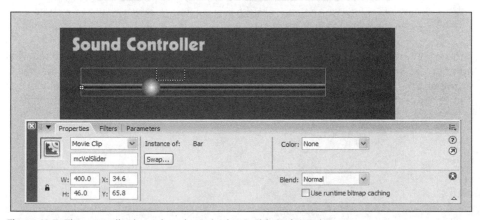

Figure 12-5. The controller is ready to be "wired up" with ActionScript.

12

5. Click the first frame in the Actions layer once, open the ActionScript Editor, and enter the following code:

```
var mySound:Sound= new Sound();
mySound.loadSound("track01.mp3" , true);
mySound.onLoad = function() {
  mySound.stop();
}
```

Nothing new here. Mind you, if you test the movie, the sound won't play because, instead of using the start() method in the function, you use the stop() method, which kills a sound. Let's deal with this one right now.

6. Press the Return/Enter key twice and enter the following code:

```
btnStop.onRelease = function():Void {
  mySound.stop();
};

btnPlay.onRelease = function():Void {
  mySound.start();
};
```

Go ahead, test the movie. Click a button, and the sound stops or starts.

Now that the easy part is completed, you'll turn your attention to using the slider to control the volume level of the audio track.

Figure 12-6 shows you the basic relationship of the ball to the volume level. The width of the bar is 400 pixels. This means the location of the center point of the ball on the bar, at any point in time, can be expressed as a percentage of distance along the bar.

Figure 12-6. The location of the ball along the bar will determine the volume level of the audio.

The neat thing about ActionScript is that distance is nothing more than a number. That number can then be subsequently used as the volume level. For example, if the ball is sitting at the midpoint of the bar, 200 pixels, it is 50% of the way along the bar, and that number is used as the value for the volume level of the audio. Here's how you do that:

1. Select the first frame of the Actions layer, open the ActionScript Editor, and enter the following code after the Play button code:

```
var nVolCheck:Number;

mcVolSlider.volBall.onPress = function():Void {
  this. startDrag (false, 0, 0, 400, 0);
  nVolCheck = setInterval(updateVolume, 100);
};

mcVolSlider.volBall.onRelease = function():Void {
  this.stopDrag ();
  clearInterval(nVolCheck);
};
```

You are going to be using a number that tells ActionScript how long to wait between "checks" for the ball location on the bar. The first line of code does just that.

The next two functions tell ActionScript what to do when the user presses the mouse and what to do when the user releases the mouse.

When the mouse is pressed, the ball—this—is made draggable—startDrag(). The parameters inside the startDrag() method tell ActionScript not to lock the center point of the ball to the mouse tip and that the ball can only be dragged a total distance of 400 pixels to the right. This 400 is the width of the parent movie clip, mcSlider, and the number starts at the left edge of mcSlider. The next line of code is similar to that in Chapter 2. It uses the setInterval() method to determine what to do when a check is to be performed—updateVolume—and how long to wait between checks—100 milliseconds.

When the user releases the mouse, the ball is no longer draggable, and the checking for the ball position stops. The final step is to write the updateVolume function used when the mouse is pressed.

2. Press the Return/Enter key twice and enter the following code:

```
function updateVolume():Void {
  var vol:Number = (mcVolSlider.volBall._x)/4;
  mySound.setVolume(vol);
  mcVolSlider.volBall.volText.text = vol;
};
```

The first line of the function performs the percentage calculation determining the ball's location on the bar. The number is constantly changing, which explains why it is given the variable name of vol. The ._x property of the ball—its location on the X-axis—is determined, and that number is divided by 4 to obtain a value between 0 and 100. That number is then used as the parameter for the setVolume() method and is also added, as text, to the dynamic text box—volText—just above the ball.

12

3. Save the movie and test it. Notice how, as shown in Figure 12-7, the number changes as you drag the ball and the volume level increases or decreases as you move the ball to the left or the right.

Figure 12-7. Everything is working as it should.

A video sound controller

Controlling the audio in an FLV file is quite a bit different from the previous exercise. Essentially, what you need to do is to pull the embedded audio track out of the FLV, put it in a movie clip, and manage the audio in the movie clip. In many respects, the audio is treated in exactly the same way an audio track in the Library would be treated. Let's see how this works:

1. Open the VidAudioController.fla file in the Basic_Flash folder. Being the nice guys we are, we have already added the video object and the ActionScript that makes the video play to the Actions layer (see Figure 12-8).

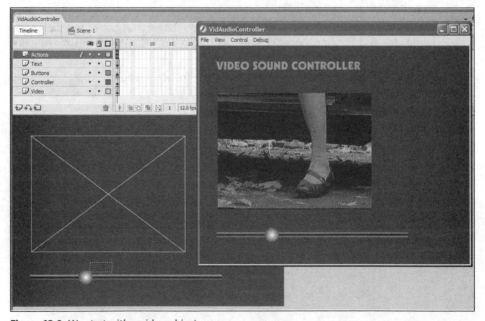

Figure 12-8. We start with a video object.

The video used in this exercise was produced by Film and TV Production students at the School of Media Studies, the Humber Institute of Technology & Advanced Learning, Toronto. Mamma Andretti's Pizza is a 30-second commercial the students in the program have to produce as a part of their studies.

2. Select the Actions layer, open the ActionScript Editor, and add this code:

```
_root.createEmptyMovieClip("mcVol",_root.getNextHighestDepth());
mcVol.attachAudio(ns);
```

Recall from Chapter 2 that this code creates an empty movie clip named mcVol, adds it to the main timeline—root—and attaches the audio track from the NetStream to the movie clip.

3. Press the Return/Enter key twice and add the following code:

```
var FLVSound:Sound = new Sound(mcVol);
FLVSound.setVolume (100);
```

The Sound object is created using the new movie clip as its target instance, and the audio level is set to 100 using the setVolume() method of the Sound class.

There is a major difference between using a Sound object to manage a streaming sound—playing an MPS file from a web server—and managing a sound playing through a movie clip. The difference is that you can't use the start() and stop() methods used in the previous exercise to turn the sound on or off.

Remember the sound is now seen by Flash as being in a movie clip, and the inference in the sound is seen as a file in the Library. This means you need to use the setVolume() method to control the volume level.

4. Press the Return/Enter key twice and enter the following button code:

```
btnPlay.onPress = function() {
  FLVSound.setVolume(100);
}

btnStop.onPress = function() {
  FLVSound.setVolume(0);
}
```

Save the file and test the movie. The buttons will turn the sound on and off.

If you don't believe us when we say the start() and stop() methods can't be used, change the setVolume code line in the Play button to FLVSound.start(); and see what happens.

12

5. In the ActionScript Editor, press the Return/Enter key twice and enter the following code to "wire up" the controller:

```
var nVolCheck:Number;

mcVolSlider.volBall.onPress = function():Void {
  this. startDrag (false, 0, 0, 400, 0);
  nVolCheck = setInterval(updateVolume, 100);
};

mcVolSlider.volBall.onRelease = function():Void {
  this.stopDrag ();
  clearInterval(nVolCheck);
};

function updateVolume():Void {
  var vol:Number = (mcVolSlider.volBall._x)/4;
  FLVSound.setVolume(vol);
  mcVolSlider.volBall.volText.text = vol;
};
```

This is exactly the same code used in the previous exercise.

6. Save and test the movie. As you drag the ball, the volume level increases or decreases, and the volume level is shown in the dynamic text box (see Figure 12-9).

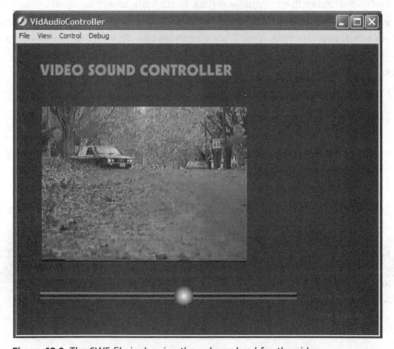

Figure 12-9. The SWF file is showing the volume level for the video.

Sound visualization in After Effects

One of things that is dead simple to do in After Effects falls into the realm of advanced ActionScript in Flash. That "thing" is **sound visualization**, which essentially is the graphic representation of an audio signal. For example, Danny Franzreb has a piece in *New Masters of Flash, Volume 3* from friends of ED that uses a third-party piece of software, FlashAmp Pro 2, that pulls the sound information out of an audio track and saves it into arrays that can then be used in Flash. The example called "sound waves" is breathtaking, demonstrating the art one can create when using audio. The problem is the ActionScript that makes all of this possible falls squarely into the realm of the master coder.

After Effects, on the other hand, has a couple of effects in its arsenal that allow you to create audio visualizations at the click of a mouse. Obviously, the difference between what you can do with After Effects and what Danny can do in Flash are separated by a universe, but they do have a common intersection: a sound wave.

Sound is nothing more than waves of compressed air. The number of waves there are per second is called **frequency** and the height of a wave is called **amplitude**. These things can be measured, and we know that anything that can be measured kicks out a number, and that number is nothing more than data that can be manipulated. Danny uses those numbers to create his art, and After Effects uses the same numbers when it visualizes sound. Here's how:

1. Open a new After Effects document, create a Comp, and add a solid to the Comp.

2. In the Chapter 12 Exercise folder is another folder named Spectrum. Inside that folder is a file named track01.wav. Import this WAV file into the project and save the project to the Spectrum folder.

3. Drag the audio file to the timeline.

4. Select the solid layer and in Effects & Presets ➤ Generate, drag a copy of the Audio Spectrum effect onto the Comp. The effect displays the magnitude of frequencies in the range you define using Start Frequency and End Frequency in the Effect Controls panel.

5. Open the Effect Controls panel and select track01.wav from the pull-down list in the Audio Layer area.

6. Do a RAM preview of the Comp. As you see in Figure 12-10, the lines will swell or shrink depending upon the frequency of the audio being played by the playback head.

Figure 12-10. The Audio Spectrum effect applied to a solid

12

As is typical of many of the effects in After Effects, the properties in the Effect Controls panel, as shown in Figure 12-11, look a lot more complicated than they first appear. Here's a quick rundown of the various properties in the Audio Spectrum effect:

- Audio Layer: This pull-down allows you to choose the audio track to be used for the effect.

- Start Point, End Point: The numbers you enter here define the start and end points of the effect on the Comp. You can also drag the handles on the Comp.

- Path: You can apply this effect to a path you select in the pull-down. You will be doing that next.

- Use Polar Path: This specifies the path is to start from a single point and the display is a radial graph.

- Start Frequency, End Frequency: You can choose the frequency range to be used by the effect.

- Frequency bands: Here you specify the number of frequencies displayed. Drag the slider to the right, and more lines are added to the effect.

- Maximum Height: This specifies the maximum height, in pixels, of the lines.

- Audio Duration (milliseconds): Here you specify the duration of audio used to calculate the spectrum.

- Audio Offset (milliseconds): This lets you choose the time offset, in milliseconds, used to retrieve the audio.

- Thickness: Here you specify the thickness of the lines in the effect.

- Softness: Think of this as applying a feather to the lines.

- Inside Color, Outside Color: Use the Color Picker to choose the inside and outside colors of the bands.

- Blend Overlapping Colors: Here you specify whether overlapping spectrums are blended.

- Hue Interpolation: If you enter a value greater than 0, the frequencies displayed rotate through the hue color space.

- Dynamic Hue Phase: When selected, and the Hue Interpolation value is greater than 0, the starting color shifts to the maximum frequency in the range of displayed frequencies. This allows the hue to follow the fundamental frequency of the spectrum displayed as it changes.

- Color Symmetry: When selected, and the Hue Interpolation value is greater than 0, the start and end colors become the same color.

- Display Options: Here you specify whether to display the frequency as Digital (the lines you see), Analog lines (the frequency looks like a waveform using lines), or Analog dots (this replaces the lines with dots).

- Side Options: Is the effect above the path (Side A), below the path (Side B), or on both sides (Side A and Side B)?

- Duration Averaging: Select this and the audio frequencies are averaged to reduce randomness.

- Composite On Original: When selected, this displays the original layer with the effect.

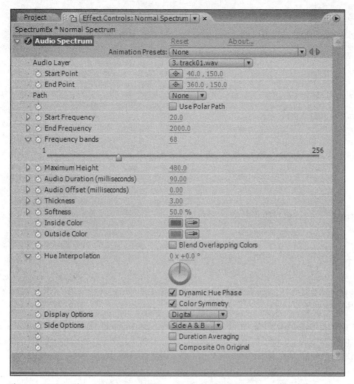

Figure 12-11. The Audio Spectrum controls aren't as complicated as they look.

The Audio Spectrum effect can also be applied to a path. Here's how:

1. Select the effect in the Effect Controls panel and delete it.
2. Select the Pen tool and draw a path with a couple of curves somewhat like the one shown in Figure 12-12.

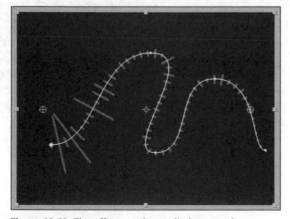

Figure 12-12. The effect can be applied to a path.

3. Drag a copy of the Audio Spectrum effect onto the Comp window.

4. Open the Effect Controls panel and use these settings:

- Audio Layer: track01.wav
- Path: Mask 1 (This is the path you just drew on the solid.)
- Start Frequency: 1
- End Frequency: 400
- Frequency bands: 50
- Maximum Height: 800
- Thickness: 5
- Softness: 75%
- Inside Color: #070DFA (dark blue)
- Outside Color: #02FFE4
- Display Options: Analog lines

You should have noticed that as you made the changes, they were instantly reflected in the curve. Scrub through the timeline, and you will see the graph constantly change.

5. You are probably a bit curious about the Use Polar Path selection. Select it in the Effect Controls panel, and the effect switches to the start point of the curve. If you scrub through the timeline, it will look like a star burst, and it expands or contracts only at that point on the path (see Figure 12-13). Save the project.

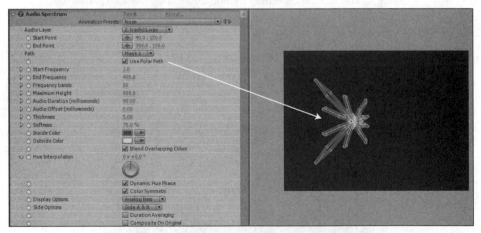

Figure 12-13. Applying the effect to a path

Have you ever seen the northern lights, Jimmy?

Now that you know what the effect can do, let's really have some fun with it. You know the effect occurs around a shape and starts at a point on the shape. You also know that selecting Use Polar Coordinates shoots the effect out of one point on the shape. Armed with this knowledge, you can create a rather fascinating effect that looks like the northern lights. Here's how:

1. Create a new project and add a new Comp with a Duration setting of 0:00:44:00. Import the audio file in the Spectrum folder into the project and create a new black solid. Drag the audio file from the Project panel to the timeline.

2. Select the Elliptical Mask tool and draw a small circle on the solid in the Comp.

> *To draw a perfectly round circle, start drawing the circle from about the center point of the Comp and then hold down Ctrl+Shift (PC) or Cmd+Shift (Mac) and continue dragging. The circle will draw out from the center.*

3. Drag a copy of the Audio Spectrum effect onto the circle, open the Effect Controls panel, and use these settings:

   - Audio Layer: track01.wav
   - Path: Mask 1
   - Start Frequency: 1
   - End Frequency: 3,000
   - Frequency bands: 100
   - Maximum Height: 2000
   - Audio Duration (milliseconds): 200
   - Thickness: 5
   - Softness: 100%
   - Inside Color: #FFFFFF (white)
   - Outside Color: #0267FF (blue)
   - Blend Overlapping Colors: **Selected**
   - Hue Interpolation: 1 x +0.0 degrees
   - Dynamic Hue Phase: **Deselected**
   - Color Symmetry: **Deselected**
   - Display Options: Analog lines

4. Select Use Polar Path, and the lines seem to shoot sideways from the top of the circle.

12

5. Do a RAM preview, and the effect looks like a crude comet with a variety of colors shooting out of its tail (see Figure 12-14).

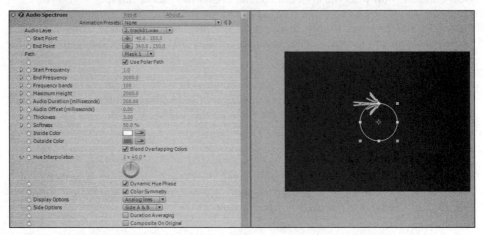

Figure 12-14. The effect starts out looking like a crude comet.

6. Twirl up the Audio Spectrum effect in the Effect Controls panel and drag a copy of the CC Radial Blur effect from Effects & Presets ➤ Blur & Sharpen.

7. In the Effect Controls panel, specify these settings:

- Type: Select Fading Zoom from the pull-down. This will fade the blur out from the bottom of the "comet."

- Amount: 250. As you change this value, the distance of the blur decreases or increases.

8. Do a RAM preview, and the effect, shown in Figure 12-15, looks like the changing colors of the northern lights.

This one may take a while to render because of the CC Radial Blur effect and the color changes. If you are impatient, click the Quality switch for the solid. It will change from \ to /. If you look at the Comp, the blur is now a low-res blur. It will give you an idea of how the effect looks, but it isn't close to the final product. Still, the low-quality RAM preview is a lot quicker.

> *This effect can also be created using the* Radial Blur *effects in the* Effects & Presets *panel. In this case, you would apply a blur amount of about* 150 *and select* Zoom *in the* Type *pull-down.*

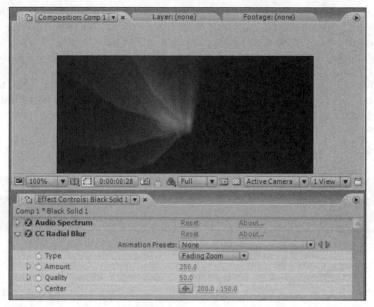

Figure 12-15. The "northern lights" effect

Building a boom box

In this exercise, you will discover that sound can be converted to an object capable of being manipulated on the stage and how to use the Ripple effect to give the illusion of the cones in a speaker working overtime. This will also introduce you to the use of **expressions** in After Effects.

Before you get going, this is the only place in the book where we will be using expressions, and even then it will be an extremely shallow exploration. Expressions in After Effects are, in many respects, just as deep and complicated as ActionScript. In fact, expressions in After Effects use the same common coding language as ActionScript: JavaScript. The technique we will be showing is a simple drag-and-drop linking of an effect to the sound amplitude. If we were to "code" the expression, we would have to assume you have a working knowledge of JavaScript.

1. Inside your Chapter 12 Exercise folder is another named Boom. Open it and open the loudspeaker.aep file in that folder. We have assembled most of the exercise for you. What you are going to do is to manipulate the sound and add an effect to the speakers.

2. On the timeline, right-click (PC) or Ctrl-click (Mac) the audio file.

3. When the context menu opens, select Keyframe Assistant ➤ Convert Audio to Keyframes. When you release the mouse, a new solid named Audio Amplitude will appear on the timeline. Drag this layer between the Loudspeaker Left and the Audio layers on the timeline. Twirl down Audio Amplitude ➤ Effects.

You will see three bars: Left Channel, Right Channel, and Both Channels. These bars, shown in Figure 12-16, represent all of the audio sources in the Comp. The really neat thing about what you have just done is, through the use of expressions, you can now link the changes in the Audio Amplitude property to other layer properties such as Scale and Opacity. For example, when a sound is really loud, the object linked to the audio can get really big and appear at 100% opacity. When the amplitude reduces, the object gets smaller and more opaque. In the case of this exercise, you are going to tie the vibration of the speaker cones to the changes in Audio Amplitude.

Select the Left Channel and Right Channel keyframe layers and delete them.

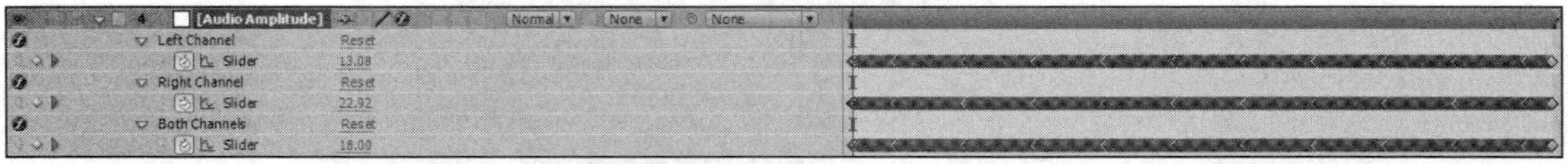

Figure 12-16. The audio keyframes in the timeline

4. Select the Loudspeaker Left layer in the timeline and drag a copy of the Ripple effect (Effects & Presets ➤ Distort) onto the speaker. Use these settings for the Ripple effect:

- Radius: 30

- Type of Conversion: Symmetric

- Wave Speed: 8

Repeat this step for the Loudspeaker Right layer.

5. In the Loudspeaker Left layer, twirl down Effects ➤ Ripple and in the Audio Amplitude layer, twirl down Both Channels.

6. Hold down the Alt (PC) or Option (Mac) key and click the stopwatch of the Wave Speed property of the Ripple effect. The Expression layer will open on the timeline. What you need to do is to link this property to the Audio Amplitude layer.

7. The icon in the Expression layer that looks like a coiled piece of rope, as shown in Figure 12-17, is called the Pick Whip. Click and drag the Pick Whip down to the Slider property of the Audio Amplitude layer. Release the mouse. When you do, the Wave Speed value turns red, telling you it is tied to an expression, and the expression will be written in the timeline.

▽ ○ Wave Speed	15.0			thisComp.layer("Audio Amplitude").effect("Both Channels")("Slider")
Expression: Wave Speed	☰ ﹏ ◎ ◉			
On/Off Switch	**Graph Overlay**	**Pick Whip**	**Expression Menu**	**Expression**

Figure 12-17. The Expression layer

8. Repeat steps 6 and 7 for the Loudspeaker Right layer. Turn off the visibility of the Audio Amplitude layer, save the project, and do a RAM preview.

There is a new club in town

This final project for the chapter pulls together all of the bits and pieces you have worked with in this chapter and the ones leading into it to create a short promo for a local club that is opening in your town. This one will be a combination of us explaining how a few of the effects were put together, and, because this is an audio chapter, you will be handling the audio chores.

1. To start, open the ClubFriday.aep file. This file can be located in the ClubFriday folder found in the Chapter 12 Exercise folder.

2. You will notice the project window contains a Comp called Maincomp and another named Girl. The Girl Comp is used three times in this piece in a rather creative manner, and you'll be adding the fourth instance. Double-click the Girl Comp to open it. When it opens, press the Home key to return the playback head to the start of the timeline.

This effect looks suspiciously like the reverse of the iPod ad–like video you did in Chapter 4. In fact, it is totally different. The only similarity is that we keyed out the background using the Keylight effect (make sure to open the Effect Controls panel to see this). Instead of applying the Levels effect from Effects & Presets ➤ Color Correction, we applied the Minimax effect, shown in Figure 12-18, from the Channels folder.

The Minimax effect enlarges or reduces a matte for a specific channel or all channels. By selecting Color in the Channel pull-down, the effect is applied to all channels in the video. The critical word is *channels*. Each pixel in a color channel in the video has a value between 0 and 255, with 0 as the "mini" and 255 as the "max" (thus the name for the effect). What you can gather from this is pixel values are shifted up (max) or down (mini) depending on the parameters of the effect. Thus, the pixels in the mask are going to move toward white (max) or black (mini).

The color of the woman in the video was removed by setting the Radius value to 42. If you set the Radius value to 0, you will see the woman appears. Change the value to 2, and she starts to appear blocky and washed out as the colors shift to those of pixels with higher pixel values within the mask. (White is the highest value. Each of the color channels has a maximum value of 255. On the RGB scale, white is 255 across the board.) At a Radius value of 42, the highest-value pixel is a white one, and the result is what you see. The Direction property tells the filter which direction to travel when scanning for values. Horizontal & Vertical scans all directions for the minimum or maximum pixel. Just Horizontal and Just Vertical scan only left and right or up and down, respectively.

If you were to select Minimum as the Operation, moving the Radius slider to the right will make the image darker as the pixels with high color values are replaced with ones containing lower values.

12

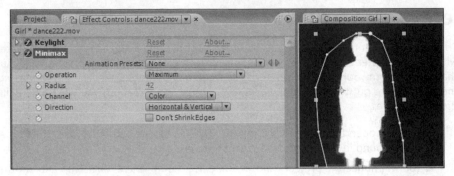

Figure 12-18. The Minimax filter

3. Double-click Maincomp in the Project window to open the main timeline for this project. Drag a copy of the Girl Comp in the Project panel directly under the Camera 1 layer on the timeline. Set the In point for this layer to 0:00:07:14 and the Out point to 0:00:11:02.

4. With the new Girl layer selected on the timeline, open Effects & Presets ➤ Blur and Sharpen and drag a copy of the Radial Blur effect onto the selected layer. Use these settings:

- Amount: 350
- Position: 184, 136
- Type: Zoom
- Antialiasing: Low

5. Twirl down Effects ➤ Radial Blur in the selected layer and add a keyframe to the Amount property at the In point of the clip. Move the playback head to 0:00:08:18 and set the Amount value to 0. Twirl up Effects and click the 3D switch.

6. Place the playback head at the In point of the layer, twirl down Transform, and specify these values:

- Anchor Point: 16, 120, 0.
- Position: 239.9, 126, –277.9.
- Scale: 30, 30, 30.
- Opacity: Add a keyframe.

7. Use the following Opacity values at the times shown:

- 0:00:08:09: 100%
- 0:00:11:03: 0%

8. Lock the layer and save the project.

Doing the audio "thing"

You are going to finish the project by adding the audio track and having some fun with it.

1. Open the Audio folder in the Project panel and drag a copy of the track03.mp3 file to the bottom of the timeline.

2. Select the audio track on the timeline and convert it to keyframes. Drag the resulting Audio Amplitude layer between the audio track and the C layer.

3. Twirl down Effects ➤ Both Channels in the Audio Amplitude layer and Effects ➤ Radial Blur in the C layer.

4. Alt-click (PC) or Option-click (Mac) the Amount stopwatch in the Radial Blur effect. When the Expression layer opens, drag the Pick Whip from the expression to Slider in the Both Channels layer of the Audio Amplitude layer.

The expression you just added applies a uniform amount of the blur to the object in the layer. What about situations where the blur can be applied in different amounts at different points in the duration of the animation? In short, the image appears to blur and sharpen at irregular times. This can be done by adding a random value to the expression. Instead of a uniform amount of blur, you are going to tell After Effects: "You apply the blur however you see fit as long as the value applied is a number between 0 and 100." Here's how:

5. Click once at the end of the expression code in the timeline. Click the Expression Menu button and when the menu opens, select Random Numbers ➤ random(). When you make the selection, you will see that random() has been added to the end of the expression.

6. Click once in front of the word *random* and enter +. Click once between the brackets after the word *random* and enter 100. The expression should now read as follows:

```
thisComp.layer("Audio Amplitude").effect("Both Channels")("Slider")➥
   +random(100)
```

With this expression added and with the Audio Waveform effect that has already been applied to the C, this large letter will function like a giant drop cap that pulses to the music and blurs as it bounces, rotates, and flips on its side to function as a platform for the four clips of the dancer (see Figure 12-19).

12

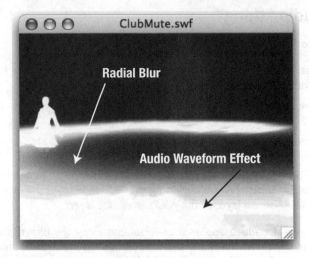

Figure 12-19. Combining effects is a good habit to develop.

The final touch to be added to this piece uses the Audio Spectrum effect. What will happen is the effect will be applied to the mask in the Big Sized Solid layer and a camera will travel along the path while the Audio Spectrum effect is pulsing.

7. Select the Big Sized Solid layer and add an Audio Spectrum effect to it. Use these settings:

   - Audio Layer: track03.mp3
   - Frequency bands: 179
   - Maximum Height: 480
   - Inside Color: #002AFF (blue)
   - Outside Color: #328EFF (light blue)
   - Dynamic Hue Phase: Deselected

If you scrub across the layer, you will see the Audio Spectrum effect, as shown in Figure 12-20, appear to move around, thanks to the movement of the cameras in the Camera 1 and Camera 2 layers.

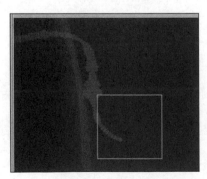

Figure 12-20.
The camera is following the Audio Spectrum effect.

The final step in the process is to render this movie out as a QuickTime video using the Animation codec. Though we have stated this a couple of times in this book, it really is worth repeating. When you render a video from After Effects, the audio track must be added manually in the Output Module Settings dialog box as shown in Figure 12-21. If you do not select the Audio Output option, the audio track won't be included in the final output.

Figure 12-21. Be sure that Audio Output is selected, or the audio won't be included in the QuickTime movie.

Streaming audio and video in Flash

Not including the audio track, in this case, is not the end of the world. In fact, it might even be an option.

Before you do a backflip, remember you can lay in the audio in Flash. In this case, you could then use the MP3 audio file as a background audio loop in other areas of the Flash site. This animation works beautifully with the audio, but the thing is, it is not tied to the audio with a Gordian knot. If it ends a bit before the animation ends, it is no big issue because the animation itself ends with the words *opening this Friday*. If the sound ends while those words are appearing, no one is going to know the difference.

The other advantage to you is you can swap out the audio track with another one of the same genre without having to open After Effects and rerender the QuickTime movie and the FLV file.

Here's how:

1. Open the ClubMute.fla file found in the ClubFriday folder in your Chapter 12 Exercise folder.

2. Select the first frame of the Actions layer, open the ActionScript Editor, and enter the following code:

```
var nc: NetConnection = new NetConnection();
nc.connect(null);
var ns:NetStream = new NetStream (nc);
myVideo.attachVideo(ns);
ns.play ("ClubMute.flv");

var mySound : Sound= new Sound();
mySound.loadSound("track03.mp3" , true);
mySound.onLoad = function() {
  mySound.start();
}
```

3. Save the movie and test it. The video plays, as shown in Figure 12-22, along with the audio. In this example, the audio playing through Flash ends at the same point it does playing through the QuickTime player. Obviously, if there were a video clip in the piece that included someone talking, this technique simply wouldn't be a viable option.

Figure 12-22. Separate audio and video streams in Flash

Summary

This chapter was designed to show you what you can do with audio in both Flash and After Effects, and we suspect you no longer regard audio as the "red-headed kid in a family of blondes." We showed you how to add and manage audio in Flash and After Effects and also showed how to stream a sound in Flash. We also showed you how to build a widget that controls the volume level of a Flash video and how to turn the sound in an FLV file on and off.

You learned three sound visualization techniques in After Effects and then learned how to animate an object on the stage by using an expression and audio that has been broken into keyframes on the timeline. You then completed a project that pulled together a lot of what you learned in this chapter and previous chapters in regard to 3D and a variety of effects. The chapter ended with you discovering that you can stream both an audio and a video track into Flash.

. . . and so our dragon hunt comes to an end. It has been quite the expedition and has taken you into territory that, over the coming years, will become more fully explored as more Flash developers and designers and After Effects pros expand the boundaries of what you have learned . . . and discovered . . . in this book. It isn't only the users of the product that are realizing that Flash and After Effects were made for each other. Adobe has also come to this realization, and what they do over the next few iterations of both applications should push the boundaries of the capabilities of both applications in the field of video and animation even deeper into Dragon Country. Still, we hope you have discovered what the authors have learned: the amount of fun you can have with these applications should be illegal.

We'll see you in jail.

12

INDEX

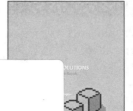

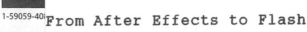